DILLINGER

THE UNTOLD STORY

G. Russell Girardin

WITH WILLIAM J. HELMER

INDIANA UNIVERSITY PRESS

Bloomington and Indianapolis

The paper used in this publication meets the minimum requirements of American National Standard for Information Sciences—Permanence of Paper for Printed Library Materials, ANSI Z39.48-1984.

 ™

Manufactured in the United States of America

Library of Congress Cataloging-in-Publication Data
Girardin, G. Russell (George Russell)
    Dillinger : the untold story / G. Russell Girardin with William J. Helmer.
       p.   cm.
    Includes bibliographical references (p.   ) and index.
    ISBN 0-253-32556-0 (acid-free paper)
    1. Dillinger, John, 1903–1934.   2. Criminals—Middle West
  Biography.   I. Helmer, William J.   II. Title.
HV6248.D5G57   1994
364.1'523'092—dc20
[B]   93-35737
  2 3 4 5 99 98 97 96 95 94

For Jessie Janette Rekemeyer
and her great-grandmother,
Myrtle Janette Helmer

And he will be a wild man;

his hand will be against every man,

and every man's hand against him.

Genesis, xvi, 12

CONTENTS

STATE OF ILLINOIS)
) SS: <u>AFFIDAVIT</u>
COUNTY OF C O O K)

    I, LOUIS P. PIQUETT, being first duly sworn,
on oath depose and say, that I was the attorney for the late
John Dillinger, that as his attorney I had access to and conversations with the late John Dillinger denied to all other persons,
that I have read the manuscript concerning the life of the late
John Dillinger and his associates, written by G. Russell Girardin
and Richard H. Walters, that the narrative is a true and accurate
history of the life and activities of the late John Dillinger and
his associates, that the said narrative is the only one written
which bears my authorization and which has been contributed to
by me, that all incidents transpiring between John Dillinger and
myself are faithfully and accurately set out and described in
said narrative.

SUBSCRIBED AND SWORN TO
before me this 4th day
of April A.D.1936.
           Louis P. Piquett

Notary Public

About the Book

In 1934, George Russell Girardin was a young Chicagoan trying to build an advertising agency in the midst of the Depression. He would eventually own a major company, and become a respected orientalist who traveled in the Far East and wrote on Chinese and Japanese history and art, which he studied as an avocation. But his immediate problem was making enough money to rent his own office. He had leased space at 139 North Clark Street from attorney Leonora Z. Meder, and if such makeshift quarters did not give his fledgling agency an image he felt would impress prospective clients, it did allow him to meet unusual people, one of whom would lead him into a memorable adventure.

One otherwise uneventful day that fall, Girardin was making light conversation with his attorney landlady while she waited for a prospective client. He arrived an hour late, and out of conventional politeness she introduced Girardin to a stocky, white-haired man of middle age whose name was then much in the news. He was Louis Piquett, also a lawyer, whose notoriety and legal problems had proved to be the occupational hazard that went with representing an even more notorious client, the outlaw John Dillinger.

The previous summer, on June 22, Dillinger had taken girlfriend Polly Hamilton to the ritzy French Casino nightclub on Chicago's North Clark Street to celebrate his thirty-first birthday (and possibly his promotion to

Public Enemy Number One, which occurred the same day). Exactly a month later, on July 22, he accompanied the same Polly and her friend Anna Sage to the Biograph Theatre on North Lincoln Avenue to see *Manhattan Melodrama,* a Clark Gable gangster movie, and was blown to immortality by the FBI. The shots that ended Dillinger's ordeal marked the beginning of Lou Piquett's, who soon found himself facing prosecution for what the authorities viewed as services far exceeding attorney-client privilege.

Girardin had followed Dillinger's exploits with the interest of most other newspaper readers, never expecting to play any role beyond that of history's witness. The chance meeting with Piquett led to something more. The young ad man called on the colorful and much-maligned lawyer, now facing criminal charges, and asked his help in writing the "inside" Dillinger story. Piquett, needing funds, consented, and brought into the project his private investigator, Arthur O'Leary, who had served as his contact man with the Dillinger gang and had presided over the plastic surgery performed on Dillinger in an attempt to change his appearance. Piquett and O'Leary signed a collaboration agreement with Girardin that resulted in a series of weekly articles published in the Saturday supplements of Hearst newspapers from October 1936 to January 1937.

Titled "Dillinger Speaks," the series was the only detailed account of Dillinger's life and criminal career by those who knew him personally, and decades later it qualified as a primary source for any researcher either diligent or lucky enough to discover it. Who G. Russell Girardin was, and why the lengthy series was never developed into a book, I had no idea. I had found the material by accident, while searching the original morgue files of the old *New York Journal-American,* now housed in the Harry Ransom Humanities Research Center at The University of Texas at Austin—the same school that had once seen fit to award me a master's degree in history despite a thesis titled "General John T. Thompson and the Gun That Made the Twenties Roar: A Case Study in Culture and Technology." (My supervising professor and guardian angel, Dr. Joe B. Frantz, had guessed correctly that such an academic mouthful would confuse the opposition enough to let me write a thrill-packed history of the Thompson submachine gun, later published by Macmillan more simply as *The Gun That Made the Twenties Roar.*)

My Tommygun research had led me to Dillinger and ultimately to G. Russell Girardin, a mystery man who was neither described nor identified, and who, I assumed, had long since followed Dillinger into history. And that's where he would have stayed, as far as anything I knew, but for a series of coincidences.

About 1987 Joe Pinkston, a long-time friend and owner of the John Dillinger Historical Museum in Nashville, Indiana, had introduced me to a (Mr.) Sandy Jones of Ft. Collins, Colorado, who was collecting Dillinger memorabilia. The items I sent him included the Girardin articles (minus chapter 11, annoyingly enough), which he evidently copied and sent to Tom Smusyn, another Chicago Dillinger buff, whom I would meet by another coincidence, and who at some point furnished Pinkston with copies of the copies (all still minus chapter 11), which by now were barely legible. In the spring of 1990, Pinkston asked me to help him locate Girardin. Since I was living in Chicago, had found the articles in a defunct New York newspaper on microfilm in a library in Texas, and they had been written over half a century ago by someone I had never heard of since, I had no suggestions. It did not occur to me to look in the Chicago telephone book. That did occur to Pinkston, however, who found Girardin to have an unpublished number that the telephone company had locked up in its computers the way banks lock up their money.

Would John Dillinger have let that stop him?

Using guile instead of a gun, I found a way into the electronic vault, which yielded an address only a few blocks from my own. The next day I located the house, knocked on the door, and a few minutes later was talking to one G. Russell Girardin. He was a frail-looking man in his eighties with thinning hair, but his mind and manner were lively, his personality outgoing, and his memory amazing. He had sold his large ad company, Girardin, Inc., some years earlier and was now living in pleasant retirement with his wife, Sue, in a splendid old two-story brick home on the North Side of Chicago.

If Girardin was surprised to be tracked down because of a single writing project in his youth, the greater surprise was mine. Not only was the Dillinger story still fresh in his memory, but from a shelf in his extensive library he pulled a timeworn, hard-bound, book-length manuscript that never had been published. He had been offered a contract by Putnam, but the syndicate that had purchased the series wanted a share of the book. After some unsuccessful negotiations, Girardin had shrugged, put the manuscript away, and gone on with his life.

Girardin knew that Dillinger would become a legendary outlaw. The night he was killed, first hundreds and soon thousands of Chicagoans called their friends and knocked on doors to share the most dramatic local crime news since the St. Valentine's Day Massacre. More than a thousand people flocked to the Biograph Theatre, turning the neighborhood into a carnival of the macabre, with some dipping handkerchiefs and scraps of newspaper, even hems of dresses, in the dead man's blood. The next day police avoided a riot only by allowing thousands more to file through the hot, reeking, fly-filled basement of the Cook County Morgue to view the corpse of a man whose exploits, style, and cockiness had created his legend even as he lived. For there was an irony to Dillinger that puzzled and fascinated even the most law-abiding citizen. Despite his reputation as a robber and gunman, Dillinger seemed to possess a fairly conventional value system not evident in such contemporaries as Baby Face Nelson or the Barker-Karpis Gang. Mindful of his image, he displayed gallantry and even playfulness when circumstances permitted, and took no obvious pleasure in violence. His admirers, and he had many, considered him crooked but not twisted. These qualities were all part of the truth, myth, and legend of John Dillinger, as widely if not always accurately portrayed.

What made this manuscript a Dead Sea Scroll to Dillinger historians (that description by me brought a laugh from Girardin) was not merely the new light it shed on Dillinger's desperate last days; after we had talked at some length he told me, with a conspiratorial smile, that he had additional information which could not be revealed at the time.

In his preface to the original manuscript, written in 1935 (and at my request not revised), he says that the book confines itself to verifiable facts and confidential information that Dillinger personally gave to Piquett and O'Leary. To me he added that O'Leary, especially, enjoyed recreating the conversations between himself and Dillinger, who was quite aware of his celebrity status and often spoke as though to an interviewer. What Girardin doesn't say in his preface, and couldn't, was that some facts had to be concealed or even falsified for his own protection and that of his collaborators. Some of the "disinformation" in the original version (as well as in erroneous news accounts) was propagated by later writers, to become permanent elements of the Dillinger story. The opportunity to correct the record at this late and safer date greatly appealed to Girardin, now that he had managed to outdistance a number of people who would have had no qualms about killing anyone with the incriminating knowledge he came to possess.

How the famous "wooden gun" jailbreak was engineered and who was bribed is described here for the first time. Dillinger's ties with his betrayer Anna Sage and with East Chicago policeman Martin Zarkovich—one of her lovers and his killers—also is revealed. Also interesting are the claims by Piquett and O'Leary that some of Dillinger's bank robberies were prearranged with the banks themselves, through local underworld contacts, to create or conceal losses. In other words, Girardin's account adds a wealth of new information on Dillinger and his associates, revises important aspects of the Dillinger story, and answers some of the questions that were baffling the police at the time.

My collaboration on the project began in the summer of 1990. For several weeks Girardin went through the original manuscript page by page, elaborating on questions I raised and adding footnotes. On August 28, barely a week after giving me the last of these, he suffered a stroke and was rushed by ambulance to Chicago's Swedish Covenant Hospital.

Sue, a native of Japan and his wife of twenty-seven years, stayed with him around the clock. After a few days Girardin not only had regained consciousness but seemed to be recovering, his memory and faculties intact. He was greatly pleased at the absence of any serious paralysis or speech impairment, but as a precaution took care of various legal matters through Raymond Krysl, his attorney and the only other person in town at all acquainted with the friendly but reclusive couple. Then, after several days of improvement, a series of new strokes left Girardin in a coma. At 4:35 A.M. on September 26, 1990, he died.

Of course I was saddened at the loss of a colleague who had quickly become a friend, and sorry that Girardin should have lived so long, only to be denied the pleasure of seeing his work of half a century ago finally become a book. On the other hand, how fortunate that Joe Pinkston had set in motion the chain of events that led me to Girardin's door while he was still alive, and to the discovery of his bound manuscript, dimly typed on onionskin, which he had long since relegated to a final resting place on a shelf in a library overflowing with rare books.

For that matter, how fortunate all this was for Girardin, a very private man whose declining health had largely confined him to the couple's comfortable house in a pleasant and secluded neighborhood. Sue remarked not only that my enthusiasm for his writing and story had flattered her husband greatly, but that our collaboration had revived his interest in life and work and made his last months especially happy ones. Still, I regret that any recognition due Russell Girardin now must come posthumously.

After a few weeks I resumed work on the project, as agreed, and was pleased to discover how much of Girardin's story is confirmed directly or indirectly by FBI records that were confidential at the time. In picking through thousands of these documents and other contemporary accounts, I also began stumbling onto characters whose interesting roles in the Dillinger case seem to have eluded both the authorities and the press at the time, and therefore the history books. Names and information briefly mentioned in different sources became like pieces of a jigsaw puzzle that only now is starting to make sense, but has yet to reveal a properly detailed picture of one Father Coughlan (for instance), a maverick Catholic priest whose flock seems to have consisted mainly of bank robbers; or of James Murray, whose brother had been killed by Al Capone's machine gunners in 1926, and whose own singleminded devotion to criminal enterprise should earn him more than a passing mention.

Both of these men, as it happens, figure in the mystery that still surrounds the death of Baby Face Nelson, who emerges from the clichés of 1930s journalism as a worthy subject for some future biographer, as does Dillinger's attorney, Louis Piquett, a P. T. Barnum of the legal profession—or maybe its W. C. Fields.

Some of these individuals and events are covered in the endnotes (see "After the Facts") in much more detail than usual, partly because they add another dimension to the Dillinger story, and partly because I simply found them fascinating.

Because social conditions and crime control have changed greatly since 1935, Girardin allowed me to divide his manuscript into five parts and introduce each with commentary that relates Dillinger to an earlier American dream which ended during the Depression, and to the emergence of the Federal Bureau of Investigation as a national law-enforcement agency.

This introductory material and the epilogue are provided by me, as are the endnotes, appendixes, acknowledgments, and sources. The on-page notes are by Girardin, who was alive to read and approve most of the initial editing. (Where I have added any on-page note, it appears in brackets with my initials.)

What follows is the original preface to Girardin's remarkable bit of history, written by an excited young ad man in 1935 when the story still was news.

—William J. Helmer

Preface

The very name John Dillinger cannot be spoken without myriad headlines coming to mind. The number of words written on his exploits is impossible to estimate—certainly the figure extends well into the millions. He was the darling of the circulation managers of newspapers, and writers for magazines and other publications found him a fertile field as well.

One would expect, therefore, that this subject has been thoroughly covered. In volume this is true; in authenticity it is quite the contrary. Much that has been written is incomplete, and much more either is based on erroneous information or bears the mark of pure invention. In fact, it is seldom indeed that one finds two accounts bearing upon the same topic that even remotely agree, except in instances all too common where one is obviously taken from the other.

Nevertheless, the greater part of this mass of printed matter has been thoroughly examined, if only to be discarded. The main exceptions are personal experiences recounted by narrators devoid of self-serving motives. Even accounts by members of the federal and state governments are considered reliable only with corroboration, as recollections often make good use of hindsight when personal and professional reputations are at stake. Much written on the subject appears to be the product of little more than rumor or imagination. When one reads detailed accounts of John Hamilton committing crimes months after he was dead and buried, or statements that John Dillinger did not understand how to use a machine gun, or when one sees the six-foot-tall Homer Van Meter referred to as "the diminutive bandit," it is impossible to give credence to anything further the writers may say.

It was therefore resolved to disregard most secondhand accounts and seek information primarily from direct and credible sources. To do this, it was necessary to meet with Dillinger's father, other members of the family, state and federal authorities, police officials, secret investigators, officers of banks, and, most important, the associates of Dillinger himself.

Chief among those in the last category were Louis Piquett, Dillinger's attorney, and Arthur O'Leary, who served as Piquett's investigator and contact man for the gang. It may be mentioned that Piquett has never heretofore broken the silence which he maintained following the outlaw's death, and has declined all previous requests made to him for information on the subject. However, so much unwelcome notoriety and unfavorable publicity have been heaped upon his head that he finally resolved to place the whole detail of his connection before the public without restraint or reservation, feeling that even the most damaging portions of the truth could not possibly be as injurious to him as the false rumors being spread. The very close relationship of attorney and client existing between the two gives his revelations a peculiarly confidential and authentic quality.

Arthur O'Leary is the one living person who was closest to John Dillinger during the period of his criminal activities. Over a period of many weeks he saw Dillinger almost every day, and there were few secrets that the famous desperado did not share. For Dillinger was not unlike the ordinary person in needing a friend and confidant, and was always amused and sometimes annoyed at the often ludicrous information published concerning him. He kept O'Leary apprised of the accuracy or nonsense of many of these stories. At one point he proposed to furnish O'Leary a full account of his career, and during the early summer of 1934, when Dillinger was laying low in Chicago and undergoing plastic surgery, six or seven conferences were devoted to this task. While the gang leader's informal memoirs were cut short by violent circumstances, much was told, and this portion stands forth as the most reliable data that can ever come to light.

It may perhaps be remarked that this account presents John Dillinger in a light more friendly than some. To this it can be said only that the Dillinger story usually is told by the men who were his enemies and who now have had their say. The "other side of the picture" is naturally more in his favor. Nevertheless, every effort has been made to combine the versions of both sides impartially, and much information favorable to Dillinger has been disallowed in the absence of proof. In fact, if there is any credit at all due the compilers of this story, it is that they made every honest effort to present the truth. Where doubt exists upon any topic, admission is frankly made that this is the case. Included in the temporary or permanent possession of the compilers are the letters written by John Dillinger, the wooden gun he used to escape from the jail at Crown Point, a radio he owned, his tobacco pipe, his field glasses, coins from his pockets, and other articles of his daily life.

In addition to Piquett and O'Leary, valuable information was obtained from numerous other persons, many of whom, because of their official positions or for reasons of a private nature, requested anonymity. The following, however, have kindly consented to lend their cooperation publicly, and the occasion is therefore taken to make grateful acknowledgment of their valued assistance:

John Wilson Dillinger, father of John Herbert Dillinger
Mrs. Audrey Hancock, John Dillinger's sister
Captain Matt Leach, head of the Indiana State Police
Edward Barce, Assistant Attorney General of the State of Indiana
Kenneth Dewees, Chief of Police, Montpelier, Indiana
D. M. Kreamelmeyer, Chief of Police, Auburn, Indiana
C. W. Coulter, Chief of Police, St. Paul, Minnesota
W. G. C. Bagley, President of the First National Bank, Mason City, Iowa
Walter A. Simmons, *The Daily Argus-Leader*, Sioux Falls, South Dakota
Meyer Bogue, intimate of several Dillinger gang members while they were inmates at the Indiana State Prison, and later employed by the state of Indiana as a special investigator in the Dillinger case

In closing, it may be pointed out that the travails of John Dillinger stand forth for all time as an example of the consequences that cannot fail to ensue when the laws of society are flouted by the criminal.

—G. Russell Girardin, Chicago, 1935

We can't all be saints.

—John Dillinger

PART I

After a period of postwar inflation and labor unrest, the 1920s roared with progress, prosperity, and a general optimism that helped Americans ignore some of the decade's less agreeable aspects. Automobiles, airplanes, telephones, radio, motion pictures, musical recording, and an endless parade of fads enthralled the nation and tended to obscure the failure of its greatest reform movement, Prohibition, to usher in the era of clean living and clear thinking that its supporters had promised. Instead of ending a scourge that was sapping the nation's vitality (according to moralists and managers), it had only transformed drunkenness from a working-class vice into a symbol of middle-class rebellion. It was good-natured rebellion to be sure—a fun and relatively safe way to thumb one's nose at propriety and authority, since the law enjoined the sale of booze but not the drinking of it. Adventurous rumrunners and cocky bootleggers provided Americans with a new form of entertainment that obscured the corruption they fostered at every level of government. Only when Chicago's beer wars exploded in the middle twenties and spread to other cities did gangland violence begin to compete with automobile accidents (another new phenomenon) for public attention; and not even then did the country realize it was witnessing the birth of a new and permanent antisocial phenomenon—nationally organized crime.

Politicians, police, and purveyors of illicit services had long been organized at the city or county level, but by the end of the decade so many billions of illegal dollars had been so blatantly lavished on public officials by professional lawbreakers that even the most cynical were becoming alarmed. In 1929, the St. Valentine's Day Massacre and the stock market crash were totally unrelated events, yet each contributed to a sense of impending disaster; and with government demonstrating no ability to protect citizens from either financial or personal harm, new atrocities such as the kidnap-murder of the Lindbergh baby seemed only to confirm that there was no one at the controls.

Thus the Depression did much to alter attitudes toward crime. Worried Americans not only lost their enthusiasm for celebrity bootleggers, but began to view lawlessness as evidence of a general breakdown of morality, authority, and leadership. The fact that only the federal government could stop Al Capone, and it could stop him only on a technicality, merely verified that state and local officials were impotent or corrupt or both, and that the criminal justice system was in shambles.

The Hoover administration had not intervened in the Capone case willingly. It did so only after a group of prominent Chicagoans descended on Washington with great hoopla in 1930 and laid the gangster problem squarely on the White House doorstep. Even then, President Hoover and his attorney general made it clear that while the national government might be expected to enforce a national law, it was not in the business of fighting crime. That was the job of state and local governments, as clearly established in the U.S. Constitution and insisted upon by a states'-rights Congress, and neither party had ever advocated the expansion of federal police power. The Comstock Act of 1873, the Mann Act of 1910, and the Harrison Narcotics Act of 1914 were passed largely out of legislators' fears of appearing soft on obscenity, prostitution, and drugs, respectively, when those perennial problems had been declared national perils mainly to wake up the electorate. Probably a truer reflection of citizen priorities was the National Motor Vehicle Theft Act of 1919, known as the Dyer Act, which gave Justice Department agents the rather pedestrian job of retrieving stolen cars that had been driven across state lines. Even when public outrage over the Lindbergh case forced the passage of a federal kidnapping law in 1932, with the usual interstate-commerce restrictions, Hoover signed it with reluctance while his attorney general grumped at Congress, "You are never going to correct the crime situation in this country by having Washington jump in." Locking up Capone on a tax beef that anyone else could have settled out of court had been more or less a favor to some politically important Chicagoans.

That philosophy of government went out with Herbert Hoover. The country's economic collapse called for emergency measures that were clearly beyond the capacity of state and local authorities, and the presidential candidate who promised action and spectacle instead of caution and patience—a

New Deal for Americans—was the think-positive governor of New York, Franklin Delano Roosevelt.

Roosevelt took office in 1933 without having dwelled on the issue of crime. He had pledged repeal of the Eighteenth Amendment not to end gangland violence so much as to create jobs and restore lost tax revenue, and hardly intended to revolutionize American law enforcement. That would have been consistent with the New Deal style of reform, but the way it began and the way it turned out owed much to one of history's flukes.

The man Roosevelt picked to be attorney general was Thomas Walsh, a seventy-four-year-old Montana senator whose earlier disputes with the Justice Department, and that department's retaliation, had created a strong and mutual animosity. Especially detested was a zealous young Red hunter and dirt digger who had been promoted to director of investigations in 1924, to clean up an office mired in corruption. But two days before the inauguration Walsh died of a heart attack, denying him the pleasure of cleaning the Justice Department house himself and no doubt sacking its chief investigator, whose men had tried to connect him with the Teapot Dome scandal a few years before. Thus was saved the job of one J. Edgar Hoover, who would thrive in the New Deal climate of activism and soon fashion in his own image an awesome agency which would be called the Federal Bureau of Investigation and which would make his name a household word.[1]

The name Americans encountered first, however, was that of Homer Stillé Cummings, Walsh's last-minute replacement. A former mayor and county prosecutor from Connecticut, Cummings was an able lawyer with progressive ideas on criminal justice but hardly known outside Democratic Party circles. The choice would prove to be propitious, however, for Cummings brought to his new post exactly the approach and energy that the New Deal philosophy wanted—and that J. Edgar Hoover needed. The two men began framing an array of unprecedented federal laws that would place the U.S. government in the forefront of the "war on crime," as it was now in the forefront of the "war" on every other national problem. The Constitution still required the Justice Department to attack crime indirectly (and sometimes quite awkwardly) through the power of Congress to levy taxes and regulate interstate commerce, but Roosevelt and most of the country now considered such restraints mere technicalities, and *Newsweek* approvingly declared Cummings to be "as enthusiastic about his new job as a small boy trapping muskrats."

While every politician had been railing against lawlessness, only Cummings and Hoover seemed to recognize that much of the problem stemmed from an American style of crime control that was hopelessly antiquated. State police forces still were mainly paper organizations—"highway patrols" for the new motoring public—and county and municipal police were often at odds over who protected which illegal enterprise when jurisdictions overlapped. In the larger cities police districts were practically autonomous, often corrupt, and given to maintaining the peace with as much brutality as public opinion would tolerate. There was little coordination or cooperation between agencies, and after a decade of Prohibition the law-enforcement profession was as despised as the politicians who usually dominated it.

American police science was just as backward. The tedious Bertillon method of identifying criminals by physical measurements, imported from France in the nineteenth century, was finally giving way to fingerprinting, but the forensic sciences had yet to find wide acceptance in either police work or the courtroom. Ballistics and other firearm identification methods were formally introduced only after the St. Valentine's Day Massacre inspired some civic-minded Chicagoans to personally fund the country's first scientific crime-detection laboratory, which became the prototype for all police crime labs, including the FBI's. So if Cummings and Hoover had both professional and personal motives for promoting reform, the fact remains that the reforms were badly needed.

Being right was not enough, however. The national mindset still distrusted centralized authority and feared that any federal law-enforcement agency would sooner or later become a secret police. So Washington needed to demonstrate the threat posed by "interstate" crime, the inability of state and local authorities to cope with it, and the urgent necessity for new federal criminal laws enforced by a professional, nonpolitical, and incorruptible bureau of the Justice Department.

When gangbusters Cummings and Hoover set to work in the spring of 1933, the "underworld army" was imagined only vaguely as the great community of wrongdoers who were breaking the law. Any law. In using the term "gangster," neither the press nor the public distinguished between businessmen whose illegal goods and services represented "consensual" crimes that were hard to prove, and robbers who stole money at gunpoint and could be arrested the same way. Some criminals worked in both camps, of course, and both types tended to use the same lawyers, doctors, bail-bondsmen, taverns, and car and gun dealers, who together amounted to an underworld support group. But for crime-control purposes, consensual offenses and crimes of violence involved different kinds of laws and required different law-enforcement strategies.

So while the country had plenty of big-city mobsters and notorious murderers like Leopold and Loeb, its last famous robber was Jesse James. Texas's Clyde Barrow and Bonnie Parker enjoyed regional notoriety as a boy-and-girl stickup team, but the only outlaw attracting much national attention was Charles Arthur Floyd, a young Oklahoma farmer-turned-bandit who was raiding small banks with a submachine gun and a flair for the dramatic. Called Pretty Boy probably by mistake (several explanations exist, but it now appears that police originally confused him with a petty crook called Pretty Boy Smith and the nickname stuck), Floyd became something of a hero among Depression-stricken farmers by looting banks and then throwing his money around. If Pretty Boy didn't exactly pay off mortgages, as described in the Woody Guthrie ballad, he apparently did go out of his way to destroy loan records as a philanthropic gesture.

By the time he received national recognition in 1932 as "Oklahoma's Bandit King," Floyd was on the run, and he might have drifted back into obscurity but for some bad shooting in Kansas City a few months later. Strapped for cash, Floyd hired himself out to a local crime boss to help deliver convicted bank robber and mobster Frank "Jelly" Nash from guards taking him to the federal penitentiary at Leavenworth. On the morning of June 17, 1933, a trio of gunmen including Pretty Boy intercepted Nash and his guards in the parking lot of Kansas City's Union Station, and when the smoke cleared, two cars had been riddled and four lawmen killed, including FBI agent Raymond Caffrey. Also dead was Frank Nash, the man they were supposed to rescue.

The Kansas City Massacre was the "Machine-Gun Challenge to a Nation" for which Cummings and Hoover had been waiting, and it came the same morning that the nation's papers were bannering the kidnapping of St. Paul brewer William Hamm, Jr. The Hamm kidnapping revived outrage over the still-unsolved death of the Lindbergh baby the year before, and even the Hamm case was overshadowed in less than four weeks by the kidnapping of Oklahoma City oilman Charles Urschel, whose abductors demanded an unprecedented ransom of $200,000.

Armed with a machine-gun "massacre" and two excellent kidnappings, Attorney General Cummings declared the country's first "war on crime" and dramatically unveiled his Twelve Point Program of federal crime control. Congress was immediately dubious about that, but Roosevelt applauded and obligingly instructed Cummings to study the advisability of turning the FBI into a "superpolice force."

When Cummings declared war on crime, the opposing armies were not very clearly defined. The public knew little of Hoover and his agents, who were not yet called "G-men"; and the big-city mobsters, who attended ball games and operas and might even give interviews, were hardly the "interstate fugitives" Cummings was talking about. The first order of business, therefore, was to personify the enemy, and with Pretty Boy Floyd now in deep hiding, the country had to make do with Machine Gun Kelly.

George F. Barnes, Jr., alias George Kelly, was a small-time Memphis bootlegger who had also robbed a few banks without attracting attention. He might have avoided notoriety but for his attractive third wife, Kathryn, whose circle of friends included some underworld characters with much more ambition than her laid-back George. Supposedly at her insistence, George Kelly helped kidnap Urschel, whom they deposited with Kathryn's slow-witted parents on a farm in Texas. After payment of the ransom, Urschel was released unharmed and, the official story goes, helped the FBI quickly break the case by remembering certain details of great use to the government's new breed of scientific detective. An unofficial story is that the FBI learned about the kidnapping from two informants. In any event, within a month the kidnappers and their accomplices all had been arrested—except for Kathryn and George Kelly, who seems to have acquired the name "Machine Gun" only after a captured Thompson was traced to a Ft. Worth gun dealer whose customer had been Kathryn. By the time he was tracked to Memphis and arrested in his pajamas on September 26, Kelly had been promoted to leader and brains of the gang. The FBI described him as a "desperate character, having served a number of prison terms [two, actually] for bootlegging, vagrancy, and other offenses," and even the conservative New York Times declared that "Kelly and his gang of Southwestern desperados are regarded as the most dangerous ever encountered." After a sensational trial in Oklahoma City, Kathryn and "Machine Gun" Kelly were sentenced to life in prison.

In the Urschel kidnapping, the Justice Department scored an early and impressive victory in its war on crime. The investigation had covered seventeen states, with arrests in five. Within ninety days the crime had been solved, the ransom recovered, and the kidnappers sent to prison, clearly demonstrating the effectiveness of the federal government in dealing with interstate criminals. Detailed news releases on the progress of the case, unprecedented newsreel coverage of the federal courtroom trials, plus theatrical precautions against the Kellys' escape, ensured that the public got the message.

With the "Machine Gun Kelly Gang" so decisively smashed, Cummings and Hoover were on a roll and needed more interstate criminals with which to make headlines. They were spared any frustrating search for Pretty Boy or for the yet-unidentified Hamm kidnappers by the timely debut of the bank-robbing gang which eventually would make their day. On September 26, 1933, while Kelly was being captured, ten convicts broke out of the Indiana State Prison at Michigan City, using guns smuggled to them by a recent parolee, and began a midwestern crime spree that soon had the entire country's attention.

The weapons for the Michigan City breakout were supplied by a thirty-year-old Hoosier named John Herbert Dillinger, who had been released from Michigan City four months previously after serving nine years for a bungled holdup in 1924. It was this stiff sentence for a first offense, many believed, that turned Johnnie Dillinger from a restless but likable farm boy into a hardened professional criminal. True or not, over the next fourteen months, Dillinger and the FBI would make one another famous—or maybe infamous, since Dillinger humiliated his pursuers all the way to the Biograph, jeopardizing Hoover's job and costing Melvin Purvis his. Dillinger's spectacular robberies, jailbreaks, gun battles, elusiveness, and impudence provided Americans with an exhilarating game of cops 'n' robbers that helped Homer Cummings ram his bills through a reluctant Congress, made J. Edgar Hoover a household name, and created the legend of the FBI. The Justice Department did the same for Dillinger, who demonstrated that if Crime Does Not Pay, it can still be a shortcut to immortality.

Writing in the style of another age, G. Russell Girardin told it like it was.

CHAPTER ONE

THE TWIG IS BENT

There is no garden in which some weeds do not rear their heads; there has been no time and no place in which some individuals have not strained at the leash and broken the restraining bonds. Upon their heads has been placed the brand of the outlaw, and to them is exhibited only the face of implacable hatred and warfare. The vast majority live and die unhonored and unsung, for the world has no laurels to place on the brow of mediocrity. But now and then, like a meteor flashing through a night sky, there arises some one of society's rebels whose exploits fill the tongues of men, and about whose name legends cluster like ivy on a gray stone wall.

From the seed of England sprang the great American republic, and as its sturdy pioneers conquered the mountains and deserts of a new land they enriched the New World culture with legends from the Old. The passage of years had gifted pirates Edward Teach and Captain Kidd with reputations, real or mythical, that gave them immortality, in the same way that folklore established highwaymen Dick Turpin and Robin Hood as legendary outlaws no modern counterparts could rival. In America, only two would venture close. Jesse James became the good badman in death; John Dillinger became a legend in his own time.

Who was John Dillinger? Was he a bold and benevolent Robin Hood, or a mad and ruthless killer? Or an ordinary human being whose life was molded by luck and circumstance into a career so strange that even before his death legend and fable had begun to weave about him?

This is the story of the real John Dillinger, as he wrote it in his letters and told it to his family, to his friends, and to his closest associates.

*   *   *

In the hills of Lorraine lies the rich wine country of the Moselle Valley, the cradle of the Dillinger family. Mathias Dillinger left his native France when about twenty years old and arrived at New Orleans on the eve of the Civil War. Shortly thereafter he settled in Indiana and married, and the Dillinger family combined with Hoosier stock. From that blend came John Wilson Dillinger, the father of America's greatest desperado.

No one who has ever visited the elder Dillinger on his farm at Mooresville can come away unimpressed with the strength of character expressed in those kind brown eyes. He was the "Honest" John Dillinger to fellow townsmen, and even at the time of his son's direst troubles never tried to protect him with false information. His weatherbeaten face is that of a man who has lived close to the soil, and there is about him an air of bleak courage mingled with private sorrow.

The Honest John Dillinger settled on the outskirts of Indianapolis and married Mary Ellen or "Molly" Lancaster, the daughter of a respected farmer from the nearby town of Cumberland. To them was born in 1889 a daughter, a small-boned, red-haired girl whom they named Audrey. And then no other child for fourteen years.

John Herbert Dillinger was born in a bungalow at 2053 Cooper Street (the present Caroline Avenue) in Indianapolis, Indiana. The mystery surrounding him begins even with the date of his birth, for over a dozen different dates are given in various published articles. The reason for these discrepancies is difficult to explain, for the records of the Department of Public Health and Charities of Indianapolis and those of the Dillinger family agree that John Herbert was born on June 22, 1903.

When he was scarcely three years old his mother died, and John began to learn that life held many blows. On the day of the funeral, the relatives and friends who had gathered at the home noticed that the youngster had disappeared, and immediately began a search. They found him on a chair he had laboriously dragged to the side of the coffin, shaking his mother to awaken her.

From this time the maternal duties devolved on Audrey, and the neighbors unite in testifying as to how well she carried out the task. Young John was a sturdy, laughing youngster, the pet of everyone who knew him, and always immaculately neat in the little suits provided by his sister. The elder Dillinger operated a small neighborhood grocery at 2210 Bloyd Avenue, and was deacon at the Hillside Christian Church in Indianapolis. Numerous Bibles in the family home at Mooresville testified to the constant presence of a religious atmosphere.

Audrey married Emmet Hancock, a pleasant, hardworking man, and went to live in the village of Maywood, just outside Indianapolis. Their progeny consisted of four boys and three girls, while little brother John was regarded equally as a member of the family. According to Audrey, "John was with me a great part of the time. He was raised up with my two older boys, and they were like brothers."

In due course Johnnie Dillinger reached school age. Public School No. 38 was located in the Oak Hill district where the Dillingers then lived, and which at that time had much of the aspect of a small country town. If John did not stand forth in school as a prodigy of learning, he attracted the attention of his teachers with his alert mind, and his invariably neat and clean appearance. Arithmetic was always a drudgery to him, but he had a passionate love of reading, and borrowed books from neighbors when his own scanty supply had been thoroughly perused.

About the same time that young John entered school, old John married for the second time. This wife was Elizabeth Fields, and much maternal solicitude went to her two stepchildren. Nor was this affection lessened by the children from her own marriage—a boy, Hubert, and two younger girls, Doris and Frances. These three never ceased to love the man the world knew as an outlaw, but who to them was their big brother Johnnie.

There is a vague feeling about John Dillinger that he must necessarily have been a criminal from the cradle, to become so notorious in later life. But there is nothing to indicate that he was markedly different or more mischievous than the average boy.[2] The consensus among friends and neighbors and schoolmates is that there was nothing really "bad" about Johnnie Dillinger. He raided orchards and strawberry patches, he sometimes snared a neighbor's chicken, and he teased the town drunk. Once he roped a farmer's outhouse to a freight train standing on nearby tracks, with a predictable result. Similar adventures among his boyhood companions did not lead them into lives of crime. The only thing that set young Dillinger apart from some of his peers was his ability to use his fists. Though not very tall, he was broad and surprisingly strong, and the undisputed cock of the walk.

Johnnie Dillinger quit school before finishing the eighth grade, and there his education ceased. It was not economic necessity that compelled him to take this step, but like other boys, he fancied himself tired of school, and so went to work in a veneer mill near his father's store. The work was hard, entailing much heavy lifting, and those who were less physically fit discovered that Dillinger would usually lend them a hand. What money he had also was available to those in financial straits. More than one fellow employee owed some part of his wardrobe to Dillinger's natural generosity.

Mooresville, Indiana: Located on the top of a gentle slope, the town sleepily scatters its ramshackle buildings over the hillside. Before State Highway 67 became a freeway, it ran through the center of town and served as "main street" to the local residents. A drug store, a post office, and a small weekly newspaper were then the most important buildings. On the outskirts of the village stood the school, a functional structure built in the best traditions of Hoosier education. Beside the school stood the church, whose tolling bells called the faithful to worship.

The countryside around is typical of central Indiana—rain-washed gullies, hilly rough fields, and yellow sticky clay. It is from this soil that the sturdy Indiana farmer eked out his livelihood and the village of Mooresville its existence. From the drudgery of his daily tasks, the farmer's only surcease was "going to town" to Mooresville, interspersed with an occasional journey into Indianapolis. Youth worked side by side with the parent until he married the neighbor's daughter, and the dreary cycle began all over again.

It was in surroundings such as these that John Dillinger spent his early manhood. He lived the normal life of any rural boy in central Indiana during the daylight hours, working with his father on the farm, helping his stepmother with household tasks, and otherwise giving assistance wherever it was needed. His youth at this point seems to have been a happy one, and by all accounts he was devoted to his stepmother, who in turn loved him and mothered him as though he were her own son.

When not working Dillinger spent time in the woods with his

dog and gun, hiking for hours and shooting at rodents and crows. He early showed a liking for firearms and was said to take much pride in his marksmanship. On most of these expeditions he preferred to be alone with his dog, claiming to derive pleasure from daydreaming beside a stream and listening to the sounds of nature. He was shy and diffident during this period of his life, and the outdoors may have somehow compensated for his lack of association with others of his own age.

As he grew older, however, this shyness disappeared, and he began to appear more and more with youths of the surrounding country. It was at this time that he developed the fondness for baseball that was to follow him through life, and which at one time in Chicago would nearly result in his demise. He joined the Mooresville baseball nine, beginning as second baseman and then, as his confidence increased, becoming the club's leading pitcher. The popularity this brought may have made his life up to then seem unbearably routine, for he began to stay out nights and hang around the local poolroom, seeking out the town's closest approximation of excitement and adventure.

The boy was now growing into the man, and with the advent of adolescence had come a new awareness of the female face and form. If not preoccupied with girls, he was also not without early sexual experiences, at least of a casual nature. But when he did feel love, he felt it with unusual intensity. For a while he attended the Quaker Sunday school in Mooresville, less to fulfill any spiritual needs than because of a girl in the class.

Frances Thornton came to Mooresville on a summer visit to a girlfriend and met young Dillinger, who happened to be her stepfather's nephew. John promptly fell in love. From statements made by him in later life the two became engaged, though this fact probably was withheld from their respective families. In any case, the parents of Frances looked with scant favor on Dillinger's courtship of their daughter, and at length the continued efforts of her stepfather were successful in ending the relationship.

With the failure of this love affair John Dillinger experienced a great sense of loss, and memories of Frances Thornton would remain with him the rest of his life. But now Mooresville was intolerable. He fled to Indianapolis, and after a period of youthful carousing and dissipation enlisted in the U.S. Navy on July 23, 1923. His naval career was of short duration, however. He was assigned to the battleship *Utah*, but he felt a certain homesickness and adjusted poorly to the military discipline. He deserted in Boston before five months had elapsed and made his way back to

Mooresville, informing family and friends that he had been discharged because of a weak heart. No serious efforts at apprehension were made by the naval authorities, and it was not until later, in 1925, when he was incarcerated in the Indiana State Reformatory at Pendleton, that an undesirable discharge was issued.

Still at loose ends in Mooresville, Dillinger worked sporadically and dated whatever girls were available and willing. One was a prosaic rural lass named Beryl Hovious, only sixteen years old to John's twenty, and on April 12, 1924, she became his wife. The general impression in Mooresville at the time was that he was not deeply attached to Beryl, and that his marriage was mainly an effort to obliterate the memory of Frances Thornton. But whatever sentiments may have actuated him then, the ties of affection would ripen and deepen.

Thus far John Dillinger's life had experienced a certain amount of turbulence, but nothing exceptional for a restless youth whose heart was not in the land or the quiet rural community. The next mistakes he would make would have more serious consequences. The bitter days were now to come.

CHAPTER TWO

THE QUALITY
OF MERCY

The narrow limits within which life moved in Mooresville could never confine the active spirit of John Dillinger. He began to enter the "wild life" of the town, which consisted of the usual run of rural youths and loafers to be found about the poolroom and the interurban station. This routine was varied by nothing more exciting than an occasional trip to nearby Martinsville, the county seat, or to Indianapolis.

Some time after Dillinger's death a story arose that he had been involved in an automobile theft, but much of it bears evidence of a long-prevalent tendency to link his name with crime. The details of the tale are these. Oliver P. Macy and his wife had parked their new car outside the Quaker church in Mooresville while they attended Sunday evening services, and found it missing when they came out. The car was returned to Macy later that night by an Indianapolis police sergeant, who stated that it had been found in the possession of a youth in that city. The young man was supposed to have identified himself as John Dillinger, but had broken away and fled while the arresting officer was at a call box. Macy, true to the traditions of his creed, refused to prosecute and allowed the matter to drop, and later received a letter from Dillinger denying the theft and asserting that he had passed the evening in question with a girl in Martinsville. The story is unsupported by police or other records, and perhaps it would be well to consign the incident to the mass of legends that attached themselves to the Dillinger name.

We now come to Dillinger's first crime of any significance and the one for which he was convicted. Among the ne'er-do-wells who frequented the Mooresville pool hall was Edgar Singleton, an older man who had served time in the Indiana State Prison in Michigan City. Singleton proved quite a lurid attraction to many of the unsophisticated town boys, who listened intently to his exaggerated accounts of his exploits and fancied him to be quite a desperate character. Among the most impressed of his disciples was young Dillinger, who traversed another step on his road to hell when he began to go out on drinking bouts with Singleton.

On the night of September 6, 1924, the drinking had been unusually heavy. Frank Morgan, the groceryman of Mooresville, was headed for his home, with the weekend receipts of $150 tucked in his pocket, when he passed by the Christian Church. On the back steps of the church were Dillinger and Singleton, their minds sadly befuddled with the quantities of moonshine liquor which they had imbibed. Possibly on impulse but more likely as part of a preconceived plan, the two rushed upon Morgan and began beating him with an iron bolt wrapped in cloth. Still struggling, the grocer seized the revolver and it discharged, inflicting a slight flesh wound between the thumb and forefinger of his hand. Morgan by this time was loudly giving the distress signal of the Ku Klux Klan,[3] and when men began rushing to his aid, his assailants fled into the night, Singleton by car, leaving Dillinger to escape on foot. He was found badly gashed about the head, and it was probably his stiff straw hat that saved him from much worse injuries.

Still staggering in a half-drunken state, Dillinger went back to town after this exploit and began asking questions as to the welfare of Mr. Morgan, which of course aroused suspicions. Then he went home, and was arrested there on Monday morning. Dillinger maintained he had no recollections from the previous Saturday night and no idea why he was being locked up. He denied having any part in the assault, and grocer Morgan was unable to identify his attackers. Singleton quietly disappeared from town, but when arrested later did not hesitate to place the entire blame on his younger companion.

Old John Dillinger felt his heart breaking within him when he learned of the trouble John was in. Pseudo-friends were showering him with advice, but afterward he said, "I just didn't have the money to hire a lawyer for my boy."

With grocer Morgan unable to make a positive identification, the case against young John was beginning to look decidedly shaky. So the Dillingers were told by court officials that they had incontrovertible proof, and if John would plead guilty he might gain a light sentence. This suited the elder Dillinger's sense of justice, and he so advised his son. Both Dillingers were unlearned in the ways of the law, and were taught a hard lesson. Judge Joseph Williams handed John Dillinger the maximum sentence— ten to twenty years for assault with intent to rob, concurrently with two to fourteen years for conspiracy to commit a felony.

Ed Singleton, hardened by prior experience with both crime and the workings of the law, hired a "smart" lawyer from Indianapolis, pleaded not guilty, and had a jury trial before a different judge. As a consequence, he received a sentence only on the conspiracy charge of from two to fourteen years, and in less than two years was back loitering like an evil shade about the smoky atmosphere of poolrooms.

There is many a tale of injustice and severity met with in courts of law, but on occasion these episodes contain a measure of truth. The disparity between the severity meted out to the youth Dillinger and the lenience accorded the ex-convict Singleton has had interesting repercussions. Ten years later Indiana Governor Paul V. McNutt would allow that the "obvious injustice" of Dillinger's first sentence could well have been the moment of concept for the future public enemy. "The judge and the prosecutor took him out and told him if he would tell certain things they would let him off with a lighter sentence. They didn't keep their word. They gave Dillinger ten to twenty years, while his partner in crime, Edgar Singleton, got two to fourteen years and was released at the end of two years. This made a criminal out of Dillinger."

Judge Williams defended himself by pointing out that the sentence he imposed was mandatory on a plea of guilty. This very statement would seem to demonstrate that Dillinger had not been told at the time of pleading what consequences would necessarily ensue. To Judge Williams's demand for a retraction, Governor McNutt replied, "All that I have said about the Dillinger case I reiterate; it is all true."

In this period of John Dillinger's life, at least, there had been certain favorable elements that a wiser jurist might have taken into consideration. He was not yet twenty-one years of age, he was married, he came from a family occupying a respected place in the community, he had no previous criminal record, and the offense in question had been committed while he was under the influence of liquor and an older individual. Judge Williams might have taken these facts into consideration and granted probation. It was certainly his moral duty not to have accepted a plea of guilty when he knew that Dillinger had no legal counsel and was obviously unaware of what such a plea would entail.

Some consideration was shown to Dillinger's youth and absence of record in assigning his place of confinement; instead of being sent to the penitentiary he was taken to the red brick building that housed the Indiana State Reformatory at Pendleton. Audrey Hancock, the tiny red-haired sister who had reared him, stood with tear-filled eyes at the window of her small white cottage as her brother passed along the road before her home.

Three months after his arrival John Dillinger made a clumsy attempt to escape from Pendleton, an attempt that gave no indication of the finesse which later enabled him to laugh at the confining walls of jails. During the next three years he was reported seven times for disorderly conduct, yet he was at no time considered a dangerous prisoner.

Pendleton was sufficiently close to Mooresville that John was able to receive visits from family and friends. The ties of family affection burned strongly among the Dillingers, and the heart of the young man confined in the State Reformatory was still warm with the memories of domestic scenes and ties. A letter to his wife, written August 18, 1928, strongly exemplifies that feeling.

My dearest wife,

Received your sweet letter tuesday even the only one this week and I'm still waiting for that interview. Gee honey I would like to see you. Hubert wrote to me last week. I would sure like to see him if he wants to come see me. Let me know and I will send him the carfare. I hope Sis is getting along allright and all the rest of the folks are well. Sweetheart aren't you ashamed for getting mad at Hubby over that letter when you ought to have known that I would have wrote if I could. You were mad now weren't you and I come very near not writing at all last time. I hope you are not worrying about how your going to keep me home with you after I get out, as sweet as you are you can let me do the worrying. Dearest we will be so happy when I can come home to you and chase your sorrows away and it wont take any kids to keep me home with you allways. For sweetheart I love you so all I want is to just be with you and make you happy. I wonder if I will get an interview monday. I sure hope so for I am dying to see you. Darling have some pictures taken, every time I see you, you look dearer and sweeter to me so I want late pictures. Now say rassberries but honey its the truth. I sure am crazy about you. . . . Write soon and come sooner.

Love from Hubby
XXXOOOXXXOOOXXX

What John Dillinger did not know at the time he wrote this letter was that his wife had decided to obtain a divorce. Shortly thereafter she came to him and told him what was on her mind. She had waited for him nearly four years, and that was a very long time, especially when there were perhaps many more years to wait as well. John could see how it was—her family and friends were constantly pressing upon her the reasoning that the devotion of a wife need not extend to the point of martyrdom. Her husband said nothing, for he could find no words.

Years later, when John Dillinger, now a national figure, was in hiding in Chicago, his thoughts would go back to Beryl Hovious and the effect of her divorce on him. "I began to know how you feel when your heart is breaking. For four years I had looked forward to going back home, and now there wasn't going to be any home to go back to."

Beryl Dillinger obtained a divorce on June 20, 1929, at Martinsville on the ground that her husband was an incarcerated felon. This blow was followed by another less than one month later: despite his efforts at exemplary behavior, the parole board turned him down. Dillinger expressed his disappointment by making an unusual request—that he be transferred to the Indiana State Prison at Michigan City. Whether or not this was influenced by a desire to play baseball on the better team in that institution, as some believe, it put him back in touch with his closest inmate friends, Harry Pierpont and Homer Van Meter, who had preceded him to that place. When he was moved to Michigan City on July 25, the event marked yet another step in the evolution of what would one day be called the Dillinger gang.

At Michigan City, as at Pendleton, Dillinger was not classed as a bad character. He involved himself in trouble from time to time, but it was never of a serious nature. Among the prisoners Dillinger enjoyed considerable popularity. His likable disposition and his ready good humor won him many friends. They knew that he could be trusted, and they found that he could not refuse help to a friend. Throughout his hectic career Dillinger's intense interest in baseball never flagged. He played on the prison baseball team, followed the Chicago Cubs with avidity, and conducted a baseball pool in the penitentiary.

Dillinger was assigned to the workshop of the shirt factory, and became a skillful operator on the sewing machine. His job was to sew on the yoke line across the back of the shirt. It was here in the shirt factory that he met more of the men who would later become members of the gang. A letter to his nephew, Norman Hancock, written about the late summer of 1929, throws an interesting light on the Dillinger of this period.

> Dear Norman.
>
> Well, where is that letter you were going to write me? I sure was glad to see you but you sure have grown. I hardly knew you. You tell Fred and Mary they had better write or I will disinherit them. Ha ha. Received Sister's letter, was sure sorry to hear that her and Mary are sick. I sure wish Sis had good health. Sometimes I think I won't have a Sister when I get out. . . . I want you to buy some things for me. It will come to about six dollars and you can have the rest. Ought to be over twelve dollars for you, you and your girl can have a swell time on that. Here is the list of what I want. One pair of suspenders real loud color about #2. One pair of supporters #1 lavender color. Three hankerchiefs like I told you. One black pocket comb. One pair of loud sleeve holders and a prophylastic tooth brush. . . .
>
> Lots of love to all.
> Johnnie.

Christmas day of the same year found Dillinger writing to his niece, Mary Hancock, who lived with her family in Maywood, Indiana:

> My dearest Niece:
>
> Received your sweet letter and was certainly glad to hear from you, it was about time you were writing. So, you hav'nt oddles of time to throw away, now I like that young lady. I will forgive you this time though providing you write oftener. Honey! I am so glad you like school so well for if you don't go their are plenty of times that you wish you had. I am sure glad to see you make such fine grades. I bet Sis and Emmett are proud of you. . . .
>
> Gee! sweetheart I can hardly believe that you are big enough to have a beau. I received my package O.K. also Sister's letter. I am sure sorry to hear she isn't any better. Sis wants me to pray for her to get better but I am not very strong for praying. I think it will take more than prayers for her to get well or for that matter for me to get out of here. Now dont think I am an Atheist for I am not, I do believe in God, but his ways seem strange to me sometimes, for if anyone deserves health and happiness it is your dear Mother who is the best and sweetest woman in the world. . . .

I know right from wrong and I intend to do right when I get out. I suppose you think that I do not try to make my time clear but honey I do try, and a lot of times when I want to do something or start to do something that might get me in trouble I think of Sis. And I dont do it. . . . Say you and Sis keep your eyes open for a sweet girl with plenty of money and ballahoo me up. Ha! Ha! Give my love to all the kiddies and you be a real good girl and help Sis to get better and when I come home I will buy you something real sweet. Well honey I guess I will ring off for this time. Merry Christmas to all of you. Lots and lots of love to all.

Johnnie.

P.S. . . . I just received a real nice letter from Clarice Mills about her picture. Hubert is mad at her over something that he shouldn't be mad about. Will you please write her a nice letter and tell her I am sure everything will be all right, and tell her I will write to her January 5. Also tell Hubert he had better behave himself and treat Clarice better.

The ceaseless efforts of the Dillinger family to effect John's freedom eventually begin to bear fruit. Dr. Charles Fillmore, the retired pastor of the church in Mooresville, went before the parole board to plead in his behalf. Judge Williams, Dillinger's former nemesis, had apparently undergone a change of heart and likewise appeared to express his belief that John was needed on the farm and that he would make a useful citizen. Grocer Morgan was more reluctant to join in the request for parole, but finally consented to sign a petition that bore the names of 184 fellow townsmen.

On May 22, 1933, John Dillinger, supplied with the five dollars the state of Indiana then bestowed upon those departing its penal institutions and a perfunctory lecture that crime does not pay, stepped beyond the walls of the Michigan City prison.

Hubert Dillinger and Norman Hancock were waiting for him at the gates in their aging automobile. It was with difficulty that they recognized the gaunt and pallid figure who now joined them as the sturdy youth whom they had known nine years before. The three began the long-awaited journey to Mooresville, and there the last drop of gall was poured into the bitter draught that fate had prepared for John Dillinger.

"Mom," the second wife of old John Dillinger, had been regarded with the affection of a true mother by both of her step-children. Several days before, while making a cake for her son Hubert's approaching birthday, she had suffered a stroke and collapsed to the floor of the farmhouse kitchen. On the same day that father Dillinger saw his son reenter the home, he witnessed the departure of his wife forever, for John Dillinger arrived to learn that his second mother had just died. For the moment, the many years spent in prisons dropped from his shoulders, and for the last time the bitter tears of sorrow and disappointment came to his eyes.

CHAPTER THREE

"AND EVERY MAN'S HAND"

There was little place for an ex-convict in the rural atmosphere of Mooresville. The jubilation that ordinarily would have attended Dillinger's homecoming had been obliterated by the death and burial of his stepmother. His fellow townsmen displayed only sympathy and friendliness, but John knew that covertly there were the usual small-town whisperings that he was a criminal, and that he had served time in the penitentiary. It is hard living down a record like that. He helped his father and Hubert in the work about the farm, but much of his time was spent in a restless promenading about the house, wandering aimlessly from one room to another.

John Dillinger took careful stock of the situation confronting him. His own mother had died in his infancy, and now his stepmother had followed her to the grave. The sweetheart of his youth was lost to him forever. The wife he had idolized had divorced him, and was married to another. An unthinking act of severity on the part of a country judge had robbed him of the most important years of his life. His home town tolerated him, but only as an outcast. Where then was he to turn? His penitentiary experience provided the answer.

On the night of July 16, 1933, Dillinger left the paternal home in Mooresville, and the greatest career in the annals of American criminal history had its inception. His companions in this early stage were one Harry Copeland, a heavy-eyed, swarthy chap, and Hilton O. Crouch, a former dirt-track automobile racer and a good man to have at the wheel of a bandit car. The following afternoon this trio held up the Commercial Bank of Daleville, Indiana, a small town situated midway between Pendleton and Muncie. It was a rather amateurish job of bank robbing and had little in the nature of thrills. Confronting them was nothing more dangerous than a nervous woman cashier and an open vault, which yielded an amount of some $3,500. There was not even a chief of police in the town.

The next job of this embryo Dillinger gang was the Montpelier, Indiana, National Bank on August 4. Kenneth Dewees, chief of police of Montpelier, writes an interesting account of this holdup:

> Three men were in the party. J. Dillinger and Copeland entered the Bank, and the third man, identity unknown (Hilton Crouch), remained in the car. This was August 4, 1933, at 2:30 P.M. At this time one of the N. R. A. committees were meeting in Wells' & Rapp's meat market directly across the street from the Bank. R. B. Shandle, Earl St. John, Glenn Arrick, Fred Rapp and Jim Wells made up this committee. They were standing in front of the large plate glass window in the meat market when a large car drove up in front, and they saw two men enter the bank. In a very few minutes they saw them leave the bank, each carrying money sacks. Jim Wells, a very short, fat man says, "What in the hell do those men have in those sacks? My God, they are robbing the bank! Fred, get that gun quick!" During this excited speech Jim was jumping up and down, which was a very laughable matter later. Jim has passed on beyond this world since. Two men, Al Wikel and John Fox, were leaning against the Kroeger store next to the Bank building, and Dillinger and Copeland passed within ten feet of these men, carrying the $6,700 that was stolen. Fox and Wikel made the remark, "Look at the money those men have. Let's hold them up," at which Dillinger only smiled. They entered their car and left town, no one knowing which way. They were not followed.

Newspaper accounts placed the amount of money taken in this robbery in the neighborhood of $12,000. In any event, the loot proved greater than at Daleville, for Mr. Dillinger was getting into the larger money. About the middle of the same month, the Dillinger gang visited the bank in the small town of Bluffton, Ohio, taking $6,000. The bandits' hideout was in East Chicago.

Those three robberies, unimportant as they seemed at the time, were to bring Matt Leach, captain in charge of the Indiana State Police, into the Dillinger picture. From this time onward Dillinger was to prove the bane of Leach's existence, for a perverse fate seemed to decree that Leach was always to reach the scene in time to glimpse Dillinger's coattails. But Leach was to continue the pursuit with a deadly earnestness, and afforded the desperado more than one uncomfortable moment. To Dillinger, Captain Leach was a source of never-ending ridicule. When he related a humorous anecdote concerning an officer of the law, Matt Leach usually was the butt of the joke. During the then-current craze for gangster pictures, there was a dark-haired character who invariably played the part of the traditional dumb detective.

"You should have been with me," Dillinger would joke on returning from the movies, "Matt Leach was in the picture."

A good deal of Dillinger's animosity was no doubt due to the fact that Leach tried to connect him with half of the crimes committed in the Middle West at this time. "Some day that guy will try to have me indicted for shooting Abe Lincoln," the desperado once remarked. To one attempting to trace the career of John Dillinger at this time, the numerous interviews given out by the voluble Mr. Leach serve only to distort and confuse the picture, and are responsible for many of the wild legends and extravagant statements surrounding the outlaw.

And now was to come the most daring exploit that the Dillinger gang had as yet essayed. This was the raiding on September 6 of the Massachusetts Avenue State Bank in Indianapolis, near the headquarters of the state police. Two patrons, George Alexander and Francis Anderson, were in the bank at the time and raised their hands at the entrance of the bandits, but were told to lower them again. Dillinger realized that men standing with upraised arms would be sure to inform passersby that a holdup was in progress. Then, as cashier A. J. Krueger looked on, the robbers helped themselves to $21,000, and were soon speeding out of range of pursuit, leaving Captain Leach to tear his dark hair and unleash every force of the law against this new menace.

Meanwhile, important events were taking place among Dillinger's former classmates at the "university" in Michigan City. Ten men were to regain their liberty in one of the most sensational of all prison breaks, and in this number were many of the names that would subsequently figure largely in the annals of the gang. The band who escaped consisted of the following:

John (Red) Hamilton, so called from his dark red hair. Although generally reputed as one of the most dangerous of the Dillinger gang, he was a quiet type of man who won the liking of all with whom he associated. Hamilton originally had been a Canadian carpenter who, for robbing a gasoline filling station in St. Joseph County, Indiana, received a sentence of twenty-five years, of which he had already served two.

Harry Pierpont was wild, desperate, and ruthless, and more in accordance with the usually accepted model of a gang leader. Pierpont came from a good family of Leipsic, Ohio, and had served eight years of a ten-to-twenty-year sentence for robbery.

Charles Makley, a former insurance agent, had arrived at the penitentiary five years before on a ten-to-twenty-year sentence for robbery. Like Hamilton, he was bold when boldness was required, but otherwise displayed a quiet and retiring nature, subordinating himself to the more impetuous Pierpont. He lacked Hamilton's serious mien, however, and was known as the drollest and wittiest member of the gang.

Russell Clark, tall and handsome, with a small black mustache, was looked upon by his associates as "just an average sort of fellow." He had served six years of a twenty-year sentence for bank robbery.

Edward Shouse plays but a small part in the Dillinger drama, and that an ignoble one. He was in his third year of a twenty-five-year sentence for robbery.

Walter Dietrich, a bold, reckless bank robber, had at this time served two years of a life sentence.

Joseph Jenkins had completed two years of a life sentence for murder.

John Burns had been in prison for thirteen years on a life sentence for murder. He had no real connection with the Dillinger gang, and was recaptured in Chicago on December 17, 1934.

Joseph Fox had completed three years of a life sentence for robbery. He was the last of the ten to be recaptured.

James Clark, no relation to Russell Clark, had served two years of a life sentence for robbery and suffered greatly from stomach ulcers. He had no desire to join the break, but was virtually compelled to do so by Dietrich, who believed he needed outside medical care.

These were the participants in the escape, but it had been carefully planned by Pierpont, Hamilton, and Dillinger before the latter's parole. The contact between Dillinger and those within the prison was to be made by Pierpont's sweetheart, Mary Kinder, who possessed the somewhat dubious distinction of having a sweetheart, a husband, and a brother all in Michigan City at this time. Mary Kinder, or Northern, was a small girl with a penchant for flashy clothes, including red shoes, and an abundance of rouge and lipstick. Scattered about midway in a family of thirteen children, she had been born in Martinsville, Indiana, but later moved with the family to the factory district of Indianapolis. Her father's death compelled her mother to work in a factory and Mary to secure employment as a waitress, and to the poverty of the family was added further suffering when her brother Earle was sentenced to Michigan City, along with Harry Pierpont, for robbing a bank in Kokomo. Later she married Dale Kinder, the son of an Indianapolis police sergeant, but he was caught robbing a grocery store in that city, and became an addition to the family group in prison. Mary was very much in love with Pierpont, and on her trips to Michigan City to see her brother, she never failed to bring him gifts and visit with him as well.

It was only after Dillinger had robbed the banks in Daleville and Montpelier that he found himself in a position to contact Mary Kinder and carry out the previously concerted plan. At the time of her next visit to Michigan City she made all necessary arrangements with Pierpont, and then joined Dillinger in East Chicago to acquaint him with the details.

A unique device was employed to tell Dillinger where to deliver the guns to the convicts. A red arrow was painted upon a white board by Leslie "Big" Homer and hung from the window of the shirt factory in such a position as to indicate where the guns were to be thrown. The prison guards and officials were either strangely blind to this conspicuous marker, or else must have discounted it as some kind of game with which the prisoners sought to amuse themselves. In any case, on or about the night of August 10 Dillinger tossed a package over the prison walls, a package containing several pistols and a box of bullets wrapped in cotton and newspaper. Early the next morning the guns were picked up in the prison yard by Dietrich and secreted beneath the bales of shirt material in the warehouse.[4]

A few days later Dillinger tossed three more guns over the walls, but these failed to reach their destination, as two other convicts, an Italian and a Negro, came upon them first. Wishing to curry favor with the officials, one watched the package while the other informed a guard. The guns were seized, and, as usually happens, the hand of suspicion fell upon the wrong persons. Daniel McGeoghagen, a Chicago hoodlum, along with his two friends, Jack Gray and Edward Murphy, were accused and placed in solitary confinement.

One may wonder why more than a month elapsed between the

delivery of the guns and the break. The principal reason is that a visit by the members of the parole board was anticipated about September 20, and it was the intention of the convicts to seize these gentlemen and hold them as hostages. But when the day of the visit arrived, the plan proved impossible to execute. Burns worked in the tin shop, Jenkins in the hospital; several of the other men were scattered about, and could not be assembled when the propitious moment arrived.

Came the fateful day of September 26. It was the fall of the year, and beyond the prison walls the red-tinted leaves of the trees dropped gently to the earth while wind whispered across the dunes of sand bordering Lake Michigan. But the prisoners knew only the unending four stone walls that circumscribed men's souls even more than their bodies. Shortly after two o'clock in the afternoon, Pierpont and Russell Clark approached George H. Stevens, superintendent of the shirt factory, and informed him that one of the officials wished to see him in the basement. Suspecting nothing, he accompanied the pair to the tunnel of the basement, where he was seized by the other eight members of the party. Stevens alone was not considered a sufficiently important hostage, so Dietrich went in search of Albert E. Evans, assistant deputy superintendent. He told Evans that two convicts were fighting in the basement, and led him into the same trap that had already snared Stevens. Next to taste the hospitality of the conspirators was foreman Dudley Triplett, who came to the basement for supplies and was promptly bound and placed behind bales of cloth.

Evans had been the cause of Pierpont receiving much severe disciplining, and now the prisoner, with a gun in hand, was prepared to exact retaliation.

"Here's one that I settle with before I go," said Pierpont, and Evans felt the breath of the angel of death cold upon his face.

Hamilton's arm shot out and seized Pierpont. "No killings," he ordered. "One shot and the whole penitentiary will know what's going on. We've got enough trouble ahead of us. Let's not make any more for ourselves."

Pierpont, amid grumbling and a flood of curses, agreed to spare his enemy's life. And now began a strange procession to the outside world and freedom. Stevens led the way, with Dietrich on his left side and Hamilton on his right, their guns concealed beneath a stack of shirts carried in their arms. The other eight men, with Evans in their midst, picked up a steel shaft and followed behind. It was necessary to traverse almost the entire length of the penitentiary, but other guards and prisoners gave no more than a passing glance to the group, believing they were witness to nothing more than ordinary prison routine.

The first steel gate they reached was guarded by Frank Swanson.

"Open the gate," said Stevens quietly. "These men are armed, and they will kill us if you don't."

Swanson obeyed, and was made to join in the parade.

More-formidable obstacles now presented themselves. Beyond a second steel gate was a third, and beyond that a corridor occupied by guards Fred Wellnitz and Guy Burklow. Wellnitz, known as "Eyebrows" to the convicts, defied their summons to open the gate. The steel shaft was now brought into play, and employed as a battering ram. Two or three thrusts shattered the lock, and the third gate was opened with the keys taken from Wellnitz. Wellnitz himself was slugged into unconsciousness for his show of resistance.

"That," later remarked Makley, who throughout the escape maintained the utmost composure and good humor, "was to teach him to be more cooperative when gentlemen are desirous of leaving the penitentiary."

The escaping prisoners were now in the inner lobby of the administration building, where eight clerks, including two women, were herded into the vaults. It was at this time that Finley Carson, a seventy-two-year-old clerk, was shot and dangerously wounded in the thigh and stomach by Burns, who then broke all of the telephone connections while the rest of the men kept guard or raided the arsenal. Warden Louis E. Kunkel, happening along at this time, was made to enter the vault along with the others.

Outside the prison the group split up. Sheriff Charles Neal of Harrison County, along with Dr. L. B. Wolf, arrived just in time to run headlong into the band. Dietrich, Burns, Fox, and James Clark immediately seized Neal's car, taking the sheriff along with them. The others made their way to a nearby service station, where Herbert Van Valkenberg, a farmer of Oswego, Illinois, along with his wife and Mrs. Minnie Schultz, a relative, had just stopped for gas. This little town of Oswego was incidentally to figure again in the annals of the Dillinger gang. The Van Valkenberg car was commandeered by Hamilton, Pierpont, Makley, Russell Clark, and Shouse. Jenkins began running in the direction of Michigan City.

It was at least four minutes after this event that a general alarm was sounded, and then pandemonium reigned. Guards and officials dashed about in wild confusion, while the news of the break was broadcast to the surrounding counties. Roads were blocked, reserve forces and vigilantes were called out, and a posse of five hundred men was organized to conduct the pursuit. Rumors flew in wildest profusion—the fleeing convicts were being sighted everywhere—and northern Indiana became gripped in panic.

Into even so serious a matter as a prison break a gleam of humor sometimes makes its way, and so it was in this case. As Captain Matt Leach and his men were driving up to a gas station, they, along with the audience of a Gary radio station, were hugely surprised to hear a bullet-by-bullet account of a pitched battle between pursuers and pursued.

"Here we are, folks," the announcer was excitedly gushing, "right on the scene of a gigantic manhunt. The troops are lined up all around here. There go more squads through that field of death, right on the trail of the felons. Do those boys ever falter? No, sirree! Listen closely now, folks, and you can hear the shots as a deadly patter of lead is rained all about. Oh, boy, is this exciting! What a battle!" And from the loudspeaker came the sounds of gunfire—machine guns, pistols, and shotguns—the eerie howls of police sirens, and the hysterical screams of women. Meanwhile, the families and friends of the supposedly besieging forces were frantically calling the authorities and the newspapers for word on their loved ones and a list of the casualties.

The cause of the uproar was this. In response to a report that the convicts were hiding in a wooded area southwest of Chesterton, Indiana, a party of five hundred vigilantes had closed in on the place. The radio station in Gary, wishing to delight its listeners with a battlefield broadcast, had rushed members of its staff to cover the proceedings. When Captain Leach arrived upon the scene, he discovered that the announcer, disappointed in the absence of any battle, had rolled out sound effects and staged a little make-believe war. After cooling applications had been placed upon the announcer's feverish brow, he was released upon a promise of a complete retraction over the air.

The first real news of the escaped prisoners came on September 29 with the reappearance of Sheriff Neal and James Clark. On the day of the escape the two had been put out of the car about three miles north of McCook, Indiana, and Clark given a gun to guard Neal. From this point they walked into Gary, where the sheriff was released by Clark, who went on to Hammond, Indiana. Clark called a cab in that city to take him to Chicago, but the driver, Vernon Moats, recognizing Clark from pictures in the papers, excused himself on the pretext that he needed permission to take the cab out of the city, and called police. A squad car hastily responded, and officers Kelly, Wilson, Dimitroff, and Mroz soon had the fugitive in custody. Clark, a very sick man, whose revolver was loaded only with teargas cartridges, offered no resistance.

On September 30 another member of the band met his end. Joseph Jenkins had managed to make his way to the vicinity of Indianapolis, where he kidnapped a motorist named Lule and drove his car until the gas was exhausted. He then continued on foot, leaving Lule sitting in the abandoned car. As he neared a small Indiana town bearing the euphonious name of Beanblossom, he was recognized by the townspeople, who were very much on the alert for the escaped men. William Alltop and Benjamin Kantor killed Jenkins with their shotguns, while Herbert McDonald, keeper of the general store, was slightly wounded in the arm during the melee. McDonald's wound, although of importance only to him, is nevertheless noteworthy in making him the first in a long parade of innocent bystanders wounded or killed in the pursuit of Dillinger or his associates.

It is with the men in the other car, however, that we are most concerned. On the day of the escape they appeared at the home of William Warner, a farmer living near Wanatah, Indiana, and made prisoners of Warner and a mailman who chanced to come along. When night fell they made their way to Chicago, where an apartment was waiting for them, and they were joined by Mary Kinder, Crouch, and Arthur McGinnis.

Fortunately for the gang, they did not remain long in Chicago, for McGinnis, a stool pigeon, was hovering about only in order that he might tip off their movements. They drove south by way of Indianapolis in the direction of Hamilton, Ohio, where Matt Leach had been advised of their coming and had prepared an elaborate reception. But the "trap" was laid with so much fanfare and official bungling that it served as a warning rather than a snare. Leach, believing the gang had just eluded him, engaged in a heated altercation with Police Chief Calhoun of Hamilton with regard to the blame for allowing the fugitives to slip out of the city unnoticed.

After this close brush with the law the party drove on to Cincinnati, where the next week was spent. But the search was still on, forcing them to keep moving. From Cincinnati they went back to Indianapolis, and then headed in the direction of Pierpont's home in Leipsic, Ohio. Before reaching that destination, however, an event of importance occurs, and John Dillinger reappears in the picture.

At the time of his parole from Michigan City, John Dillinger had promised several fellow prisoners that he would call upon their relatives and friends. Among them was Joseph Jenkins, one of the ten who would later escape. Jenkins had a sister living in Dayton, Ohio, named Mrs. Mary Jenkins Longnacre, an attractive young divorcée, and when Dillinger found himself in the neighborhood he stopped by her place. One call led to another, and soon Dillinger was a steady visitor at the Longnacre apartment. More than that, he took Mrs. Longnacre and a girlfriend to the World's Fair in Chicago, and there amused himself by asking a policeman to pose for snapshots.

Word soon reached Captain Leach, by way of his stool pigeons, of Dillinger's infatuation, and the information was immediately passed along to Dayton. On the night of September 25, 1933, Inspector S. E. Yendes of the Dayton Police Department raided the Longnacre residence. Dillinger, although heavily armed, was taken by surprise and surrendered without resistance. From him the police took six pistols, maps of the Michigan City prison, and a large sum of money.

Matt Leach lost no time in demanding the return of the prisoner to Indiana, but the state of Ohio had different ideas. Dillinger was wanted there for the robbery of the Bluffton bank, and as a consequence was conveyed to the Allen County jail at Lima, Ohio.

A letter was written by John Dillinger to his father from the Lima jail on September 29, and conveys insight into his feelings at this time.

Dear Dad,

Hope this letter finds you well and not worrying to much over me. Maybe I'll learn someday Dad that you cant win in this game. I know I have been a big disapointment to you but I guess I did to much time, for where I went in a carefree boy, I came out bitter toward everthing in general. Of course Dad most of the blame lies with me for my environment was of the best, but if I had gotten off more leniently when I made my first mistake this would never have happened. How is Doris and Frances? I preferred to stand trial here in Lima because there isn't as much prejudice against me here and I am sure I will get a square deal here. Dad dont believe all that the newspapers say about me for I am not guilty of half of the things I am charged with and Ive never hurt anyone. Well Dad I guess this is all for this time just wanted you to know I am well and treated fine.

From Johnnie

This letter seems to indicate that Dillinger was expecting to stand trial, and that he was not looking forward to rescue or escape. The allusion to newspaper reports refers to tales which had Dillinger shooting a watchman in Monticello, Illinois, and robbing banks as far away as Pennsylvania.

About half past six on the evening of October 12 a car drove up to the red brick jail at Lima. Harry Pierpont led the way into the office of Sheriff Jesse Sarber, followed closely by Charles Makley and "Red" Hamilton, while Russell Clark and Harry Copeland remained outside in the car.

"We're officers from Indiana," said Pierpont. "We've come to take John Dillinger back to Michigan City."

This appeared plausible, as Sarber knew Ohio and Indiana were negotiating the matter of Dillinger's custody.

"All right," the sheriff replied. "Let's have your credentials."

"Here are our credentials," said Pierpont, and pulled an automatic pistol from the pocket of his coat. Sarber, with a foolhardy courage, reached for his revolver in a holster hanging on the wall. A report rang out, and the sheriff sank to the floor as a bullet tore into his abdomen. Mrs. Sarber and deputy Wilbur Sharp came running into the office at the sound of the shot, only to face the guns of the invaders.

John Dillinger at the time was playing cards with another prisoner, Art Miller, unaware of the bold rescue undertaken by his friends. Startled by the gunfire, he looked from his cell to see the three men, now in possession of the keys, herd Mrs. Sarber and Sharp into the lockup. Moments later, John Dillinger was seated in a car that was speeding out of Lima.

The party drove to Pierpont's home at Leipsic, Ohio, where the other members of the gang awaited them. The following day, October 13, was Pierpont's birthday, and a party had been prepared by his mother. In spite of the many accusations brought against her son, she always maintained in her usual assertive manner that he had "never done a wrong thing in his life." Her husband, a small, balding man, also entertained a firm belief in his son's innocence. He was later described by attorney Louis

Piquett as "continually talking in a whining nasal voice. He must have been vaccinated with a phonograph needle."

Thus a gay birthday party climaxed the brutal slaying of Sheriff Sarber.

CHAPTER FOUR

THE GANG ATTAINS MATURITY

The Dillinger gang was now to abandon its comparatively petty operations in favor of criminal activities on a much larger scale. It had been reinforced, not only in numbers, but with men who had confidence and trust in one another and understood what they were expected to do. It was the reckless, quick-triggered Harry Pierpont who really led the band at this time, although Dillinger's nerve and native intelligence were bringing him to the fore.

The outlaws had the men, but they lacked armament. Their foes, the police, had plenty of guns. What could be more logical, then, than to take the guns they needed away from the police? And so began a unique phase of the Dillinger operations—holding up police stations.

After dark on the evening of October 14, the day following the birthday party, the caravan pulled out of Leipsic. Shortly before midnight they arrived at the little police station of Auburn, Indiana, and Pierpont, Dillinger, and Makley, flashily attired in new clothes, strode boldly in. Makley remained in the corridor, while the other two continued to the office, where policemen Henry West and Fred Krueger were on duty. Before the officers were aware of their presence, Dillinger and Pierpont covered both with .45-caliber automatics. West was made to open a metal gun case, after which the two policemen were locked up in cells. Within ten minutes of their arrival, the entire arsenal had been cleaned out, and the bandits were on their way.

According to Chief of Police D. M. Kreamelmeyer, the Auburn police department was robbed of a Thompson submachine gun,[5] a "Type L" [50-round] drum magazine, a 20-round Thompson magazine, two bulletproof vests, a lever-action Model 1897 .44-40 Winchester rifle, a .401 automatic rifle, a .30-caliber army rifle, a .45-caliber automatic pistol, a .38-caliber revolver, a German Luger pistol, a .25-caliber Spanish automatic pistol, a .38-caliber "hammerless" revolver, a .44-caliber revolver, and 1,245 cartridges.[6]

The police station at Peru, Indiana, was the next to be visited, with Dillinger leading the raiders. Here the collection was augmented by two automatic rifles, riot shotguns, a teargas gun, and a half-dozen bulletproof vests.

Following these exploits they proceeded to Chicago, chosen to be gang headquarters, and for the next few days were occupied in finding apartments. But before Indiana could recover from the shock of having its police stations stripped, the state suffered another blow.

On the afternoon of October 23 two cars, each containing four men, entered the pleasant city of Greencastle, Indiana, the home of DePauw University, located to the west of Indianapolis and Mooresville. Six of the members of the party were Dillinger, Hamilton, Pierpont, Makley, Russell Clark, and Harry Copeland; the identity of the other two has never been definitely established, but may have been Shouse, Leslie Homer, or Crouch. For about an hour they drove around the town, then just before closing time they stopped at the doors of the Central National Bank and Trust Company.

Leaving two men in the cars, the other six entered the bank with overcoat collars turned up, in order to partially conceal their faces, and pulled out guns. There were twelve customers in the bank at the time, in addition to the employees, and these were quietly herded to one side. One of the bandits approached Harry Wells, the cashier.

"Just open the vault, brother, and do it fast."

Wells, facing the muzzle of a gun, had no choice but to obey, and the robbers scooped up $20,000 in cash and about $56,000 worth of negotiable securities. For some reason no attempt was made to take the stacks of money showing on the counters. But the bandits did take the time to rob two customers who entered while the affair was in progress. One, High Hammond, lost $300 and the other, Postmaster E. R. Bartley, turned over $285 of government funds.

Meanwhile, one of the bank employees managed to notify the police station, but the police took a roundabout route, and by the time they arrived the gang had already left. A deputy sheriff and a state policeman were in the sheriff's office across the street, but seem to have been unaware that a robbery was going on.

The peculiar circumstances attending this Greencastle robbery led to certain speculations, and it was decided to bring the rumors directly to the attention of the Central National Bank. A letter was written containing the following questions.

"We would like to know if it is true that Dillinger ignored money left on the counters, and took only that which was in the vault. Is it true that it took the police over twenty minutes to answer the alarm? Inasmuch as the newspaper accounts of the story place the loot in excess of $70,000, and John Dillinger often said to intimates here in the city that all he got was $32,000, we would like to ascertain just what the proper figure is."

The reply, signed by President F. L. O'Hair, consisted of only one sentence: "Replying to your letter of April 9th we are not seeking any publicity in connection with our experience with Mr. Dillinger."*

Panic was now at its height in Indiana. The state police were ordered on twenty-four-hour duty. On October 26 the Indiana National Guard was called out to confront the menace, and 70 officers and 560 enlisted men, all picked for their marksmanship, were sworn in as special deputies under the command of Al Feeney, superintendent of the state police. Mr. Feeney suggested calling upon the American Legion to again take up arms in the service

---

*It may be mentioned that some of the Dillinger bank robberies were prearranged affairs. We were then in the Great Depression. Insurance covered a bank's loss in case of failure but not that of its depositors, and many were ruined in the epidemic of bank closings during the Hoover era. Banks were held in scant esteem, and there was no shedding of tears on the part of the general public when they were robbed.

As for the banks themselves, a staged robbery represented an opportunity for profit or for covering any losses that might otherwise be difficult to explain, for any amount could be reported as a loss. Most of the scheduled robberies were concerted with the underworld connections of the gang in East Chicago, Indiana. The day and hour of the robbery were arranged, the money to be taken was to be in readiness, no resistance would be offered, and pursuit would be delayed until the gang had made their escape. In later conversations with Arthur O'Leary, Dillinger mentioned the Greencastle robbery as a specific example of this. [An insurance investigator told federal agents that he suspected Greencastle was staged, and one of the gang's later associates claimed this in connection with other robberies.—W.J.H.]

of their country. The next day the warfare extended to the air, as Lieutenant Howard Maxwell, in a National Guard airplane, was ordered to circle over the state highways. The entire state of Indiana became an armed camp. In addition to the National Guard, a special force of two thousand men was mobilized and armed. Five airplanes were stationed in readiness at the Mars Hill airport. Highways throughout the state were barricaded with sandbags. As a most unusual precaution, Governor McNutt ordered that the firing pins be removed from all guns in the arsenals of the police stations. This is perhaps the first time in history that government officials felt obliged to protect the police from the men whom they were employed to capture. The Dillinger gang was rapidly attaining a national rating.

About this time Captain Matt Leach received an addition to his library. The book, sent to him by John Dillinger, was entitled *How to Become a Detective.*[7]

While the state of Indiana was mobilizing its forces on land, sea, and in the air, John Dillinger was falling in love again. He had met Evelyn Frechette in a nightclub on the North Side of Chicago, and henceforth she would be a loyal companion in his dangerous activities, and the ''Maid Marian'' of the Dillinger gang.[8] The father of Evelyn, or ''Billie,'' was a Frenchman, while her mother was a member of the Menominee Indian tribe, and she was born on a reservation in Wisconsin in 1907. She remained there until she was about thirteen, and for the next four years attended the Indian school at Flandreau, South Dakota. Her primary education completed, she moved to Milwaukee, and thence to Chicago, obtaining employment in both cities as a nursemaid and a waitress. In Chicago she married a man named Walter Sparks, who soon left her to reside in a penitentiary.

At the time of her meeting with Dillinger, Evelyn had just passed her twenty-sixth birthday. She was a handsome girl, of about average stature and weight. Her Indian ancestry was denoted in a cream-colored complexion, rather high cheekbones, very dark hair, and large brown eyes. There was nothing of the ''gun moll'' type about Evelyn Frechette. She possessed an air of refinement and stoical calm, while her speech and manners were singularly devoid of vulgarity. In view of the slight advantages afforded her by ancestry, education, and environment, these facts are all the more noteworthy. Dillinger claimed she was the best bed partner he ever had.

For the two months following the rescue of Dillinger from the Lima jail, the gang members and their girlfriends were scattered about Chicago and moved from one apartment to another. Upon their arrival in that city Dillinger, Pierpont, and Mary Kinder had stayed for a brief time in the apartment of Harry Copeland at 115 North Parkside Avenue. These three, soon joined by Billie Frechette, also used an apartment at 901 Addison Street, just east of the Chicago Cubs' baseball park, and occasionally the apartment of Billie's half-sister, Frances, or Patsy Frechette. Their longest stay, however, was in a third-floor six-room apartment at 4310 Clarendon Avenue, where they conducted themselves with all decorum and were regarded by their neighbors as merely two young married couples.

Russell Clark, with his sweetheart, Opal Long, also known as Bernice Long and Bernice Clark, lived at four or five different addresses in the Uptown district of Chicago's North Side, and most of the time Makley and Shouse resided with them. Opal was perhaps the only one of the gang's girlfriends not possessed of physical attractiveness. She was a large, heavy-set red-haired girl, wearing glasses, and with a freckled face, huge bust, and well-padded buttocks. But what Opal lacked in beauty she made up for in an intense devotion to Russell Clark, who, ironically, was perhaps the most handsome member of the gang.

About this time Homer Van Meter enters the Dillinger saga. Van Meter had known Dillinger when both were at Michigan City, had been paroled shortly before him, and stayed in contact with the members of the gang. Van Meter was a lone wolf, however, and desired the fewest possible dealings with his fellow men. One sudden descent by his outlaw friends and their female companions upon his one-room apartment thoroughly aroused his apprehensions, and he immediately moved to St. Paul, where he will remain for the time being. The whereabouts of "Red" Hamilton during this period will be discussed later.

During his stay in jail Dillinger had contracted a ringworm infection that was continuing to bother him. Being unacquainted in Chicago, he asked Arthur McGinnis to recommend a doctor. McGinnis had been a fellow prisoner in Michigan City, but he had become a paid informer and was about the last person in the world deserving of trust. McGinnis immediately notified Matt Leach, who permitted Dillinger to make his first visit unmolested to the offices of Dr. Charles H. Eye at 4175 Irving Park Boulevard, to allay any possible suspicions.

Dillinger had his second appointment the evening of November 15. Lieutenant John Jenkins and Sergeant O. W. Ryan of the Indiana State Police had joined with the Chicago police in laying a trap, while McGinnis waited in the drugstore below the physician's office to signal the desperado's arrival. In addition to the Indiana car, three Chicago squad cars, carrying Sergeants Howard Harder, Andrew Carrol, and Walter Bailey, were waiting in readiness. Shortly after nine o'clock Dillinger arrived in a small, fast car with Billie Frechette.[9]

The offices of Dr. Eye were located on the southeast corner of Irving Park Boulevard, running east and west, and Keeler Avenue, running north and south. Dillinger turned from Irving Park south onto Keeler, parked on the west side of the street across from Eye's office, and went in. McGinnis signaled from the drugstore, and the police cars began moving closer. One took up its station near the Dillinger car, facing it. Another was parked on Keeler Avenue just north of Irving Park Boulevard, with the other two on Irving Park on either side of Keeler Avenue, thus blocking all four directions of escape. Evelyn Frechette, waiting below, saw the trap, but was unable to sound a warning.

Now fate stepped in. Dr. Eye, while treating his patient, chanced to walk past a window.

"Look at all the police cars outside," the physician observed. "I wonder what's happened."

In an instant Dillinger was at the window, and comprehended at a glance. The next instant he was running down the stairs with a gun in each hand.

Dillinger fired two shots as he stepped from the office, and his waiting companion started the car. Before the startled police understood what was happening, he had run across the street, jumped into the car, and discarded his pistols for a machine gun. Billie hurriedly backed into Irving Park Boulevard, ramming and disabling a police car waiting there, and headed east. By the time the police could take up the pursuit, the outlaw's machine was traveling eighty-five miles an hour, and the slower Chicago squad cars were soon hopelessly outdistanced. Dillinger had broken the glass in the rear window, and his machine gun was returning the rain of lead from the police. Lieutenant Jenkins, with a faster car, was able to keep close behind until the chase reached Elston Avenue, running diagonally southeast. Dillinger's car made the turn but the police car skidded past, and by the time it could be turned around, the quarry was nowhere in sight. Dillinger and Billie arrived breathless and excited at a party at the apartment of Russell Clark and recounted their adventure.*

On the following day the car used by Dillinger was found abandoned by the police, riddled with fifty-two bullets. The license plates had been issued to a Joseph Harris, 2847 Washington Boulevard, the name which Dillinger was using at that time. The same night Deputy Chief of Detectives William V. Blaul raided the apartment at 4310 Clarendon Avenue with four squads of police, but found it empty. Matt Leach joined Lieutenant Eugene Butler and detectives Arthur Keller and Eugene Ryan, and remained in the city to continue the search.

On November 19 policemen Edward McBride and John Ryan found a man and a girl seated in a car at the corner of North and Harlem avenues in Chicago, engaged in a heated argument. Particularly attracting their attention was the man's waving of a revolver to emphasize some point. He was arrested and taken to the station, where he gave his name as John Santon, but fingerprints revealed him to be Harry Copeland. The Dillinger panic which gripped Indiana had by this time spread to Chicago, and Lieutenant Richard Barry placed machine-gun and shotgun squads at both front and rear doors to prevent a possible jail delivery. Copeland was taken back to Indiana for violation of parole, and identified as one of the participants in the rescue of Dillinger from Lima, Ohio.

Meanwhile, what of Arthur McGinnis, ace stool pigeon? McGinnis was never quite able to reconcile his new role of law enforcer with his former profession of law breaker, and during lapses of uprightness had used official cars in the commission of crimes. He was rendering himself not only obnoxious but also useless to the authorities, for his character as informer was now so well known that his attempts to ensnare Dillinger had only made the outlaw more alert. When he held up a bridge party of twelve prominent women at the home of Mrs. Henry G. Zander in Kenilworth for $3,000 worth of jewelry, it was decided to retire Mr. McGinnis for the good of all concerned. The armed robbery

---

*There are various police reports of this Dr. Eye incident, some of which are conflicting and patently exculpatory. The account given here is that told by Dillinger to Arthur O'Leary, and it is possible that one or both embellished the narrative. A report by the Indiana officers has nothing good to say about their faint-hearted Chicago colleagues, but states that no shots were fired by Dillinger. The officers did not bother to contradict reporters whose stories described police bullets bouncing harmlessly off the escaping vehicle's armor while a machine-gunner inside poured withering fire at them through a specially built gun port.

earned him one year to life in the Illinois state penitentiary, and attempts to receive probation were resolutely opposed by women's organizations in the Chicago suburbs.

Situated just to the south of Milwaukee, on a snug little harbor on Lake Michigan, lies Racine, second city of Wisconsin. Its varied industries, its many streets of neat and attractive homes, and the civic spirit of its residents have stamped it as a flourishing and progressive community.

It was the afternoon of November 20, shortly before 3:00 P.M., and a few depositors were hastening to enter Racine's American Bank and Trust Company before closing time. Two cars had driven up, and four men got out and mingled with the customers of the bank. One of the men stopped at the door, and from beneath his overcoat he suddenly produced a machine gun. Two of the others walked to the cashier's cage, thrust aside Barney Cowan, who was endeavoring to make a deposit, and pushed a pistol into his ribs. H. J. Graham, the cashier, standing with his back turned, heard a curt command to "Stick 'em up!"

"What's the hurry?" jested Graham, without bothering to turn around.

A bullet tearing into his arm advised him that the order was no joke.

A bank employee stepped on the alarm button, inspiring the bandit at the door to fire a burst from his machine gun. Reinforcements from the cars outside rushed in to scoop up money. The clanging alarm meanwhile had attracted a crowd, some of whom were peering through the windows. This invasion of privacy evidently irked the intruders, for Leslie Homer pasted a large Red Cross poster in the window, shutting off the gaze of the curious.

The Racine police lost no time in reaching the scene, but the forces dispatched consisted of no more than a sergeant and two policemen. Policeman Cyril Boyard, entering first with a machine gun, was seized by the robbers and disarmed before he could fire a shot. Sergeant Wilbur Hansen, likewise dashing in, was met with a hail of bullets and fell to the floor badly wounded. Policeman Frank Worsley, the third member of the party, wisely beat a retreat.

By this time the robbers had gathered up a loot of $28,000, but the streets outside were crowded, and might perhaps include lawmen and armed vigilantes. Policeman Boyard, bank president Grover Weyland, and Mrs. Ursula Patzke, an employee, were therefore taken along as living shields.

Police reinforcements had arrived on the scene, but were forced to hold their fire for fear of hitting the three hostages. Boyard was carried on the running board of one of the cars, and then dropped after about a mile of flight. Mr. Weyland and Mrs. Patzke, however, were forced to accompany the bandits for some thirty-five miles before they were released unharmed. The machines of the band headed northwest into Waukesha County, then turned about and followed a circuitous route into Chicago.

Thus Wisconsin joined the group of sister states vowing death and extermination to the Dillinger gang.

Back in Chicago, the gang divided the loot obtained in the Racine robbery and scattered about the city. Meanwhile the hue and cry increased. Wisconsin was aghast at the boldness of the Dillinger gang. The Chicago police were frantically raiding hideouts and hangouts. In Indiana, Governor McNutt was seeking a grand jury investigation of the Michigan City break, which had unleashed this cataclysm upon society. Senator J. Hamilton Lewis of Illinois intimated there would be a shakeup of officials in the federal Department of Justice. J. Edgar Hoover would resign, and Melvin Purvis, agent in charge of the Chicago office, was likewise to be ousted, he claimed. Supposedly Purvis would be replaced by Hinton G. Clabaugh, a former Justice Department official now with the Commonwealth Edison Company.

The next blow was to fall on December 13, and it is noteworthy in that this was the only escapade of the gang attempted in Chicago. About one o'clock that afternoon the bandit cars appeared before the former Unity Trust and Savings Bank at 3909 North Avenue.[10] The bank itself, like many others, had been closed for two years, but its safety-deposit vaults were still in use. The attendant on duty, Joseph Kinch, was trussed up by the first three men who entered and ensconced in what had formerly been the cashier's cage.

Four more men now appeared carrying cold chisels and hammers, and began working on the safety-deposit boxes in a most leisurely manner. A portable radio was plugged into the wall socket and tuned to pick up police calls.[11] John Dillinger directed the operation. David Kolber, an elderly vendor of Christmas candy, picked this inopportune time and place to offer his wares. As he entered he was seized by Dillinger, and in the process one of his candy boxes fell, scattering its contents about the floor.

"Pardon me, Dad," said Dillinger, "I seem to have busted up your store."

"That's all right, sir. It's all right."

"No, it isn't. This is a bank job, not a candy store robbery. Here's three dollars for you. You keep quiet and you'll be all right."

Mr. Kolber, at least, profited by the robbery.

During the afternoon three other clients, Joseph Bara, William E. Nelson, and Frank Destree, entered and were sent to the cashier's cage. All this time the leader and the men at work on the boxes were keeping up a continual chatter.

"Hurry it up. This is no picnic."

"Look at all the 'slum' in this box."

"What did this cheapskate want with a deposit box? There's not enough in here to throw a drunk on."

"Here's a good one. This fellow certainly isn't suffering in the depression."

It was nearly three hours before the gang moved out in an unhurried fashion, taking their hammers and chisels in addition to the loot. They had smashed a total of 96 boxes, leaving some 250 untouched. The amount taken was estimated to be $8,700, but the true figure could never be ascertained, and counting the jewelry the total may have exceeded $50,000.

In this bank vault robbery the Dillinger gang had taken a direct slap at the Chicago police. The wild rumors in circulation became wilder. Hamilton and Makley were identified as members of the robber band, but the police tried to hook up the Touhy gang, consisting of Tommy Touhy, Basil (The Owl) Banghart, Charles (Ice Wagon) Connors, and Frank (Porky) Dillon, as well, inasmuch as Tommy Touhy had served time with Dillinger. The various official bodies seeking to capture the gang fell to quarreling among themselves over whom to blame for what had already happened. Captain Daniel Gilbert of the state's attorney's office in Chicago assigned responsibility to Indiana, declaring that Chicago authorities had had crime well under control, with Al Capone in prison and the Touhy mob broken, when Indiana allowed the Dillinger crowd to escape and sneak into town. At this time the state of Indiana was taking a considerable ribbing because of Dillinger, and it would soon take a lot more.

Now "Red" Hamilton reappeared on the scene to add to the confusion. He had shared the various hideouts of the gang until about November 19, when he rented rooms in the Loganwood Apartment Hotel, 2530 North Sacramento Avenue, under the name of Orval Lewis. During the short space of a month he shared these quarters (consecutively) with no fewer than three female

John Dillinger, age three and a half. *John Dillinger Museum*

Molly Lancaster Dillinger, John's mother, died in 1906 when he was three. *John Dillinger Museum*

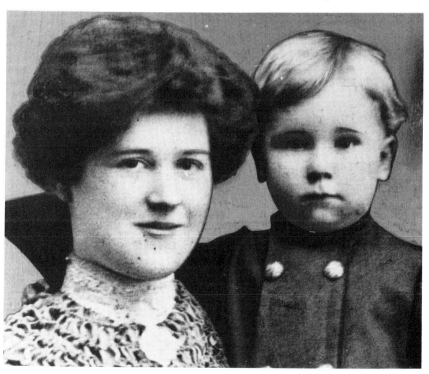

Dillinger's married sister, Audrey Hancock, raised him like a son. *John Dillinger Museum*

Dillinger, age 10, in Mooresville. *John Dillinger Museum*

Dillinger as a teenager with his father. *John Dillinger Museum*

Dillinger, 19, before enlisting in the Navy. *John Dillinger Museum*

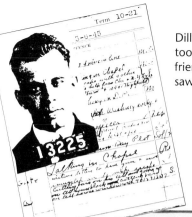

Dillinger irritated prison officials by talking too much, cutting into line, and writing friends to ask them to smuggle in guns and saws. *Goddard Collection*

Paroled in May 1933, Dillinger committed several robberies to raise funds for a gang and was arrested at a girlfriend's house in Dayton. In freeing him from the Lima, Ohio, jail, his escaped-convict friends killed Sheriff Jesse Sarber. *Sandy Jones*

The Dillinger gang's bank-robbing campaign prompted four state governors to jointly offer a $15,000 reward for his capture, dead or alive. *Chuck Schauer*

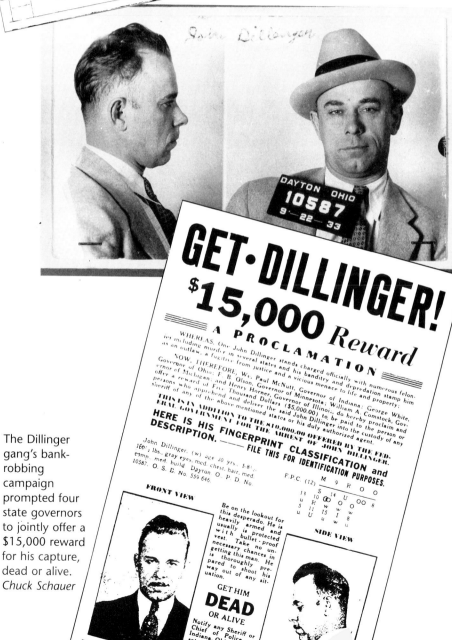

GET·DILLINGER!
$15,000 Reward
A PROCLAMATION

WHEREAS, One John Dillinger stands charged officially with numerous felonies including murder in several states and his banditry and depredation stamp him as an outlaw, a fugitive from justice and a vicious menace to life and property;

NOW, THEREFORE, We, Paul McNutt, Governor of Indiana; George White, Governor of Ohio; F. B. Olson, Governor of Minnesota; William A. Comstock, Governor of Michigan; and Henry Horner, Governor of Illinois; do hereby proclaim and offer a reward of Five Thousand Dollars ($5,000.00) to be paid to the person or persons who apprehend and deliver the said John Dillinger into the custody of any sheriff of any of the above mentioned states or his duly authorized agent.

THIS IS IN ADDITION TO THE $10,000.00 OFFERED BY THE FEDERAL GOVERNMENT FOR THE ARREST OF JOHN DILLINGER.

HERE IS HIS FINGERPRINT CLASSIFICATION and DESCRIPTION. —— FILE THIS FOR IDENTIFICATION PURPOSES.

John Dillinger, (w) age 30 yrs., 5.8½,
160¼ lbs., gray eyes, med. chest. hair, med.
comp. med. build. Dayton O.P.D. No.
10587. O. S. B. No. 559.646.

F.P.C. (12)   M   9   R   O   O
                        13   S   14   U
                        u   10   ⊙⊙   U   OO   8
                        5   R   11   w   I
                        u   U   15   w   8
                             u   u   u

FRONT VIEW

Be on the lookout for this desperado. He is heavily armed and usually is protected with bullet-proof vest. Take no unnecessary chances in getting this man. He is thoroughly prepared to shoot his way out of any situation.

SIDE VIEW

GET HIM
DEAD
OR ALIVE

Notify any Sheriff or Chief of Police of Indiana, Ohio, Minnesota, Michigan, Illinois.

Evelyn "Billie" Frechette met Dillinger in the fall of 1933. She stuck with him through two gun battles, cross-country flights, and capture by the police. *Ellen Poulsen*

Dillinger is led off an American Airlines plane at Chicago's Midway Airport en route to the "escape-proof" jail in Crown Point, Indiana. His easy capture by Tucson city police caused him to complain, "I'll be the laughingstock of the country." *Mike Johnson*

Lake County Prosecutor Robert Estill promised Dillinger the chair, but this chummy pose for photographers ended Estill's career.
Dennis Hoffman

At his arraignment for murder, Dillinger's life of crime seems ended and his future bleak. *Neal Trickel*

companions, the last of whom was Mrs. Elaine DeKant Dent, a waitress in the Stevens Hotel. For several weeks Lieutenant John Howe of the Chicago police had been on the trail of Hamilton's green roadster, and it was finally traced by Sergeant Dan Healy to the repair shop of Carl A. Blomberg at 1135 Catalpa Avenue. Blomberg said Hamilton had come to him for some repair work, but to have a fender straightened he had been sent to the garage of Frank Leihn and Arthur Ulness around the corner at 5320 Broadway.

On December 14, by coincidence the day following the Unity vault robbery, Chief of Detectives William Shoemaker dispatched Sergeant William T. Shanley, a detective squad leader, to the garage to arrest the owner of the green roadster. Accompanying Shanley in the squad car were detective Frank Hopkins and patrolman Martin Mullen, the driver. After waiting some time in the garage, Shanley sent Hopkins to instruct Mullen to return the squad car to headquarters for use by the night squad. It was while Hopkins was engaged on this errand that Hamilton entered, accompanied by Mrs. Dent. Shanley stepped forward and flashed his star.

"Is this your car?"

"Well, no, not exactly," said Hamilton. "It belongs to my wife. Show him the papers."

Mrs. Dent fumbled in her purse and produced the license receipt.

"All right," said Shanley. "Keep your hands out of your pockets." Shanley had been warned by Chief Shoemaker merely that the occupants of the car might be dangerous.

Hamilton whipped a gun out of his shoulder holster and shot Shanley twice, wounding him mortally. The sergeant fell to the floor, the license receipt still clutched in his hand.

"I'm shot!" he cried. "Call the police!"

Hopkins, hastening back to the garage at the sound of the gunfire, saw Hamilton running down the street, pulling his companion along with him. The two separated after a short distance, and Hopkins elected to pursue the woman, who was less fleet of foot and, incidentally, unarmed. Hamilton cut across a vacant lot and escaped, but the terrified Mrs. Dent was soon overtaken and brought back to the garage. Shanley was lying on the floor in a pool of blood and died within twenty minutes.

It was at first believed by the police that the killer was Harry Pierpont, and only after the questioning of Elaine Dent did Hamilton's identity become known. Her friend, she said, bore the remarkable cognomen of John Smith, and was known as "Three-fingered Jack" because two fingers on his right hand were missing. She had moved in with him after losing her job at the hotel, and believed him to be the son of a wealthy family. Once he had shown her $70,000 in thousand-dollar bills, she said. Hamilton probably showed her a roll of bills and told her it was $70,000. In any case, her family considered Hamilton a great catch, and had encouraged her to make every effort to marry him.

"He was awfully nice," she said between sobs. "He used to take two baths a day, and he never said any swear words."

The outcry against the Dillinger gang increased. First, there had been the slaying of Sheriff Jesse Sarber, and now the murder of Sergeant Shanley. The bank robberies had been generally regarded with apathetic humor. The man in the street had in recent years nursed a grievance against bankers, and if they were now losing some of their money he refused to become very upset about it. But brutal killings were another matter, and now "every man's hand" was raising against John Dillinger and his associates.

CHAPTER FIVE

A FLORIDA VACATION

With the killing of Shanley following close upon the heels of the Unity bank robbery, Chicago became decidedly "hot" for the Dillinger gang. Dillinger, Pierpont, Evelyn Frechette, and Mary Kinder were at this time living at 1850 Humboldt Park Boulevard, with other members of the band nearby. The search for Hamilton was especially intensive because of the Shanley murder, but he felt he could hide more successfully in a large city rather than in the country or on the road.

The Humboldt Park apartments were hastily abandoned, however, just in time to miss the police, and the others headed southward, their destination Florida. Four cars conveyed the party—Dillinger and Evelyn Frechette in one, Pierpont and Mary Kinder in another, Russell Clark and Opal Long in the third, and Charles Makley in the fourth. There was nothing stealthy about the trip. They caravaned down Chicago's Michigan Avenue, then traversed the entire state of Indiana, which had been turned into an armed camp in their honor.

An overnight stop was made at a hotel in Nashville, Tennessee. In the morning, Harry Pierpont took Mary Kinder to a jewelry store across from the hotel and bought her both an expensive diamond ring and a wedding band. The trip required some five days, and the group did not arrive in Daytona, Florida, until about the nineteenth of December.

Once in Daytona, the Dillinger party quickly settled down. They were fortunate in securing an entire seventeen-room house, with a front porch facing the ocean, for only one hundred dollars a month. As was customary, the machine guns and pistols were locked in a closet, carefully out of sight of the maids who came to clean. The members of the gang had come to Florida for a vacation, and they took every precaution against arousing any suspicions.

John Dillinger, always a meticulous dresser, took the opportunity to restock his wardrobe, and was quite a natty figure in white trousers, white shoes, and sports sweater. The girls likewise presented charming pictures in their fashionable organdy dresses. To avoid unnecessary observation, they cooked most of their meals within the house. Amusements consisted mainly of swimming and movies, along with the less righteous pastimes of playing poker and shooting craps. Chicago papers were anxiously perused, and over the radio they learned with great amusement that the police were "positively identifying" them here, there, and everywhere throughout the Middle West. One day Dillinger read that he had just shot a dog in Chicago.

"Hell!" he chuckled, "that's going too far. How could I hit a dog in Chicago from way down here in Florida? I wonder if the dog's name was Matt."

Christmas day was a merry one, though for some members of the party it was the last they would spend on earth. While their Florida neighbors were shooting firecrackers, the Dillinger group shot craps. Mary Kinder received a diamond watch from Harry Pierpont, and a box of cosmetics from Dillinger and Billie. Mary gave Billie silk underwear, while she and Pierpont presented Johnnie with a pen and pencil set.

There was a big celebration on New Year's Eve. The original intention had been to attend a movie, but too many others had the same idea and the theater was sold out. The reins of self-restraint were relaxed nevertheless, and the whole party became gloriously intoxicated. Dillinger, thoroughly drunk for perhaps the first time since that fateful night in Mooresville, emptied his Thompson at the moon. The noise might have attracted much undesired attention, but on this occasion it was adequately masked by their neighbors' fireworks and alcoholic jubilation.

During their entire stay in Florida, members of the Dillinger gang traveled openly in Daytona, Miami, and other places with little fear of detection. Dillinger used the name of Frank Kirkley and Pierpont that of J. S. Evans, with Billie Frechette and Mary Kinder posing as their wives. Their neighbors seemed to entertain no suspicions.

Even into Paradise does discord find its way, however. John Dillinger had fallen deeply in love with his Indian sweetheart, and to one in love the voice of jealousy invariably can be heard. He fancied that Harry Pierpont was being too attentive to Billie, and for some time there was a coolness between the two men. But he also felt that Billie was too receptive, and it was against her that his resentment was chiefly directed.

One night John Dillinger took Billie for a "ride" along the Florida sands. Suddenly he stopped the car.

"You've been playing around too much with Harry," he said in a voice cold with anger. "Do you have anything to say before I give it to you?"

Billie Frechette never flinched.

"You know it isn't true. But I'm not afraid to die. I don't want to live if you believe a thing like that about me."

What little convincing Dillinger needed came from the courageous manner in which she stood up before his threat. "All right, kid, get back in the car, and forget it."

Nevertheless, Evelyn Frechette was sent back to visit her mother at the Indian reservation in Wisconsin, with instructions to rejoin him in St. Louis. It was time to break camp in Florida anyway, for Dillinger and Pierpont had a "meet" in Chicago. Makley, Russell Clark, and Opal Long were to proceed to Tucson, Arizona, where Makley had friends, and to make preparations for continued "cooling off."

While John Dillinger and his principal associates relaxed in Florida, in Chicago some minor characters of the gang were experiencing a heat wave. The Shanley killing led State's Attorney Thomas Courtney to coordinate the efforts of federal, state, and local law-enforcement agencies. Photographs were distributed of the Dillinger gang, the Touhy gang of Chicago, the Harvey Bailey and Verne Miller gang of Oklahoma, and the Jack Klutas gang of southern Illinois. Amid the general consternation it was believed that a formidable hookup had been effected of all of these bands, and that the authorities were now confronting the greatest hoodlum ring that the world had ever known.[12] Captain John Stege, veteran Chicago policeman, was placed in charge of a special "Dillinger squad" consisting of forty hand-picked quick-trigger men divided into ten groups.

The first victims of the Dillinger squad were Arthur (Fish) Johnson, a gambler, and his companion, Helen Burke, who were charged with disorderly conduct.[13] Next to fall into the net were a man known as Ted Lewis and his wife, Agnes, who were taken into custody for questioning. On December 20, Captain Stege gave out the license numbers of twenty-two automobiles reportedly in use by the Dillinger gang, along with a warning that if any of these cars were sighted, police should wait for help before attempting a capture.

In Wisconsin, on the same day, Milwaukee police seized Harold Trimby and Helen Smith in an apartment supposedly used by Dillinger while trying to dispose of bonds taken in the Racine bank robbery. The only charges brought against them, however, were for vagrancy and lewdness, on which they received sentences of ninety and sixty days respectively.

Also on December 20, the first capture of importance took place at Paris, Illinois. Captain Matt Leach, acting on a tip from one of his stool pigeons, arranged with Addison Crable, Paris chief of police, for the arrest of Edward Shouse when Shouse drove into town. The streets were crowded with Christmas shoppers as Shouse, accompanied by a man and two women, parked nearly opposite the La France Hotel. Shouse surrendered without resistance to Paris policeman Albert Stepp, as did the women, who proved to be Mrs. Frances Cohen of Fort Worth and Ruth Spencer of San Diego, California. However, the other man leaped from the car and escaped amid a shower of lead. Eugene Teague, an Indiana state trooper, was accidentally shot and killed by another Indiana policeman, the bullet entering the back of his head and coming out his mouth. Thus Teague takes his place on the ever-mounting list of victims of police gunfire.

The next day a similar scene took place in Chicago. Captain Stege received a tip that John Dillinger and several of his gang had taken an apartment at 1428 Farwell Avenue, and a raid was planned for that night. The squad was led by Sergeant Frank Reynolds, whose gun already had many notches, and all entrances to the building were guarded. Reynolds and a party of men crept up the stairs and knocked, and as the door was cautiously opened they forced their way inside. Three men in the living room scrambled for their guns, but Reynolds's pistol barked rapidly and all

three fell. As one lay wounded on the floor, he pointed his gun at Reynolds, but Sergeant John Daly kicked it from his hand and shot him through the head.

First reports of this shooting had the police killing Dillinger, Hamilton, and Pierpont. Mayor Kelly of Chicago and State's Attorney Courtney applauded the squad for its valor, and Coroner Walsh exclaimed, "I want to congratulate all of you brave men for your fine effort. This sort of thing will bring back the police department." After the smoke had cleared, it was found that the three dead men were Louis Katzewitz, Charles Tattlebaum, and Sam Ginsburg, a trio of minor hoodlums. The three had earlier robbed the Union National Bank at Streator, but in so doing had usurped the job assignment of a rival gang. The other gangsters had then "hijacked" them in a North Shore suburb of Chicago, seizing the Streator loot as rightfully their own. The luckless Katzewitz, Tattlebaum, and Ginsburg were later arrested for the robbery and jailed at Ottawa, Illinois, but had succeeded in escaping, only to become victims of mistaken identity.

"We got them," Reynolds told Stege after the raid. "But it wasn't Dillinger."

"Well, they were probably good ones," the captain replied.

These three must likewise be reckoned among the innocent who fell during the reign of terror, although they were innocent only in not being Dillinger. And, as Captain Stege said, they still were "good ones."

Another associate of the Dillinger group was picked up on Christmas Eve. In tracing the license number of one of the alleged Dillinger cars, Chicago police found that the machine belonged to George Drumm, owner of a tavern at 4433 Broadway. Drumm declared that the car belonged to his partner, Price, who was living at 420 Surf Street with his sweetheart, Violet Baretti. Price turned out to be Hilton Crouch, who admitted his part in robbing the Massachusetts Avenue State Bank of Indianapolis. He was returned to Indiana and sentenced to twenty years in Michigan City.

On the same day John Rowe, a paroled Indiana convict, was arrested while asleep at Chicago's Belmont Hotel, at Belmont Avenue and Sheridan Road, by Lieutenant Arthur Katt. He admitted knowing Dillinger and Pierpont, and having seen them in Chicago.

The lull in robberies during Dillinger's Florida vacation led Captain Stege to issue a formal statement that he had chased the gang back to Indiana. The day after Christmas he again received the thanks of State's Attorney Courtney, and his men were given an increase in salary of three hundred dollars per year.

On December 28 Illinois issued a new list of twenty-one public enemies, and John Dillinger was declared Public Enemy Number One. The complete list follows:[14]

1. John Dillinger	12. Ed La Rue
2. Harry Pierpont	13. Basil Banghart
3. John Hamilton	14. Charles McGuire
4. Charles Makley	15. John Klutas
5. Russell Clark	16. W. A. Hendrichsen
6. Walter Dietrich	17. Ludwig Schmidt
7. Joseph Fox	18. Homer Van Meter
8. Pearl Elliott	19. Joseph Burns
9. Mary Kinder	20. Merritt R. Longbrake
10. Tommy Touhy	21. George "Baby Face" Nelson
11. Charles Conners	

John Dillinger was "positively identified" by the doorman and the manager of the Beverly Gardens roadhouse in Evergreen Park, Illinois, as the leader of seven robbers who had perpetrated a New Year's Eve holdup. Two county highway police were wounded in the robbery, and a water spaniel first reported killed was later found to have been unharmed. For the benefit of Mr. Dillinger, the dog's name was Sandy.

The fourth of the ten Michigan City escapees to be taken was Walter Dietrich, captured on January 6 by police from the state's attorney's office in Chicago. Working on a tip from an informer concerning Theodore (Handsome Jack) Klutas, Captain Daniel Gilbert led two squads to a bungalow in Bellwood, Illinois, occupied by Mr. and Mrs. Ray Nischwitz and their eighteen-year-old daughter, Alice. The police rushed the house and seized Earl McMahon, a friend of the Nischwitz family, and Dietrich, who gave his name as Paul Stroud and whose real identity was not discovered until he was fingerprinted.

The capture of Dietrich was totally unexpected, as the police were looking for Klutas. Captain Gilbert took his prisoners back to the state's attorney's office, leaving Lieutenant Frank McNamara, Joseph Healy, and four other men behind. Toward evening Klutas arrived at the house in an automobile driven by Adolph Anzone. Sensing a trap after he rapped on the door, Klutas pulled a gun, but before he could shoot, the police had turned their machine guns on him, and he fell with six bullets. Anzone was caught a block down the street when he stopped to get gas for the car.

Several days later Dietrich was taken back to Michigan City, where he denied any connection with the Dillinger gang. At this time he also gave the false story that the guns for the break had been smuggled into the prison in a shipment of goods. This was said principally because Dillinger was still at large, and Dietrich, to disassociate himself, desired to cover Dillinger's complicity in the break.[15]

While Dillinger, Pierpont, and the others were in Florida, "Red" Hamilton had been staying at various hideouts in Chicago with Harry Copeland's former sweetheart, Patricia Cherrington. Pat, like her sister, Opal Long, was red-haired and inclined to plumpness, but unlike Opal, she was small and rather pretty. Hamilton had kept in touch with Dillinger and Pierpont, and informed them of arrangements to rob a bank in East Chicago, Indiana. A "meet" was scheduled to take place in Chicago at noon on January 15, 1934.

Dillinger and Pierpont, however, had dallied too long in Daytona, and noon of January 14 found them still in Florida. Their presence in that state and at that time has been verified, and officials have constantly been mystified as to how to account for them in East Chicago the following day. It would have been almost impossible to motor that distance within so short a time, and yet that is exactly what they did. Driving like madmen, stopping only for a few minutes at a time, they took a route through Jacksonville, Atlanta, Chattanooga, Nashville, Evansville, and thence into Chicago. They arrived shortly after midday, both utterly exhausted, but they made their meet with Hamilton.[16]

After a short rest in Chicago they set out for the First National Bank of East Chicago, Indiana, which they reached shortly before the closing hour of 3:00 P.M. Pierpont remained in the car, while Hamilton and Dillinger entered the bank, the latter with his machine gun in a trombone case. Once inside, Hamilton stood in the vestibule, while Dillinger unlimbered his Thompson.[17]

"This is a stickup!" he shouted. "Up with your hands, everybody!"

The command was electrifying. There were about a dozen employees at work, and some fifteen or twenty customers at the windows, but all obeyed without hesitation. Vice-President Walter Spencer managed to hit the alarm button.

First to appear on the scene was policeman Hobart Wilgus,

who entered with drawn pistol. Dillinger quickly took his gun and lined him up with the others. Hamilton was busily gathering up the money, which amounted to some $20,000. Dillinger glanced out of the window and saw eight policemen lined up and waiting for him.

"There's been an alarm," he called to Hamilton, "but don't hurry. Get all that dough. When we're ready to go, we'll blast our way through. Take your time."

Hamilton was now ready, holding the loot in one hand and a gun in the other. Dillinger grabbed Spencer and thrust him forward as a shield. Directly outside the door stood Officer William P. O'Malley, pistol in hand, resolutely refusing to retrace a step of ground. He fired four shots directly at Dillinger, all of which were stopped by the outlaw's bulletproof vest. Dillinger raised his machine gun, and O'Malley fell dead, a martyr to his own reckless valor.[18]

The police were forced to withhold their fire, for fear of hitting Spencer. At the car the banker fell, and the rain of bullets began in earnest. Hamilton was hit in the right hand, necessitating amputation of a finger. Dillinger jumped into the car unscathed. As Hamilton lifted up his bulletproof vest to do likewise, four bullets struck him in the groin. His bloodstained pistol dropped to the ground.

The bandit car tore away in the direction of Indianapolis with police shooting at it from all sides. Once on the road it easily shook off pursuers, who were also respectful of the machine-gun fire which Dillinger was pouring in their direction. The robbers headed for Chicago, where the next day their car, a blue Plymouth bearing Ohio license plates, was found at Byron Street and California Avenue. The wounded Hamilton had been deposited with Pat Cherrington, who called in the underworld's favorite physician, Dr. Joseph P. Moran.[19]

Who killed Officer O'Malley? Most believe it was Dillinger. Yet a number of competent witnesses declare that it was Hamilton, and not Dillinger, who carried the machine gun, and Dillinger strenuously affirmed this to his attorneys and others.

Yet it must be borne in mind that at the time of his denials Dillinger was awaiting trial on this very charge, while Hamilton was still at liberty. After his escape from Crown Point, he again spoke to Attorney Louis Piquett on the subject.

"I've always felt bad about O'Malley getting killed, but only because of his wife and kids. He had it coming. He stood right in the way and kept throwing slugs at me. What else could I do?''*

Evelyn Frechette was waiting in Chicago with a new car for Dillinger and Pierpont, and they left at once for St. Louis. They remained in that city until about January 20 and then set out for Tucson, arriving there two days later.

---

*Dillinger never told O'Leary that this was one of the prearranged robberies, or if he did, O'Leary never told me. The fact that it took place in East Chicago, where the gang had their hideout and where many of their bank robberies were planned, would suggest that it was fixed and the killing of Officer O'Malley was an unanticipated tragedy. On the other hand, a vice-president, Walter Spencer, touched off the alarm and the police came quickly to the scene. It is possible that the job was fixed by others in the bank, and since good sense dictates against everyone knowing this, Spencer was not advised. Personally, I believe that it was prearranged.

CHAPTER SIX

PROSECUTOR ESTILL POSES FOR A PICTURE

While Dillinger, Pierpont, and Hamilton were giving the Indiana police grief at East Chicago, Charles Makley, Russell Clark, and Opal Long had proceeded to Tucson, Arizona, and were preparing a temporary hideout. It is around this time that Lester Gillis, better known as George "Baby Face" Nelson, enters the Dillinger picture. Nelson, always known to the gang as "Jimmy," was small, only a little over five feet in height, but extremely agile and powerful. Born in Chicago, he was the original "problem child" who graduated from neighborhood terror to full membership in a gang of petty thieves and hoodlums. These activities won him three terms in the reformatory at St. Charles, Illinois, but each time his studied exemplary conduct caused him to be paroled for good behavior.[20]

Nelson's wife, Helen, was likewise from Chicago, the daughter of Polish parents and a graduate of Harrison High School in that city. She was a small, pale type of girl, not beautiful, but with large dark eyes that lighted up a pleasing countenance. From the time of her marriage Helen and her husband lived the life of hunted animals, yet she bore Lester Gillis two children and was always extremely devoted to him. Nelson probably became acquainted with the gang through Van Meter, and his travels between Reno and San Antonio likely included business in Tucson, but their relationship at this time was not close.

Makley, Clark, and Opal Long had rented rooms at the Congress Hotel in Tucson while scouting for more permanent dwelling places. And here Fate, usually reserving her fairest smiles for John Dillinger and his companions, dealt them what proved a very hard blow. A fire broke out in the hotel, and to the efforts of the firemen the outlaws owed the rescue of their belongings, including suitcases full of guns and a trunk containing their portion of the loot. Makley and Clark, duly grateful, rewarded the firemen with fifty-dollar bills, and such generosity led to their undoing. Back at the station the men began to wonder what might motivate so rich a recompense. Detective and crime magazines were a firehouse staple, and now the pictures in those publications began to undergo review. The firemen's discoveries were shared with the local police.[21]

John Dillinger, Harry Pierpont, Mary Kinder, and Evelyn Frechette, traveling as Anne (or Ann) Martin, arrived in the Arizona city from St. Louis on January 22. Three days later took place the famous roundup of the Dillinger gang, at that time scattered in various parts of the city.

Russell Clark was the first to fall into the net. The address of the house where he was living with Opal Long became known, and four members of the Tucson police force, all dressed in plain clothes, were sent to bring him in. Patrolman Chet Sherman went ahead with a piece of paper in his hand as though searching for a house number, while close behind him came Chief of Detectives Dallas Ford, Frank Eyman, and Kenneth Mullaney. As the door was opened, Sherman drew his gun and rushed in. Clark leaped from the sofa, grabbed the barrel of Sherman's gun, and pulled the policeman into the room. The three other officers reached the entrance of the house, but Opal Long slammed the door, breaking Ford's finger as she did so. Clark, after a fierce struggle, had overpowered Sherman and was drawing his own gun when Eyman and Mullaney broke down the door and clubbed him with the butts of their pistols. In the house the police found, in addition to a large sum of money, four machine guns, four bulletproof vests, and considerable ammunition.

Meanwhile squads of police were cruising about the city seeking other members of the gang. Makley was captured on a downtown street and surrendered without a fight. Harry Pierpont and Mary Kinder were taken as they drove into a tourist camp. Disarmed and locked up, Pierpont sneered at the small-town police.

"I'll remember you," he threatened, staring at each officer intently. "I'll be back."

John Dillinger, the last to be captured, was not taken until later in the day. The arrest of the other three already had made afternoon headlines, but for once Dillinger failed to read the papers. He and Evelyn Frechette drove serenely to the house they had rented three days before and started up the walk, Dillinger carrying a "baby" machine gun. As he put the key in the lock, fifteen police, headed by Chief C. A. Wollard, sprang out of nowhere. The outlaw took in the situation at a glance, dropped his weapon, and raised his hands in the air.

When surprised in Mrs. Longnacre's apartment in Dayton, Dillinger had surrendered without resistance when he found himself covered. Here at Tucson, holding a weapon, he again "went up" when he found himself outgunned. It is well to bear these instances in mind when seeking to penetrate the mystery surrounding his death.

With Dillinger securely handcuffed, the police bore their prize back to headquarters in triumph, taking Miss Frechette along with them. Their prisoner's emotions were a mixture of his customary bravado and chagrin at being so easily captured.

"How did you know I was in town?" he asked. "What a laugh! To be picked up by a bunch of hick cops!"

There was great elation among the Tucson police, for rewards of $8,000 were on Dillinger's head, and the others were worth $1,000 each. When arrested Dillinger was carrying about $9,000, which the police immediately identified as a part of the East Chicago loot. The $30,000 found on all six members of the party was hastily attached by the surety companies. Dillinger, Pierpont, Makley, and Clark were placed in solitary confinement and guarded by fifteen policemen.

"I feel relieved," said old man Dillinger in Mooresville. "I don't believe they have a thing on him in any of these killings."

Told that his father had rejoiced at learning he was no longer a fugitive, Dillinger remarked, "He's a good old scout. I wish for his sake I had taken up some other line of business."

The next day all those arrested were arraigned before Justice of the Peace C. V. Budlong. Dillinger, Pierpont, Makley, and Clark were held on bonds of $100,000 each, while the bond for each of the three girls was $5,000. Governor B. B. Moeur of Arizona arrived to look at the men in their cells.

"I'm sorry to see you in jail, too, governor," greeted Pierpont.

As Dillinger was brought into the courtroom, he smiled at Evelyn Frechette. She smiled back, and he leaned over and kissed her.

"Keep hold of yourself, honey," he whispered. "They've got nothing on you. We'll all get out of this yet."

Otherwise Dillinger was scornful and defiant. A large crowd of curious citizens attended the arraignment, and the captured machine guns were prominently displayed. Later the guns would be conscripted into the service of the Tucson police department.

John Van Buskirk, a Los Angeles attorney, represented the gang and stated that he could prove they had been in Florida continuously for seven weeks before coming to Tucson. He announced that he would fight extradition, file a habeas corpus writ, and try to get the bonds reduced.

Pierpont was in a talkative mood, keeping up a string of running comment, and had to be silenced on several occasions. Clark said little. Makley scornfully repudiated an accusation that he and Dillinger had been involved in the Bremer kidnaping in St. Paul, declaring that he "was a bank robber, and wanted nothing to do with the snatch racket." He said the Tucson jail was "good enough, but I have been in better bastilles."

"I suppose one gets used to it eventually," Evelyn Frechette replied in answer to an inane question as to how she liked her new quarters. When she was called under her alias of Anne Martin, Harry Pierpont informed the court, "There ain't no such animal." Mary Kinder gave the name of Mary Thompson, and begged that her small silver crucifix be returned.

The prisoners were taken back to their cells pending settlement of the extradition question. In the evening Dillinger asked if he might have more supper.

"Tell him he had plenty," Sheriff Belton bravely retorted. "We don't expect to keep that gang in luxury while they are with us."

The eyes of the nation were now focused on the jail at Tucson. Indiana, Illinois, Ohio, and Wisconsin sent their congratulations. Governor McNutt of Indiana and Captain Stege in Chicago had words of praise for the Tucson police.

What was to be done with the Dillinger gang, now that they were in custody? That was the burning question, and soon all of the states concerned would be tearing at each other's throats. The Tucson police opposed any extradition until the rewards were paid. When they were ignored by the court, their trust of their fellow men fell correspondingly, and they began to suspect that their recompense was to be laudatory rather than financial.

Requests for extradition came from Wisconsin, Ohio, and

Indiana. Wisconsin wanted them for the Racine bank robbery. Prosecutor Ernest Botkin of Lima, Ohio, stated, "We want Pierpont, Makley, and Clark. They have been positively identified as the killers of Sheriff Jesse Sarber in Lima. Indiana can have Dillinger."

"Governor White of Ohio and myself will have no trouble over that matter," declared Governor McNutt. Indiana also had warrants against Mary Kinder and Opal Long for aiding and abetting in the Michigan City breakout, and the bonds of the two girls were raised to $100,000 each.

Now there was a perfect exodus of officials from Indiana. Attorney General Philip Lutz, Jr., left from Indianapolis. Prosecutor Robert G. Estill and Chief Deputy Sheriff Carroll Holley set out from Crown Point. From East Chicago came Chief of Police Nicholas Makar. And, of course, among the first arrivals was Captain Matt Leach. The perverse fate that hovered over Captain Leach seemed to decree that he would spend his time chasing Dillinger, while others captured him. Upon reaching Tucson, Leach extended his hand to Dillinger, who took it with some reluctance. His reception from Harry Pierpont was even less cordial.

"I should have killed you when I had the chance, you dirty son of a -----!" he raged. "You threw my old mother in jail to make her tell you where I was. I'll never forget that. When I get out of here, the first thing I'm going to do is to kill you, you rat!"

Pierpont's mother had been arrested by the police of Terre Haute, Indiana. Leach himself had desired her to remain at liberty, as he felt confident that sooner or later Pierpont would communicate, and he had reproved the Terre Haute authorities for their precipitate action.

What Mr. Pierpont said to Mr. Leach is comparable only to what the various states now began saying to each other over the matter of extradition. As for Dillinger himself, he was perfectly content that the fight go on indefinitely.

"I'm in no hurry to return to Indiana," he remarked. "I haven't a thing to do when I get there."

The bitterest quarrel was between Wisconsin and Indiana. Bad blood already existed between the Wisconsin authorities and Captain Leach over the matter of Leslie "Big" Homer. When Homer was arrested as a parole violator, he confessed his part in the Racine bank robbery, and Prosecutor John Brown and Chief of Police Grover C. Lutter of Racine set out to bring him back. Upon their arrival, the Racine authorities accused Leach of breaking the story to the newspapers.

"They put us on the spot," they declared. "The Dillinger mob knew that Homer had confessed, and were out to shoot him."

But they returned safely with their prisoner, and within twenty-four hours Homer was tried, convicted, and in prison. Some two years later he was wounded in an escape attempt at the Wisconsin state penitentiary at Waupun.

Wisconsin cited the Homer trial and other instances of swift "Wisconsin justice" as reason to receive the prisoners. But Wisconsin had no capital punishment. This was attractive to the prisoners themselves, and Dillinger readily signed a waiver for extradition. Wisconsin's efforts to gain control of the gang caused a storm to sweep the country. The state was bitterly exercised elsewhere in editorials, which proclaimed the only protection against man-killers to be execution, and accused her of attempting to obstruct justice.

Indiana, meanwhile, had a large number of officials on site who were vigorously presenting her case. She stressed the question of capital punishment, and promised legal aid to the Lake County authorities at Crown Point to send Dillinger to the chair.

"To hell with Wisconsin," spoke Prosecutor Clarence Houston of Tucson. "I wouldn't hand the gang over to that state's officials under any consideration." Wisconsin received some pretty rough handling in this Dillinger matter, but her turn to laugh would come later.

Eventually Wisconsin found herself frozen out, Indiana charging possible corruption in that state's efforts to win the prisoners. Governor Moeur of Arizona awarded custody to Indiana, on the understanding that she was to keep Dillinger and turn Pierpont, Makley, and Clark over to Ohio. All three of the girls were released.

John Dillinger, heavily shackled and guarded, was taken from the jail on January 30, an hour before Van Buskirk arrived with a writ of habeas corpus. An airplane was waiting to take him back to Indiana.

"Where's my lawyer?" he shouted. "He told me this was illegal. They can't take me back east without a hearing."

Stormy scenes and squabbling continued to the very end. At the airport Captain Leach became involved in an altercation with Chester Sherman and Frank Eyman of the Tucson police which threatened to end in gunplay. Later the two Tucson officers came to Indiana. Leach stated that they had been sent by their chief to apologize for their rudeness. According to other reports, J. Parker Hale Chandler, a wealthy resident of Tucson, paid for their trip in order that they might testify in Dillinger's prosecution. In any event, the two ended up joining a vaudeville show and cashing in on the publicity they received.

The whir of the propellers sounded, and John Dillinger went for his first airplane ride, closely guarded by Carroll Holley and others. Pierpont, Makley, and Clark started eastward at the same time, conveyed in a more prosaic railroad train. While Pierpont was in jail at Tucson, a marriage license, paid for by the sheriff, had been issued for him and Mary Kinder, but no ceremony would ever be performed.

Quite a cavalcade gathered at the Chicago airport on January 30 to greet America's premier public enemy. With Dillinger were Carroll Holley of Lake County and Chief of Police Nicholas Makar of East Chicago. Following in another plane were Lake County prosecutor Robert G. Estill and East Chicago policeman Hobart Wilgus. On the ground were thirty-two of Captain Stege's Dillinger squad, clad in armor and carrying machine guns and shotguns. Present also were sixty other Chicago policemen and twenty-nine members of the Indiana State Police to escort the shackled prisoner. Thirteen cars, loaded to the gunwales with heavily armed police, made up the procession to the jail at Crown Point, the seat of Lake County, Indiana.

The sheriff of Lake County at this time chanced to be a woman, Mrs. Lillian Holley. She had succeeded to the office a year before, following the death of her husband, Sheriff Roy Holley, in a battle with a maniac. Mrs. Holley was forty-two years old and the mother of twin daughters, Janice and Janet, nineteen years of age. Carroll Holley, her nephew, acted as her chief deputy, and was expected to succeed her in office.

Seated next to the outlaw on the trip to Indiana was Sergeant Frank "Killer" Reynolds, right-hand man of Captain Stege. Eager to add another notch to the formidable number already on his gun, Reynolds taunted Dillinger constantly.

"Well, John, why don't you try making a break? Don't you want to jump out of the car?"

Late that night John Dillinger was securely housed in the Crown Point jail, and joy reigned unconfined. His amiable and garrulous manner delighted the mass of reporters, but the smile faded, and his face became set and resolute, when they questioned him about the East Chicago bank robbery.

"I never killed O'Malley. I never had anything to do with that stickup. I was in Florida when the East Chicago job was pulled, and I can prove it. They can't hold me for that."

He said that McGinnis had put him on the spot in the Dr. Eye incident. He told of his capture in Tucson, and how the careless generosity of Makley and Clark had been their undoing. What about Hamilton?

"Poor Red! He died from the wounds he received in East Chicago. Caught a whole flock of bullets in his stomach. I wasn't with him when he got it, but one of the boys told me about it. I think they dumped his body in the Calumet River. Hamilton has some kids, and before he died he sent me some money to take to them. That was the dough that was in the sacks that the Tucson police took away from me."

Needless to say, Dillinger knew Hamilton was still alive, but taking off some "heat" would allow him a freer hand to work for his release. Captain Stege and others scoffed at the story, but even when Hamilton's grave was located at a much later date, some uncertainty remained as to when and where he received his mortal wounds.

Beer, supplied by Sheriff Holley and Chief of Police Makar, soon flowed freely. Captain Stege and his thirty-two knights in armor sat around a barrel in the dining room of the jail. It was a gathering of jolly good fellows, and the atmosphere became convivial. Dillinger was asked how he felt toward Prosecutor Estill.

"I like Estill."

"How about Sheriff Holley?"

"Mrs. Holley seems like a fine lady."

The photographers clamored for more pictures, and everyone obliged. Prosecutor Estill was positioned in the middle, with John Dillinger to his left and Mrs. Holley on his right. Dillinger placed his arm affectionately around Estill's shoulder. The prosecutor put his arm about the outlaw's neck. It was quite a happy family portrait.

The morning after found many headaches among those who had made up that jolly throng, but they were nothing compared to the headache the group photograph caused Prosecutor Estill when copies of it reached every voter in Lake County at election time.

The next day life at the jail settled down somewhat. No fewer than ten persons came to view Dillinger and identify him as the man who had shot Officer O'Malley. Included among them were bank vice-presidents Walter Spencer and Edward L. Steck, cashier James A. Dalton, and Michael Obermeyer and Peter Bartok, two state game wardens who had also witnessed the killing. Dillinger doggedly maintained that he was in Florida at the time, and that it was all a mistake.

Only one message came to gladden the heart of the desperado. It was from his aged father in Mooresville, who never for a single moment faltered in his loyalty. If he was needed, he said, he would come to Crown Point, but his departure might be delayed because all of his shirts were being laundered.

Now the burning question in all minds was, which great attorney would represent the greatest criminal of the age?

John Dillinger soon settled that. He said, "Get me Louis Piquett."

Not many people knew the name. How did Piquett, a former Chicago municipal prosecutor turned criminal lawyer, whom Dillinger had never met, come to enter the case?

We do not expect to have any trouble with our newest prisoner. Of course, I warned him the first thing that we would stand for no monkey business.

—Sheriff Lillian Holley, Lake County, Indiana

PART II

With the Dillinger gang rounded up like sheep by Tucson city police, and with Dillinger securely lodged in a new Indiana jail, guarded by heavily armed deputies, soldiers, and possemen, Cummings and Hoover were left twiddling their thumbs. The fact that local and state authorities seemed to have the situation well in hand was a definite setback for the Justice Department's interstate-criminal promotion plan. With the Kansas City Massacre still unsolved and the abductors of William Hamm still unidentified, it was beginning to look like the FBI's slick and quick solution to the Urschel kidnapping was merely a fluke. Moreover, Homer Cummings's federal anti-crime bills had been ambushed in Congress by conservative southern legislators insisting that such laws would "do violence" to states' rights, and that any federal agency empowered to enforce them could turn into a European-style secret police. In short, the Roosevelt administration's sales force was encountering stiff buyer resistance to its Twelve Point Program of federal crime control.

Hoover still craved a celebrity bank robber who qualified as an "interstate" criminal. But robbing banks, taking hostages, even shooting policemen and interstate flight were not yet federal crimes that would give the FBI a chance to show what its "briefcase cops" could do. And now Dillinger was out of reach, locked up in a hicktown slammer and charming the pants off the press with the kind of good-natured cockiness that Americans admire in their out-laws. He was accused of killing Patrolman O'Malley during the East Chicago holdup, but eyewitnesses weren't positive that Dillinger was the shooter, and some even thought the killing was unintentional. Thus Dillinger's sense of public relations was paying off. A display of gallantry, when conditions allowed, usually made it into the first or second paragraph, and if reporters felt obliged to condemn the crime, one could still detect their admiration of the perpetrator's boldness and coolness under fire. Dillinger was viewed as tough but not sadistic, crooked but not twisted, and if his outlaw days might now be over, he had given the cops a good run for the money, and turned hundreds of townspeople into local celebrities, once their knees stopped knocking. Most wouldn't mind it if he beat the murder rap.

What happened next was an instance of life imitating art, except that the stunt Dillinger pulled was too improbable for any novelist. On March 3, 1934, using a fake gun, Dillinger bluffed his way out of Indiana's supposedly escape-proof jail, and three days later was back to robbing banks. That earned him not only a permanent place in American criminal history, but also the grati-tude of J. Edgar Hoover. For in fleeing to Chicago in a stolen auto, John Dillinger finally interfered with interstate commerce in the form of the Dyer Act, and became fair game for the G-men. Hoover and Cummings finally had their dragon to slay, and did not dwell on the fact that they were mobilizing the entire U.S. Justice Department to catch a car thief.

The story of the Crown Point jailbreak has been told countless times with-out resolving two questions: whether Dillinger had inside help in making his escape, and whether the wooden pistol he flourished was merely to cover the smuggling of a real gun. Deputy Sheriff Ernest Blunk first would claim that the gun was a phony, and later that it was real. Suspicion immediately fell on Judge William Murray, who was handling the Dillinger case, had unsupervised access to the prisoner, and had declined to transfer the outlaw to the greater security of the state prison. (By an irrelevant coincidence, Murray was the divorce lawyer who had once represented the wife of an East Chicago police-man, Martin Zarkovich, after he had become too friendly with a local brothelkeeper named Anna Sage.)

In the following chapters, Girardin reveals that the man who engineered Dillinger's escape was not Judge Murray, in spite of appearances, or Sheriff Lillian Holley, who also came under suspicion, but the maverick Chicago attorney Louis Piquett, who had decided the famous outlaw was his ticket to legal stardom. How Piquett employed a ruse to become Dillinger's lawyer has never before been told, nor has the inside story of the breakout. From the wooden gun to the bribery of jailers, Crown Point was Piquett's show—with a little help from a friend.

CHAPTER SEVEN

PIQUETT TAKES THE CASE

Louis P. Piquett had behind him a colorful and exciting career, quite in keeping with the stirring events that were to come. One of a family of nine children, he was born September 24, 1884, at Benton, a small town in southwest Wisconsin. His father, a blacksmith, and his mother, both in their eighties, had just celebrated their sixtieth wedding anniversary before the Dillinger episode.

Piquett finished the grade school in his home town, and then, about the beginning of the century, the spirit of adventure caught hold of him. He reached California by "riding the rods," and there somehow managed to enroll in Stanford University at Sonora. His athletic prowess attracted some attention, and in 1903 he accompanied the Stanford track team on a tour of Australia. He then turned his attention to the prize ring, and for the next year or two was a professional pugilist. With the money thus gained, he opened a wholesale cigar store at Fourth and Market streets in San Francisco, only to be wiped out by the San Francisco earthquake and fire in 1906.

Again penniless, Piquett returned to Platteville, Wisconsin, where his family was then living, and on September 12, 1906, married Nell Draper, a girl of sixteen with her hair in beribboned braids. About a year and a half later they came to Chicago, where for several years Piquett led the uneventful life of a dishwasher, waiter, and bartender in restaurants and saloons. His opportunity came when an article he wrote for a liquor magazine was called to the attention of Chicago mayoral candidate William Hale Thompson, who saw it as a welcome endorsement by the liquor interests. Piquett soon found himself a precinct captain and later a ward committeeman and political boss of the then-turbulent 21st Ward, now the equally turbulent 42d Ward.*

When Thompson was elected mayor in 1915, Piquett was rewarded with the position of chief clerk in the office of City Prosecutor Harry B. Miller. He devoted all his spare time to "reading the law," and received his license to practice in 1918. In 1920 he stepped into Miller's shoes as the city prosecutor. This was the "whoopee" era of Chicago politics, and Piquett was not to emerge wholly unscathed. In 1922 he was indicted in the school-board scandal for alleged grafting on coal contracts, but the charges were dismissed.[22] A change of administration brought the Democrats to power in 1923, but Piquett managed to retain his position for a short time longer, and had the satisfaction of presenting a voluntary resignation.

From this time on Piquett devoted himself exclusively to the private practice of law, at first with the late state senator Arthur A. Huebach, later on his own. His magnetic personality, his ability as an orator and knowledge of courtroom procedure, and his great mane of prematurely white hair made him a colorful figure and would win him a place among the foremost criminal lawyers of the Middle West. Perhaps his most notable case was that of Leo Brothers, convicted in 1931 of slaying Alfred Lingle, a Chicago newspaperman with somewhat shady connections. Piquett regarded Brothers's relatively light fourteen-year sentence as a "moral victory."[23]

---

*In 1915, William Hale Thompson, the Republican candidate, was engaged in a bitter mayoralty battle with Robert Sweitzer. The Democrats had held the mayor's office in Chicago for many years, and Sweitzer, who was a powerful figure in Catholic organizations, was a favorite to win. Piquett at this time was a Republican precinct captain in a Catholic precinct which was conceded to Sweitzer. When the polls closed on the evening of the election, Piquett proposed that the officials lock up the store which was the polling place and have dinner before they began the arduous work of counting the ballots. Piquett had another key to the store, and when all were at dinner a friend entered through the back door and replaced the ballot box with another that was stuffed. When the votes were counted, it was consequently found that the Republicans had carried the precinct by a margin of about nine to one. Thompson, who won the election, wished to congratulate the precinct captain on this remarkable achievement. Piquett modestly declared that it was due entirely to his hard work. Piquett was an important figure in Chicago politics during all the years of the Thompson administration. He never graduated from a law school, but obtained a license through his own studies and political influence.

About this time Piquett became acquainted with Arthur O'Leary, another figure who would play a major part in the Dillinger drama as Piquett's investigator. O'Leary, in spite of a difficult beginning, including a childhood in an orphan asylum, had made the most of his opportunities and gradually amassed considerable wealth. A series of financial reverses wiped out his holdings, and he started over again in Chicago as a bond salesman and legal investigator. For many years he worked with Lewis W. Mack, a prominent Chicago attorney disbarred for his propensity to appropriate the funds of clients. Mack, incidentally, took advantage of O'Leary's later incarceration on the Dillinger charges to defraud Mrs. O'Leary of a thousand dollars which she had entrusted to him to aid her husband. O'Leary was known for his expensive attire, a suave and ready wit, and the manners of a bon vivant.[24]

While Dillinger languished in Tucson, a frequent caller at Piquett's offices was one Meyer Bogue. Bogue was a tall, middle-aged man with graying dark hair who spoke in a low, insinuating voice. He had been confined in the Michigan City penitentiary much of the time that Dillinger was there, and the two were reasonably close. He had been invited to go along at the time of the break, but declined to do so, inasmuch as he had but three months longer to serve.

"I think I can get you to be Dillinger's lawyer," he told Piquett. "I'm a good friend of Hymie Cohen and I know Sheetz. I'm sure Dillinger doesn't have a lawyer and he'll be glad to take whoever they recommend."

"I know the East Chicago people, too," O'Leary added.

The "fix," or underworld kingpin, in that part of Lake County was Sonny Sheetz, who ruled with a hand of iron. Dillinger had bought protection from him in the past, and made payment from bank robberies that were arranged through East Chicago.

Hymie Cohen, a right-hand man of Sheetz, was an underworld figure in East Chicago and the operator of gambling and disorderly houses.

Another character was Jimmie Regan. Regan was employed as an investigator by Prosecutor Estill and was well acquainted in Crown Point and East Chicago, both with the underworld and with police and political circles.

"That would be wonderful if you boys can get me that case," said Piquett. "If I land that, it will make me the most famous lawyer in the United States."

Which it did.

O'Leary and Bogue proceeded to East Chicago and talked with Cohen and Sheetz. O'Leary wrote the following message on the back of one of Piquett's cards:

"Call no attorney but this one. Gang raising necessary funds for defense. Happy."

The "Happy" referred to was "Happy" Miles, a former convict and friend of Dillinger at Michigan City with whom O'Leary was acquainted.

The East Chicago people arranged to have the card passed to Dillinger by Sam Cahoon, a trusty and handyman at the Crown Point jail.*

When Piquett and O'Leary arrived on the scene, they discovered that the same thought had occurred to a small army of other attorneys, among whom were William McAleer and Joseph H. Conroy of Lake County, Indiana, and W. W. O'Brien, perhaps the most prominent criminal lawyer in Chicago. They found this awesome array of legal talent cooling their heels in the lobby, striving desperately to see the country's most publicized prisoner.

From throughout the state the armed forces of the law had gathered to form a thoroughly disorganized army. Constantly in each other's way were the jail guards and police from Crown Point and neighboring cities, along with detachments of the Indiana State Police and the Indiana National Guard. From far and wide "embattled farmers" had left their fields or firesides and hurried to the scene of the action, some armed with antiquated muskets, pitchforks, baseball bats, and wagon staves. One could scarcely take a step without encountering weaponry. At the door of the jail stood a huge "sodbuster" with flashing eyes who seemed to take a fiendish delight in thrusting a large rifle into the faces of all who wished to enter. Within the outer lobby were heavy tripod-mounted machine guns, manned by nervous farm boys in the uniforms of the National Guard.

Piquett and O'Leary stayed about Crown Point until late in the afternoon. On the way back to Chicago, Piquett stopped off to

---

*My account of the Crown Point escape published in 1936 was deliberately incorrect. O'Leary and Piquett later seemed to have no compunction about disclosing their part in the break, but O'Leary insisted that there be no mention of the East Chicago mob and their associates, for his and my protection. "They won't hesitate a minute to blow your head off," was his cautionary remark. Consequently, a story was invented that O'Leary arranged to have the card passed to Dillinger by Jim Dexter, the chef at the Crown Point jail, whom O'Leary knew. Cahoon played but a minor part in the jailbreak, and it was not a criminal offense to pass the card to Dillinger, but O'Leary wished his name to be withheld because he was too close to others in the escape.

telephone his wife, and was very much delighted to learn of reports in the late editions that Dillinger was demanding to see Louis Piquett of Chicago. The ruse had worked even more quickly than expected. They immediately returned to Crown Point, but arrived too late to be admitted that day.

The following day, Thursday, February 1, Piquett again called at Crown Point's overly garrisoned bastille. He was met by Lou Baker, the warden, who told him that Dillinger had been calling for him constantly. Every precaution was being taken to safeguard Lake County's most important guest.

"I'm sorry, but we'll have to search you," Warden Baker said. "We have to search everybody."

"That's all right," assented Piquett. "I want to be searched."

In view of what transpired later, it should be noted that on every occasion Piquett visited his client, he insisted on being searched.

Piquett was introduced to Dillinger, and was permitted to converse with him alone.

"I'd like you to represent me," said Dillinger. "I didn't have anything to do with that job in East Chicago."

"I don't believe you did."

"I can prove that I didn't. Here's what happened."

"Just a minute, before we take up too much of each other's time. Innocent or guilty, you're in a pretty hot spot here. I suppose you know that it is going to cost money to present a strong defense. How much have you got?"

"My father in Mooresville has about three thousand dollars."

"Is that all you have?"

"Yes, that's all."

"Hell, you don't need a lawyer. You need a doctor."

"The cops in Tucson cleaned me out. You don't want the case, then?"

"Don't you understand? You're the most talked-of criminal in America today. Any lawyer who represents you is going to get dirtied up plenty. I'd like to help you, but I can't see myself taking all that on for only three thousand dollars."

At this moment a telegram was brought to Dillinger. It was from his father in Mooresville, stating that he was on his way to Crown Point and was bringing with him Joseph Ryan, a one-armed lawyer from Indianapolis. Dillinger passed the wire over to Piquett.

"Well, looks like you don't need me now."

"I don't know anything about this fellow Ryan. Give me a little time. I think I know where I can raise some more money."

"We'll leave it at that. I'll see you again in a couple of days."

On Friday John Dillinger was reindicted, inasmuch as the first indictment had been hastily drawn and might not have sustained a conviction. The senior Dillinger and Ryan arrived on the scene, and a continuance was asked in order to prepare a defense. The only other noteworthy event this day was the arrival of a "mystery" woman, drunk as a hoot owl and posing as a New York journalist demanding to interview John Dillinger. Taken into custody, she proved to be a Mrs. Josephine Hunt, the divorced wife of Captain Jonathan Hunt of the United States Army. The inebriated lady was held for arraignment the next day on charges that she had failed to pay a cab bill of $32.70.

Piquett went to see Dillinger again on Saturday, but the arrival of Ryan provided the outlaw with an attorney, and Piquett announced his intention to withdraw.

On Monday, February 5, Dillinger was arraigned before Judge William J. Murray. Fifty guards stood about the courtroom, and the shackled prisoner was brought in by four men armed with machine guns. Piquett and O'Leary occupied a prominent place in the foreground, but in the capacity of spectators.

Ryan apparently was in a quandary over just what to do. He had appeared before Judge T. Joseph Sullivan and filed for a writ of habeas corpus, challenging the indictment on the grounds that Dillinger was a law-abiding citizen of the state of Arizona, based on a residency of three days. The petition was of course denied. Ryan then moved for a continuance, which was granted until Friday. Dillinger was led away visibly displeased with his one-armed attorney. Ryan spoke in so low a voice that he could scarcely be heard in the courtroom.

As Piquett left the courtroom, Warden Baker advised him that Dillinger was demanding to see him at once. There was no mistaking the outlaw's agitation.

"Mr. Piquett," he said, "I must talk to you alone."

Baker led Piquett to a cell where he could converse with the prisoner in private, but the attorney, suspicious that the place indicated might be wired, selected a cell in another part of the jail. During the conversation he kept tapping with a coin to discourage any recording by dictaphone.

"Mr. Piquett," Dillinger said nervously, "I can't have that fellow Ryan. My God, he's going to send me to the hot seat! He all but convicted me just in asking for a continuance."

"I wouldn't feel like that. Ryan's all right."

"I want you to represent me. How about it?"

"I'll be frank with you. It's going to cost you money."

"All right."

"Where is this money coming from?"

"I haven't any with me. But—" and Dillinger bent closer—"I have a third interest in a quarter of a million dollars hidden in northern Wisconsin. I'll arrange with the boys to have your fee cut out of that."*

The next day Piquett was again at Crown Point for a conference with his client. The matter of a defense was discussed in detail, with Dillinger steadfastly denying any part in the East Chicago affair. It was known that he had been in Daytona on the noon preceding the robbery. Dillinger insisted he could prove he was still there late in the evening. At the conclusion of the interview, Warden Baker informed Piquett that he could see his client without the necessity of a court order, and Piquett's subsequent visits are therefore unrecorded except when he brought some other person with him.

It was Thursday, two days later, when Piquett returned to the Lake County Jail. This time the principal topic of discussion was Piquett's fee. Father Dillinger had turned over twenty-five hundred of his three thousand dollars to Ryan, and Piquett had not as yet seen a cent. Dillinger promised him ten thousand dollars of the money supposedly in Wisconsin, and said he would send someone to get it.

The arraignment of Dillinger on Friday, February 9, hardly resembled that of the previous Monday. Piquett was on his feet constantly, fighting for every point, and Dillinger was as delighted as a small boy at a carnival. The outlaw had been brought in heavily shackled, as usual, and with the machine-gun escort poking him in the back.

"Your Honor," Piquett addressed the court, "are we to have a hearing in accord with the spirit of the laws of this state and of this nation, or are we to witness merely a mockery of the name of justice? Is the state to be permitted to continue inciting an atmosphere of prejudice and hatred? The very air reeks with the bloody rancor of intolerant malice. The clanging of shackles brings to our minds the dungeons of the czars, and not the flag-bedecked liberty

---

*Although stories of a hidden Dillinger treasure still circulate, there seems never to have been such a quantity of money. Dillinger was possibly referring to a cache of negotiable securities that had been taken in previous bank robberies.

of an American courtroom. I request the court to direct that those shackles be removed.''

"This is a very dangerous man, Your Honor," objected Prosecutor Estill.

"Remove the handcuffs from the prisoner," directed Judge Murray.

Piquett was quick to press his advantage.

"Thank you. May I also point out to Your Honor that this is a civil court, and not a military court-martial. Could anything be more prejudicial than machine guns pressed into the defendant's back, and an army of guards cluttering up the room? May the court direct that all guns be removed from the courtroom?"

Carroll Holley rushed forward. "I'm responsible for the safe-guarding of the prisoner."

"Who are you?" thundered Piquett. "Are you a lawyer? What right have you to address the court?"

The judge ordered Holley to sit down, and the deputy's face reddened as he glowered at Piquett. "Take those machine guns out of this court."

Things were now moving rapidly, and in a decidedly belligerent atmosphere. Piquett was arguing for a delay of thirty days and a date in March in order to prepare his defense.

"Ten days should be plenty," declared Estill.

"That would be legal murder," shouted Piquett. "There is a law against lynching in this state!"

"There is a law against murder, too!" Estill shouted back.

"Then why don't you observe it? Why don't you call back your men with their machine guns? Why don't you stand Dillinger against a wall and shoot him down? There's no need to throw away the state's money on this kind of mockery. Why isn't John Dillinger entitled to the consideration of a hearing? Your Honor, even Christ had a fairer trial than this!"

Judge Murray granted a delay until March 12, and as he did so Estill's nervous irritability reached the breaking point.

"Your Honor," he said bitterly, "why don't you let Mr. Piquett take Dillinger home with him, and bring him back on the day of the trial? You've given him everything else he has asked for."

As court adjourned, Dillinger grinned broadly at Piquett. "Atta boy, counsel," he whispered.

A truce was declared for the weekend, but on Monday the war-fare resumed. Jailbreaks were becoming so frequent nationwide that local officials remained in a constant state of worry over rumors they were hearing, and Prosecutor Estill joined Sheriff Lillian Holley in discussing with Judge Murray the advisability of transferring their special guest to the state prison for safer keeping.

Dillinger's face whitened when he heard the news.

"Don't let them take me to Michigan City," he begged Piquett. "I never want to see that place again. I want you to fight this thing for me."

"Of course I'll fight it," Piquett assured him. "Quit worrying. You're not going to Michigan City."

Piquett sat in on the conference and found Estill and Mrs. Holley very determined in their desire for Dillinger's removal, and pressing Judge Murray strongly. His first efforts were directed to winning over the sheriff.

"I think that's a very nice jail you have. What makes you think there's anything wrong with it?"

Mrs. Holley's professional pride was touched. "There isn't anything wrong with it," she retorted. "It's the strongest jail in Indiana."

"That's what I thought. But, of course, I don't want to embarrass Mrs. Holley. I appreciate that she's a woman, and if she's afraid of an escape—"

"I'm not afraid of an escape. I can take care of John Dillinger or any other prisoner."

Mrs. Holley now intimated a definite desire that Dillinger be left with her, and Piquett played his trump card against Estill and Judge Murray.

"I wish to protest very vehemently against Dillinger's removal to Michigan City," Piquett said. "There's nothing wrong with the jail in Crown Point. You've been telling me ever since Dillinger was brought there that it's an escape-proof jail. My offices are located in Chicago. It's far enough to come to Crown Point, and I don't see why I should be obliged to travel all the way to Michigan City every time I want to talk to my client. Furthermore, I object to Dillinger being transported back and forth, in and out of the jurisdiction. If you're not capable of giving him a fair trial here, I intend to ask for a change of venue."

The prosecutor and the judge glanced at each other, and a look of understanding passed between them. Neither of the men was a publicity-seeker, but the nationwide attention had not proved unpleasant. If the most famous criminal of the times was to be tried, they were the ones who wished to do it. So Piquett won, and Dillinger did not go to the state penitentiary.

"I told Mr. Estill that I felt Dillinger was being adequately guarded where he was," Judge Murray stated later, "and that a hundred armed men could not take him out of that jail. I explained that the statute did not contemplate the transfer of a prisoner unless there was danger of mob violence, and that no such danger existed here."*

Thursday of that week, February 15, Arthur O'Leary accompanied Piquett to Crown Point and met John Dillinger for the first time. Both men were thoroughly searched. It was Piquett's intention to send O'Leary to Florida for information helpful to Dillinger's defense, and this was the main topic of discussion between the investigator and the gang leader. As O'Leary was preparing to leave, Dillinger said to him, "Wait a minute. I'm going to give you a note for Billie."

The note was a bit thicker and shorter than a cigarette, and wound with a rubber band.

"Dillinger slipped me a note for Frechette," O'Leary whispered to Piquett.

"It's probably a mushy love note. You better let me have it. They're liable to search you when we go out, but they can't touch me."

While Carroll Holley and Warden Baker led Dillinger around the corner and back to his cell, Piquett bent over as if to lace his shoe and slipped the message into his oxford.

"I think we ought to look at what Dillinger gave you," Piquett remarked on the return trip to Chicago.

The note was written on a piece of rough brown paper of about ordinary letter size, and had been carefully folded and creased with typical Dillinger neatness. On one side was a complete floor plan of the Crown Point jail. The other side contained a message addressed to "Red" Hamilton, and gave detailed instructions for an escape. Hamilton was requested to make a sudden and bold

---

*Judge Murray was later to receive much abuse and criticism for his failure to send Dillinger to Michigan City. A motion picture described the Crown Point escape by saying, "Louis Piquett, an underworld lawyer, bribed a dishonest judge." Whether the former Chicago city prosecutor may be described correctly as an underworld character is a matter of opinion, but I heard nothing to suggest that Judge Murray was dishonest in the Dillinger case, much less that he accepted a $6,000 bribe to smuggle Dillinger a real gun, as eventually was claimed.

Judge Murray, remember, had become the focus of national attention, and he was determined not to be accused of running a "kangaroo" court and railroading Dillinger to the electric chair, a result which might be overruled by an appeals court. In all matters that came before him he was therefore inclined to give Dillinger the benefit of the doubt and display the utmost fairness. Piquett told me that he sensed this inclination on Judge Murray's part and pressed it to his advantage at every opportunity.

LAKE COUNTY JAIL

LILLIAN M. HOLLEY
SHERIFF

CROWN POINT, INDIANA

Dear Sis and all.,

Received your letter O. K. and was sure glad to hear from you. I am well and getting along fine. I would sure like to see all of you. Mrs. Holley will let any of you in to see me so whenever any of you have an opportunity you and Frances can come along to see me. Tell Dad to send me ten dollars right away, he can send it in a letter. I hope Hubert is feeling better by now. Both of my attorneys were here friday to see me and everything is progressing along fine.

How does Francis like her schooling Does Dad let you and Francis go to the show as often as I used to take you? I would sure like to see all of you kids, was sorry I didnt get to take you to the worlds fair, maybe though you will get a chance to go this summer the fair will be bigger and better this year. I wish you kids could see the country Ive seen the last few months it would sure have been a treat to you.

I am glad you are such a big help to Dad, for he is getting along in years and he needs your help. Mr. Ryan says Hubert is thinking of quitting his job. I think he had better reconsider as scarce as jobs are now. Well honey I guess Ill ring off for this time tell everyone hello and love to all from your brother Johnnie.

John Dillinger

Dillinger writes a typically cheerful letter to his family from Indiana's Lake County Jail, which proved to be less escape-proof than advertised. *John Dillinger Museum* descent on Crown Point with other members of the gang. They were to first dynamite the southwest corner of the jail, which would blow away the brickwork and leave only the inside steel. With blowtorches this could be cut through in minutes, while any guards who tried to interfere were to be dissuaded with machine guns. Dillinger told of a peephole in his cell through which he might be watched and covered, and therefore requested that the attempt be made about eleven o'clock in the morning, when the prisoners were out of their cells.

Piquett and O'Leary looked at each other.

"What do you think of that?" O'Leary whistled. "Shall we give this thing to Frechette?"

"I don't know. It would place us in a bad light to take it back and give it to Baker. I'm going to burn the damn thing up."

"Just a minute. Sooner or later Dillinger will find out from Frechette that we didn't give her the note, and then what do you think will happen? Let's give her the note, tell her we've read it, and then show her how impossible it is. We can even bring her down here and let her see the situation for herself, and then talk Dillinger out of it."

Shortly before this Evelyn Frechette had been brought to Piquett's offices late one night by Joe Ryan. She stated that she was trying to raise funds for Dillinger's defense, and after that was an almost daily visitor.

Two days later Piquett was back in Crown Point. Dillinger asked him if Bogue had contacted the people in East Chicago.

"Yes, I think so."

"I'd like to talk to Bogue myself. There are some things I need to tell him. Is there any way you can get him in here to see me?"

"I'll do my best."

Piquett and Bogue appeared in Crown Point on Monday, February 19, and were summarily refused admittance by Sheriff Holley. They then resorted to Prosecutor Estill, and met with no greater success. Piquett finally called upon Judge Murray.

"Bogue is an old friend of Dillinger's," he declared. "He knew him in the 'university.' "

The judge looked surprised. "I was not aware that Dillinger had attended a university. What did he study?"

"I think it was shirtmaking."

Everyone laughed, and the judge signed an order authorizing Bogue's admittance on Warden Baker's assurance that a screen would separate him from Dillinger.

According to Bogue, Dillinger wanted to know if he had contacted the people in East Chicago.

"I talked to Hymie. They want 25 G's."

"I can't get it to them until I'm out of here."

"They'll wait."

"Red's not in shape yet to come and get me, and I don't have time to wait until he gets better. They're afraid of me around here. If I had a gun I could take myself out. How about getting one to me?"

"I'll try. Blunk is in the know, and it might be possible for him to slip it to you."

"Do your best."

Piquett made two more trips to the jail during that week. On the first he informed Dillinger that an unexpected snag had developed. Ernest Blunk, a deputy and fingerprint expert at the Crown Point jail, would have no part of smuggling in a gun. A gun would lead to a thorough investigation, and he did not want to take a chance of being implicated.

Piquett also spoke of his fee on that visit. He asked for fifty thousand dollars for past, present, and future services. Dillinger promised that he would try and get some money to him.

It was Arthur O'Leary who conceived the idea of a wooden gun. He had read a newspaper account that on October 26, 1933, Earl Loveday, a prisoner in the Wisconsin state penitentiary at Waupun, had attempted to make his way out with such a weapon. The effort was frustrated, however, by the alertness and courage of a deputy. Warden Oscar Lee stated that the gun had been colored with ink and was a good imitation.

O'Leary declared that he knew where he could obtain such a gun. If the escape attempt failed, Dillinger could say that he had carved the gun in his cell and so no one would get into trouble.*

*My first trip to Mooresville was with Louis Piquett, at which time I spent most of an afternoon with Dillinger's father and his sister, Mrs. Hancock. When Piquett explained the purpose of our visit, they were most cooperative. They permitted me to borrow the wooden gun and some other articles of John Dillinger, and when I so requested, they said that I might keep a few copper coins that were in his pocket at the time of his death. I had the wooden gun in my possession for a period of several months. When Arthur O'Leary and I were about to leave for New York to arrange for the syndication of the story, I expressed a hope that the Dillinger family would not ask for the return of the gun, as I wished to take it with me and exhibit it there. O'Leary suggested that we could have a duplicate gun made and return that to them. I turned down this idea, as the Dillinger family seemed to have a great regard for this item and I had promised to return it to them whenever they asked. O'Leary then said he felt it was still advisable to have a duplicate, as we could take that with us to New York.

On his second visit Piquett told Dillinger of the wooden gun. Dillinger, after some hesitation, agreed when told there was no chance that Blunk would bring in a real gun.

Piquett was becoming convinced that if the case ever went to trial he could bring Dillinger off with an acquittal, and he urged him to consider the possibility. A number of witnesses could be brought from Florida to testify that Dillinger had been in Daytona on the evening preceding the East Chicago bank robbery. To add the note of sensationalism that Piquett relished, one of the country's leading dirt-track race drivers would be hired to drive a fast car from Daytona to Chicago and demonstrate that it would be impossible to cover the distance in so short a time. He argued that there was still some doubt in the minds of the Indiana authorities and the public as to whether it was Dillinger or Hamilton who had killed Officer O'Malley, and that the feeling toward him had changed to almost one of friendliness.

Dillinger listened, but indicated that he still placed greater reliance on a jailbreak.

Upon his return to Chicago, Piquett confronted another situation that made him feel the Dillinger connection was not all he had once hoped it would be. Bogue had been in East Chicago and related that they needed some advance money immediately. Sheetz and the others were willing to wait for Dillinger, but Blunk and Ernest Saager, the garage mechanic who was to have a fast car ready for the getaway, wanted part of their money now. Dillinger had been approached, but said that he had no ready money and told them to ask Piquett to advance it.

"How much do they want?" Piquett asked.

"Five thousand now."

"Where do I come in at? I haven't seen a cent yet in this Dillinger business. I don't have five thousand dollars."

"You can get it from Ada," O'Leary offered.

In Chicago's State-Lake theater building was located one of the city's leading abortion mills. It was run ostensibly by Dr. Jose-

One afternoon O'Leary drove me about three or four miles northwest of Chicago's Loop. We walked through a gangway or passage along the side of a large gray frame house, and came to a two-story brick house in the rear. I noted what appeared to be living quarters on the first floor as we went up a dirty wooden staircase to a carpentry or woodworking shop on the upper floor. There we were greeted in a friendly fashion by a bald man with a beard and a heavy German accent. I had given the wooden gun to O'Leary, who pulled it from his pocket. "Oh, ja, I remember that," the German said. O'Leary then took the man by the arm and led him to a corner, where they conversed for several minutes. I felt later that I should have paid greater attention to the location of the house and the identity of the man, but at the time I did not have much enthusiasm for the idea of a duplicate wooden gun.

phine Gabler, a short, stout, middle-aged woman, but all of the actual abortions were performed by her "nurse," Ada Martin, a close friend of Louis Piquett, who was the lawyer for this abortion ring. In the event of the death of a patient, which once happened, it was Piquett's job to pay off the husband of the victim so that he would not take the case to the authorities. Ada Martin, born in Scotland, was a square-jawed blonde woman who was distinguished by a violent temper and an unswerving loyalty to Piquett, although she vehemently denied that their relationship was anything but platonic.*

Ada Martin, of course, was not told that the money was to be used as part payment for a jailbreak. Piquett said he had received nothing from Dillinger and needed the money for ordinary expenses.

Piquett gave the five thousand dollars to Bogue, but told O'Leary to go along and make sure that the money reached the right people.**

Evelyn Frechette, accompanied by Louis Piquett, visited her sweetheart for the first time on Monday, February 26, representing herself at the jail as Mrs. Dillinger. Before seeing the prisoner, she was stripped nude by Mrs. Holley, and every article of her clothing was thoroughly searched. On the way to Crown Point she had stopped and changed a hundred-dollar bill, and she gave Dillinger ten dollars of this amount. While Piquett engaged the guards in conversation and diverted their attention, she was able to tell Dillinger that she had contacted "Red" Hamilton, and that the gang did not look with favor on the idea of dynamiting the jail.

---

*In a rather close association with Piquett, I never knew him to express interest in women other than his wife and Ada Martin. On one occasion when he was in my offices with his wife, another attorney who was present recounted that a prominent Chicago lawyer had privately settled a bastardy charge.

"If that had been me," exclaimed Piquett, "I would have been so proud that I would have paid off in Marshall Field's window."

"If that had been you," interposed Nell Piquett, "I could have told them they had the wrong pig by the ear."

Ada Martin financed Piquett's appeal efforts after his conviction on the charge of harboring Van Meter, and supported Mrs. Piquett during the time that he served in Leavenworth.

**Dillinger told Piquett that he would try to pay him $25,000, plus the $5,000 that he had advanced. As a matter of fact, Piquett and O'Leary never received any great amounts of money from Dillinger—certainly not what they had anticipated or enough to compensate them for their ordeal. Dillinger indicated to O'Leary that he had paid the balance due in East Chicago in two installments. Blunk was paid two thousand dollars and Saager half that amount for their roles in the jailbreak. Today, the amounts obtained by Dillinger in his robberies and what he paid in the Crown Point escape seem paltry indeed. It must be remembered that these events took place when jobs were scarce and wages and living costs unbelievably low. What Blunk and Saager received was probably more than they had ever dreamed of possessing.

Later, when an army of investigators were endeavoring to fathom the Crown Point escape, some suggested that Billie had managed to smuggle in a loaded gun and a sum of money. It would have been impossible for her to have done either. Likewise, the story that she conversed with Dillinger in a jargon of numbers arose solely in the imagination of a guard probably too much addicted to detective fiction.

Piquett saw Dillinger for the last time in jail on Wednesday, February 26. Dillinger was calm and appeared in high spirits. The break had originally been planned for Friday, March 2, but Piquett told him that it might have to be put off, as they did not yet have the wooden gun. O'Leary did not receive the gun, as a matter of fact, until about noon on that Friday, and it was late afternoon before he delivered it in East Chicago. Who passed it to Blunk I do not know, but Blunk passed it to Dillinger only on the morning of the escape.[25]

CHAPTER EIGHT

THE VANISHING AMERICAN

Just what happened in the Crown Point jail that eventful morning of Saturday, March 3, 1934? Federal, state, local, and private investigators spent months of time and thousands of dollars seeking the answer, with the net result of only raising more questions. Clues, suspicions, rumors, and politics became so hopelessly entwined that the truth was finally adjudged inextricable, and as if by mutual consent the matter was dropped, with everyone believing what it pleased him to believe.

Accepting that some aspects of the escape will forever remain secret, one might still expect a clear and unvaried account of the actual happenings in the jail. Yet, despite the intense investigation, no one person seems to be in complete agreement with any other person. This is not for any lack of information; it is the quality that leaves so much to be desired. Warden Baker, Trusty Cahoon, and various of the guards and prisoners have told their tales, but inasmuch as they spent most of their time locked in cells, they can necessarily tell only a small portion of the story. Deputy Ernest Blunk, the jail's fingerprint expert, could and did give a very full account, which, although credible on the whole, is nevertheless interspersed with obvious falsifications. His second account, claiming that Dillinger made his escape with a real pistol, was patently concocted at a future date and bears no elements of truth.

The person who should know more about this matter than anyone is John Dillinger, and it is Dillinger's account we will follow in the present instance. Dillinger excitedly related the entire story to Piquett and O'Leary on the night of his escape, and on later occasions referred back to it in conversations with O'Leary. The versions, as recounted separately by Piquett and O'Leary, vary only in inconsequential detail.

Saturday, March 3, was a chill, rainy day of early spring. About 9:15 A.M., Sam Cahoon, turnkey and handyman, entered with an armful of soap as Dillinger and fourteen other prisoners were exercising in the corridor outside of the lower tier of cells. Cahoon, sixty-four years old, had become acquainted with the jail through several occasions of drunkenness, but of late had been maintaining a tenacious perch upon the water wagon. As he passed Dillinger, the prisoner thrust the wooden gun into his side at the waist.

"Do as I tell you, or I'll blow you apart," the outlaw commanded. "Call Blunk."

Cahoon obeyed, and Blunk responded without delay. He likewise found an object thrust into his ribs. Dillinger turned back to Cahoon.

"Now call Baker," he ordered.

"John, I can't do it," the old man pleaded.

"All right. You don't have to. I'm not going to hurt you. Blunk will do it. But I'll have to lock you up. Blunk, give me a hand here!"

Blunk opened the barred doors and locked Cahoon in one of the cells. Then he called Warden Lou Baker. As Baker ascended the ramp to the new section of the jail, he became the third of the wooden-gun prisoners.

"I don't like to have to do this, Mr. Baker," Dillinger apologized. "I'll put you in where Cahoon can keep you company."

The siren voice of Blunk was again pressed into service. One by one he called guards Kenneth Houk, Marshall Keithley, and Mack Brown, and as each man appeared he found himself a prisoner.

Dillinger called to Herbert Youngblood, a Negro prisoner, to accompany him, while Blunk locked the other inmates in their cells. Youngblood, awaiting trial on a charge of murdering a Gary fruit peddler, was a likely candidate for the electric chair, and Dillinger knew he could be depended on to stake his all on an escape.

Outside of the cell tiers the first person encountered was John

Kowaliszyn, who, though merely a trusty, had been given a full set of keys. He was quickly cowed and the keys were taken from him. Dillinger and his supporting cast now proceeded to the office of the jail, where the guns and ammunition were kept.

One of the guards, a machine gun on his lap, sat half-dozing in a chair in the jail office with his back to the door. Walking up behind him, Dillinger pressed the barrel of the wooden gun into the back of his head, while with his other hand he lifted a machine gun from the rack.

"This is Dillinger," he curtly informed him. "If you move a muscle, I'm going to blow your head off your shoulders."

Youngblood, at Dillinger's command, stepped forward and took the machine gun from the guard's lap. Blunk looked on.

With a machine gun in his hand and one in that of his colored companion, Dillinger now was truly dangerous. Marching his prisoners before him, he made a tour of the first floor. Warden Hiles of the Indiana National Guard happened along and was disarmed of his .45-caliber pistol. The escort was now becoming too numerous for comfort, and Dillinger marched his prisoners back to the cells, taking only Youngblood and Blunk as he resumed his adventure.

The next stop was at the kitchen, where three more guards fell into the bag, along with Mrs. Lou Baker and her mother, Mrs. Mary Linton.

"Don't be frightened, Mrs. Baker," Dillinger reassured her. "We're not going to hurt anybody. You two be good girls, and nothing will happen to you."

Feeling the two women were entitled to some degree of privacy, the desperado locked them in the basement laundry. The guards were taken back up the ramp, and added to the collection in the cell block.

Once more Dillinger and associates set off in search of jail guards. It was necessary to explore almost the entire building before five more guards could be discovered and conveyed to the common place of security. The jailers began to complain of overcrowding.

Dillinger, having now locked up every living thing but the cat, took Youngblood and Blunk with him for a look at the great outdoors. Two cars were standing in the jail garage, but they could not be started without the keys.* Back went the three into the

---

*Saager intended to have Mrs. Holley's Ford gassed up and waiting in the jail garage, but the escape was hastily arranged and the mechanic did not have the car

jail, and Dillinger rummaged about the warden's desk. Then he said, "We're liable to need some money. Let's see what the boys upstairs have got in their pockets."

The army of imprisoned guards, believing they had gazed upon Dillinger's face and form for the last time, looked with open-mouthed surprise as he again entered the cell tier.

"I'm afraid we need to take up a collection," he said. "I want all of you to give, and give generously."

The collection netted fifteen dollars, which Dillinger put in his pocket. He was now in high spirits, laughing and rapping the wooden gun on the cell bars before their startled faces.

"See what I locked all of you monkeys up with?" he chortled. "Nothing but a little piece of wood. Well, so long, boys. I'll have to be moving on."

His face became serious as he passed Warden Baker.

"I'm sorry to have to do this to you, Mr. Baker," he said. "But you can see how it is."

"Yes, John, I can see how it is."

The Crown Point jail faces west on Main Street. To the north of it is the Lake County Criminal Court building, and beyond that the Main Street Garage. Behind these buildings lies South East Street.

Dillinger, taking care to lock all doors as he went out, emerged with Blunk, Youngblood, and three trusties through the kitchen door of the jail and traversed the side yard. The party, with the two prisoners openly carrying machine guns, then walked about fifty yards up South East Street and entered the Main Street Garage by the rear door.

This garage was owned by Clyde Rothermel, whose sister was married to "Red" Hamilton's brother. Rothermel was aware of the escape plan but wanted no active part, as he reasoned that his connection with the Hamiltons was sure to make him a suspect. Yet, for some reason, Rothermel was never subjected to any intensive investigation.

Rothermel made it a point to be away from the garage on the morning of the jailbreak, and the place was in the charge of Edwin J. Saager, the mechanic who was to have the getaway car in readiness. Also present in the garage at this time was Robert Volk, a mail-truck driver, who had a pistol in a belt slung across his

---

ready as soon as expected. Dillinger was willing to take any car that was handy and began searching for keys, but was told by Blunk that Mrs. Holley's machine probably was nearby in the Main Street Garage.

shoulder, but attempted no resistance when he saw the two men with machine guns.

"What's the fastest car in the joint?" Dillinger asked, for the record.

Saager pointed to Mrs. Holley's Ford, which now was all primed to go. Dillinger climbed into the rear seat with Young-blood. The three trusties could have escaped, but elected to return to the jail.

"You drive," Dillinger told Blunk. He was clad in a brown shirt, blue trousers and vest, and Sam Cahoon's raincoat, but with no coat, hat, or necktie, and rode beside Blunk in the front, a machine gun on his lap. The car swung out of the garage and started down the streets of Crown Point.

"Maybe I ought to go back and tell Mrs. Holley I'm leaving," said Dillinger. "She seemed like an awfully nice lady, and I don't want her to feel hurt about all this."

Volk, the mail-truck driver, was now dashing out of the garage shouting at a volunteer guard of the Farmers' Protective Association stationed across the street. The startled eyes of the sentinel opened wide. "You don't mean it! Dillinger's got away?"

"Sure! Can't you hear all the hollering over at the jail?"

The jailed jailers were calling loudly from the windows to be let out. All in all, Dillinger had locked up more than thirty persons.

Meanwhile, the escaping party were leaving Crown Point far behind. They headed north for about a mile, turned west to the town of St. John, and then proceeded south and west along gravel roads, stopping once so that the car's conspicuous red light could be twisted off the front.

"Take your time, take your time," Dillinger kept telling Blunk. "There's no hurry. Thirty miles an hour is fast enough."

Rain was beating against the front of the car, but there was no rain in the heart of John Dillinger. He began singing "The Last Roundup," repeating the line, "Get along, little dogie, get along," and showed off his wooden gun to his companions. Saager asked if he might have it as a memento of the occasion, but the outlaw laughed and shook his head. This did not deter Blunk, however, from later palming off a faked wooden gun, complete with affidavit of authenticity, to the owner of a large chain of drugstores.[26]

At one point the car skidded off the muddy road and into a ditch. Blunk and Saager were ordered out and told to put on skid chains.

"That will take a little time," Blunk pointed out.

"What's time to me?" said Dillinger. "I've got plenty."

The job of actually installing the chains fell to Saager, he later complained, while Dillinger and Blunk stood in the road supervising.

Blunk and Saager were let out of the car at a rural crossroads known as Lilley's Corner, about two miles northeast of Peotone, Illinois. Dillinger shook hands and offered Blunk four dollars in case they needed funds to get back home. Blunk declined, but Saager accepted the bills, and then the fugitives headed the car in the direction of Chicago, some twenty-five miles due north. A passing farmer picked up the lawman and the mechanic and gave them a ride into Peotone, where they told their story to an audience of astounded listeners before making their way back to Crown Point.[27]

"I was never scared of Dillinger," said Blunk later. "I knew he wouldn't hurt me. He was too nice for that."

At a later date Louis Piquett had some difficulty explaining why he picked up O'Leary and arrived at his law office at half past seven on a Saturday morning, when all of the courts were closed. Evelyn Frechette appeared on the scene at eight o'clock, and Meyer Bogue came in about an hour later.

It was shortly after half past nine, earlier than expected, when the telephone rang and Piquett's nephew, Bob Allen, called to say that he had just heard a radio report of Dillinger's escape.

"Seems that everything worked out," O'Leary told the assembled group.

"I think I'll call Warden Baker," said Piquett. As he waited for the long-distance connection, he could hear excited voices in the Crown Point exchange chattering about the event.

"Hello! Mr. Baker? This is Lou Piquett, in Chicago."

"Yes. Hello, Lou."

"What truth is there in the radio report that my client just broke jail?"

"That's right. He just left us."

"Anybody killed or hurt?"

"No, nobody was hurt."

"That's good. I'm glad to hear that. Say, he didn't leave any forwarding address, did he?"

"No, he didn't say where he was going, but I can guess."

"That's a hell of a client to have."

"Well, Piquett, give him my regards when you see him today."
Piquett hung up the phone. "By golly, it's true! He got away!"
Evelyn Frechette emitted a short scream.

"Poor Johnnie!" she cried, putting both hands to her face. "They'll kill him! Oh, my God, they'll kill him!"

"Quit your squawking," gently admonished Piquett. "They'll probably never get another look at his coattails."

After the first flurry of excitement, a spirit of jubilation began to fill the office. Bogue went out to buy newspaper "extras" that were beginning to appear on the streets, as well as the ingredients for making gin rickeys. By eleven o'clock Billie Frechette, who had little alcohol tolerance, began to lose consciousness of her surroundings, and was placed on the couch in Piquett's office.

Piquett surmised that Dillinger would get in touch with him before long, and the group remained in the office awaiting some call. He knew his client would desire a conference, and he was debating in his mind as to where the talk might best be held. Dillinger was familiar only with the North Side of Chicago, and while his own residence was located conveniently on Irving Park near Pine Grove, he knew it would be the first place under surveillance. Then there came to mind the name of a former employee, Esther Anderson, known not surprisingly as "Andy," who lived at 434 Wellington Avenue, in a neighborhood with which Dillinger was familiar.

Shortly after noon Billie Frechette, still under the weather but now cognizant of events, was sent to Miss Anderson's apartment. About half an hour later Piquett, only a bit less undermined by the gin rickeys, left to join her there. O'Leary and Bogue remained in the office for the anxiously awaited telephone call. It came about three o'clock in the afternoon.

"Where will I go?" were the only words Dillinger spoke.

"Go to 434 Wellington Avenue. Piquett will be waiting." And O'Leary hung up. Knowing the danger of mentioning an address over the telephone, he calculated that sufficient time had not elapsed for the wires to have been tapped; and under the circumstances it was a chance that had to be taken.

Dillinger, after separating from Blunk and Saager, had proceeded to Chicago at a leisurely pace and circled the outskirts of the city for an hour or more before telephoning Piquett's office. He then headed directly into the city by way of Torrence Avenue, although the streets were crawling with squad cars anticipating his arrival. On Broadway, several blocks south of Belmont, Detective

Lorimer Hyde of the state's attorney's office sighted the Dillinger car and immediately gave chase. For almost half a mile both cars traveled at a breakneck speed. Dillinger, fearing that Hyde might give a general alarm, suddenly brought his car to a stop and grabbed a machine gun. He and Youngblood prepared for action, and Detective Hyde sensibly drove on with the intention of gathering reinforcements.

With the immediate danger past, Dillinger drove directly to the Wellington Avenue address. Outside was Louis Piquett, hands plunged into his coat pockets and hat pulled down, leaning against the side of the building. Dillinger drove up to the front door in the stolen sheriff's car, while Youngblood lay sprawled on the back seat, tightly gripping both Thompsons.

"H'yah, counsel," he called, waving his hand.

Piquett hurried over to the car.

"Is this the place I'm going to stay?" Dillinger asked.

"No. I just want to bring you up here for a few minutes so we can talk."

The two entered the front hall of the building, where Evelyn Frechette was waiting to throw herself into Dillinger's arms. By this time, Miss Anderson had heard news of the escape and had begun to entertain suspicions about Piquett's mystery guest. A large, high-strung woman, she met them at the door of the apartment, and with much weeping, shouting, and waving of hands, managed to convey the impression that she wanted no part of the whole affair.

Dillinger, with a snort, went back to the car, while Billie ran out and jumped into the front seat beside him. Piquett joined them shortly.

"Billie says we can go over to her sister's place on Halsted Street," the outlaw informed him. "Come over there this evening about half past seven. And I need some money. Let me have whatever you've got with you."

Piquett reached in his pocket and handed his client three hundred dollars.

"Thanks, counsel, I'll see you soon."

The next move was to separate from Youngblood, who, because of his color, rendered them conspicuous. Detective Hyde had spread the word of his encounter, and Chicago's Near North Side was now swarming with police. Dillinger nevertheless managed to weave his way through and drove about three miles west. He then gave Youngblood one hundred dollars in twenty-dollar bills and two of the pistols taken from Crown Point, and placed him on a southbound Western Avenue streetcar, after which he and Billie made for a place of security.

By now Detective Hyde, after searching for some time, had despaired of finding the elusive outlaw and again started homeward. He was therefore doubly surprised to meet up with the fugitive for the second time, on Halsted Street, near Belmont Avenue. Once more the two cars raced for several blocks. Dillinger was driving with one hand and holding a machine gun in the other, and Hyde again was forced to give up the chase.

Meanwhile, Piquett had returned to his office to inform O'Leary of his meeting with Dillinger and of the appointment that had been arranged. That evening the two drove to the apartment that Patsy Frechette shared with her girlfriend Marge Edwards, on the second floor at 3512 North Halsted Street. As they entered the door, Dillinger emerged from the kitchen with the wooden gun in one hand and a real one in the other. He laughed as he recognized Piquett and O'Leary and the three exchanged greetings.

The conversation that evening centered around Dillinger's recital of his escape from Crown Point. He sat on the davenport in the living room, with Evelyn cuddled closely in his arms. The other two girls, Patsy and Miss Edwards, spent most of their time in the kitchen working on the contents of a case of beer. The last thing they had desired was a visit from the country's most celebrated bank robber, but as long as he was there, they decided to make the best of it. Piquett asked Dillinger if he could keep the wooden gun, but O'Leary interrupted. He knew that Piquett had been drinking, and feared that he might exhibit the souvenir and betray the hiding place.

"Say, Dillinger," the attorney then inquired, "when am I going to see some money? I haven't had a dollar yet, you know."

"What? Didn't Ryan give you anything? He took my dad's last five hundred dollars, and he was told to turn it over to you. You tell him to cough up those five C's, or I'm coming down and take care of him."

Piquett and O'Leary departed after hearing Dillinger's animated account of the escape, leaving the outlaw and his sweetheart to themselves. Patsy and Miss Edwards occupied the only bedroom, while Dillinger and Billie made up for a long abstinence on the davenport in the living room.

On the afternoon of the following day, Sunday, O'Leary went

to his office and called Ryan, whom he located at the Hotel Sherman in Chicago.

"I want to see you about something very important," he told him. "Come over to my office right away."

In a few minutes Joe Ryan made his appearance.

O'Leary came to the point without delay. "Where's that five hundred dollars from Dillinger that you were to give us?"

"Why, I meant to give you that, but I haven't got it right now."

"Well, you better get it damn quick. Dillinger's all burned up about it, and he says that unless you kick back he's coming down and take care of you."

"I'll pay. You'll have to give me a little time."

"I'm giving you one hour. It's four o'clock now. You be in this office by five o'clock with five hundred dollars, or I'm getting in touch with Johnnie."

Ryan departed, ashen-faced, and was seen no more in Chicago. In fact, he never returned to the hotel to pick up his baggage or the bill. Later he became involved in certain difficulties in his home city of Indianapolis, and has since disappeared from there as well.

Early Sunday evening Piquett again went to the apartment where Dillinger was hiding. O'Leary was to follow later, along with Meyer Bogue, whom Dillinger had expressed a desire to see. Before entering, O'Leary and Bogue stood for a few minutes by the drugstore on the southwest corner of Halsted and Cornelia, to make sure they had not been followed. While they were waiting there, a dark green Ford drew up containing a man whom O'Leary later learned was Tommy Carroll. Carroll beckoned them over.

"You're O'Leary and Bogue, aren't you?" he asked.

"Yes."

"Johnnie won't be able to see you. He's leaving right now, sooner than he expected."

"Just a minute," said O'Leary. "Johnnie told me he wanted to see Bogue, and that's why I brought him. You'd better tell Johnnie that he's here."

"Well, maybe he can see him for just a minute. I'm driving around the block. Walk slowly until you get in front of the house and then wait there."

The two did as instructed. In a few minutes Dillinger and Evelyn came out of the side door of the building, each with a grip in one hand and a machine gun held under their coats. They lost no

Law Offices
LOUIS P. PIQUETT
Suite 2110
228 N. LaSalle St.
CHICAGO

Telephones Central 8847
8848

March 7, 1934

Mrs. Eulalia Callender
Galion,
Ohio.

My Dear Mrs Callender,

Yours of March 7th, received and read with great deal of interest. Let me say in behalf of my client I certainly appreciate a very tender feeling reading between the lines of your short message. I can clearly realize the trend of your beautiful heart.

I will undertake seriously to have the message delivered to my client in person. You may rest assured that I am perfectly safe in saying that the party in question will be most appreciative of your very sweet offerings and thought. I, like you believe that it was the hand of God that enabled this young Christian soul to live on.

From my experience with the party in question, I can safely tell you that he will rob no banks, but it is his firm intention to travel in the path of righteousness. He is a great student of the Bible. The last conversation I had with him he had told me that it was his intention to give the balance of his life in this world to God, and beyond any doubt your sweet prayers have had a great deal to do with this deliverance.

I will be most happy to talk in person with as sweet a mind as I think you have, so if any time in the near future you feel well enough to come to Chicago you may meet me at my office address. I will be more than glad to discuss this matter with you further.

With very deepest appreciation for your very kind and thoughtful message, I beg to remain yours very sincerely and truly,

LPP/MB

Louis P. Piquett

Piquett writes a flowery and reassuring response to Mrs. Eulalia Callender, an elderly Ohio woman who wrote rambling letters contending that Dillinger could have escaped from Crown Point only with the help of God, and that it might therefore go hard on whoever shot him down.

time in scampering into the back seat, while Tommy Carroll remained alone behind the wheel. O'Leary and Bogue advanced toward the car.

"Hello, Bogue," called Dillinger. "Sorry I can't talk to you, but I haven't a minute to lose. See you again soon."

With that the car started, and was soon lost in the darkness of the early spring night. *

*In the syndicated story and in other published accounts, Piquett supposedly preaches to Dillinger that he was wrong to break jail in Crown Point and asks that he go with him to a nearby police station and turn himself in. This is pure nonsense and was written at Piquett's urgent request. He had wished at the time to divert suspicion of complicity in the escape and to create a more favorable atmosphere during his appeal from the Van Meter conviction.

CHAPTER NINE

WOODEN GUN, INDIANA

John Dillinger, in escaping from the Crown Point jail, left in his wake a storm that shook the nation. The imprisoned guards, looking somewhat sheepish, were released from their own jail about ten minutes after the desperado's departure. Word was flashed about the country, and the highway police of Indiana and Illinois established a joint headquarters at Bradley, Illinois, near Kankakee, to direct the stopping and searching of all suspicious cars. The washboard whittled on by Dillinger was found under his mattress, and wood shavings lay on the floor of the cell.

Chief Deputy Carroll Holley, off duty, was asleep while Dillinger was making history. Mrs. Holley had just finished dressing when one of the released guards burst into her room to inform her that their prize had unexpectedly departed. She immediately strapped on a pistol and announced that she would lead the search in person. Said Mrs. Holley, "Don't blame anyone else for this escape. Blame me. I have no political career ahead of me, and I don't care." The world took her at her word.

Deputy Blunk and garageman Saager soon returned and enjoyed a fleeting moment of glory. Newspapermen and officials crowded around them as they related their stories. Sheriff Holley returned from her tour of the surrounding country and questioned the pair, remarking that the whole affair was "too ridiculous for words." Prosecutor Estill declared, "From what I hear, it seems strange that Dillinger didn't serve tea to the guards before he went away."

Elsewhere, those occupied with Dillinger business were loud in their disparagement of the Lake County authorities. Captain John Stege of Chicago's Dillinger squad, momentarily forgetting the Dr. Eye fiasco, stated that the desperado's escape "smelled to the high heavens." United States Marshal H. C. W. Laubenheimer expressed his opinion that "there's something wrong with those guards." Frank J. Loesch, president of the Chicago Crime Commission, striking a note that was rapidly becoming popular, said, "That's what might be expected of having a woman for a sheriff."

Commented Mayor Edward J. Kelly of Chicago, "I'm sick about it. It couldn't have happened in Chicago. Dillinger won't come here because he knows it's too hot for him." At this particular time Dillinger, having cruised about Chicago's police-ridden streets for hours, was enjoying peace and security in that city.

The *Chicago Tribune* expressed itself editorially: "The probability of collusion in Dillinger's escape is too large to be dismissed. Other explanations must deal with more feeble mindedness and imbecility than are expectable even in Indiana politics."

Naive old dad Dillinger sat at his radio in Mooresville and anxiously awaited further tidings of his son. "It makes me feel a little better, of course," he said. "But at the same time I'm worried. You know Johnnie was always kind of reckless. He wrote me for ten dollars last week, but he didn't say what he wanted it for."

In the state of Indiana, Democrats and Republicans were engaged in a perfectly joyous carnival of mudslinging. Republicans pointed with pride to the Michigan City jailbreak and the Dillinger escape as evidence that their opponents were totally incapable of administering state and local affairs. Democrats rejoined that they were merely reaping the evils sown by the previous Republican administration, and hinted broadly that certain Republican politicians had connived at Dillinger's escape in order to embarrass the local officials. Governor McNutt said he didn't know what comment to make, but ordered a complete investigation. His secretary, Wayne Coy, pointed out that Mrs. Holley had declined an offer to place Dillinger in the state penitentiary, and Warden Louis Kunkel of the Michigan City prison said he had twice made this suggestion to the sheriff.

Although a veritable army was searching for Dillinger, by Sunday he had completely vanished. Every road was being carefully watched in Indiana, Illinois, Ohio, and Missouri, and he was being sought as far east as New York, and west to Oklahoma and Arizona. At the request of Governor McNutt, federal Department of Justice agents in Indianapolis cooperated with Attorney General Lutz, who placed Assistant Attorney General Edward C. Barce in charge of the investigation.

On Monday the search for Dillinger was intensified on Chicago's North Side when Mrs. Holley's car was found abandoned next to an apartment building at 1057 Ardmore Avenue. It had been left there by Billie Frechette early Saturday evening. The gas tank was dry, and in the side pocket was Sheriff Holley's .32-caliber revolver. O'Leary followed in another car and drove her back to her sister's apartment.

What were the general public saying about the Dillinger escape? The general public considered it a huge joke, and were having their best laugh since the Teapot Dome scandal. Vaudeville and radio comedians utilized it to the utmost, and newspaper cartoonists likewise had a field day. One paper published a drawing based on the celebrated photograph of Estill and Dillinger draping their arms around each other, captioning it, "The Law's Embrace in Indiana." Another showed Mrs. Holley sitting disconsolately on the steps of her deserted Crown Point jail, while the gag line described her as "The Girl He Left Behind Him."

About this time an occurrence became known which aroused no little surprise and suspicion. Warden Baker, in broadcasting the alarm on Dillinger's escape, had given out the license number of Sheriff Holley's car as 679-929, whereas the correct number was 674-549, a considerable discrepancy. This led searchers to look for the wrong plates, a circumstance that certainly had not hindered the prisoner's escape. Baker offered no explanation.*

Sheriff Holley went about with large hollows under her eyes, and her face devoid of makeup. She readily stated that her men were "yellow." "I'm not a sissy," she said. "I can take it on the chin. But I feel that I am getting the blame for this just because I am a woman."

The usual rumors added to the confusion. Dillinger was "sighted" simultaneously in Lincoln, Havana, Peoria, and El Paso, all in Illinois, as well as in towns in Iowa. The question of greatest interest to the investigators was whether Dillinger had had any outside assistance. Speculation centered on the mystery

---

*Warden Baker could not understand how the mistake occurred. The truth of the matter, as Dillinger told Piquett and O'Leary, was that Blunk had managed to substitute the wrong number. The mechanics of how this was done I do not know.

woman who had visited Dillinger in the company of Louis Piquett. Sheriff Holley believed her to be Hamilton's companion, Elaine Dent, but it was soon discovered that Mrs. Dent had been in a hospital for a month. Piquett declared that he knew her only as "Billie," and that he believed her to be Dillinger's wife. "She was in my office Saturday morning when we got news that Dillinger had broken jail," Piquett told the newspapers. "She ran out of the office and I haven't seen her since. No, I haven't heard from Dillinger. I don't ever expect to hear from him, because he owes me money. He probably figured me for as big a sucker as anyone." Meyer Bogue was likewise suspected, but took advantage of his acquaintance with Dillinger to sign on with the state of Indiana as a paid informer at fifteen dollars per day.

Suspicion fell heaviest upon Ernest Blunk and Sam Cahoon, and they were accused in formal affidavits filed before Judge Murray on Tuesday, March 6. Blunk collapsed when the affidavit was read. Murray, however, declared himself convinced that there had been no bribery of the jail workers, and released Blunk on his own recognizance. "Blunk didn't have any nerve, that's all that was wrong with him," said the judge in discussing his action.

Perhaps the saddest man in all this sorry mess was William J. Schroeder, the president of the Lake County council. The special guards hired to prevent Dillinger's escape had cost the county $150 per day, Mr. Schroeder glumly pointed out.

Attorney General Lutz announced that he had sufficient information to discount Blunk's story, and that he believed the escape was planned. His assistant, Edward Barce, said that indisputable evidence showed that Dillinger had practically walked out of the jail with the assistance of certain prison attachés. The federal government had all eight of its own prisoners transferred from Crown Point to lockups elsewhere.*

*The indisputable evidence gathered by Edward Barce was the fairy tale told him by Meyer Bogue and which only Barce would have believed. I made the trip to Indianapolis with Bogue to talk to Indiana state officials connected with the Dillinger case. He had offered his services to me several times, but I regarded him as somewhat of a slimy character and did not relish his company. To my surprise, Bogue was received cordially and with apparent credulity. I met Matt Leach and Barce and at the time was favorably impressed with Barce, who told me that Blunk and Saager had been fixed, which I knew to be true. Recently I received copies of FBI reports from Mr. Tom Smusyn, a diligent student of the Dillinger era, who had obtained them under the Freedom of Information Act. Among them was the report of Edward Barce to Governor Paul McNutt and Attorney General Philip Lutz of Indiana, and an interesting FBI memorandum of Bogue dated April 24, 1935, addressed to J. Edgar Hoover. Bogue was very free in his allegations. Among those implicated were Judge Murray, Warden Baker, who he said received a bribe of $3,500, Blunk, Saager, Hymie Cohen, James Regan, Estill, Piquett, O'Leary and his wife Grayce, Martin Zarkovich of the East Chicago police, and others. He did concede that one

By this time Dillinger was being seen everywhere. Squads of police rushed about the streets of Chicago in answer to more than one hundred false reports. The detective bureau heard that the outlaw intended to rob the National Builders Bank, located in the

Meyer Bogue was also present, but only as a more or less innocent bystander desirous of obtaining information for Mr. Barce, to be paid for at the usual rates.

The evidence of Barce against Judge Murray was that he had engaged in real-estate deals with Hymie Cohen, who was a lawyer as well as an underworld character. This may very well have been true, but it does not mean that he was fixed in the Dillinger case. He knew he was the center of national attention and that the Dillinger case could not be handled like a petty local affair.

Barce explains why he never questioned Cohen. "The reason that Cohen was not talked with was that he was considered a very important witness in the matter, but we believed that he would not disclose any facts that would incriminate himself unless we were really able to confront him with sufficient evidence to cause him to make a full statement." In other words, Barce had no evidence against Cohen.

James Regan had at one time been the chief of police in East Chicago. Barce relates of Regan "that we had Bogue with us and must be working on the Lake County investigation, and that this was very foolish for us to be doing for he knew all about Bogue, and that Bogue was absolutely undependable, and that no information which he gave to anyone could be believed." The faith of Barce in Meyer Bogue remained unshaken.

Bogue had no evidence whatsoever against Estill.

I knew Grayce O'Leary well over a period of several years. She was an attractive woman who was completely devoted and loyal to her husband, but she never gave me the impression of having any deep interest in his affairs.

Probably the most ridiculous evidence that Bogue palmed off on Barce were the copies of seven letters which O'Leary is alleged to have written to Regan, Cohen, and Zarkovich and which would have been highly incriminating, to say the least. I knew the very cautious Arthur O'Leary over several years, and he would never under any circumstances have placed his neck in any such noose. Common sense would dictate that the escape be discussed privately, and certainly not in correspondence. Bogue claimed these letters were handed to him on October 29, 1934, by Marguerite Becker, who until recently had been Piquett's secretary. Ms. Becker was fully cognizant as regards Bogue. The previously mentioned FBI memorandum mentions that "O'Leary further stated that subsequent to Dillinger's escape from Crown Point, Bogue was employed as a 'stool pigeon' and finally ordered Bogue out of the office, and told him to stay away."

The origin of these letters becomes evident in this memorandum: "In the nature of documentary evidence, Bogue sold copies of seven letters at $15 each to Mr. Barce, which letters are reported to have been dictated at the office of Piquett to his secretary Marguerite Becker by Arthur O'Leary. These letters are addressed to 'Jimmy,' 'Zark,' and 'Hy,' and reference is made in several of the letters to the payment of certain sums of money to certain suspects mentioned in connection with Mr. Barce's investigation. Both O'Leary and Miss Becker, who ceased her employment with Piquett on October 1, 1934, upon being interviewed by Special Agents, denied any knowledge of these letters."

Arthur O'Leary would have had ample opportunity to destroy the incriminating letters had they ever existed. Furthermore, it is scarcely conceivable that Ms. Becker, nearly a month after she left Piquett, would have possessed any such copies or for no reason turned them over to Bogue, whom she knew as a disreputable character. Finally, it was not in O'Leary's nature to write letters at all. [Even if phony, Bogue's letters indicate O'Leary to be on first-name terms with the East Chicagoans, including Zarkovich, which would tend to confirm their roles in smuggling Piquett's business card to Dillinger and handling the Crown Point bribe money.—W.J.H.]

The letters were composed by Meyer Bogue to sell to the utterly gullible Mr. Barce.

same building as Piquett's office, and soon the lobby contained so
many detectives there was scarcely room for customers. Twenty-
five police swooped down upon the Rokeby Hotel, at 3831 Rokeby
Street, but found nothing. An attendant at a filling station at 73d
Street and Stony Island Avenue told police that he had talked with
a man he could positively identify as John Dillinger. Several persons telephoned to say that they had seen Dillinger and a woman
speeding in an auto past the Southmoor Hotel. He was sighted by
a motorist in Evanston, Illinois. He was identified as the man who
had riddled a pursuing police car with machine-gun bullets in
Schiller Park, Illinois. A private chauffeur reported that Dillinger
had made off with his car from in front of 2440 Lake Shore Drive.
While Dillinger was playing all this mischief with the peace of
Chicago, he was likewise being recognized in Mason City, Iowa,
Youngstown, Ohio, and Buffalo, New York. Oddly enough, no
reports were received from Dillinger's actual hideout at St. Paul,
Minnesota, or from any of the points en route.

Meanwhile an ever-growing horde of federal, state, local, and
private investigators were tramping stealthily about the streets of
Crown Point, scowling at each other and constantly tripping over
themselves. Judge Murray discharged the Lake County grand
jury, whose foreman was Clyde Rothermel, owner of the Main
Street Garage, on the ground that its members were unfit to investigate the escape. He then summoned a new jury, to be headed by
a special prosecutor instead of Estill. "You're putting me on the
spot," Estill complained to the judge when he heard the news.

The new grand jury, with former circuit judge Martin J. Smith
as special assistant prosecutor, was scheduled to meet on Monday,
March 12. Barce announced that he would present evidence showing that Dillinger had the active and willing assistance of Blunk,
while Judge Murray declared that he could not believe Blunk had
entered into any conspiracy. In keeping with the farcical spirit of
things, the investigation then had to be postponed because two of
the six special grand jurors failed to show up. The tentative plans
to reenact the escape were abandoned because it was feared that
more prisoners would take the opportunity to walk out.

By Wednesday the grand jury had been rounded up and the
investigation began. Warden Baker was the first witness, and
showed the jurors Dillinger's route through the building. James
Dexter, who had resigned as jail chef two days before the escape
in order to manage the election campaign of Estill's political oppo-
nent, was also called to testify. Sheriff Holley, Sam Cahoon, and
numerous others followed in a wearisome procession over the next

few days. The event was enlivened mainly by rumors, utterly false, that Governor McNutt's wife was John Dillinger's first cousin. The reports were emphatically denied both by the governor and by Dillinger's father.

Deputy Blunk, the fingerprint expert, soon found more troubles coming his way. On Thursday, March 15, he was arrested by detectives Harvey Hire and Ray Hullett, conveyed to Indianapolis, and placed in the city jail. The next day he was taken to the Severin Hotel, thoroughly grilled by Barce and three Indianapolis detectives, and then released. His instinct for self-preservation thus stimulated, Blunk suddenly decided that he had been intimidated by a real rather than a wooden gun, and changed his statement accordingly. "I think I'm going to be made the goat in this case," sighed Blunk upon returning to Crown Point.

The Indianapolis Council of Women on April 3 adopted a resolution urging a state law against the manufacture, sale, and importation into Indiana of wooden or other imitation guns or pistols. This action may have been motivated by the fact that the Crown Point post office was receiving large numbers of letters addressed to Wooden Gun, Indiana; Clown Point, Indiana; and other derisive misnomers.

On that same day the special grand jury made known its findings on the escape. Blunk and Cahoon were indicted for the jailbreak, but the jurors announced that no alliance existed between crime and politics. Prosecutor Estill was held blameless, and Judge Murray was censured for not taking his advice on sending Dillinger to Michigan City.

The usually genial Judge Murray found himself considerably incensed after perusing the report. "Why," he asked, "should I take the advice of a prosecutor who had just finished hugging Dillinger? If I had Dillinger again I would put him right back in that jail." The passing of time apparently failed to soothe his aroused feelings, and on April 6 he brought contempt proceedings against the members of the jury.

"This report," declared Judge Murray, "is worded in language not contemplated by law. It is lacking in the respect due to courts of justice and to judicial officers, and is particularly disrespectful to this particular Court and its present Judge. It is a defamation of the Judge, and contains language which scandalizes the Court." The dispute was settled, however, short of jail terms or fines. A week later Judge Murray accepted the apology of the grand jurors, and the report on the jailbreak was expunged from the record.

In spite of his favorable treatment by the grand jury, Prosecutor Estill was to find that Mr. Dillinger's little stunt was his political demise. He was dubbed the "Wooden Gun Prosecutor" by his opponents, who widely distributed copies of the now-famous photograph and toy wooden guns. In the May primary elections he found himself defeated for renomination.

About the same time, Ernest Blunk was being tried before Judge Maurice Crites of East Chicago, sitting in Crown Point. Various witnesses told of Blunk's sauntering about the jail with Dillinger, and extending every courtesy to facilitate the escape. Mr. Blunk continued to insist that Dillinger's gun was real and not a wooden one, and that all of his friendly activities stemmed from fear. He was acquitted of complicity on May 11, and a week later Sam Cahoon was freed on a motion of the state.

Here the Dillinger escape rested, still a mystery as far as official investigation was concerned. Dillinger himself was dead by July, and anyway the local authorities had grown sick and tired of the entire matter.[28]

CHAPTER TEN

HOW DILLINGER DID IT

How did John Dillinger make his escape from the Crown Point jail? The question now produces a scratching of heads and a shrugging of shoulders. The federal government, the state of Indiana, the local authorities of Lake County, newspapers, and private investigators have all spent many months of time and thousands upon thousands of dollars trying to find out just how Dillinger managed the most amazing jailbreak of all time. So far, no conspiracy has been proved, and no single explanation stands up under scrutiny.

John Dillinger, of course, knew his part of the story, and before his death he revealed the essential details. The simplicity of his account strikes one immediately, and it is supported both by the known parts and by common sense.

The complicity of Piquett and O'Leary is now known. How far their subsequent activities in behalf of Dillinger have served to create a prejudice against them in this Crown Point matter cannot be determined. Certain more definite allegations have been made, however, and it is upon these that suspicions have been based.

According to an affidavit made by Meyer Bogue for Ed Barce, Piquett, O'Leary, and Bogue went to a saloon operated by Harvey Keiser on Main Street in Crown Point, where they were said to have been joined by Warden Baker. The claim was that Piquett received a package from Baker containing the complete plans of the jail, whereupon O'Leary paid Baker $1,800 in cash.

Another meeting was supposed to have taken place at the White Star barbecue, north of Crown Point, where Piquett, O'Leary, Bogue, and Baker were joined by Keiser and Blunk. The owners of the place, Mr. and Mrs. Terry Garland, according to the affidavit, said that Louis Piquett freely admitted to them that he had engineered the entire Dillinger escape in return for fifty thousand dollars; that he met the fugitive after the break near the border of Illinois and Indiana; that he then gave him one hundred dollars and told him where to go to be safe.

The indefatigable Mr. Barce, investigating Mrs. Vera Garland and her associates, came up with the following piece of astounding information: "All of these witnesses are of Crown Point, Indiana, where they operate a saloon the second door west of Lanson's Restaurant. This saloon has a Schlitz beer sign on the front of it."

Agents of the FBI questioned Baker, Blunk, Keiser, and his wife, all of whom flatly denied that these meetings had ever taken place. Mrs. Garland stated that she could not remember ever having made the statement attributed to her. Moreover, the allegations in the statement were completely contrary to the facts. Dillinger did not have fifty thousand dollars to give Piquett, and, indeed, borrowed three hundred dollars from the attorney when they met on the North Side of Chicago the evening after the escape. What motive Piquett might have had for confiding such incriminating information to total strangers escapes human understanding.

All of these meetings were pure inventions of Meyer Bogue for the edification of Ed Barce and to justify his fifteen dollars per day retainer.

The truth of what actually happened has been ascertained from two sources. First, there is the account of the escape as related by John Dillinger to Piquett and O'Leary that same evening, and later to O'Leary while Dillinger was staying at the house of Jimmy Probasco. Second, certain exhibits and evidence were unearthed in the course of researching the present biography.

The Dillinger account given to Piquett, and included under his affidavit, is related virtually as told by the outlaw:

Red got busy right after the cops grabbed us down at Tucson. He was getting lonesome, with Pete (Pierpont), Mak and Russ locked up in Lima, and me down in Crown Point. But he was hard up just then, and he wasn't in shape to go out and take any banks. He had been shot in

East Chicago, and he was just getting better in some hideout on the North Side. So Red got in touch with Van and Jimmy [Van Meter and Gillis], who were doing some casing around St. Paul, and asked to borrow some money on principle until he made his first score. They were planning that Sioux Falls heist then, and Red tells Van that if he can get me out of jail in time, we could kick it back to him out of our share.

Van and the boys sent Tommy Carroll down right away with some money. Van had done time with me in Michigan City and he was pretty hot around here, but nobody knew Tommy.

We had one hell of a time trying to figure a way to spring me. I wanted to use dynamite, but Red didn't think much of that idea. When Billie came she told me that the boys thought it would be better just to walk in the front door, like they had done in Lima. I figured that I might have a long wait ahead of me, because Red was still in pretty bad shape, and it might be some time before he could get the rest of the gang down from St. Paul. If I was tried and convicted, they would be sending me to Michigan City.

But after East Chicago got the fix in, it made it much easier. I got to know the layout of the jail, and I figured if I could only get a gun I could take myself out.*

I wanted to go out the day before I broke, but things weren't set, so I had to wait until the next morning. After I started locking up the guards, I thought sure one of them would see that I only had a wooden gun. I kept it pretty well down and covered with my hand, and most of the time I had it slipped in my pocket so they wouldn't get a good look at it. Once I got my hands on the choppers, there was nothing going to stop us.[29]

Certain other evidence verified Piquett's narrative. A letter written by Dillinger to his sister, Audrey Hancock, goes into some detail, and an allusion to his having been wounded places its date as shortly after the Mason City bank robbery of March 13, 1934.

Dear Sis,

I thought I would write you a few lines and let you know I am still perculating. Dont worry about me honey for that wont help any, and

*In the 1936 account it was stated that the wooden gun was smuggled to Youngblood, who was not so closely guarded, and Youngblood passed it to Dillinger. This is not true. O'Leary and I were casting about for an explanation as to how Dillinger obtained the gun, inasmuch as O'Leary insisted that the East Chicago underworld be kept out of the picture.

"How about Youngblood?" he suggested. "Lots of people are curious why Dillinger took him out with him. We can say that Youngblood's lawyer brought the gun into the jail and Youngblood then passed it to Dillinger."

Dillinger wished to help Youngblood, who was a likely candidate for the electric chair, and he knew also that a desperate man armed with a machine gun might prove useful to have along in the escape. Neither O'Leary nor I knew if Youngblood even had a lawyer.

besides I am having a lot of fun. I am sending Emmett my wooden gun and I want him to allways keep it. I see that Deputy Blunk says I had a real forty five. Thats just a lot of hooey to cover up because they dont like to admit that I locked eight Deputys and a dozen trustys up with my wooden gun before I got my hands on the two machine guns. I showed everyone the wooden gun after I got a hold of the machine gun and you should have seen there faces. Ha! Ha! Ha! Pulling that off was worth ten years of my life. Ha! Ha! Ha! Dont part with my wooden gun for any price. For when you feel blue all you will have to do is look at the gun and laugh your blues away. Ha! Ha! I will be around to see all of you when the roads are better, its so hot around Indiana now that I would have trouble getting through so I am sending my wife Billie. She will have a hundred dollars for you and a hundred for Norman. I'll give you enough money for a new car the next time I come around. I told Bud I would get him one and I want to get Dad one. Now honey if any of you need any thing I wont forgive you if you dont let me know. I got shot a week ago but I am all right now, just a little sore. I bane one tough sweed. Ha! Ha! Well honey I guess I'll close for this time. Give my love to all and I hope I can see you soon. Lots of love from Johnnie.

The wooden gun is a matter of some interest. I understand it was delivered by Billie Frechette to Mrs. Hancock, who later allowed my use of it for some months. The gun was taken to an experienced woodworker, and examination revealed that the hole in the barrel had been made with a three-eighths-inch standard wood bit. The barrel itself was formed of the brass shaft of the handle of a safety razor, from which both ends had been filed. The heads had also been filed from the two small nails which were used as sights on the imitation pistol. Certainly the equipment necessary for turning out so complicated a copy of a gun would not be available in a jail cell, and even if it were, it could hardly have been employed without arousing the attention of even moderately vigilant guards.*

As for the exact route taken by the wooden gun, anyone

*A wooden gun may be seen in the John Dillinger Historical Wax Museum in Nashville, Indiana. Mr. Joe Pinkston, the owner of the museum, states that the gun was found in a house in Dubuque, Iowa, occupied by Arthur O'Leary at the time of his death. This may very well be true. As I did not wish to make a special trip to Mooresville, and knowing O'Leary's desire for the gun, I gave it to Louis Piquett to be returned. With the wooden gun obtained by Pinkston came a memorandum evidently written by Piquett to O'Leary, and therefore serving as a kind of receipt, in which he says that he is giving O'Leary the gun to deliver to the Dillinger family. It would not surprise me if O'Leary kept it for himself.

Mr. Pinkston kindly brought the gun to my home for examination. The original gun had been covered with black shoe polish and highly polished, and while in the course of years it seems to have lost some of the shine as I remembered it, I am quite certain it is the same wooden gun Dillinger used in his escape and which I once had in my possession.

acquainted with the underworld knows it is bad and dangerous form to ask questions of this nature. The "East Chicago mob" included Hymie Cohen, Jimmie Regan, Sergeant Martin Zarkovich, Captain Tim O'Neil, and others, but no one knows if all of these men were involved. Following Dillinger's departure, both O'Neil and Zarkovich announced that they were conducting their own investigations of the escape. Inasmuch as the East Chicago police had no direct concern in the matter, their unsolicited efforts served only to divert suspicion of themselves.

Suspicion did fall on Cohen and Regan, although neither man could be definitely hooked up with the conspiracy. A few days before the November elections of 1934, Meyer Bogue and Assistant Attorney General Barce visited Arthur O'Leary at the county jail in Waukegan, Illinois, where he was awaiting trial on charges of harboring Dillinger and Van Meter. A one hundred dollar bribe secured them admittance, and Barce waited outside while Bogue went in to talk to O'Leary. The proposal was that in return for a statement linking Cohen and Regan with the escape, O'Leary would receive five thousand dollars and, if convicted, a pardon.

O'Leary knew Bogue had no authority of any kind and knew nothing of the break, but the next day he read in a Chicago newspaper that he had paid eleven thousand dollars to take Dillinger out of the jail.

Although Blunk was tried and acquitted of aiding in the escape, the Indiana authorities seem to entertain no doubts on the question of his involvement. One would expect a prison guard to make some small effort to deter an escaping prisoner, or at least express dismay at seeing him leave. According to testimony, however, Blunk opened cell doors, disarmed guards, and served as a cicerone to Dillinger about the jail. The outlaw at no time exhibited distrust of his deputy.

The other person displaying a similar spirit of cooperation is garage mechanic Edwin Saager. It will be remembered that there was a connection through marriage between his employer, Clyde Rothermel, and "Red" Hamilton. In his testimony at the trial of Evelyn Frechette in St. Paul, Saager stated that he gave the two escaping prisoners a car because he thought they were deputy sheriffs. Working only a few doors from the jail, the mechanic

[The Dillinger family told Pinkston some years ago that the wooden gun was eventually returned to them but later disappeared or was stolen. It now seems likely that O'Leary talked Piquett into giving him the gun, returned a duplicate to the Dillingers, and it was that duplicate which disappeared, while O'Leary kept the original.—W.J.H.]

might have been expected to at least recognize Blunk and other jail personnel. He must certainly have known Dillinger from the countless pictures of him in the newspapers, and it is hard to imagine his mistaking Youngblood for a Crown Point deputy sheriff. Saager seems to have thought of these points, too, for in testimony at the Piquett trial he changed his story to the effect that Dillinger had intimidated him with a machine gun. The mechanic had finished tuning up the fastest car in the garage ten minutes before Dillinger arrived, and had the tank filled with gasoline. Merely by taking the red light off the front, Dillinger concealed the fact that it was an official car, and with Warden Baker unknowingly broadcasting the wrong license number, it is no great marvel that the fugitives were not captured.

All in all, this entire escape from Crown Point presents nothing that can be regarded as particularly surprising. The Crown Point jail may be one of the strongest in Indiana, but stone walls alone do not a prison make. The alliance between politics and crime in Lake County is very close, and Dillinger possessed influence in both quarters. It was only a question of making the necessary arrangements for Dillinger to keep his "meet" with the gang in St. Paul.

The essentials of the story are as given above. This much more can be said—the entire mystery of all that concerns John Dillinger's escape lies in East Chicago, Indiana.*[30]

*Years later, in a conversation with J. Edgar Hoover in Washington, I pointed out this paragraph as an effort to go as far as I then dared in revealing the Lake County involvement in Dillinger's escape. Mr. Hoover intimated that he knew of the East Chicago connection, but Dillinger was dead by then and his escape was a matter for the state of Indiana. [Girardin died before I could ask him more about O'Leary's connections with the East Chicago hoodlums, who headquartered in a part of the city called Indiana Harbor. Part of O'Leary's value to Piquett may have been these associations, which included former police chief James W. Regan, Sergeant Zarkovich, lawyer (and sometimes city attorney) Hyman Cohen, and Sonny Sheetz, who operated an illegal casino called the Big House and had close ties with the Chicago Syndicate. Although Girardin believes Judge Murray had no personal involvement in the Crown Point escape, Murray was suspected of corruption in other cases, with Zarkovich as his bagman; and he is said to have gotten Deputy Blunk his fingerprinting job at the Crown Point jail. Also, Murray was virtually Cohen's partner in developing the Washington Park neighborhood in the "Harbor," where he became a neighbor of Sonny Sheetz. Dillinger supposedly operated out of the Harbor district following his release from prison, headquartering at or near Sheetz's gambling house and occasionally staying at Sheetz's apartment on Euclid Avenue, where some of the prearranged robberies allegedly were set up. Zarkovich moved to a nearby address on Euclid, where his widow still resides. —W.J.H.]

Red, have Carroll contact East Chicago people they will fix it with B for him to pass gun to Yungblood

Johnnie

Dillinger's note to gang members John "Red" Hamilton and Tommy Carroll concerning delivery of the fake gun. The "B" presumably stands for Deputy Sheriff Blunk, later acquitted of helping Dillinger escape.
G. Russell Girardin

POLICE DEPARTMENT CHICAGO INFORMED ME JOHN DILLINGER ESCAPED
CROWNPOINT JAIL NINETHIRTY THIS MORNING WITH NEGRO FURTHER DETAILS
UNKNOWN
END
RMW
OK   RCV

Dillinger's wooden pistol was not whittled in his cell but was made in Chicago and smuggled into the Lake County Jail the morning of his escape. His flight across state lines in a stolen car unleashed the FBI. The actual pistol (*left*) had a machine-bored barrel press-fitted with a tubular handle from a safety razor. A "counterfeit" pistol (*below*) was sold by Deputy Ernest Blunk to drugstore owner Charles Walgreen, who later donated it, with Blunk's affidavit of authenticity, to the Chicago Historical Society, which only recently learned it was not the real thing.

Jut, When and where Hooters and Girardin is through with the wooden gun, I want you to be pure and see that it goes back to Dillinger

Sister.   Piquett

Object of the "greatest manhunt in U.S. history," Dillinger correctly assumed that no one would think him foolish enough to simply go back home, where he spent a peaceful weekend in Mooresville with his family, eating his favorite meals and posing in the yard for snapshots. *John Dillinger Museum*

After getting it wrong a few times, police finally identified Polly Hamilton (Rita Keele) as the girl in the picture found in Dillinger's pocket watch—to the annoyance of his supposed true love, Evelyn Frechette. *Jeff Maycroft*

Polly Hamilton had been married to a Gary, Indiana, policeman named Roy Keele, but was a friend of brothel owner Anna Sage at the time she met Dillinger. *Richard Crowe*

Anna Sage received a federal reward of $5,000, but felt betrayed herself when the G-men did nothing to prevent her deportation on morals charges. *Kathi Harrell*

East Chicago police sergeant Martin Zarkovich, dapper as he was corrupt, supposedly participated in the FBI trap to make sure Dillinger didn't live to talk. *Neal Trickel*

GIRL TRICKS DILLINGER

U. S. Agents Slay Gunman at Movie

SPORTS · CRIME'S END! · Betrays Outlaw to Get Reward

HOW DEATH WAS DEALT TO DEATH-DEALING JOHN DILLINGER

This photo-diagram illustrates how America's most notorious criminal was trapped and shot to death last night. The final act of the Dillinger melodrama began at 10:45 p. m., when the desperado, who had watched—on the screen—the rise and fall of another gangster, stepped from the Biograph Theater at 2433 Lincoln av. Obviously, he did not suspect that he was being watched, that the denouement was near, as he strode south. In the doorway of the tavern two doors south of the theater stood Melvin Purvis. Dillinger passed him. He continued on to the alley. Purvis and two other men followed. Three men closed in from across the street. Two stood on the other side of the alley. Now Dillinger saw the peril. He tried to duck down the alley, tried to pull a gun. The man hunters beat him to it. They fired—a bullet went into the heart; a second found the same vital organ. As Dillinger toppled a third bullet entered his neck. He died a few minutes later.

SCENE OF DILLINGER KILLING AND HOW THE TRAP WAS SET FOR HIM

FIVE GOVERNMENT AGENTS STATIONED IN ALLEY

This photodiagram shows the elaborate plans made to insure against the escape of John Dillinger in which fifteen federal agents and five members of the East Chicago (Ind.) police force participated. When the plan to seize the bandit-killer before he entered the Biograph theater (shown in center) at 2433 Lincoln avenue was abandoned because of the surging crowd of theatergoers, police were stationed on all sides of the theater entrance to block his flight when he came out.

The positions of the agents and police at the time Melvin Purvis, chief investigator in Chicago for the department of justice, gave the signal to close in are shown, according to numbers, as follows:

1—Sergt. Martin Zarkovich, partner of Policeman Patrick O'Malley who was slain by Dillinger last Jan. 15 in East Chicago. Sergt. Zarkovich was the key man in the capture plans should Dillinger have turned to the right when he left the theater.

2—Sergt. Glenn Stretch.

3—Melvin Purvis, federal director, who gave the signal to close in and fired the first shot at Dillinger.

4—Government agent.

5—Man informer who verified identification of Dillinger as he walked along.

6 and 7—Dillinger and girl friend who betrayed him.

8, 9 and 10—Samuel P. Cowley, assistant to Purvis, and two federal agents.

11—Government agent.

12—Sergt. Walter Conroy.

13—Policeman Peter Sopsic.

14—Government agent.

15, 16 and 17—Capt. Timothy O'Neil and two government agents.

Five other government agents were placed in the alley to the right at the entrance of which the familiar "X" marks the spot where Dillinger fell. After the signal from Purvis the police and agents quickly closed in from all sides to bar any possible exit to the trapped bandit.

The federal agents and the Indiana officers ambushed Dillinger outside the Biograph Theatre without advising the Chicago police, leaving the local cops and reporters equally frustrated in their efforts to reconstruct the shooting from eyewitness accounts.

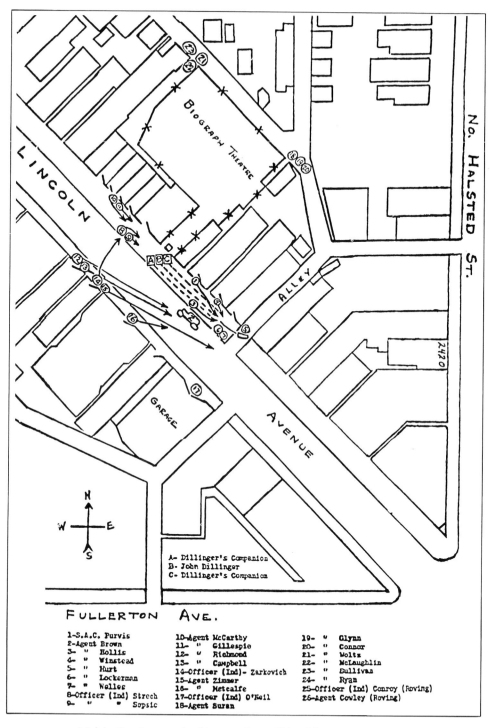

Melvin Purvis occupies his prominent "No. 1" position in the
official diagram of the Biograph ambush (slightly altered here)
that went into FBI files. He disappeared, however, in a simplified
version the Bureau released to the press.

Dillinger's body in the Chicago police patrol wagon that took him to the Alexian Brothers Hospital. *Neal Trickel*

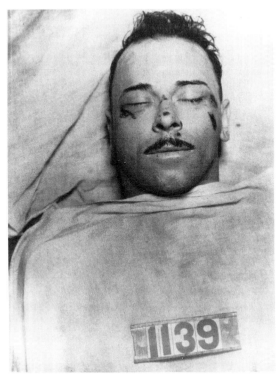

The fatal bullet, fired at close range by Agent Charles Winstead, entered the back of Dillinger's neck and emerged beneath his right eye. *Neal Trickel*

Insull Hopes for 'Justice'

Only Chicago Evening Newspaper With All Leading News Services—Associated Press, International News and Universal Service

CHICAGO AMERICAN

FINAL MARKETS Closing Prices

DILLINGER AT ST. PAUL!
ESCAPES IN NEW BATTLE

2 CENTS

Chicago Daily Tribune **Final**

HUNT DILLINGER IN CHICAGO

INDUSTRY PUTS
JOHNSON IN OWN
GOLDFISH BOWL

Will Rogers Says

COURTNEY ASKS McDonough
U. S. AID IN
STRIKE HERE

2 CENTS

Chicago Daily Tribune **Final**

SPEED DILLINGER EAST BY AIR

Columbus Evening Dispatch

Roosevelt
READY TO SIGN
BILL AND ISSUE
PROCLAMATION

DILLINGER USES WOODEN GUN TO ESCAPE

Today

The Herald Examiner
THE LIFE OF OUR LORD
by Charles Dickens

2 CENTS FINAL

CHARGE GUARD HELPED DILLINGER FLEE

New Dillinger Gang Blamed for Bank Robbery

The Marietta Daily Times

KEEP OF AIR FORCES PLANNED

The Marietta Daily Times

DILLINGER ON RAMPAGE AGAIN

Cleveland Plant Under Guard of Police

Only Chicago Evening Newspaper With All Leading News Services—Associated Press, International News and Universal Service

CHICAGO AMERICAN

FINAL MARKETS Closing Price

BIG TAX BOOST BILL TO ROOSEVELT
ALL POLICE JOIN DILLINGER HUNT

Coast

Racket To
Jury Today
Verdict I

MORE SUMMER
FOR CHICAGO

2 CENTS

Chicago Daily Tribune **Final**

KILL DILLINGER HERE

SLAIN BY U. S. AGENTS AS HE LEAVES THEATER

HOME, VIOLENCE NEWS SUMMARY
IN TWIN ATOM CE
IN MINNEAPOLIS

ARE KILLED
23 OTHERS HURT

STORY OF POWEL
LEADER IN LONG
DESPERATE HUNT

THE LADY OF THE LAKE

Heat Routed
Along Lake,
Inland Bakes

THE WEATHER

7/24/34

The *Chicago Tribune*'s cartoonist implicitly criticizes the public's fascination with Dillinger—but a closer look detects the family bookshelves stocked with stories glamorizing outlaws and pirates.

I guess my only bad habit is robbing banks. I

smoke very little and don't drink much.

—John Dillinger

PART III

Dillinger's wooden-pistol jailbreak was as sensational as the St. Valentine's Day Massacre, but with an important difference. That cold-blooded mass murder had shocked even apathetic Americans and probably did more than any other single event to tip public sentiment in favor of Repeal. Dillinger's escape, on the other hand, made headlines not for its violence but for his audacity and cleverness in outwitting the superior forces of the law, which made him not only a Robin Hood (in the loosest sense) but also the trickster of folk tradition. Although the press referred to both Capone and Dillinger as "gangsters," the public was beginning to distinguish between the urban mobsters who were capitalists corrupting the system and the outlaws who were rebelling against it. If the embarrassed authorities wanted to give him a real gun to explain the achievement, most people liked to think that a wooden pistol was all that a man like Dillinger needed.

This was a problem for the Justice Department. In spite of its improving image and increasingly effective efforts to mobilize public opinion against crime in general, Dillinger still represented—as city mobsters did not—the traditional American virtues of courage and resourcefulness. After 1930 especially, the self-made millionaire was not as admired as the rugged individualist who could cope with adversity, which now existed in abundance. For the symbols of wealth that had become so attractive in the Roaring Twenties had almost overnight turned into symbols of privilege and exploitation, and more than a few disgruntled citizens probably wished they had what it took to rob banks.

To counter a national tradition of rooting for underdogs, the government needed to field a new and improved crimefighter who embodied the outlaw's virtues of fearlessness and ferocity, but had loftier motives, superior intelligence, and God on his side. Hoover had been working on that righteous combination, for public contempt for cops required that he disassociate his new breed of incorruptible and scientific manhunters from the local flatfoot on the street and the riff-raff in the Prohibition Bureau. To amplify the distinction (since federal agents might work for any branch of government), Hoover's publicists began promoting the nickname "G-man," which had been around for years but had never found a worthy federal agency to denote. The official post-Hoover FBI story has that term being coined on September 26, 1933, by Machine Gun Kelly, who is supposed to have thrown up his hands and pleaded, "Don't shoot, G-men!" Since the Urschel kidnapping was still the Bureau's chief source of favorable publicity, any reporter or magazine writer attracted by the new "scientific criminology" was given the details on a platter—with "how the G-men got their name" as its centerpiece.

This worked like a charm. Americans, if somewhat soft on bank robbers, loved the excitement of the new war on crime, which of course needed warriors, who needed a catchy name. "G-man" sounded like a gunshot, and took off like one. And what the news and feature writers liked, screenwriters liked even more.

The motion picture industry already stood accused of aiding and abetting criminality with its glamorous portrayals of amoral gangsters who lived fast and died young but meanwhile had a great time. Only when threatened with censorship did Hollywood abandon such a lucrative product, which it had defended on the ground that exposing America's terrible crime situation would galvanize an informed public into demanding reforms. It was a dirty job, in other words, but somebody had to do it.

So the New Deal's war on crime was the moviemakers' salvation. Under a self-imposed code that now banned gratuitous violence—at least by criminals—James Cagney could no longer be a pint-sized, tough-talking, psychopathic killer in *The Public Enemy* (1931), but he could be a pint-size, tough-talking, morally justified killer in *"G Men"* (1935).

Simply by switching from gangster movies to G-man movies, Hollywood took the glamor it had been wasting on criminals and bestowed it on G-men and their crusading director, J. Edgar Hoover. Attorney General Cummings thus became an early casualty of his own war on crime. The top billing he enjoyed in the press during 1933–34 did not make it into either the movies or the history books, which now barely give him a supporting role during the FBI's exciting formative years.

Although serving its purpose, the G-man image required much patching and polishing after the treatment accorded it by Dillinger. When unleashed by the outlaw's Dyer Act violation, the FBI failed to demonstrate the invincibility Americans had been led to expect of it. Over the next five months the Dillinger gang still made Hoover's men often look like Keystone Kops as they blundered along in pursuit, antagonizing local police and other federal agencies alike, with an unrefined policy on lethal force that prompted Will Rogers to crack, "Dillinger is going to accidentally get with some innocent bystanders sometime, then he will get shot."

Cummings responded to Dillinger's depredations by declaring war on Dillinger personally, calling him Public Enemy Number One and pleading for airplanes and armored cars. The government's melodramatic measures tended to inflate Dillinger's reputation at the expense of the FBI's, to the point where most people guffawed upon learning that Public Enemy Number One, during the "greatest manhunt in U.S. history," had dropped in on his family at Mooresville to enjoy home cooking and pose in the yard for snapshots.

It was just such impudence that encouraged Congress to pass nearly intact the package of major federal laws that Cummings wanted and Hoover needed to personally fashion the most formidable and scientific (if often eccentric and selective) crimefighting organization in the history of the world. Not that it looked very good at the time.

CHAPTER ELEVEN

ENTER UNCLE SAM

In driving Sheriff Holley's automobile from Indiana to Illinois, John Dillinger violated the so-called Dyer Act, a federal law which prohibits that very thing. It has been said that if Crown Point had only been in Illinois, Dillinger would not have run counter to the G-men. In truth, his breaking jail at Crown Point put Mr. Dillinger too much in the spotlight. The federal warrant issued on March 7 merely furnished the federal government an excuse to enter the case; failing that, some other reason would soon have been found.

Let us glance for a moment at the much-publicized G-man, known as "whiskers" to the underworld. The Division of Investigation of the U.S. Department of Justice, under the direction of J. Edgar Hoover, already had taken on the vast hoodlum rings that were spawned in part by the Eighteenth Amendment. In the spring of 1934 its ranks comprised an interesting and varied collection of about four hundred men. Qualifications included a background in police work, graduation from a law school or college, or training as a certified public accountant. In practice, the emphasis was heavily upon the law students and college degrees, and most of the agents fell into these categories. Within the ranks were many who carried out their assignments conscientiously and well, and who knew how to handle their guns and handle themselves. Some had years of detective and police experience that entailed knowledge of scientific techniques, while others employed methods that never rose above third-degree savagery. Perhaps a few too many have had nervous and inexperienced trigger fingers that placed the lives around them in peril.

The Chicago bureau at the time was in the charge of Melvin Purvis, a diminutive South Carolinian, who worked later with Inspector Samuel P. Cowley. Attorney General Homer S. Cummings called the Dillinger escape a "disgraceful episode," while Director Hoover sent a score of federal investigators to Crown Point and transferred many more to the Chicago office.[31]

With heaven and earth thus being moved in Washington, the Dillinger gang was rounding into its final form in St. Paul, a city that has been an asylum for criminals of all sorts as long as they behave themselves while in residence. Thither came Homer Van Meter, who had served time with Dillinger at Indiana State Prison, and "Baby Face" Nelson, born Lester Gillis, a young Chicagoan who had graduated from petty thievery to bootlegging to armed robbery and whose most wholesome activity seems to have been a few dirt-track races at Chicago's Robey Speedway around 1930.

Homer Van Meter was a large man, almost six feet in height, with broad shoulders, tapering waist, and sinews and muscles of steel. His eyes revealed the mind of a hunted animal and the soul of a killer. "Red" Hamilton was also a member of the gang, but the wounds he received in the East Chicago robbery and other problems kept him in Chicago. Tommy Carroll, a paroled convict from Iowa, was also in Chicago at the time, more or less waiting for Dillinger. Carroll was a husky, fine-looking, dark-haired chap, about the same height as Van Meter, but more inclined to fleshiness.

Inasmuch as Dillinger's jailbreak had been delayed a day, he was running late for the March 6 meet in St. Paul. With Tommy Carroll driving and punishing the car all the way, the party arrived in the Twin Cities on the fifth, in time to keep the appointment. Dillinger and Billie Frechette immediately rented an apartment at 3352 Girard Avenue, Minneapolis, under the name of Mr. and Mrs. Irving Olson.

On that Tuesday, March 6, the reconstituted gang commenced operations. The bandit car that headed southwest on this morning bore Kansas license plates and contained John Dillinger, Homer Van Meter, "Baby Face" Nelson, Tommy Carroll, and Eddie Green. Hamilton had been expected, but found it impossible to cover the distance from Chicago in time. The object of the expedition was the Securities National Bank and Trust Company (the present Northwest Security National Bank) of Sioux Falls, South Dakota, which they reached at the customary hour, just before closing time. Carroll and Green remained outside, while the other three, Dillinger leading with his machine gun, entered the bank.

The employees were quickly lined up by the bandits and covered by Dillinger and Van Meter with their machine guns. The catlike Nelson was scampering over the cages and gathering up the money, but the robbers found that the door of the vault had been closed and locked.

Dillinger waved his machine gun menacingly.

"Get that safe open," he ordered the employees. "Which one of you knows the combination?"

No one volunteered.

"Come on, speak up. I'm not going to monkey around with you. Tell me who can open that safe, or I'm turning this chopper loose and wipe out the whole bunch of you."

The fear-stricken employees recovered with miraculous rapidity, and a half-dozen of them pointed to a small and much-embarrassed middle-aged man.

"Well, what in the hell are you waiting around for? Get busy and get that safe open!" The incensed Dillinger accompanied his words with a kick to the banker's posterior.

"That was one awful kick you gave that jugger," commented Van Meter afterward. "I thought your boot was going right through his body."

Outside the bank, the inhabitants of Sioux Falls were being treated to a thrilling spectacle. Eddie Green, at the car, was directing traffic to keep motorists moving in the right direction, while Tommy Carroll stood on the sidewalk using his machine gun to wave away intruders. A hurried call to the police station had stated only that there was trouble at the bank. Chief of Police M. W. Parsons and a detective, wondering if that meant citizens were engaged in a brawl, drove to the bank armed only with their pistols. To their chagrin, they found themselves staring into the machine gun of Carroll, who forced them to get out of their car and stand helplessly on the sidewalk. Motorcycle policeman Hale Keith, hearing shots and hastening to investigate, suddenly found himself in the danger area, and suffered wounds in the abdomen, one leg, and both arms. This was the only casualty of the day, and fortunately the wounds did not prove fatal.

A large crowd had gathered in the street about a block from the bank, watching the robbers as they worked. Spectators gaped from doorways and windows, and craned their necks from behind poles and mailboxes. One intrepid photographer managed to get a picture of Tommy Carroll standing on the sidewalk with his machine gun and firing over the crowd to keep anyone from venturing too close.

The bandits within the bank, having acquired a loot of $49,500, now departed in the company of four women employees and teller Leo Olson. Olson was released at the city limits, but the women were carried some distance farther. Close behind the bandit car followed a posse of vehicles headed by Sheriff Melvin L. Sells and Deputy United States Marshal Art Anderson. The bank robbers were blazing away with their machine guns, and their pursuers were throwing bullets back. A slug tore through the windshield of Anderson's car, while a volley of machine-gun fire raked the headlights and hood of Sells's machine. Across the state line, just north of Luverne, Minnesota, the gang managed to shake off the posse. Although all roads were guarded, and while authorities scoured the highways and soared overhead in airplanes, the bank robbers suffered no further interference on their return trip to St. Paul.

It was only a considerable time afterward that the Dillinger gang was definitely connected with this Sioux Falls robbery. China R. Clarke, president of the bank, stated that Dillinger was not in the party. But Piquett and O'Leary had no doubts about the gang's identity. For the next few evenings O'Leary remained in the office until late, hoping to receive some definite word regarding the fee promised by Dillinger. On Friday, March 9, he received a mysterious telephone call directing him to the lobby of the Copeland Hotel at four o'clock that afternoon. Scarcely had he entered the doors when a tall man in a dark overcoat, his face concealed by the collar, approached, thrust a package into his hands, and hurried out the door. Back at the office Piquett and O'Leary unwrapped the package and found it to contain $976, $24 short, for some reason, of $1,000. O'Leary was due one-third of all fees in the Dillinger case, but reimbursed Piquett for half of the $300 he had given to Dillinger on the night of his escape, leaving his total share of this payment a modest $175.33.

Regarding the Sioux Falls affair as a success, the gang prepared for further operations. A word here would not be out of place as to the careful technique employed by the Dillinger gang in their profession of robbing banks. Operations were never conceived or carried out on the spur of the moment. The bank to be robbed was selected at least a week or two beforehand and "cased" by some member of the gang, usually Homer Van Meter. He would visit it one or more times on some pretext of business, taking careful note of the general layout and the presence of any balcony (always a menace to bank robbers), as well as peekholes, bulletproof cages, or evidence of gas guns. Other matters of interest were the strength of the tellers' cages, the location of the vault, and the existence of alarm buttons, gongs, and other protective devices. The distance from the closest police station and the strength of the police department would also be recorded.

What particularly distinguished the Dillinger gang was their invariably successful getaways. After the route had been planned, the gang would travel over it three or four times before the robbery, constructing their own maps which showed towns, distinguishing landmarks, and the exact mileage between spots as indicated by the speedometer. Cans containing from ten to twenty gallons of gasoline were hidden in haystacks close to the highway, along with kegs of nails to puncture their pursuers' tires. The driver closely followed the instructions called to him by the front-seat passenger. "Two miles straight ahead to the bridge," this man would say. "Prepare for sharp turn to the left a half-mile ahead. Two and a half miles straight down the road to the haystack with the gas cans." Those in the rear seat would have broken out the rear window glass for the convenience of their machine guns.

Exactly one week after the Sioux Falls stickup, on March 13, the gang descended on the First National Bank of Mason City, Iowa, one of the largest banking institutions of that state in a thriving community of 25,000 people. The same five members of the gang were present, plus John Hamilton, who had since arrived in St. Paul to join his associates.

The bandits parked their machine on the south side of the bank, close to the back door. Tommy Carroll, the driver, remained in the car, while Eddie Green guarded the rear of the bank. Van Meter took up a strategic position in the entrance of a drugstore across the street, asking the proprietor and a lady customer to stay there and keep him company. The other three, Dillinger, Hamilton, and Nelson, to create a commotion, dashed into the bank shouting at the top of their voices and brandishing their machine guns. Mr. Willis G. C. Bagley, president of the bank, describes the event in a letter:*

---

*This letter was sent in answer to my inquiry. I have no reason to suspect that the Mason City robbery was prearranged.

This robbery occurred on the afternoon of March 13, 1934, about twenty minutes before three o'clock—twenty minutes before our closing time. The writer was at his desk just outside his private office. The first intimation that I had that anything was wrong was someone hollering like a Comanche Indian. I naturally turned toward the lobby to see what the confusion was all about, and as I did so, I faced into a fellow with a gun pointed at me. He said nothing—just hollered. My impression was that some crazy fellow with a gun was running wild; not thinking that it was a holdup. My first thought was to get into my office, being next to my desk I ducked in. He followed me through the gate and before I could get the door closed, his gun was in the door. He tried to push it in and I tried to shut the door. Finally he pulled his gun out of the door and said, "Come out of there, you S. of a B.," and fired through the door, missing me by about an inch.

Pandemonium reigned in the bank lobby. There were thirty-one employees and between twenty-five and thirty-five customers, all stricken with terror as the bandits fired machine guns over their heads. Nelson scampered back of the cages and into the vault, taking H. C. Fisher, the assistant cashier, with him. Hamilton covered the customers, while Dillinger rounded up a group of employees.

"Lay face down on the floor!" he barked. The frightened employees hastened to do so, and in their excitement some of the young women lay on their backs.

A grin came over Dillinger's face. "I said on your faces, not on your backs. This is a stickup, not a directors' meeting."

"Red" Hamilton spotted Tom Walters, a bank guard, in a glass cage overlooking the lobby, and turned his machine gun on him. The cage was struck in a dozen places, but none of the bullets pierced the shatterproof glass. Walters was unable to return the fire, however, for fear of hitting employees and customers. The only attempt at resistance was a gas bomb thrown into the lobby by one of the bookkeepers, a man named Barclay.

The usual large crowd was gathering outside to watch the holdup, despite bursts of bullets fired over their heads. One of the spectators, R. H. James, secretary of the Mason City school board, was hit in the leg by a stray slug. Police and vigilantes climbed to the vantage points of nearby roofs and upper-story windows to attack the bandits when they emerged from the bank.

Meanwhile, the gas from the hand bomb was rendering the bank interior insupportable.

"If Jimmy [Nelson] could have held out five minutes longer,

we would have taken another two hundred grand,'' Dillinger remarked later. "But the gas was so bad we had to get out." Still, the gang made off with $52,000, all in cash.

This while bullets were pouring into the bank from the outside, and while the bandits within continued shouting and firing their guns. Dillinger and his companions finally herded their hostages from the gas-filled interior by way of the rear door, where Green and Carroll seized sixteen to serve as shields. As Dillinger and Hamilton were hurrying out, both were wounded in the shoulder. The shots came from a second-story window, and struck near their necks between the tops of their bulletproof vests and their inner clothing. The injuries were not serious, however, and both men successfully reached the car.

The hostages—four bank employees and twelve customers— were crowded onto the machine, hanging on to the running boards and across the back of the car. The glass was knocked out of the windows to accommodate machine guns, which protruded from both front and rear. In this manner the police and vigilantes were frustrated, and as no serious pursuit occurred, the captives were released at the city limits.

This was the largest bank yet robbed by the Dillinger gang, and the way they had terrorized an entire city caused consternation throughout the Middle West. Within a short time the bankers of this region were paying more than a thousand dollars a day for extra bank guards, and the private agencies supplying them were unable to fill many requests. Thus, while the federal government was gearing up to hunt him, John Dillinger was helping solve the unemployment problem.

Herbert Youngblood, Negro companion of John Dillinger in the exploit that had made Crown Point so wooden gun–conscious, appeared in the headlines one last time. No trace could be found of him after the escape, and some police convinced themselves that Dillinger had put him to death as a now-useless encumbrance. But Youngblood, rendered hale and hearty by the sweet air of freedom, had managed to make his way to the neighborhood of Detroit, Michigan.

The night of Wednesday, March 14, found him in the city of Port Huron, flashing a bankroll in the colored saloons of the city, and boasting of his acquaintance with Dillinger. His big moment had arrived, and he was making the most of it. Word reached police headquarters on Friday morning that a thoroughly intoxicated man was making himself obnoxious in the small store of

Mrs. Pearl Abraham, and Sheriff William Van Antwerp, accompanied by Undersheriff Charles Cavanaugh and Deputy Howard Lohr, responded to the call.

Cavanaugh seized Youngblood and took his automatic pistol, but Youngblood, stepping back, drew another gun and opened fire. As Cavanaugh tried to shoot back, a bullet pierced his lungs and he fell dying. During the battle Lohr was critically wounded in the chest, Van Antwerp was shot in the left arm, and a customer named Fields was hit in the shoulder. Fields picked up a gun from the floor and shot Youngblood twice. Van Antwerp and Lohr were likewise hitting their mark, and the escaped convict dropped with seven bullets in his body.

Youngblood lived for four hours and was true to the last, declaring that he had been with Dillinger only the night before. It surpasses belief how such an obvious attempt to throw the authorities off was eagerly received as a clue of great importance. Captain Matt Leach, hurrying to Detroit, wired Governor McNutt that "the Dillinger trail was hot." Dillinger was reported to have been seen crossing into Canada near Sarnia, Ontario. Several officers from Crown Point hastened to Port Huron the next day. American and Canadian police maintained a careful watch on both sides of the boundary, while nearly five hundred peace officers occupied the Michigan shore, blockading roads and stopping and searching cars. Another report had Dillinger reaching Canada by crossing the St. Clair River into Ontario in a rowboat. Two loads of state police were rushed to Marysville, Michigan, on nothing more than a rumor that two men had asked directions to the Marysville airport.

While Dillinger was being hunted everywhere else, the outlaw and his associates in the Mason City robbery returned to their hideouts in St. Paul and Minneapolis, arriving there the same evening of Tuesday, March 13. Dillinger and Hamilton found their wounds minor and medical attention unnecessary, but the accidental discharge of a pistol in the apartment, coupled with the sense that they had stayed long enough in one place, decided them to return to Chicago. Not wishing to make the trip without proper dressing on their wounds, on March 15 they paid a visit to Dr. N. G. Mortensen, the city health officer of St. Paul. Although no law required him to report bullet wounds to authorities, Dr. Mortensen found himself showered with criticism and was suspended by John McDonald, the commissioner of public safety, when the facts became known. In justice to the physician, however, he may well have been telling the truth in claiming he did not know the true identities of his patients until he later saw their pictures in the newspapers.

The same day the outlaws were being treated in St. Paul, Chicago police raided an apartment at 640 Wrightwood Avenue on a report that Evelyn Frechette lived there. Two couples were seized, Anthony and Lucille Fontana and Thomas and Alice Dyer, but all survived interrogation by Captain Stege.

On the following day, Friday, March 16, Dillinger and his Indian sweetheart arrived in Chicago and telephoned Piquett's office. O'Leary answered and said that the attorney had left for the day.

"Be in front of your office, on the Wacker Drive side," the voice told him. "I'll pick you up in about fifteen minutes."

As O'Leary surmised, the man who drove up for him was John Dillinger, and at his side was Evelyn Frechette. O'Leary entered the car, and the three drove around the streets for a short time. Dillinger told him that Billie wished to divorce her imprisoned husband so that the two of them could marry. Whatever O'Leary may have thought of Dillinger's sense of priorities, he promised to take the matter up with Piquett, and advise him in the next day or two.

The next meeting occurred on Sunday afternoon, March 18, while Piquett was in Lima, Ohio, seeing Harry Pierpont. Billie Frechette telephoned O'Leary and asked him to meet her at four o'clock at Madison Street and Homan Avenue. From there they walked a block south to Monroe Street, where Dillinger was waiting in a car, and the three drove around for about half an hour. O'Leary had discussed the Frechette divorce with Piquett, but the attorney, mentioning that his services for Public Enemy Number One had so far brought him more trouble than money, showed little interest in the case. Dillinger was told that Piquett was not a divorce lawyer, and it was suggested that he seek out someone who specialized in that field.

Dillinger dropped the divorce idea for the time being, and the next day Billie set out for Mooresville, conveying the letter in which the wooden gun episode is mentioned, along with that famous weapon and small sums of money for Mrs. Hancock and old John Dillinger. Before leaving she called at O'Leary's apartment and left a package containing twenty-three hundred dollars, together with a note instructing that one thousand dollars should go to Pierpont's parents, another thousand to Piquett, two hundred to Meyer Bogue, and the remaining one hundred to O'Leary. Arriving back in Chicago early on Tuesday morning, Piquett made his first stop at O'Leary's apartment to pick up the package.

Mrs. J. G. Pierpont, the mother of Harry, already had made several trips to Piquett's offices, pleading with him to locate Dillinger and obtain much-needed funds. Piquett at this time was likewise strapped for cash. He explained this to Mrs. Pierpont, yet gave her five hundred dollars and told her that more would be forwarded within a few days. As for Meyer Bogue, Piquett and O'Leary had begun to suspect his connection with the Indiana authorities and gave him only fifty dollars, deciding to retain the balance until they could determine his loyalties.* This same day, Wednesday, Billie Frechette returned from Indianapolis and was greeted at the Chicago airport by Piquett, Pat Cherrington, and Opal Long.

Friday, March 23, Dillinger slipped away from Chicago and paid a visit to the Pierpont family. He sat with Mrs. Pierpont on the front porch swing and discussed Harry's troubles and his hopes that his friends might be able to take him out of jail. Mrs. Pierpont mentioned her visit to Piquett's offices and the fact that he had given her money.

"How much did he give you?"

"Five hundred dollars."

"That was all?"

"Yes."

Mrs. Pierpont did not explain that Piquett was short of cash or that the rest was promised, and from this misunderstanding grew an incident with nearly serious consequences. A flock of rumors began to circulate that Dillinger and Piquett had had a violent falling out, and fictitious letters, supposedly from Dillinger, have even been concocted to support the tale. Its only likely basis is this Pierpont incident, which proved to be a matter soon amicably adjusted.

Dillinger returned to Chicago the next day, and immediately had Billie arrange another meeting with O'Leary at the same corner of Homan and Madison. Dillinger was waiting nearby.

"Get into the car," he said curtly as O'Leary approached.

---

*My last contact with Meyer Bogue was not a pleasant one. I had been introduced to Louis Piquett by Mrs. Leonora Z. Meder, a prominent Chicago lawyer with whom I shared office space at 139 North Clark Street. I chanced to introduce Bogue to Mrs. Meder, who appeared interested in his tales, true or false, of his exploits. One day Bogue came when I was out and said he would wait until I returned. Mrs. Meder had just received a legal fee of about six hundred dollars and put the money in her purse, which she placed in a drawer. She then left Bogue alone in her office while she talked to another lawyer in the building. When she returned, Bogue was gone and so was the money from her purse.

The latter was mystified at the absence of Dillinger's usual cheery "H'yah, Art!"

For nearly ten minutes the three drove around without a word being spoken. From the grim expression on the outlaw's face, O'Leary sensed that something was wrong.

"What's on your mind, Johnnie?" he ventured.

Dillinger snorted. "What kind of a skunk are you working for?" he said in reply.

"What are you talking about?"

"What happened to that grand I sent for Mrs. Pierpont?" he demanded.

"I turned it all over to Lou."

"How is it she only got half?"

O'Leary was mystified, inasmuch as Piquett had forgotten to tell him of the arrangement for paying in two installments.

"How do you suppose that makes me look with the rest of the gang?" Dillinger went on. "Here I have been telling them all about what a great lawyer I've got, and then he holds out on a man that's lying in jail. If it was my money, I wouldn't say anything, but Hamilton sent that money for Pierpont. Is he down at his office now?"

"No, he's left for the day," O'Leary answered, not knowing if Piquett was there or not.

"You're covering up for him," Dillinger said and stopped the car. "Billie, run into that drugstore and call Piquett's office. I want to find out if Art's lying to me."

The few minutes that Evelyn Frechette was in the drugstore were like years for O'Leary, but fortune smiled on this occasion.

"He's not in," said Billie on her return to the car, and O'Leary's fluency of speech returned.

"Be reasonable, Johnnie. What if Lou did keep some of the money? What do you expect? You know what we have been up against, risking our lives and liberty for you. And how much money have you given us for it?" O'Leary turned to Dillinger's companion. "Why don't you tell him, Billie? You've sat in our offices day after day. You know sometimes we didn't have a quarter for lunch."

But Miss Frechette was not disposed to cooperate. "I don't know a thing about it," she said, tilting her nose in the air.

So O'Leary went on talking, and the outlaw's ill humor gradually dissipated. Dillinger possessed a natural geniality, and his outbursts of anger were seldom of long duration.

The desperado looked at O'Leary's anguished face and grinned. "All right, Art. I'll take care of the other five hundred myself. Let's forget about it."

Soon the matter was clarified to everyone's satisfaction. Dillinger forwarded another five hundred to Mrs. Pierpont, and Piquett credited him with that amount against his still-unpaid legal fees.

On the evening after O'Leary's sweat of blood, Dillinger and Billie returned to St. Paul. By now more false reports were making the rounds, leading police to search the forests of upper Michigan and northern Wisconsin. At the same time, he was "positively" identified as the robber of a bank in St. Cloud, Florida, and Florida officials commenced combing that state.

CHAPTER TWELVE

STORM IN THE MIDWEST

Now that the new Dillinger gang was attaining national renown, let us glance back to see how the members of the original group were faring after the roundup at Tucson. While Dillinger returned by airplane, Pierpont, Makley, and Clark were transported by train, arriving in Chicago on February 1. They refused comment on reports that during November and December 1933, the gang had paid protection money of one thousand dollars a week to certain Chicago police officials.

Escorted by a guard of one hundred officers, the three were taken to the penitentiary at Michigan City, Indiana, pending their transfer to Ohio to stand trial for the killing of Sheriff Sarber.

"Do me a favor," Makley begged his guards as they came in sight of the prison walls. "Shoot me through the head, so I won't have to go back in there."

The sense of humor which had caused Pierpont to jest throughout the Tucson proceedings now gave way to frequent outbursts of bitterness.

"Every day for years something has happened to make me hate the law," he exclaimed.

Clark was quiet and uncommunicative as usual, but his face was set in hard, angry lines.

The reception they received did not improve their moods. They were immediately thrust into solitary confinement on a diet of bread and water. Pierpont, Makley, Clark, Copeland, and Shouse were all indicted for the Sarber killing in Ohio, but Copeland remained in Indiana for arraignment on a charge of robbing the Greencastle bank. Hilton Crouch, the companion in Dillinger's earlier adventures, received a sentence of twenty years for the Indianapolis bank robbery. Mary Kinder was held to the grand jury in Indianapolis for aiding in the Michigan City prison break.

Harry Pierpont, Charles Makley, and Russell Clark were arraigned on February 15 before Judge R. E. Everett at Lima, Ohio. All three stood mute during the proceedings, and Judge Everett entered "not guilty" pleas in their behalf. Separate trials were granted all three, with Pierpont's set for March 6.

On March 3, however, Dillinger escaped from Crown Point, and the repercussions of that event quickly reached Lima. Pierpont, Makley, and Clark put on suits as though expecting his imminent arrival, and from that moment until the removal of the prisoners, the citizens of Lima lived in constant dread of a descent upon them by the most fearsome horde since that led by Gengis Khan. Orders were issued to double the guards inside the jail and to construct sandbag emplacements outside for heavy machine guns. There can be few instances in history where one man so thoroughly frightened a city as did John Dillinger, as even National Guardsmen were ordered to Lima for the protection of that city. The jury was completed two days later, and Sheriff Don Sarber, the son and successor of the murdered man, was called as the first witness. He stated that his father, dying on the floor, told him, "I did not know any of the men. They were all big men." During the remainder of the trial young Sarber sat in court with a machine gun on his lap.

Deputy Sheriff Wilbur Sharp, who was locked up by the raiders, insisted that one was Harry Copeland, but that Pierpont had fired the fatal shot.

The strongest witness for the state was Edward Shouse, who testified against the man who had escaped with him from prison. Shouse was conveyed from the Michigan City penitentiary in a bulletproof automobile, and hung his close-cropped head when brought into the courtroom.

"Pierpont was the guy," Shouse muttered from the witness stand. He was then returned to Michigan City under a heavy guard.

Although there seems little doubt that Pierpont killed Sarber, there is room for discussion as to what credence can be given to

Shouse's testimony. John Dillinger, who should have known something about the matter, later stated that Pierpont, Makley, and John Hamilton were the three who entered the jail, and that Clark and Copeland waited outside in the car. But by this time Hamilton was no longer among the living, and perhaps John Dillinger was shielding someone else.

The jury deliberated only forty-five minutes before finding Harry Pierpont guilty of first-degree murder, and with no recommendation of mercy, death in the electric chair became mandatory.

Pierpont, hands and feet shackled in chains, was asked if he had anything to say before the verdict was read. He replied, "No, not a word"; and when told he was condemned, he only grinned.

There had been a stormy scene in the courtroom that day. Pierpont on the stand had admitted that he led the Michigan City break, but denied the Sarber killing. His father and mother testified that he had been in their home that day. The closing argument of Prosecutor Ernest M. Botkin had been interrupted by the prisoner shouting, "If you had never heard of Matt Leach of the Indiana State Police, you would never have heard of me!" When the death penalty was imposed, Pierpont's mother rushed to his side and held a scarf before his face to shield him from photographers.

The Dillinger fear was tightening its tentacles about Lima. General Harold M. Bush of the state militia assumed command of the National Guard and ordered the machine-gun defenses strengthened. Arrangements were made so that in the event of attack an alarm could be spread throughout Ohio, Indiana, and southern Michigan in fifteen minutes. Rumors had Dillinger expected in Lima at any time to shoot Pierpont out of jail. The Ohio State Sheriffs' Association added to the general tension by warning police in northwestern Ohio to watch for a car containing three heavily armed men.

In Columbus, two National Guard squads were assigned on March 12 to guard Governor White of Ohio and his daughter, Mary White, after threats of abduction had been received. The governor, one of the few men in the state to maintain a level head, scoffed at the idea, but Adjutant General Frank D. Henderson insisted on precautions and the executive acquiesced.

The same day, Charles Makley went on trial for murder in Lima's nest of machine guns. Judge Everett opened the proceedings with the boggling announcement that Dillinger was en route to Lima at that very moment with a jail-wrecking crew. Judge Everett enjoyed a high reputation for his deportment on the bench, but the glare of publicity and drama of the occasion seem to have swept him off his feet. Although the city was an armed camp with a barricaded courthouse, and although the courtroom was filled with machine guns, a defense motion for a change of venue, on the ground that such large-scale military preparations were prejudicial, was summarily overruled.

Charles Makley, a pleasant-faced man, walked into the court with his hands in iron cuffs. For further melodramatics, his legs were placed in chains as soon as he was seated. Judge Everett then issued contempt citations against defense attorney Clarence C. Miller and two members of the grand jury who stated they had talked with Miller in his office. The three were each fined twenty-five dollars and costs, but the fines were suspended with a strong warning.

The Makley trial involved four days of jury selection and testimony. The evidence indicated that the defendant had been present with Pierpont in the jail office at the time, but was not the actual killer. This time the jury deliberated all night Friday, March 16, and did not return until ten o'clock Saturday morning. But the verdict was the same—guilty of first-degree murder, with no recommendation of mercy, which meant death in the electric chair.

There is small need to mourn the ranting, cursing, violent Pierpont, but sympathy for the genial and mild-mannered Charles Makley is not totally out of place. There was no stain of murder upon his record, and no thought of murder in his mind when he went to take Dillinger from the Lima jail. It was solely the act of the trigger-happy Pierpont that was now sending him to his death.

Makley's sisters, Florence and Mildred, and his half-brother Fred had come from Kansas for the trial. He stood before the bench with face tense and slightly pale, and as the verdict was read he clenched his fists and teeth, but made no comment.

The death sentences of Pierpont and Makley were the first in the history of Allen County.

Pierpont and Makley had been tried and convicted—it was Russell Clark's turn next. But Clark had one true friend who worked unceasingly to save him from the fate of his associates. Every day found the frumpy Opal Long at Piquett's offices to learn of any news and do anything she could to help. On the morning of Friday, March 16, she took $485 from her purse and placed it on the attorney's desk.

"Here's every cent I have, Mr. Piquett," she said. "I want you to go to Lima with it and try to save Russell."

That afternoon Piquett boarded the train. Scarcely had he left the office than a phone call came for O'Leary.

"You'll find a package and letter for Piquett marked 'Urgent' in his desk," O'Leary was told. "Be careful it doesn't fall into the wrong hands, and get it to him right away. Send a special messenger if you have to." And before O'Leary could answer, the party had hung up.

O'Leary found the note, but had no way to reach Piquett. He knew it was from Dillinger and that it must be important. He thought of Esther Anderson, in whom he knew Piquett placed much confidence. He explained the situation to her briefly by telephone, not mentioning Dillinger, and she set off by train for Ohio that same night, bearing the mysterious letter.

Piquett found Lima under virtual martial law. National Guardsmen patrolled the streets and worked busily on the sandbag defenses. Special guards with machine guns were stationed everywhere. A couple of planes flying over the town caused additional consternation, for one rumor in circulation had Dillinger coming by airplane.

Miss Anderson quickly located Piquett and gave him the correspondence. It was, of course, from Dillinger, requesting him to determine if any legal maneuver might save the men from death. If there was no possibility of rescue by legal methods, then, Dillinger stated, he would leave for Lima immediately with six or seven men and take the jail by storm. Piquett immediately burned the note and hoped only that he would have an opportunity to talk Dillinger out of such a mad project.

Piquett immediately contacted Clarence Miller, Clark's attorney, and arranged to join the defense. Meanwhile, the news of his arrival in the company of a woman was causing a stir among the police.[32] What was Dillinger's attorney doing in Lima? It was recalled, with knowing looks, that Piquett and a woman had also visited Dillinger shortly before he escaped from the Crown Point jail. Perhaps Piquett had been sent by Dillinger to reconnoiter the enemy defenses.

It was a time when men's minds no longer functioned clearly. About one o'clock on that Saturday afternoon Piquett found himself rudely escorted to the city jail. Prosecutor Botkin was soon on hand and the two were introduced.

"You've been very successful, Mr. Prosecutor," Piquett said. "You've just sent two innocent men to the electric chair."

Whereupon Botkin's affection for Piquett increased by leaps and bounds.

Piquett was searched and a list of prospective jurors, furnished by attorney Miller, was confiscated. Released, he immediately went to Miller and obtained another list. About four o'clock the police again took him into custody and seized the second list.

Now thoroughly incensed by the attentions lavished upon him and by the refreshments imbibed between these encounters, Piquett began to forcefully express his opinion of Lima's hospitality. He stopped before the courthouse and contemplated the militiamen toiling at the barricades.

"I'm Lou Piquett," he announced. "I've got a client up in Chicago who may be coming down to see you boys. Better throw on a few more sandbags."

Mr. Piquett now became the most popular man in Lima.

About six o'clock he was escorting Esther Anderson back to the railroad station when one of the National Guardsmen advised that General Bush would like a word. The commander was headquartered in a nearby hotel room.

According to Piquett's account, General Bush, flanked by four militia officers, was waiting with a whip in his hand.

"So you're down here from Dillinger," the general snapped. "I have a good mind to let you have this across the face."

"I'd be a little careful about who I hit with that whip, General."

"What are you doing here in Lima, anyway?"

"It's no secret," said Piquett. "I'm here to help defend Russell Clark. His mother, Mrs. May Clark, sent me."

"You're sure Dillinger didn't send you to case the jail?"

Piquett snorted.

"Well," the officer grumped. "We'll put you in a place where you won't do any harm."

So Piquett spent his first night in Lima in the hoosegow. Sunday morning he was released to the custody of an attorney, Francis W. Durkin, who announced that Piquett was off the case. Another distinguished visitor in Lima this day was Captain Matt Leach, who had just finished looking for Dillinger in Port Huron and was now trying to pick up the trail in Ohio.

Whatever plans lawyer Piquett may have had for a comfortable Sunday night in his hotel were rudely shattered by another encounter with the authorities. Lima apparently could not rest easily with Lou Piquett on the loose, for the city was in a state of mind that found nothing too improbable. Piquett was next accused of offering Lima's guardians fifty thousand dollars for the escape of the three prisoners. Even the policeman who escorted him all day said that was ridiculous, but the lawyer found himself in jail for the second consecutive night—despite the offer of some much smaller bribes in his own behalf.

Monday morning the trial of Russell Clark opened. Jury selection took two days, and it was Wednesday before testimony began. By then Louis Piquett had ceased to be a thorn in Lima's flesh, however. Monday evening he had been picked up yet again and had made his fifth visit in three days to the city bastille. The trip was now becoming monotonous. His attorney secured his release about midnight and, feeling that the route to the hotel had become altogether too familiar to the police, took him to a private club for the remainder of the night. Tuesday morning fresh woes were heaped upon the lawyer's head, for Attorney General Lutz had arrived from Indiana with a detachment of the state police and a warrant charging him with implication in the Crown Point jailbreak.

Piquett hailed a taxi and ordered the driver to take him to the next town. At the railroad station more police were gathered.

"Go over and see if you can find out what those policemen are doing there," he told the driver.

In a few minutes the cabby returned.

"They're looking for a Chicago lawyer named Louis Piquett."

"That's what I wanted to know. Drive me on to Fort Wayne."

At Fort Wayne he learned that rumors travel faster than lawyers. He was supposed to have already been there and gotten off the train, and police were checking the hotels.

"Take me to Chicago," sighed Piquett.

About midnight the frazzled attorney and his loyal driver arrived, after numerous stops at taverns along the way. The taxi meter showed a staggering bill of forty-two dollars. The damage done to Mr. Piquett's feelings and pocketbook was greatly assuaged, however, when he reached O'Leary's apartment later that same night and found Dillinger's package to contain stacks of bills totaling twenty-three hundred dollars. With overcoat pockets bulging, the weary lawyer turned his steps homeward, and this particular adventure reached its conclusion.

Back in Lima, Russell Clark was fighting for his life. The guard about the courthouse had been strengthened, and orders were given to frisk spectators even more thoroughly. Judge Everett continued to issue bulletins on the expected Dillinger raid, and warned that the "danger" had increased.

Few men tried for murder have ever seemed as apathetic as Russell Clark. He yawned and dozed off from time to time as he heard witnesses describe his role in Sarber's murder. Knowing the short shrift given to Pierpont and Makley, he looked upon his own condemnation as a foregone conclusion.

But the thirst for blood had now been somewhat quenched. Clark also was found guilty of first-degree murder, but with a recommendation for mercy, which meant a sentence of life imprisonment. At the same time Judge Everett set the execution date for Pierpont and Makley as July 13, and overruled their motions for a new trial.

All of this happened on Saturday, March 24. On the previous night John Dillinger, the most wanted man in America, had been in Lima for several hours. He determined the strength of the garrison, and inspected the barricades, machine-gun nests, and protective measures in the jail. He came away convinced that it would require an army to take the jail, and that if his friends were to be freed, it would have to be through some surprise move or legal stratagem.

Following their conviction, Pierpont, Makley, and Clark were transported under heavy guard to the Ohio state penitentiary at Columbus, where special reinforcements had been hired. In fact, so largely was attention concentrated on these celebrities that on April 29, three other convicts disarmed one of the guards and climbed over the walls to freedom.

CHAPTER THIRTEEN

HOMECOMING

Meanwhile, Dillinger, before leaving the Twin Cities, had requested Eddie Green to arrange a hideout for use upon his return. Eddie's wife Beth, a comely woman with bright red hair, accordingly rented a furnished apartment at 95 South Lexington Avenue, in St. Paul. Dillinger and Evelyn Frechette arrived a few days later, and were joined by John Hamilton, his sweetheart Pat Cherrington, and her sister, Opal Long.

On Friday, March 30, this group staged a party which lasted most of the night. Hamilton left early Saturday morning, and about ten o'clock Opal Long and Pat Cherrington, clad only in housedresses, went out to the store. No sooner had they left than things began happening.

Federal agents in St. Paul had received, along with other reports, a tip that suspicious characters were living at the Lexington Avenue address. J. M. Ladd, in charge of the St. Paul office, dispatched Special Agent Rufus C. Coulter, accompanied by Detective Henry Cummings of the St. Paul police department. The two rapped on the door, and a woman attired in a negligee opened it a crack.

"Is Carl here?" asked Coulter. John Dillinger had borrowed Pearl Hellman's name and was living in the apartment as Carl Hellman, but in the confusion of their many aliases Billie had forgotten it.

"Carl who?"

"Hellman."

"Oh! No, Carl isn't in. He may be back later this afternoon."

"Well," said the officers, "we can talk to you."

"Who are you?"

"Police officers."

"I'm sorry, but I'm not dressed. You'll have to wait a minute until I can get some clothes on."

Billie closed the door and bolted it. Dillinger was still in bed.

"Get up, Johnnie! It's the police!"

Dillinger was out of bed in an instant.

"What are we going to do?" Billie cried. "We're trapped."

"Keep your shirt on and hurry up. Get your grip and throw a few things into it."

Dillinger, meanwhile, was hastily dressing, and throwing money and clothes into his suitcase. Coulter left Cummings on guard, found a telephone to call for reinforcements, and raced back to his post in the hall.

At this crucial moment Rosser L. Nalls, another federal agent stationed outside, saw a man pull up in a green coupe and enter the building. That much was nothing out of the ordinary, but the next sight to greet Mr. Nalls was that of Agent Coulter running out of the building with the unidentified man chasing and shooting at him. Coulter escaped, and Homer Van Meter hurried back into the apartment house.

The bewildered Nalls called out to Coulter that his assailant had driven up in the green coupe, and Coulter immediately sent a bullet into its tire to flatten it. While this was going on, Van Meter slipped out the rear door of the building and gained a nearby street. A large coal truck chanced to drive by, and the bandit clambered into it. Opal Long and Pat Cherrington returned from the store about this time, and decided to keep walking. Pat went to join Hamilton, while Opal stopped at a nearby shop only long enough to purchase a black dress with a white collar, and the next morning was in Chicago breathlessly telling her story to Piquett and O'Leary.

While Coulter was escaping from Van Meter, Detective Cummings waited at the end of the hall for the occupants of the apartment to emerge. Dillinger, working rapidly, but with the utmost coolness, finished with his packing and then proceeded to clear a path for his and Evelyn's departure. With a specially made machine pistol, he raked the door with a volley of bullets and stepped out into the hall. Cummings emptied his pistol from around a corner, then fled downstairs to reload, hurried along by another burst fired in his direction. Dillinger and Billie made for the back stairway, the girl going ahead with the luggage while he covered her retreat.

Panting with exertion, Billie stumbled and fell in the alley, dropping the suitcases. Then she ran to the garage and brought out the car, pointing it toward Lexington Avenue. A moment later Dillinger appeared.

"Not that way," he called, as he saw the direction the car was facing. "Turn it around!"

Billie drove the car into the garage again, then backed it out in the direction indicated. Dillinger threw in the suitcases and climbed into the back seat.

"You drive," he told her. "I've been hit."

Billie saw his gray trousers soaked with blood and started to scream.

"It's nothing," he reassured her. "Drive to Eddie Green's. I'll tell you how to go."

This gunfight took place in a populated section of a large city, and the ease with which Dillinger escaped is almost unbelievable. Of course it was not known at the time that the gunman was Dillinger; that was established only after the police identified fingerprints found in the apartment.

Before long the Dillinger car reached Eddie Green's apartment on Fremont Avenue, and Evelyn hurried inside.

"Johnnie wants you down in the car, Eddie," she exclaimed. "He's hurt." Green slipped on his coat and ran downstairs.

"The police raided us," Dillinger told him. "Have you got a place where we can hole in? I caught a slug in the leg."

"We'd better get you a doctor."

"It's not bad. Do you know a doctor that will stand up?"

"I'll get Doc May. I've known him for years. He's a right guy."

Dr. Clayton E. May had practiced medicine in Minneapolis for many years, although, like many other basically reputable physicians, his standards had some flexibility. Green rushed to his office and told him he had a friend in urgent need of medical attention. The physician immediately drove with Green to the alley where Dillinger was waiting, examined the injury, and said, "We'll have to take him someplace where I can treat him. How about your apartment?"

"No," said Green. "It's too hot. Don't you know of some place, Doc?"

Dr. May had a working agreement with a nurse, Mrs. Augusta Salt, also known by her daughter's stage name of La Delle. Mrs. Salt maintained a sort of private nursing home in Minneapolis where she handled cases of abortion and venereal disease for Dr. May and others. It was here the wounded outlaw was conveyed with the help of Billie Frechette. The bullet had passed completely through the fleshy portion of the lower left leg, and the physician cleansed and dressed it.

Saturday evening Dr. May again visited his patient. Later that night he picked up Miss Dolores Smart, a gorgeous twenty-two-year-old blonde and the most beautiful of all the women associated with the Dillinger gang. The two drove up to Green's apartment, and while Beth Green entertained Dolores, Green and Dr. May talked privately in another room. It was at this time that Green revealed the identity of the injured man, and the first payment of money was made. All in all, Dr. May received a total of one thousand dollars, although on the witness stand he maintained that he had received no compensation whatever.

Thrilled, frightened, and elated at the events of the day, the adventurous Dr. May joined his platinum-haired companion, and the two passed the night in her room at the Ritz Hotel. Sunday he informed Green that Dillinger's wound was healing satisfactorily, and on Monday morning he made another call at the home of Mrs. Salt. His fourth and last visit was on Tuesday evening. He found Dillinger dressed and walking about, and decided that no further medical attention was necessary. On the morning of Wednesday, April 4, Dillinger and Billie informed Mrs. Salt they would be leaving, and on that same evening departed Minneapolis.

Among the many items found by federal agents in the hastily abandoned apartment was a telephone number scribbled on a slip of paper, and from it they learned where Green was staying. Concealing themselves in the apartment, the federal men soon bagged two colored maids, Lucy Jackson and Leona Goodman, who, amid much chattering of teeth, admitted that they had been sent by Green to pick up his clothing and take it to their home, where he would call for it. The agents accompanied the women and laid a new trap. On April 3 Green drove up with his wife, got out of his car, and knocked on the door. One of the maids opened it only enough to practically throw out the suitcase. As Green ran toward his car, a G-man in the living room shoved his Thompson's muzzle through the glass of a window and fired a burst of shots. Other agents also commenced firing at Green and at the car. Beth Green emerged from the machine.

"Please don't shoot anymore," she pleaded. "We're all alone."[33]

Mrs. Green ran to the side of her mortally wounded husband, but was pulled away by the federal men and taken into custody. Green was moved to a hospital, where he lingered in a semi-delirious condition until April 11. Questioned constantly during this time, and scarcely knowing what he was saying, Green told the investigators about Dr. May and furnished other information of much value.

The shooting of Green determined Dillinger to leave Minneapolis without delay. It likewise frightened Dr. May, who, fearing arrest, went into hiding, after counseling Mrs. Salt to do likewise. About a week or so later the two took up residence together in an apartment in Minneapolis. On April 17, federal men called and told Mrs. Salt that they wished to see Dr. May. As the physician entered the room, one of the agents said, "I suppose you know what we want you for."

"Well, I guess they have got us," was all he said.

As stated, John Dillinger and Evelyn Frechette fled Minneapolis on Wednesday, April 4, after hearing the news about Eddie Green. But where to go? All roads were barred, and federal, state, and local authorities had launched what newspapers were headlining as the greatest manhunt in U.S. history. So John Dillinger decided to go home. Mooresville, Indiana, he reasoned, was the last place in the world anyone would think to look. He reasoned correctly.

They left Minneapolis shortly after dusk, traveling by stealth and by roundabout routes. Dillinger's leg was not bothering him to any great extent, but the limp might attract attention, and he wanted to avoid the thousands of eyes that were searching every face for his. It took three days to reach Mooresville. Evelyn damaged the car in an accident near Noblesville, Indiana, on Saturday, April 7, but they purchased another machine and reached the old Dillinger home that same night.

Sunday was perhaps the last day of true happiness and rejoicing that the Dillinger family was ever to know. Old John Dillinger welcomed his son with real tears of joy, and his loved ones were ecstatic. John's sister, Mrs. Audrey Hancock, came down from Maywood and baked three of his favorite coconut cream pies. That was what he really had come home for, he told her, and so she offered to make some more for him to take with him when he left. But he took her in his arms, patted her head, and told her that she had already done enough. Nearly two years were to pass before Mrs. Hancock could bring herself to bake another coconut cream pie.

In the afternoon the sun shone brightly, and they went out to the side of the white farmhouse to take snapshots. John Dillinger stood in the yard with his wooden gun in one hand and a machine gun in the other. They also took a picture of Billie, whom Johnnie presented to the family as his wife. Where were the G-men and the police, who were supposed to be watching Mooresville as a matter of routine? For weeks they had been scouting overhead in airplanes, training high-powered field glasses on the house from the adjacent woods, and driving up and down the road in front. But no official automobiles traversed the road this day, and thus an incredible sight was missed: the most wanted man in America posing for family pictures, wearing a grin and holding his phony pistol and a very real submachine gun. The G-men had evidently assumed that he would never have the effrontery.

Virtually everyone in Mooresville knew that the town's most famous citizen had returned home for a family reunion, but it was some time before the authorities learned that the man they so desperately sought had come and gone under their very noses. Old John Dillinger discussed the visit without reluctance. His religious beliefs forbade him to lie, but he felt it was only right to wait until he was asked.

"Yes, John came down to look in on me," he said simply. "He was hurt in the leg, but not much. I talked with him for some time. But he isn't in Indiana now."

Al Feeney in the Indianapolis office of the state police denounced the people of Mooresville for not informing the authorities of Dillinger's homecoming, but Captain Matt Leach took an oddly tolerant view. "What good will it do?" he said. "Dillinger's come and gone, and under the law the old man's got a right to protect him."[34]

The citizens of Mooresville never felt unkindly toward John Dillinger. At this time they even were circulating a petition requesting Governor McNutt to grant amnesty if the outlaw would surrender.

Dillinger and Billie left Mooresville before sunup on April 9—a day destined to be eventful for Evelyn Frechette—and drove to Chicago. That afternoon Billie called O'Leary and arranged a meeting for three o'clock at Sacramento Avenue and Augusta Boulevard. Dillinger was in high spirits after his visit with his father, and spoke of the fine reception accorded them in Mooresville. He also told O'Leary about the gunplay in St. Paul, of how he had shot his way out of the trap. He mentioned the leg wound, and said that it no longer bothered him.

"How's Mr. Piquett?" then asked Dillinger, pronouncing the name, as he always did, "Pikwatt."

"He's fine," O'Leary answered. "He's in Washington right now."

"When he comes back, tell him that I expect to get some money to him very soon. I know that he's having a pretty tough time of it. And tell him to forget about the Pierpont thing. I've fixed it up."

They drove in silence for some minutes.

"By the way," Dillinger asked, "doesn't Piquett know a doctor who does plastic surgery work?"

O'Leary asked him why.

"I'd like to have him work on me. I want to live like other people. Billie and I would like to be married and settle down somewhere."

"I'll speak to him about it."

After leaving O'Leary, Dillinger telephoned Larry Strong, supposedly a friend, and spoke to him about arranging a hideout for a few days. An appointment was made to meet Strong at his tavern, the State-Austin Inn, 416 North State Street, at eight o'clock that evening. Unknown to Dillinger, "friend" Larry had recently turned informer, and he immediately did what informers do. John Dillinger was at heart a country boy and, despite his prison experience, still somewhat naive in the ways of the underworld. He was still learning that while this society may possess a few characters endowed with some redeeming qualities, on the whole it consists of conniving outcasts who mock the very notion that there is honor among thieves.

At the appointed time John Dillinger drove to the restaurant and parked around the corner while Billie Frechette went in. Before she could walk back out and mistakenly signal Dillinger that it was safe, five or six federal agents surrounded her with pistols and machine guns.

Dillinger, watching intently, saw the commotion and drove away unnoticed. Billie would irritate her captors greatly by insisting that Dillinger had been elsewhere in the room when the agents pounced, and had simply strolled past them out the door.

Billie was taken to the federal offices in the Bankers' Building and, according to her story, was handcuffed and questioned throughout the night. The following morning, Tuesday, April 10, Agents Harold H. Reinecke and Murray C. Falkner arrived on the scene, and for the next two days took charge of the questioning. During her harboring trial in St. Paul a few weeks later, some serious discrepancies marked the testimony concerning her interrogation. Miss Frechette stated that she was given nothing to eat Tuesday or Wednesday, and was not permitted to sleep. The agents insisted that they had sent out for whatever she wanted whenever she wanted, but inasmuch as they were not present at night, they had no way of knowing if she slept or not.

The testimony likewise conflicted as to the manner in which the questioning was conducted. The following extract is from the cross-examination of Agent Reinecke by A. Jerome Hoffman, Billie's attorney.

Q. Isn't it a fact, Mr. Reinecke, that you yourself slapped this girl in the face?

A. I did not slap this girl at any time.

Q. Isn't it a fact that you continually went like that to her under the chin? (Indicating with right hand)

A. I think I can explain what you are alluding to, if you will permit me.

Q. Alright, go ahead.

A. Miss Frechette had a manner of not looking me in the eyes when I was talking to her. When her head would be down, I would take the tips of my fingers, on one or two occasions, and raise up her chin, and I said, "Please Evelyn, look at me when you are telling me, and answering my questions."

Miss Frechette told the story differently.

Q. By the way, did you hear Agent Reinecke say that he on several occasions lifted up your chin with his finger, and asked you, "Please Evelyn, look me in the eye."

A. Yes, I heard him say that.

Q. Did that occur?

A. Well, he didn't lift up my chin, and he didn't say "Please."

Q. But he did have his hand under your chin?

A. Yes. I would say he hit it up, instead of lifting it up.

Q. And were you, or were you not, faced with a lot of lights in that room?

A. Well, when I first got in this building Monday night I was. I remember one fellow coming over there and saying, "Well, maybe Evelyn wouldn't like these lights," and he shone them right in my face.

Wherever the truth may lie, there was no doubt in John Dillinger's mind that Agent Reinecke had struck the girl he loved. It was only the outlaw's death that saved Reinecke, for the federal agent's name was marked above all others as one Dillinger firmly intended to kill.

Billie states that on Wednesday night she was permitted to sleep for a few hours on the chairs in the federal offices. Inasmuch as Piquett was now striving desperately to secure her release, she was awakened during the night and taken to the Lansing Apartments, at 1036 North Dearborn Street. Three federal agents, she testified, remained with her in that apartment until a warrant was obtained from United States Commissioner Edwin K. Walker for her removal to St. Paul.

It was only a few minutes after Billie Frechette's arrest that Dillinger reached O'Leary at his apartment hotel on Pine Grove.

"Hello, Art. The G's just picked up Billie in a restaurant at State and Austin" [now Hubbard Street].

"How did it happen?"

"I was sitting in my car right around the corner. There were too many of them for me to take her away. It was that rat Larry Strong who put her on the spot. Where's Mr. Piquett? Is he still in Washington?"

O'Leary said he was.

"Well, phone him right away, and tell him to try and get a writ to get Billie out."

O'Leary telephoned Piquett that same night at the Willard Hotel in Washington and told him the news. During his trial Piquett stated that this call came from Dillinger, but the incident was evidently confused in his mind. Piquett asked attorney Paul Pomeroy to obtain a writ of habeas corpus, and arrived in Chicago himself on April 11. The government had tried to maintain secrecy about Evelyn Frechette's arrest. Some newspapers got wind of it, but reporters could get details only from Piquett. Melvin Purvis refused to comment.

About this time John Dillinger reverted to his former amusement of holding up police stations. On the night of April 12 policeman Judd Pittinger was walking his beat around the streets of Warsaw, Indiana, when he suddenly found himself in the custody of Dillinger and Van Meter. He was forced to accompany the pair back to the Warsaw police station, where they forced the gun case, took out two revolvers and four bulletproof vests—a disappointing haul—and then went on their way.

Dillinger and Van Meter returned to Chicago immediately, as the former was anxious for news of Billie Frechette. During this time they were variously reported in Pittsburgh, Pennsylvania; South Bend and Elkhart, Indiana; Niles, Michigan; and other places, but in reality they never left Chicago except for the Warsaw excursion.

Dillinger did not mention his place of residence during this week, but from various intimations the gang probably had their hideout above a barbecue stand and restaurant at North and Harlem avenues, operated by Jimmy Murray.[35]

Evelyn Frechette was arraigned on Friday, April 13, before Commissioner Walker on the proceedings for her removal to St. Paul. Louis Piquett was on hand to represent her. The district attorney, evidently considering the girl a dangerous and important prisoner, requested that her bond be set at $200,000.

"That's asinine!" shouted Piquett, and the bond was finally set at $60,000 by Commissioner Walker. Either amount was beyond the financial capacity of John Dillinger.

O'Leary had another meeting with Dillinger the next night at Belden and Campbell avenues. A light spring rain was falling. Walking along one side of the street, O'Leary thought he saw Dillinger on the other, and tipped his hat. The other man did likewise. This is the accepted underworld signal used by one party to the other that he is "clean," or not being followed. To walk with one or both hands on the lapel of the coat, or to expectorate, is a danger signal warning of a "tail." O'Leary crossed the street.

"Hello, Art. Get in the car."

As O'Leary climbed into the front seat, he noticed two men in the back. Dillinger's hat was pulled down to conceal his face, and O'Leary suddenly feared that he had walked into a police trap.

"Johnnie!" he said. "Is it you?"

"Of course it's me.

"Take off your hat."

"Okay. What's the matter?"

"I just wasn't sure, especially with those fellows in the back."

Dillinger laughed as he introduced "Red" Hamilton. O'Leary noted the missing fingers as he shook the man's hand. No introduction was made for the other dark, tall individual, but from occasional glances and the fact that Dillinger addressed the man as "Van," he surmised it was Van Meter. Van Meter evidently wanted to form his own opinion of O'Leary before revealing his identity.

The men discussed the Frechette arraignment on the preceding day. Dillinger requested that Piquett find out when and how Billie was to be conveyed to St. Paul, so that the gang might liberate her from the federal officers.

Another meeting was called two days later, at four o'clock on the afternoon of April 16, at North and Kedzie avenues. Dillinger had arranged it by telephone, simply giving the time and "32 west and 16 north," to denote the location of the streets. Hamilton sat in the rear of the car with a machine gun under a lap robe. Pat Cherrington was in the front with Dillinger, but when O'Leary arrived she clambered into the back.

O'Leary reported that so far he had been unable to find out how Billie Frechette would be taken to St. Paul for trial. The truth was that neither he nor Piquett wanted anything to do with such a potentially bloody venture, and they had made no efforts to obtain the information. Dillinger was visibly disappointed, and O'Leary counseled him to try to win Billie's freedom by legal means.

"Will Mr. Piquett go to St. Paul and help defend her?" the outlaw asked.

"I'll have to speak to him, but I'm sure that he will."

"That's fine, Art. Here, give him this five hundred dollars. By the way, did you hear anything more about the doctor who does the plastic surgery?"

"Yes. Lou says his name is Dr. Ralph Robeind."

"Did you find out what he charges?"

"It will cost you five thousand dollars."

"Five grand! Don't you think that's pretty high?"

"Not when you consider how dangerous it is. Hell, man, don't you realize that you're the hottest person in the whole United States?"

"Well, then I guess it will have to be all right, if he does a good job. Keep in touch with him. And I also want you and Mr. Piquett to see about finding me a good hideout somewhere here in town. We're all leaving for St. Paul right away to hole in for a while. I'll get in touch as soon as I get back."

Dillinger, Hamilton, and Pat Cherrington headed north after leaving Chicago to visit Hamilton's sister, Mrs. Anna Steve, who lived in Algonquin, a suburb of Sault Ste. Marie, Michigan. They arrived late on the night of Tuesday, April 17, and departed the next morning for St. Paul, where they would meet the other members of the gang.

This visit to Hamilton's sister had been tipped off to federal agents by a stool pigeon. The next evening two planeloads of G-men arrived at the home of Mrs. Steve, taking over the house and conducting a search of the surrounding country. No trace of the outlaws was found, although Mrs. Steve was taken into custody.

For affording a night's shelter to her brother when in the company of an interstate car thief, Mrs. Steve was tried and sentenced on June 7, 1935, to three months in jail.[36]

CHAPTER FOURTEEN

SLAUGHTER OF INNOCENTS

The events in St. Paul, including the raid on Dillinger's apartment and the killing of Eddie Green, disrupted the Dillinger gang. During the next few weeks word circulated in favor of a meeting where plans would be laid for future operations. Although St. Paul was most convenient, they were too well known there for safety or comfort, and so, after initial contact was made, they immediately set out for a more secluded spot.

About thirteen miles from the northern Wisconsin town of Mercer, in the midst of a wild hunting and fishing region, lies the lodge of Little Bohemia, so-called by its proprietor, Emil Wanatka, in tribute to his native land. The lodge itself is a large, rambling two-story affair, the lower portion constructed of logs, while the upper story has wood siding painted white. A long, narrow road leads to it from the main highway, and on one side of the building are a number of cottages for the accommodation of surplus guests. Behind the complex is a small lake.

This place was chosen by the Dillinger gang for what would be their last general reunion, and here they began arriving early on the afternoon of Friday, April 20. In some respects the selection was not a judicious one; the hunting and fishing season had not yet opened, and the arrival of a large party aroused the curiosity of the few inhabitants of this desolate region. However, the very remoteness of the lodge afforded the outlaws a measure of security.[37]

John Dillinger was there, of course, but he was deprived of a female companion since the arrest of Evelyn Frechette; John Hamilton and his current love, Patricia Cherrington, had arrived with him. Homer Van Meter had come up from Chicago, bringing along his sweetheart, Marie Comforti. Marie, a small Italian girl, had attracted Van Meter with her pertness and free and easy manner. She had piercing dark eyes and was naturally a brunette, although during this period of her life she had transformed herself into a blonde. She was given to displays of irritability, while her amusements included cabarets, dancing, and an occasional off-color joke.

The remainder of the party comprised "Baby Face" Nelson and his much-devoted wife, Helen Gillis; Tommy Carroll and his wife, Jean Crompton; and Pat Reilly, a one-time mascot of the St. Paul baseball club and now a hanger-on with underworld characters, although not an inside member. Thus there was a total of ten persons—six men and four women—five of the men constituting what is generally spoken of as the Dillinger gang.

Emil Wanatka and his wife may have viewed the off-season group as a windfall, but they kept their eyes and ears wide open to learn the identities of their guests. At a later date, when Mr. Wanatka had tasted publicity and found it to his liking, he blossomed forth with an outlandish tale of Dillinger and his gangsters sweeping down upon them with machine guns and taking the lodge by force; of how he was constantly guarded by the desperadoes but managed to slip out a note in a package of cigarettes; and much more of a like nature which he thought would make good reading.

The truth of the matter is that the gang had no other thought in mind than finding a safe retreat. They tried to conduct themselves like any other guests, and certainly at no time went about proclaiming themselves gunmen and bank robbers. Except for an occasional conference among the men, the three days at the lodge were passed by playing cards, strolling in the woods, and the customary eating and drinking. The guns were kept out of sight, but, as John Dillinger afterwards remarked, "you couldn't whisper your own thoughts to your pillow without Mrs. Wanatka knowing all about it ten minutes afterward."

The Wanatkas and their relatives, Henry Voss and his wife, talked the matter over and concluded that Emil's guests were none other than the infamous Dillinger gang. As good citizens they felt obliged to report this to the authorities. Though not entirely oblivious to the prospects of fame and fortune, they knew this entailed some risks, and decided to give out the information from Rhinelander, Wisconsin, located about fifty miles away.

It was shortly after midday on the eventful April 22, a Sunday, when Melvin Purvis received word from Rhinelander that the much-wanted Mr. Dillinger was sojourning at Little Bohemia. Purvis acted with celerity and dispatch, and soon the Bureau's Chicago office was a scene of wild confusion. Agents were hastily recalled from other assignments, and frantic telephone calls were made to Washington and St. Paul.

The considerable distance involved, and the fact that the Dillinger party might pack up at any moment, made it imperative that airplanes be used. Within hours, two planeloads, carrying eleven agents with machine guns, teargas guns, rifles, and steel vests, took off from the Chicago airport, while arrangements were made for reinforcements to follow in two automobiles. The federal office in St. Paul was at the same time sending five men by plane, with more to follow by motor.

It was early evening when the Chicago expedition reached the airfield at Rhinelander and found the St. Paul plane already there. The problem of securing automobiles for the fifty-mile journey to Little Bohemia proved a serious one. Five cars of differing vintage and mobility were commandeered, but two of them broke down, forcing their eight occupants to complete the journey in frozen misery on the running boards of the other machines. The caravan's progress was excruciatingly slow, recent rains having rendered the gravel roads almost impassable.

The G-men left their cars a short distance below Little Bohemia, and silently made their way through the dense woods to the driveway leading to the lodge. Purvis and five other agents, clad in bulletproof vests, were to make a frontal attack, while two other parties, consisting of five men each, were ordered to approach the building from the right and the left. The lodge itself was brightly illuminated, and cast its light into the dark wilderness of trees.

Three men, two wearing blue denim overalls and the other clad in a mackinaw, emerged from the lighted doorway and entered a parked automobile. The federal agents, their minds filled only with thoughts of Dillinger, began shouting at them to halt. The men heard no one say they were officers. Confused by the yelling all around, perceiving only that there was trouble, the driver threw the car into gear and tried to escape. Nervous fingers went to the machine guns, and the agents, forgetting there might be innocent people in the lodge, blazed away. Eugene Boisoneau, an adviser at one of the government's CCC camps, died. John Morris, the chef at the CCC camp, was struck four times. John Hoffman, an oil station attendant at Mercer, Wisconsin, was wounded in the arms, but managed to run off.

The strains of a dance orchestra from the radio in the bullet-riddled machine, mingled with the cries of the wounded men who lay in it unattended, added a touch of the macabre as the excited agents tried to decide what to do next.

The federal agents would blame that night's ever-worsening fiasco on the barking of the dogs about the lodge, and the warning this supposedly gave the outlaws. In justice to the canines, it should be said that the members of the gang had become accustomed to their frequent outbursts and paid them no attention. Dillinger later declared that he had been playing cards with some of the others, and that the first intimation of the danger was the roar of gunfire outside. He and the others dashed up the stairs to their rooms, and soon machine guns were protruding from the windows in the second story of the lodge. Emil Wanatka, at the first sound of shots, opened the trapdoor in the barroom and made for the security of the cellar.

For a few minutes a pitched battle raged. The gangsters, believing at first they were surrounded, fired away at unseen attackers in the woods. The group under Purvis lost no time in replying, but for some time heard nothing from their two supporting columns. The party approaching the right side of the building had become entangled in barbed wire and saw no service while the battle lasted. The quintet coming up on the other side were delayed by stumbling into a drainage ditch, but regrouped in time to add their own fireworks to the display.

It took the agents some time to realize that the firing from the house had ceased. But the outlaws had already noted the absence of any assault from the rear, and decided on that avenue of escape. Climbing from the rear upstairs windows, they slid down the sloping roofs of the lodge, and proceeded toward the lake. Once they gained the security of the woods, the gang split up. Nelson and Carroll each went in separate directions, while Dillinger, Van Meter, and Hamilton elected to stay together. Feeling their way around trees and bushes, the three covered nearly a mile before coming to a resort owned by E. H. Mitchell, an elderly gray-haired man. Dillinger went ahead.

"Don't be afraid," he told Mitchell. "We're not going to hurt you. We're looking for a car."

Mitchell had only a small truck, but an employee, Ray Johnson, owned a coupe which they took over. Johnson was ordered to drive them to Park Falls, Wisconsin, where they ejected him from the car and continued on their way.

Purvis, when the shooting began, had dispatched agents W. Carter Baum and J. C. Newman to try to telephone for reinforcements. The local exchange was located in a nearby hotel resort owned by Alvin Koerner, and the pair were driven there by Deputy Constable Carl Christensen of Spider Lake. As they drew up in the yard, "Baby Face" Nelson, attempting to escape in that direction, stepped from the shadows.

"Who's there?" he shouted.

"We're federal agents," they called back, mistaking him for one of the members of the raiding party.

"Get out of the car!" he ordered.

Somewhat mystified, the three started to comply. As they stepped to the ground, Nelson opened fire. Baum was killed instantly with a bullet in the head. Christensen fell with several slugs in his body. Newman attempted to seize the outlaw's gun, but was knocked unconscious by a bullet which grazed his forehead without doing serious damage.

Nelson drove off in the wounded constable's car, which was found several days later about twenty miles east of Mercer. From there he made his way through sparsely populated country to the Indian reservation at Lac Du Flambeau, and for a period of four days took up residence with an Indian named Ollie Catfish. Any dog in the vicinity which ventured to bark risked death by the gangster's gun, and the unfortunate Indian saw his slender stock of provisions entirely consumed by his unwelcome guest, until at the end of the visit the two were reduced to eating lard. Tiring of this unpalatable fare, Nelson stole the automobile of Adolph Goetz, a mail carrier, and made his escape from the neighborhood.

At Little Bohemia, Purvis and his men had continued to besiege the house, now garrisoned only by Helen Gillis, Marie Comforti, and Jean Crompton. Earlier in the day Pat Reilly had driven Patricia Cherrington to St. Paul, and the outlaws were expecting their return about the time the shooting began. The two arrived shortly after the first attack had subsided, but another blast of federal machine-gun fire convinced them to turn their car around. In their own flight, they encountered the machine in which Dillinger, Van Meter, and Hamilton were making their escape. Van Meter was tossing bundles of money out of the car, evidently part of the ransom from the Bremer kidnaping. Pat Cherrington stopped to pick up the money, which she returned to him later.[38]

For over six hours the federal agents huddled outside in the cold, not venturing to light fires for fear of revealing their positions. No sign of life came from the lodge, where the three women clung to each other in terror while Emil hunkered in the basement.

About four o'clock in the morning Purvis, his party now reinforced by more agents and members of a local posse, gave the word to advance. The storming party approached on the right side of the house, and began shooting teargas shells through the windows. Several of these bounced off the log walls and exploded, sending their fumes back upon the attackers. A woman's face appeared at one of the windows.

"Don't shoot anymore," she called. "We'll come out." Three white-faced girls, hands in the air and shaking with fear, came filing through the door.

The three prisoners, Helen Gillis, Marie Comforti, and Jean Crompton, were conveyed to Madison, Wisconsin, and indicted on May 19. On May 25 they were sentenced to a year and a day, but were placed on probation by Federal Judge Patrick T. Stone with an injunction to return home and behave themselves in the future. This apparent leniency was granted in the expectation that the girls would lead federal agents to their men. Nor did any of the three fail to violate her probation within a short period of time.

Thus ended the Battle of Little Bohemia, and the federal agents never lived it down. The net result was one federal agent and one citizen killed; one federal agent, one local police officer, and two citizens wounded; and no gangster captured—only three women they had to leave behind. A wave of indignation not only swept this country but occurred throughout the world. Reports from Washington hinted that Director Hoover would be demoted or even fired if Dillinger remained at large. Senator Schall of Minnesota declared, "The Bureau of Investigation needs fewer politicians and more detectives." Berlin saw in the entire Dillinger affair a vindication of Hitler and the Nazi program of sterilization. Britain likewise took considerable notice, and certain London papers informed their readers that red Indians had taken to the warpath, hunting Dillinger with their bows and arrows.

A citizens' committee in Mercer, Wisconsin, brought forth a petition blaming the fiasco on Purvis and demanding his dismissal from federal service. Chambers of commerce passed resolutions of censure, and a grand jury investigated the killing of Eugene Boisoneau. The federal men had not fired upon the CCC workers with murderous intent, of course, but their apparent recklessness brought almost unanimous criticism.

In fairness to Mr. Purvis, he accomplished much in the time he had, and he demonstrated personal bravery in leading his men while under fire. In retrospect, a closer cooperation with local authorities and citizens familiar with the area might very well have made the difference between victory and acute embarrassment. The citizens of Mercer concluded, fairly or not, that the federal agents had wanted to "hog all the glory." In any case, the federal government found itself forced to stoop very low indeed for allies before the career of John Dillinger was finally brought to an end.[39]

Little Bohemia left the nation feeling that the government had suffered an ignominious defeat. But the hurried transportation of agents, the painful hours in the cold, even the appalling number of casualties, were not to prove in vain. The backbone of the gang had been broken, and it was never able to reunite in its once-formidable power. The crest was reached at Little Bohemia—and thereafter began a steady decline that ended in death and extinction.

The first blow was to fall with sudden and terrible force. Following the ejection of Ray Johnson from his own car at Park Falls, Dillinger, Hamilton, and Van Meter raced toward St. Paul. While still on the road, they learned that news of the resort battle had preceded them, and the city was on the alert. They quickly turned and headed south, in the direction of Chicago, but a short distance south of St. Paul, in the vicinity of St. Paul Park and Hastings, Minnesota, they encountered deputies Joseph Heinen, Larry Dunn, and Norman Dieter. Newspaper accounts described the usual police heroics: orders to stop met with a rain of bullets, a ten-mile running gun battle, a truck suddenly emerging from a side road and enabling the bandits to escape. What really happened was told by both Dillinger and Van Meter to O'Leary and other persons.

By the afternoon of April 23, the three fugitives found themselves utterly exhausted. They had been driving steadily since the previous night, and the constant sense of danger had badly frayed their nerves. Their eyelids were refusing to remain open, and finding themselves away from St. Paul and on a lonely country road, they stopped the car to sleep for an hour or two. All three dozed off sitting in the coupe—Dillinger behind the wheel, Hamilton in the middle, and Van Meter next to the passenger-side door.

The distant crack of shots and the shirring of bullets awakened them with a start. Hamilton's hands clutched at his two companions.

"I'm hit!" he gasped, and then slumped forward.

Dillinger and Van Meter looked out the back window and saw a police car stopped in the road nearly a quarter of a mile away, with the three deputies shooting at them with high-powered rifles. Dillinger stood on one running board, Van Meter on the other, and returned the fire with pistols. After an exchange which lasted a minute or two, the police car turned around and sped off, probably to secure reinforcements, and possibly because Dillinger had placed one or two bullets dangerously close.

"What hurt us was that we didn't have a rifle in the car," Dillinger said afterwards. "If I'd had a good rifle, not one of those cops would have come away."

The two outlaws jumped back into the car and left the neighborhood before the deputies returned with increased forces. Dillinger drove while Van Meter administered as best he could to the stricken Hamilton. A rifle bullet had punched through the trunk lid and the car seat, entering his back and lodging in his intestines. There was a hole "the size of a silver dollar," as Dillinger later described it, and blood soaked the entire seat cushion.

The gun battle had of course rendered Ray Johnson's stolen coupe somewhat conspicuous, and every police car in the state would soon be looking for them. Dillinger spotted a new maroon sedan approaching and blocked the road with his own machine. The driver, Roy E. Francis, was forced to stop.

"Get out!" the gang leader commanded, and Francis and his wife quickly obeyed.

"Stand over there and keep your backs turned." This order was necessary because Dillinger had to pocket his gun while helping Van Meter carry Hamilton from the one car to the other.

Leaving the Francis couple and the shot-up coupe, they continued south, following pretty closely the eastern bank of the Mississippi. Hamilton was in excruciating pain, and it became apparent that he would never survive the trip to Chicago. Late that night they decided to stop and do whatever they could for their dying companion. They found an old shack at the abandoned Reisbeck mine, near the hamlet of Jenkinsville. This spot is located in the southwestern corner of Wisconsin, and incidentally only about five miles from Piquett's home town of Platteville.

Early the next morning the two left Hamilton in the hut and drove to Dubuque, Iowa, the nearest large city, where they purchased surgical supplies and newspapers reporting the Little Bohemia affair. After returning, Dillinger plied a farmer with liberal sums of money for some milk, eggs, and other articles of food. This farmer committed suicide a short time afterward, conceivably out of fear that his assistance to the outlaws would be discovered. "Red" Hamilton proved to be mortally wounded, and they were able to do little for him. Dillinger and Van Meter both stated that Hamilton died on the fourth day after he had been shot, in extreme agony until the last. This would place the date of his death on Friday, April 27, 1934.

Where was John Hamilton buried? On August 28, 1935, federal agents dug up a body in a shallow grave just outside Oswego, Illinois, in the vicinity of Aurora. According to the official explanation, they were directed to this spot by workmen reporting that the grass and weeds there were stunted in growth. The face and hands of the body were so badly eaten away by lye and the effects of decomposition that it could not be recognized, but the federal men declared that they knew it was Hamilton because the dentist at the Michigan City penitentiary identified it by the teeth.

As for the disposition of Hamilton's body, Piquett's and O'Leary's stories differ. Louis Piquett does not believe that the Oswego body is that of Hamilton. He says Dillinger told him specifically that they passed the entire time until the death of Hamilton at the abandoned mine. Further than that the outlaw would not go, but Piquett reasons that it would be both dangerous and senseless to convey a dead body in a car from western Wisconsin to Oswego. On a subsequent visit to Platteville, Piquett visited the Reisbeck mine. The shaft of the mine is a straight one, filled with perhaps twenty feet of water. He found the hut just as Dillinger had described it, and within it a few articles which the outlaws had used. Close to the mouth of the shaft was a huge abandoned bull wheel, weighing perhaps a ton, and which many years before had been cracked and broken into three pieces of about equal size. Inquiries in the neighborhood revealed that about the time of the outlaws' visit, one of these pieces disappeared. The supposition is that Dillinger and Van Meter, both powerful men, weighted Hamilton's body with this heavy section of wheel and pushed it into the waters of the flooded mine.

O'Leary's story is as follows. Shortly after their return to Chicago, he questioned Dillinger and Van Meter about Hamilton, but both only looked downcast and made no reply. A few days later, however, they told him the story in some detail. Dillinger stated that it was his desire to bury Hamilton in the sand dunes that line the Indiana shores of Lake Michigan. He went on, "Van and I dug a good deep grave, and after we put Red's body in it we poured four cans of lye over it, so they can never recognize him even if they do find him."

"There's only one other person that knows where Red's buried beside Van and myself," Dillinger went on, "and that's Jimmy [Nelson]. But I don't mind telling you, if you'd care to know. Maybe you can use it to bargain with, if you ever run into trouble."

"Count me out," said O'Leary. "I don't want to know. If they ever find him, I don't want you thinking that I was the one who did the talking."

O'Leary believes that the Oswego body may be that of Hamilton, but he does not feel at all certain. There is no doubt that the fugitives spent some time in the neighborhood of Platteville and Dubuque, but he is of the opinion that they stopped at the mine only long enough to doctor Hamilton. The wounded man would therefore have died somewhere between Dubuque and Chicago, and in that case the burial at Oswego would be explained. On the other hand, Dillinger specifically mentioned the dunes. It is possible that the gang's associates in northwestern Indiana, not wishing to have Hamilton's body found in their back yard, dug it up and reburied it at Oswego.

One naturally wonders if the remains exhumed at Oswego are really those of Hamilton. This is supported by the discovery of bullet fragments lodged in the back, where Dillinger and Van Meter described the wound. Likewise, traces of lye were found. Efforts of the state of Indiana and others to see the coroner's report have been unsuccessful, as the entire matter appears to be a jealously guarded secret of the federal government. However, if it is true, as reported, that the body had only two fingers missing from the right hand, it will be recalled that Hamilton had a third digit from the same hand shot off in the East Chicago holdup. Moreover, Dillinger and Van Meter both said that they had dug a deep grave, whereas the scant two-foot excavation at Oswego could certainly not be so described. It is regrettable that the government has not chosen to reveal further details regarding the dental identification, as well as the qualifications of the dentist and any possible remuneration he may have received.

How did the federal agents learn of the mysterious grave at Oswego? The explanation of the stunted grass is less than plausible. The discovery took place after a year had afforded plenty of time for new growth. Furthermore, there are thousands of spots of stunted grass where government agents were not observed digging.

There is one other possible explanation. Dillinger remarked that Nelson knew the place, and Nelson, for all his less endearing qualities, was devoted to his wife. He may have placed the secret in her keeping for use in securing clemency, should the occasion ever arise. It could be significant that the day after the discovery of Hamilton's body, newspapers reported that Helen Gillis would be released from the federal prison at Milan, Michigan. She was, moreover, placed on probation that included an injunction to secrecy.

One or two other matters relate to John Hamilton. Shortly after the Little Bohemia incident, O'Leary and Piquett found themselves besieged day after day by Pat Cherrington. She was not only eager for news of Hamilton, but in straitened financial circumstances, and begged them to so inform Dillinger. O'Leary brought this to Dillinger's attention on several occasions, adding that he was having difficulty answering her questions and pleas.

"Pat Cherrington was in the office again today," he told Dillinger one night when they met outside the city.

"Give this to her," Dillinger replied, handing him a sealed letter. "Tell her I'll send her some money in a few days."

It was almost midnight when O'Leary arrived back in Chicago. He went directly to Miss Cherrington's room in the Chateau Hotel, 3838 Broadway, but found her out and left a note to call him at the office. About two o'clock in the morning, however, there was a knock on O'Leary's door, and Pat Cherrington and Opal Long came rushing into the apartment.

Not wishing to disturb his sleeping family, he took the two girls into the bathroom, closed the door, and handed Dillinger's note to Pat. The missive described the shooting near St. Paul, and stated that Hamilton had died in his arms four days later. It went on to say that "Red" had only a small sum of money, and that Van Meter had appropriated it toward debts Hamilton owed.

Pat Cherrington became hysterical, weeping and screaming despite all efforts of Mr. O'Leary to calm her before she awakened the entire hotel. She heaped curses on the head of Homer Van Meter, and told of how she had recovered and restored to him the money he had tossed from the car after Little Bohemia. Finally O'Leary persuaded the two girls to leave, and then destroyed the note sent to Pat by Dillinger.

A few days later, Pat Cherrington and her sister Opal received a sum of money from John Dillinger sufficient to relieve their wants if not their minds.

The other incident relates to Hamilton's final resting place. About a month or so before Dillinger's death, Louis Piquett conceived the thought that if Hamilton's grave was offered to the government, a tidy sum might come their way, and he told O'Leary to propose it to Dillinger. The desperado flew into a rage at the suggestion, and O'Leary quickly changed the subject.

As John Dillinger said one time, "Red sure was a hard-luck guy. Whenever we went on a job he came back full of lead. They wounded him at East Chicago, they wounded him at Mason City, and then they killed him in St. Paul. He was a cinch to get it, sooner or later."

John Hamilton is dead—there is no doubt about that. Perhaps circumstances attending his burial will someday be revealed.[40]

CHAPTER FIFTEEN

THE SAFEST PLACE
IN AMERICA

After the shooting episode near St. Paul and the resultant death of Hamilton, John Dillinger again disappeared. Yet scarcely was a crime of violence committed anywhere in the country without his being suspected or identified. Three police officers held up by hoodlums in Bellwood, Illinois, declared at first that it must have been the Dillinger gang. On that same day, April 30, the Dillinger home at Mooresville was raided by more than a score of Indiana state police and G-men, three weeks after the desperado's visit. They found old John Dillinger repairing the fence, but nothing of greater moment. It was reported on May 5 that Dillinger and Van Meter had robbed the bank in Fostoria, Ohio.

About the same time arose the flurry of reports that America's Public Enemy Number One had departed for Europe. The genesis of these totally unfounded rumors was a jesting remark made by Louis Piquett to a newspaper reporter who by his persistency had made himself a pest. One day Piquett, seeking at least temporary deliverance, took him by the arm and led him aside.

"I'll let you in on something," he confided. "I don't know where Dillinger is right now, but the last time I heard from him he told me that he was setting out for England."

Instantly the stories flew about that the famous fugitive was on the high seas. A close watch was kept in the ports of Glasgow,

Greenock, Belfast, and Liverpool, and the steamship *Duchess of York* was searched three times in one day. Even Scotland Yard took cognizance of the yarns, although apparently not crediting them heavily.

Where did the Dillinger gang hide after the death of John Hamilton? The answer is that, like the snail, they carried their house with them. Of all the bizarre and amusing adventures in the life of this extraordinary criminal, this is perhaps the most fantastic.

On the fifth day of May or thereabouts O'Leary received a telephone call from Dillinger instructing him to be at a place in South Chicago that evening. Driving by the appointed spot, O'Leary saw Dillinger and picked him up. They proceeded along the road to a rather desolate spot about four or five miles west of East Chicago, Indiana, and then stopped next to a closed truck that was bright red in color. Much to O'Leary's surprise, Tommy Carroll was occupying the driver's seat, while the face of Homer Van Meter peered from the window in the rear.

Dillinger remained in O'Leary's car and recounted their recent adventures. They had arrived in Chicago around the end of April, and remained there for a few days while purchasing the truck. About May 1 they went on the road, but spent much of their time in a timbered region near East Chicago. Dillinger said they were sleeping in a small wooden shack, but that it was in terrible condition, with windows broken or missing and a leaking roof. When not staying in the hut, and particularly after dark, they passed the time by driving about the roads of northwestern Indiana.

A few days before, Tommy Carroll had joined them from St. Paul, arriving on a freight train dressed as a hobo and carrying his money in a belt about his waist. Dillinger and Van Meter went to meet him at Indiana Harbor and conveyed him to East Chicago, feeling that he could reside there unrecognized and provide them with supplies. Carroll was contacted about every other day and furnished them with cooked food, as well as canned goods which they stored in the truck along with a double mattress that provided an alternate sleeping arrangement.

This night Dillinger particularly wanted news of Evelyn Frechette, who was then in St. Paul. He also told O'Leary to remember the appearance of the truck, in the event that they should arrange further meetings. O'Leary, noting the color, said he doubted he could miss it.

Two weeks elapsed before O'Leary again saw Dillinger, on May

19. This night he drove out to the rendezvous in a borrowed Packard instead of his customary Ford, and proceeded to a tavern on Indianapolis Boulevard, on the outskirts of Chicago. After about an hour, the red truck appeared. O'Leary followed it several miles into the country. The truck stopped and he pulled up behind it at the side of the road.

O'Leary found Dillinger desperately ill with a cold, evidently contracted while sleeping in the drafty truck and the abandoned shack in the woods. His temperature had reached 104 degrees, and it was feared that the fever might culminate in pneumonia. Dillinger was in fact so sick that he could no longer remain at the wheel, and O'Leary drove the truck around the back roads of Indiana from about eight o'clock until midnight. Van Meter remained in the back throughout this time, watching out of the two small windows in the rear doors while holding a machine gun. Dillinger was afraid to seek medical attention in his old haunts in East Chicago, and requested O'Leary to return the following night with medicines.

Piquett had arrived in Chicago earlier that day on a weekend recess from the Frechette trial, bringing with him a note from Billie, which O'Leary delivered to Dillinger. There had evidently been some previous correspondence between the two, for much of her letter was taken up with dissuading Dillinger from attempting her liberation. Her reason, she declared, was that he might be killed, and she assured him that if found guilty she would do her time cheerfully in the knowledge he would be there waiting upon her release.

Dillinger was much affected by this communication, and read and reread it many times. He gave O'Leary six hundred dollars to pay Piquett for his services in the trial, and promised him that the balance would be forthcoming soon.

It was on this night that Dillinger told O'Leary the circumstances of Hamilton's death, and also gave him the note to deliver to Pat Cherrington. An amusing bit of conversation likewise occurred. Dillinger related that they had spent several days in a tourist camp in Crown Point.

"Weren't you afraid to go back there?" O'Leary asked.

Dillinger chuckled. "Why, Crown Point's the safest place in America."

As promised, O'Leary drove out the next night with a bottle of cough syrup and a pint of whiskey for the ailing Dillinger. The meeting was arranged for a side road on the outskirts of Indiana Harbor, and O'Leary was to flash his lights four times as a signal.

The headlight glare from an oncoming car prevented him from seeing the truck until he was nearly on top of it, however, and he remembered with some apprehension that Van Meter's machine gun would be pointing straight at him. The truck pulled over without incident, fortunately, and Dillinger came back to join O'Leary in his car.

The meeting on this night lasted only half an hour. Dillinger thanked O'Leary for the medicine and the whiskey, but the thoughts uppermost in his mind concerned Evelyn Frechette, and he talked mostly of her. He gave O'Leary a note for Piquett to deliver to Billie, and which, as with the other, Piquett and O'Leary exercised the postman's prerogative of reading. Much of the letter was taken up with expressions of affection. It also informed her of his somewhat rustic situation, while assuring her that she had nothing to worry about regarding him. Although expressing a willingness to comply with her desires, Dillinger repeated his offer to rescue her from jail. He deprecated the danger, declaring in a fit of schoolboy romantics that he asked nothing more than to be allowed to die while holding her in his arms.

During this visit Dillinger also asked O'Leary if arrangements had been completed for the plastic surgery operations. O'Leary said yes, and was told by Dillinger that he would instruct him further within the coming week.

The next time O'Leary encountered John Dillinger was in the house of Jimmie Probasco.

The scene once again shifts to St. Paul, and to the supporting characters in the Dillinger drama. The federal government was now actively campaigning to exterminate or imprison all members of the gang and their associates. Beth Green had entered a plea of guilty on May 5, and received a sentence of fifteen months.

The joint trial of Evelyn Frechette, Dr. Clayton E. May, and Augusta Salt opened on May 15 in the United States District Court in St. Paul before Judge Gunnar H. Nordbye. Dr. May and Mrs. Salt were represented by Thomas McMeekin, while A. Jerome Hoffman and Louis Piquett acted for Billie Frechette. On the very first day, the trial was nearly halted by the disappearance of one of the defendants. As the court recessed for lunch, Billie simply got up and joined the departing jurors and spectators. She had succeeded in reaching the corridor before a court officer recognized her and brought her back. Her absence had not been noticed by the bailiffs, and Billie innocently explained that she had merely intended to go out and have lunch with the others.

The following day Piquett had one of the greatest surprises in his life. As he left the courthouse he heard his name called softly by a voice in a waiting automobile. He turned, and there was Dillinger sitting at the wheel of the car and grinning broadly.

"What the hell are you doing here?" Piquett exclaimed.

"Just thought I'd run up and see how the trial was coming along," he chuckled.

"You're hotter than a firecracker in this town!"

"What's happening? Can you get Billie off?"

"I can't tell yet. It's a hard case to beat, but we'll do our best."

"Do everything you can for her. I'll see that you and the others will get paid. Well, so long, counsel. See you in Chicago!"

The trial itself was taken up largely with an account of the shooting at the St. Paul apartment and identification of finger-prints. Several federal agents were called to testify that Miss Frechette had talked glibly to them of her relations with Dillinger, and that in the course of her questioning she had made many damaging admissions. They were subjected to a severe grilling by the defense attorneys, while she denied on the stand that she had made any statements to them whatsoever.

Dr. May related his part, claiming that he had received no pay for his services, that he consented to care for the wounded outlaw only after Dillinger had menaced him with a machine gun, and that he had afterward received several threatening telephone calls warning him not to report the matter to the authorities. Mrs. Salt declared that Dillinger had given her one hundred dollars for her services and ten dollars for supplies, and that she was unaware of his identity until after he had left her home. Evelyn Frechette's defense was concerned mainly with the story of her life and of the events leading up to her arrest.

During the closing arguments, Piquett delivered a fiery oration in behalf of his client. "Dillinger is the most overestimated, the most overrated man in America," he declaimed. "Evelyn Frechette loved Dillinger, and although she knew he was a desperado, she was willing to take a chance with him. We all know where Dillinger belongs, but are we going to punish three people because they were innocently drawn into this net? Miss Frechette was willing to go the limit with this Public Enemy Number One because she loved him. She did not harbor him under the statute. I appeal to you—give her back her freedom!"

The jury remained out all night and returned its verdict on the morning of May 23. In spite of Piquett's appeals, Evelyn Frechette was convicted and given two years in the federal prison at Milan, Michigan, plus a fine of one thousand dollars. Dr. May received a like sentence, except that he was committed to Leavenworth penitentiary. The nurse, Mrs. Salt, was acquitted.

Piquett, after announcing that Billie's conviction would be appealed, returned to Chicago to see if Dillinger would provide the funds. Brokenhearted at the loss of the girl he had truly grown to love, he readily agreed to do so. Piquett was reluctant to thus place his connection with Dillinger in so open a light, however, and publicly announced that Patsy Frechette, Evelyn's sister, had managed to raise the money.

The appeal on the Frechette case was for unknown reasons transferred to the federal court in Denver, Colorado. Attorney Hoffman, Piquett's associate, went to Denver and was assured by the clerk that the case would be given all possible dispatch, but that the dockets were so crowded that it might not be heard for six months, or a year, or two years.

"In the event the case comes up," the clerk went on, "you'd better leave your address."

Hoffman signed and muttered, "Timbuctoo, Africa."

Tragedy occurred late on the night of Thursday, May 24—the murder of officers Martin O'Brien and Lloyd Mulvihill of the East Chicago police. The two were an experienced team of detectives who had been present at the East Chicago bank robbery and the killing of Officer O'Malley, and had thenceforth been active in the Dillinger hunt. They left the police station shortly after eleven o'clock, supposedly on a tip as to Dillinger's whereabouts.

Less than half an hour later the police car was found standing in the middle of the old Gary macadam road, in a lonely and swampy area. The bodies of the occupants were still in the machine, both riddled with bullets about the face and neck. Mulvihill was the father of six children, O'Brien the father of three.

A flock of rumors circulated. O'Brien and Mulvihill supposedly had learned the identities of the Dillinger gang's East Chicago connections and had been murdered because they might reveal their information. A high police official of the state of Indiana said in an interview that he suspected Captain Tim O'Neil of involvement, while others believed that O'Neil and Sergeant Martin Zarkovich had killed the two personally.

O'Neil and Zarkovich were not the actual murderers of their fellow officers, although the accusations indicate how state authorities felt toward the pair. Statements by Dillinger and Van

Meter throw light on the events of this dark night. Dillinger was driving the red truck when Mulvihill and O'Brien drove alongside and ordered him to pull over. In the rear of the truck was Homer Van Meter with his ever-ready machine gun. He realized that it was a case either of their being captured and confronting the electric chair, or of shooting their way out. Before the detectives had a chance to step out of their car, Van Meter expressed his decision in a spray of machine-gun bullets.

Dillinger placed the blame for these killings on Sergeant Martin Zarkovich. Zarkovich was a hoodlum in police officer's clothing. Dillinger had been in contact with the East Chicago people while sojourning in the red truck, and they, including Zarkovich, knew he was in the area.

"Those two police should never have been bumped off," Dillinger later told O'Leary. "They were just trying to do their job and there's nothing wrong about that. Their trouble was that they were getting to know too much and Zark was getting antsy. They were sent off to shake down a couple of suspicious characters who were driving around in a red truck. I think Van felt bad about it, too, but there was nothing else that he could do, and Zark knew what was going to happen. If we had given ourselves up we both would have got the hot seat."[41]

Immediately after the slayings, Dillinger and Van Meter abandoned their nomadic existence and returned to Chicago. According to statements made by Jimmie Probasco, they passed at least a part of the three days before coming to his house at the establishment of James Murray.[42]

The hue and cry after Dillinger became even more intense, and on May 25 five states joined in offering a reward of five thousand dollars for his apprehension. Meanwhile the state of Indiana began to investigate the political and criminal situation in East Chicago. Three men were taken into custody in that city in a raid on a saloon believed to be a rendezvous for Dillinger.

But East Chicago's dirty linen will be washed later in this account.

I'd like to have enough money to enjoy life; be

clear of everything—not worry; take care of my

old man, and see a ball game every day.

—John Dillinger

PART IV

For all their mistakes and bad luck, Hoover's G-men were taking their toll on the Dillinger gang. After the Battle of Little Bohemia, Dillinger himself was too hot to find good hideouts except at exorbitant prices from unreliable people. To the newspaper-reading public he still seemed to be leading a charmed life, and could be imagined living somewhere in luxury on the proceeds of his robberies. It reflects the primitive state of police work of the day that it still seemed possible for an outlaw to lead two lives simply for want of identification; or to literally retire from a life of crime once enough loot had been amassed. It's possible that some unusually self-disciplined robbers did just that, for one heard only of those who were caught, after all. This was implied in many prison movies, and was virtually a subplot in *I Am a Fugitive from a Chain Gang,* based on a more or less true story. The constant preaching of "Crime Does Not Pay" suggested that not everyone was convinced of this.

So while Dillinger's life was fast becoming the desperate one of a hunted animal, it did not seem totally out of the question to him or the public that he might yet elude capture by means of the new plastic surgery, marry his girl-friend Evelyn, and go straight—in this or some foreign country. Such was the state of unscientific crime control by the country's uncoordinated, untrained, and generally inept lawmen who had proved no match for professional crimi-nals throughout the 1920s.

Whatever personal quirks and dubious villains might later obsess its director, the FBI changed crucial aspects of American police work almost overnight. Its new centralized files of crime statistics, criminal records, and fingerprints, along with its nationwide teletype network, state-of-the-art crime lab, and police-training academy, made the Bureau a role model of professionalism and the provider of indispensable services for every police department in the country. Nor did local authorities have much choice in the matter once the news and entertainment industries agreed that fingerprints, ballistics, test tubes, comparison microscopes, and radio would lick the national crime problem.

For some lawbreakers, that was true. Once Congress passed the laws that gave the Justice Department as much actual as moral leadership in the crime war, and once that leadership had been thrust upon a more-than-willing Hoover by enormous amounts of publicity, the FBI became the instrument that converted American law enforcement from a sieve through which the most witless criminal might slip into a web that doomed any worthwhile fugitive—as soon as the Bureau's crime lab and records division yielded the rascal's name.

What rescued Cummings's federal crime bills from emasculation in Congress and empowered Hoover's FBI were the front-page exploits of John Dillinger during March and April 1934. The irreverent have since credited Dillinger with sacrificing his life to give this country its first comprehensive criminal code and make Hoover a national hero. He just didn't do it intentionally.

CHAPTER SIXTEEN

LOESER WHETS HIS KNIFE

It will be remembered that Dillinger had been talking to O'Leary about a secure hideout and plastic surgery which would enable him to move about with less fear of detection. O'Leary had communicated all this to Piquett, who said he would deal with it.

Strange as it may seem, Piquett had been approached by a number of persons wanting to harbor the famous outlaw. Some of these Piquett knew only slightly or not at all, but there was one among them, James J. Probasco, whom he had known casually for almost twenty years. Probasco was a bronze-skinned Italian, rather below medium height and slight of build, with a turbulent career behind him and a reputation in underworld circles for always beating raps.

Probasco had been divorced some years earlier by the sister of Thomas Bowler, head of the Sanitary District of Chicago. At various periods of his life he had been a teamster, a prize fighter, a rather dubious sort of veterinary, and a fence for thieves. He had been arrested in 1921 on charges of burglary and receiving stolen property, but after some months, the charges were dropped. Several years later he was suspected of being the fence for a ring of diamond thieves whose operations extended into the millions of dollars, and there were stories that he had made a payment of forty thousand dollars to a police captain. He was arrested in

1927, and police found ten thousand dollars' worth of loot stolen from a prominent Lake Forest family, but again he seems to have slipped through the clutches of the law. During Prohibition he was picked up for selling liquor, yet this case, like the others, shows no record of prosecution.

But Probasco was hard up. Although he was still dwelling in the underworld, his schemes were not generating enough money for him to realize his immediate ambition to buy the Green Log Tavern at 1525 Howard Street. The sight of Piquett one day at the Criminal Court building reminded him of Dillinger and an idea he had hatched. Piquett, however, was responding to a hurried call from "Boss" McLaughlin, and told him to come around some other time.[43]

Several days later Probasco was a caller at Piquett's offices.

"What kind of a guy is this fellow Dillinger?" he asked.

"What do you mean?"

"Jimmy Murray tells me that Dillinger wants to hole in for a while. I've got just the spot for him—that cottage of mine on Crawford Avenue [now Pulaski Boulevard]. I'm a bachelor now, you know, and we'd be all alone there. You can vouch for me to Dillinger that I'm a stand-up guy and don't talk."

Such a place would meet Dillinger's needs, Piquett believed, but doubts persisted. "I don't know, Jimmy," he said. "You realize you would be going into a very serious matter. The penalty for harboring is six months, and for conspiracy to harbor, it's two years. They would probably hook you on the conspiracy charge."

"I know. I'll take my chances on beating the rap."

"Do you realize how dangerous it is? If the police or the federal men came, you'd be killed right along with the rest of them."

"Hell, I'm not afraid. I'm an old man. I'm telling you, Mr. Piquett, I have to raise some money. If you see Dillinger, speak to him about me, and tell him the price is fifty dollars a day."

A short time later Probasco called for his answer, and Piquett summoned O'Leary into the office.

"This is Jimmy Probasco," he said by way of introduction. "I've known him for years, and he's all right. He needs money, and he wants to hide Dillinger. He's a bachelor, and he's got a good place on North Crawford. When you see Johnnie again, mention it to him."

The negotiations for the surgery were proceeding simultaneously. As chance would have it, Piquett was acquainted with one Dr. Wilhelm Loeser,[44] a German immigrant and long-time

U.S. resident who had studied medicine at Kansas and Northwestern universities. His wife had become insane some fifteen years previous, and he had taken up residence with a woman named Anna Patzke, a tall brunette with a penchant for chewing gum. In July of 1931 he was convicted under the Harrison Narcotics Act and sentenced to three years in Leavenworth, but he managed to gain parole in December of the following year. Dr. Loeser immediately violated his parole by traveling to Mexico, where he obtained a divorce from his wife. Returning to the United States, he assumed the name of Dr. Ralph Robeind, by which he was known throughout the Dillinger transactions. According to Dr. Loeser, he and Anna were married in Kansas City, but he admitted that Anna had never seen the marriage license and consequently did not consider herself married.

Piquett had known Dr. Loeser and his paramour over a period of several years, and sometimes assisted them in legal matters. Following Dillinger's request for plastic surgery, Piquett called on the doctor at his apartment at 536 Wrightwood Avenue one evening and broached the subject in a general way. Loeser showed Piquett the results of a process he had used in Mexico to remove his own fingerprints. He added that, as a matter of fact, he needed money to get his furniture out of storage, in case Piquett knew of anyone in need of his services. Piquett said that he might. Loeser of course understood that Dillinger was being referred to.

It was only a few days thereafter that Piquett took O'Leary to Loeser's place to discuss the proposed operation. An assistant for Loeser was mentioned, and O'Leary thought of Dr. Harold Bernard Cassidy.[45] Cassidy, a young, dark-haired, dark-eyed physician, was then being sought by the police on a charge of perjured testimony in a bank robber's trial at Ottawa, Illinois. O'Leary had known him for some years, and suggested him only with the thought in mind that it would earn him some easy money. In the end, Cassidy would have scant reason to thank O'Leary for his well-intentioned act.

The all-important question of price was also discussed. In view of the danger attending any involvement with Dillinger, and the necessity of dividing the money several ways, the figure arrived at was five thousand dollars. Six hundred dollars would go to Dr. Cassidy, and the balance would be divided equally among Loeser, Piquett, and O'Leary.

All arrangements were now concluded—it remained only to contact John Dillinger and advise him what had been worked out.

John Dillinger moved into the two-story frame cottage at 2509 Crawford Avenue on the night of May 27. Piquett and O'Leary drove there in the former's car, and stood in front of the brightly illuminated filling station next to the Probasco house. In a few minutes Dillinger came walking down the street, greeted the two, and then excused himself for the moment. They watched as he walked to a car parked close by, the same light tan sedan in which Tommy Carroll would meet his death some ten days later. Dillinger leaned in and spoke to three dark figures, presumably Van Meter, Nelson, and Carroll, who were on hand in the role of bodyguards. From the rear of the car Dillinger brought forth a machine gun, a bulletproof vest, two or three pistols, and a number of drums of bullets, all of which he carefully wrapped in a lap robe.

Jimmy Probasco was totally unaware that a guest was coming to his home that night.

"Jimmy, this is my famous client, John Dillinger," Piquett announced as soon as they were inside. "Have you got someplace where we can all sit down and talk?"

Probasco's face was wreathed in smiles as he nervously shook the desperado's hand and led the group to the kitchen.

"So this is it," Dillinger said without great enthusiasm. "Have you worked out the price, Mr. Piquett?"

"Jimmy says it will cost you fifty dollars a day," Piquett answered.

"Don't you think that's high?"

Probasco broke in. "Well, you're pretty hot, you know, but I want you to be satisfied. What do you think is fair?"

"How about thirty-five a day?"

"That's all right with me. Thirty-five bucks a day, then, for room and board."

Dillinger's greatest interest lay in the operations. He was told of the arrangements made with Loeser and Cassidy, and was assured by Piquett and O'Leary that they were both competent and trustworthy. Because of his wish to proceed without delay, it was decided to operate the following night. Dillinger counted out three thousand dollars and handed it to Piquett.

"There's the down payment," he told him. "You'll get the rest after the operation."

While Dillinger and O'Leary sat in the kitchen, a stout woman in her thirties came out of the rear bedroom and walked across the kitchen to the bathroom. The outlaw gave O'Leary a look of great annoyance.

"Who's the woman?" he demanded.

"Damned if I know."

"I thought you said this guy was a bachelor."

"That's what he told us. I'll ask Probasco."

Probasco, who had been in the front of the house with Piquett, hurried back when O'Leary informed him of what had happened.

"That's Peggy Doyle, my housekeeper," he told Dillinger. "She's a nurse, and she works during the day. But if you don't want her around, I'll get rid of her while you're here."

"Is she a good cook?"

"The best cook you ever laid your eyes on. And she knows how to keep her mouth shut."

"All right. As long as she's seen me, you'd better let her stay."

Piquett drove O'Leary home and gave him fourteen hundred dollars, of which six hundred would go to Cassidy. He then proceeded to the apartment of Dr. Loeser and told him to be ready the following night. He also gave him a part of the money, which Dr. Loeser declares was five hundred dollars and Piquett claims was eight hundred.

The next morning, Monday, May 28, O'Leary drove to 1117 North Dearborn Street, where Cassidy was living at the apartment of a friend.

"I've got a job for you," O'Leary informed him. "You're to assist another physician in some surgery, and then act as a male nurse to the patient. There will be about six days' work at a hundred dollars a day."

"That's pretty high. What's the matter with him?"

"He's a red-hot. That's all you need to know."

O'Leary paid Cassidy the six hundred dollars in advance.

"Go out and rent a car, and be at my apartment at six o'clock this evening," he told him.

Cassidy arrived at the appointed hour and they drove over to pick up Loeser. The doctor was waiting with his black bag of surgical equipment and supplies. Upon their arrival at Probasco's, Dillinger and Loeser discussed the operation.

"Do you want a general or a local anesthetic?" Loeser asked.

Dillinger hesitated. "A general would put me completely out, wouldn't it?" he inquired.

"Yes, it would."

Dillinger turned to O'Leary. "Are you going to be here, Art?"

"I'll stay if you want me, Johnnie."

"I want you to stay."

The reason for having O'Leary remain was that Dillinger did

not know how far he could trust Probasco, Loeser, and Cassidy, who might decide they could make even more money—legally—by turning him in while he was unconscious. O'Leary was unarmed, it is true, but he knew where Dillinger's guns were and could easily have reached them had the need arisen.

Dillinger decided on general anesthesia, and the physician asked whether he had eaten much that day.

"Just grapefruit, toast, and a cup of coffee for breakfast." This was untrue, for Dillinger had eaten two full meals, but he was anxious to proceed with the operation.

The outlaw removed his shirt and reclined on the cot in the small bedroom. Loeser went into the bathroom, which had been scrupulously cleaned for the occasion, and commenced to sterilize his hands, while Cassidy placed a cone wrapped in a towel over Dillinger's face and began to administer the contents of a can of ether.

"Are you there, Art?" Dillinger kept asking from time to time.

"I'm right with you, Johnnie," O'Leary reassured him. "Try and relax."

Dillinger, however, seemed to be fighting the anesthetic, and Cassidy administered the entire contents of the can in an effort to put him under. Suddenly a bluish tint began to creep over his face, as his breathing and heartbeat stopped. Cassidy's countenance whitened and he staggered against the wall, unable to utter a word. O'Leary, noting the consternation of the young physician and alarmed at Dillinger's appearance, shouted for Loeser.

The German fairly flew into the room and began applying artificial respiration. Probasco, hearing the commotion, hurried to the scene and stood in the doorway.

"My God, he's dead!" he kept shouting, sobered probably for one of the few times in recent years. "Oh, my God, oh, my God!" O'Leary threw open the bedroom window to allow the ether fumes to escape, and then hastened to silence the clamoring Probasco.

Nearly fifteen minutes elapsed before Dillinger fully revived, and it was decided to continue the operation under local anesthetic. Loeser and Cassidy first cut away three moles on his forehead, then removed a small scar on the upper lip. Loeser next made a slit under the lobe of each ear, removed about an inch of flesh, and pulled back the skin in order to remove the heavy lines under his cheeks and raise the drooping corners of his mouth. A cut was then made at the point of the chin and the entire nose was slit open. With the tissue taken from the cheeks the dimple on the chin was filled, and the nose built up in order to make it perfectly straight. The cuts were closed with sutures, and the patient's face was wrapped in gauze bandages.

Dillinger remained in a groggy state even under the local anesthetic, and would wince and squirm as the cuts were made. He bled profusely, so that the bed was soaked, and the doctors were much hampered by his violent vomiting throughout the operation.

Within a fairly short time Dillinger recovered his senses, although he was still a trifle dizzy.

"How are you feeling?" O'Leary asked. "Did they hurt you much?"

"Pretty good. No, I didn't feel much pain."

"Well, there's something I want to tell you. You pretty nearly died on us. We had a hell of a time bringing you back."

Dillinger laughed. "It might just as well have been now as some other time."

"Well, I don't want it to happen while I'm around. I would have had a swell time trying to explain to the gang that we didn't put you on the spot."

"It's all over with now, so don't worry."

"Do you want me any longer, Johnnie?"

"No, you can go any time now."

Loeser had packed his things and departed immediately after the operation. Cassidy remained in the house to take care of Dillinger.

O'Leary met Piquett at the office the next morning and related the events of the night before. In the evening he again went to the Probasco house, and remained about half an hour. Dillinger was up and full of fun, joking a great deal as to how his passing out had frightened everyone.

The next visit that O'Leary made was on the night of Thursday, May 31. Cassidy had removed the bandages earlier in the day. Although the marks from the cuts were still conspicuous, Dillinger was greatly pleased with the change in his appearance, and always said afterward that he was satisfied with the results. O'Leary felt that it had altered his looks considerably, and after Dillinger's death there was at first some doubt as to whether the right man had been killed. On the other hand, Piquett told Dillinger that he looked as if he had been in a dogfight, and later remarked that Loeser couldn't remove feathers from a pigeon's tail.

Dr. Loeser's reputation in the facelifting field was to bring him a new patient nevertheless, and mire him still deeper in underworld medicine.

Cassidy, sleepworn and haggard, went to O'Leary's apartment at the Lincoln Park Arms late on the afternoon of Saturday, June 2, to report that his work was completed. O'Leary telephoned Piquett and asked him to come over.

"Cassidy's here," O'Leary told Piquett. "He's all through over at Probasco's. We'd better go over there tonight and get the balance of our money."

As soon as it was dark, the two drove to Probasco's house on the Near Northwest Side, and Piquett lost no time asking Dillinger for the two thousand dollars still owed them.

"I have a friend who wants the same thing done," Dillinger said. "Get those doctors over here for tomorrow night. He'll also pay five grand, and I'll have the rest of what I owe you."

Dillinger then gave Piquett an enthusiastic account of the operation, and the attorney assured him that it had altered his appearance considerably. Unless there had been a substantial change in Dillinger's features, it is most doubtful that Dr. Loeser's next customer, the parsimonious Van Meter, would have parted with five thousand dollars for a similar operation.

After leaving the hideout, Piquett went to Loeser's apartment the same night and instructed him to meet O'Leary at Clark Street and North Avenue the next evening at half past eight. The following morning, Sunday, O'Leary went to see Cassidy, who now had moved into his uncle's apartment in the Lincoln Park Arms, where O'Leary lived. Cassidy was still in bed recuperating from his nervous and sleepless nights at Probasco's place.

"I want you to go back over there," O'Leary told him. "Dillinger has a friend who wants the same work done. You'll get the same pay as before."

"Count me out," Cassidy nearly shouted. "I don't want any part of it."

O'Leary reported Cassidy's adamant refusal to Piquett, who did not want to take no for an answer. With O'Leary in tow, he called on the frightened physician, and whether it was because of Piquett's powers of persuasion or the six hundred dollars advanced to him on the spot, Cassidy relented.

O'Leary met Loeser at the appointed place, and the two rode to Probasco's house by streetcar. Piquett and Cassidy arrived separately about the same time. Homer Van Meter had come to the house during the afternoon, bringing his arsenal of guns and ammunition. Piquett took Dillinger to one side.

"The doctors say they won't touch the job unless they get their money in advance," he told him.

Dillinger called Van Meter, who followed him into the small bedroom. The two outlaws took their respective stacks of money from a dresser, and began counting it out. Piquett was seated on the couch, Loeser stood in the doorway, and O'Leary went into the kitchen to have a gin fizz with Probasco, who seemed in continual need of liquid refreshment. Dillinger finished counting first and gave two thousand dollars to Piquett, which settled his account. A minute or two later Van Meter handed his five thousand to Dillinger, who in turn passed it to Piquett. Piquett took the bundles of money and wrapped them in a newspaper.

Piquett declares that Dillinger told him to retain three thousand dollars of this amount as his expenses and fee in the Evelyn Frechette case. The government maintains that the money was given him as his share in the Dillinger and Van Meter operations.

After receiving the money, Piquett and O'Leary left the house, and Loeser began work on Van Meter. A vertical scar running up Van Meter's forehead into the hair was excised and transformed into a smaller horizontal scar, in order to prevent his being readily identified by this feature. His nose was slit and laid open, a hump left over from an old break removed, and the large pedicle of flesh at the tip cut away. Van Meter had a prominent lip, and about half of this was also reduced. A tattoo in the form of an anchor, about four inches long and bearing the legend "Good Hope," was removed from his forearm with acids. All of this work was done under local anesthetic, which only partially suppressed the excruciating pain. Loeser returned home exhausted about three o'clock in the morning, while Cassidy remained with an extremely unhappy patient.

The next day Piquett, O'Leary, and Loeser met at noon at Loeser's apartment. Piquett brought the newspaper-wrapped bundle of money and spread it out on the couch. He counted out $2,100 and handed it to O'Leary, who immediately left. Loeser was then given $1,700, Piquett explaining that he had to keep some toward an unexpected bail bond arising out of charges on a questionable stock transaction, and promising to pay the balance within a few days.

On Tuesday, June 5, two days after the second operation, Loeser again called at the Probasco cottage to complete the work on Van Meter's fingertips. Dillinger's hands had been done the preceding week, a few days after the facial operation. The method Dr. Loeser had devised for removing fingerprints involved a "secret" formula of two parts of hydrochloric acid and one of nitro-hydrochloric acid, to be used with an alkaloid, usually of sodium, called caustic soda. After the hands were sterilized, the outer skin or epidermis was cut away, exposing the derma, which was then treated with alternating applications of the acid and alkaline solutions. The scalpel was used to remove any ridges not burned away by the chemicals.

It is scarcely necessary to point out what intense pain this method involves. The stoical Dillinger endured the torture silently, and betrayed his suffering only by wincing occasionally and by the perspiration which broke out on his forehead. But Van Meter gave loud vent to his discomfort with sharp exclamations and outbreaks of cursing, and from time to time would dance about the room while waving his hands in the air. Afterward, neither man had the use of his fingers for a period of several days.

Piquett and O'Leary arrived shortly after Loeser had departed. "Baby Face" Nelson had also called and was sitting in the living room when they came in. Van Meter was standing, with the look of a wounded animal, two very sore hands held out before him. Nelson, although in and about Chicago during the time Dillinger and Van Meter resided with Probasco, refused to "hole in" as the others had done. He boasted that he never remained two nights in the same place, and made it a practice to sleep in tourist camps or at tourist homes. It was about this time that Helen Gillis violated her probation and rejoined her husband. After she failed to report to the probation authorities, an arrest warrant was issued on June 14.

O'Leary and Piquett merely called "Hello" to Nelson and the others and went on back to the kitchen to imbibe gin fizzes with the ever-willing Jimmy Probasco. Nelson was having a hearty laugh at the expense of his two associates.

"So you two decided to go out and buy yourselves a pair of new mugs," he chuckled. "Well, maybe you needed them!"

"At least I'll be able to go out on the street and get around now," Dillinger rejoined.

When Piquett and O'Leary returned to the living room, they found that Nelson had gone. The bandages had been removed from Van Meter's face that day, and he was contemplating the results with ill-concealed ire.

"What a mess they made out of me!" he stormed. "I paid out five thousand dollars, and what did I get for it?"

"You look all right, Van," O'Leary said. Then, turning to Dillinger, "You're satisfied with your job, aren't you, Johnnie?"

"Sure, I'm satisfied."

"You got a good job," Van Meter told Dillinger. "I got a rotten one."

Van Meter sat down in a corner, grumbling to himself. In a few moments he broke forth again.

"Look at those fingers," he demanded. "That's going to leave nothing but a bunch of scars."

"Your fingers are going to be all right," O'Leary told him. "Look at Loeser's fingertips. They're as smooth as anything you can want."

Van Meter continued gazing at his acid-eaten fingers. "That's a lousy job," he muttered. Then, going to a mirror, he contemplated his mangled features. "And that's a hell of a lot worse."

O'Leary's anger was also mounting. "Wait until your face and hands heal before you go popping off. What do you expect two days after the operation? Give it a chance, instead of going around yelling like a big palooka."

"I paid for a good job, and damn it, I want a good job!" Van Meter raged. "Those two are nothing but a couple of butchers. You tell those doctors they'd better come back and take care of me right, or I'm going to them!"

Inasmuch as the complaining was now threatening to turn into something more serious, Dillinger hastened to restore peace. Piquett reported the stormy scene to Loeser, and the physician returned in a day or two and did some additional work on Van Meter which, if anything, made him look worse.

Dr. Loeser, visibly worried by the threats and abuse heaped upon him by Van Meter, gave birth to an idea that stands forth as a classic model in inanity. Dillinger and Van Meter, he proudly announced, would not only have new faces, but he would give them new identities as well. Dillinger was to become Joseph C. Harris, and with a few scratches of the pen the German provided him with a birth certificate, dated March 5, 1904.

It reads: "Received $25.00 from Joseph C. Harris of six miles south of Byron, Oklahoma, in full for confinement of Joseph C. Harris, Jr., born January 11, 1904 to Joseph C. Harris and Mary Jackson Harris (maiden name of mother Mary Jackson)."

But this was not all. To account for the facial transformations he received the following receipt, which bore the date of March 15, 1931.

"Received from Joseph C. Harris of Chicago, Illinois, $44.00 in full for care of injuries to chin, to nose, to distal phalanges of both hands palmar aspect, to upper lip on left side near median line, to both cheeks below the ear, to chest."

Homer Van Meter, now transformed into Henry J. Adams, also received a full set of documents. His receipt for medical fees attending birth was dated March 5, 1899, and shows that it cost his parents five dollars more to bring him into the world than it had Dillinger's.

"Received $30.00 from Henry J. Adams four miles west of Amorita, Oklahoma in full for confinement of Henry J. Adams, Jr., born January 2, 1899, to Henry J. Adams and Mollie Johnson Adams (maiden name of mother Mollie Johnson)."

His plastic work was to be concealed under the following, dated June 17, 1930.

"Received from Henry J. Adams of Chicago, Illinois, $37.00 in full for care of injuries to distal phalanges palmar aspect of both hands, to ventral surface of right forearm, to forehead of left side near median line."

It was Loeser's intention to rewrite these documents on pieces of paper bearing the marks of age, and forge to them the signatures of physicians already dead. The originals were penned at the Probasco hideout, but in his excitement from having Van Meter glowering over him, the physician walked out and left them on the table. O'Leary placed them in his pocket, and it is thus that they still remain in existence.

The facts concerning these operations are that Dillinger, with his chubby cheeks and regular features, was of the type whose facial characteristics could easily be altered. Van Meter, on the other hand, with his elongated jaw, large nose, thin bony face, low brow, and mop of black hair, was so fashioned that nothing short of dynamite could have made an appreciable change.

CHAPTER SEVENTEEN

DILLINGER GOES TO THE PARK

While Dillinger and Van Meter were learning that the road to artificial beauty runs through the torture chamber, Piquett and O'Leary found that life continued to offer excitement. Just prior to Dillinger's arrival at Probasco's, Pat Cherrington and Opal Long, who were then living together at the Chateau Hotel, came by Piquett's office to moan of their financial hardships.

"The worst part of it," sighed Pat, "is that I've got a lot of slum and some money in that bank up at Diversey and Clark. There are two large diamond rings and a diamond wristwatch in a safety-deposit box, and several hundred dollars in an account."

"Maybe we can help you out," volunteered Piquett. He called in an elderly lawyer named McGehran who was waiting in the outer office.

"Mac," said O'Leary, "this is Pat Cherrington, Red Hamilton's girl. She's got some money in a bank on the North Side. How would you like to go up there as her lawyer and get it out?"

"Sure."

"I want to tell you," warned Piquett, "that it's awfully hot."

"Do I get paid for it?"

"I'll give you fifty dollars," Pat offered.

"Mac," armed with power of attorney, departed shortly before midday, promising to return as soon as possible. The four sat around in the office, waiting and quaffing various alcoholic mixtures as the hours dragged on. Late in the afternoon the lawyer burst into the office, his collar wilted and his face about six shades whiter than a sheet. The much-disconcerted McGehran sank into the closest chair and relaxed with a loud sigh.

"What an experience!" he groaned. "I'm through with this kind of thing for life."

"What happened?" all four asked simultaneously.

"What happened? Plenty! The G-men were watching the bank, and they grabbed me the minute I got your money. They took me down to the Bankers' Building and I've been there for the last two hours. Luckily I had dated that power of attorney from two days ago, and I finally convinced them that I haven't seen you since."

"Have you still got the money?" Pat inquired worriedly.

"Yes, here's your money, less fifty dollars for my fee. And as for your jewelry, it can stay there until hell freezes over before I go back."

O'Leary would have the next harrowing experience, which occurred at his apartment in the Lincoln Park Arms about the last day of May. The telephone rang, and on it was Piquett, somewhat intoxicated.

"Did you see that guy?" the attorney mumbled.

"What?" exclaimed the startled O'Leary.

"Did you see that fellow? You know who I mean."

O'Leary hastened to hang up, but it was already too late. Piquett's lines were tapped, and the listeners rightly took this less than cryptic exchange as referring to the elusive Mr. Dillinger.

Within fifteen minutes five police squad cars reached the hotel. The number of O'Leary's apartment was 1202, but in their excitement the raiders began pounding on the door of 202. As it so happened, the inmates of that apartment were dope peddlers, and finding the police pouring in upon them, they lost no time in dumping their narcotics out the window.

O'Leary's wife and two children had just retired, and he was preparing for his bath when a loud rapping came at the door.

"Who's there?" he called.

"Police officers. Open that door, or we'll break it in."

Complying with the request, the half-nude Mr. O'Leary found himself confronted with machine guns held by Captain Stege, Sergeant Reynolds, and a crowd of police.

"Who's in there with you?"

"Nobody but my wife and my two children."

"Anybody else?"

"Come on in and see for yourselves," said O'Leary, stepping away from the door and into the bathroom.

Inside the apartment and directly opposite its entranceway was the door to the room in which O'Leary's daughter was sleeping. The officers looked at each other, evidently with the same thought in all their minds. If Dillinger was in that room with a machine gun, he would have a straight line of fire all the way to the front door and could mow down any who advanced into the room. In the absence of probable cause, or the desire to take the chance, O'Leary's word was accepted.

"All right," they said. "Let's go." O'Leary, watching from his window, saw the squad cars drive away.

A few minutes later there was a second, less violent knock, and manager Fred Clare of the hotel appeared in the doorway.

"Are you really alone here with your family, Mr. O'Leary?" he asked.

"Certainly I am. Come in and see for yourself."

The manager made a tour of the apartment.

"Do you know, those police gave me an awful fright," he remarked. "They said you had John Dillinger up here."

"Dillinger? If they thought Dillinger was here, why didn't they come in? After coming all the way up here on a raid, surely they weren't going to take my word for it."

"I thought of that, too. I wonder why they didn't come in?"

O'Leary smiled. "Your guess is as good as mine."

On the afternoon of the division of the money at Dr. Loeser's apartment, following the Van Meter operation, O'Leary had his second encounter with the police. He was sitting in the car reading a newspaper and waiting for Piquett to come down from his apartment when he felt a pistol touch the back of his head. A voice commanded that he raise his hands and get out of the car. A squad of police surrounded him.

"What's your name?" demanded the officer in charge.

"Arthur O'Leary."

"What do you do?"

"I'm an investigator for Mr. Piquett."

"What did you do before that?"

"What's that to you?"

"Answer the question."

"It's none of your damned business what I did before," O'Leary retorted. At the same time he began pressing the car's horn button. Piquett heard the signal on his way down the stairs.

"What's going on here?" he called as he emerged from the doorway.

O'Leary explained the situation in a few choice words.

"Where's your warrant?" shouted Piquett. "Where's your warrant?"

After a minute or two of low conversation between Piquett and the officer, the police reentered their car and drove away.

A couple of days before this incident, on June 2, Pat Cherrington and Opal Long were picked up by police after trying to claim their jewelry from the safety-deposit box, and the same day Helen Burke, the sweetheart of Arthur "Fish" Johnson, was also arrested. Pat at first gave the name of Virginia Hughes, and the officers believed her to be the sweetheart of Harry Pierpont. Three days later she was arraigned as Patricia Young, while asserting that her true name was Pat Cherry. On June 21 airplanes secretly flew Opal Long to St. Paul and Pat Cherrington to Madison, Wisconsin. On July 7 Pat received a sentence of two years for harboring John Dillinger and Tommy Carroll.

For some days Dillinger and Van Meter had to cool their heels in the Probasco cottage, inasmuch as their faces bore the marks of battle. But their restless natures and long-pent-up desires to go about openly like other men led them to seek the outdoors long before the scars had healed.

Piquett had declared on the night of the Nelson visit that the lawyers in St. Paul were requesting payment of their fees, and therefore the next evening, June 6, O'Leary was dispatched to Mooresville with a note from Dillinger to his father. O'Leary spent the night in the Claypool Hotel in Indianapolis, and the next morning sought out John's half-brother, Hubert, who operated a gasoline filling station in that city. Hubert took O'Leary to one side.

"Be careful what you say," Hubert whispered. "That fellow hanging around here is Art McGinnis."

O'Leary had either learned or figured out that McGinnis had tipped the police to Dillinger's visit at Dr. Eye's in Chicago.

"What's that rat doing here?"

"I want him around where I can keep an eye on him."

"I have a note from Johnnie for your dad," O'Leary informed him. "McGinnis will be asking you who I am. Tell him that I'm a G-man, and that you're driving me out to Mooresville to talk to your father."

Within a half-hour they had arrived at the white farmhouse in Mooresville. Old man Dillinger saw them coming and walked out to meet them in the road. He read the note O'Leary handed him, then took a match from his pocket and burned it. The real G-men hidden in a nearby wood watched the proceedings with high-powered field glasses.

"How is Johnnie?"

"He's fine, Mr. Dillinger."

"Come in the house, Mr. O'Leary. I'll be with you in a few minutes."

Old John Dillinger walked to the barn behind the house, and in a short time returned with a neatly wrapped newspaper package containing three thousand dollars.

"If you see Johnnie when you get back, mention to him that Art McGinnis is at the filling station with me," Hubert Dillinger told O'Leary on their drive back to Indianapolis.

O'Leary returned to the Probasco hideout on the night of June 7, and found Dillinger and Van Meter in a disconsolate mood.

"What's the matter?" he inquired.

"We got some bad news today," Dillinger told him. "Van and I were listening to the radio and heard that Tommy Carroll's been killed." Carroll stood high in the affections of his associates, and played a much larger part in the activities of the gang than the authorities seem to realize.

"How did it happen?"

Dillinger gave him the basic details and he read more in the papers. Jean Crompton, or Jean Delaney Carroll, had lost no time in violating her parole and rejoining her husband, and the two were casing banks in Iowa. They had stopped in Waterloo to have repairs made on their large tan sedan and left the garage for a few minutes while the work was being done. Carelessly they had left a machine gun on the back seat hidden under a lap robe, and an inquisitive mechanic, peering under the robe, hastened to call the police. When Carroll returned, he found policemen Emil Steffen and P. E. Walker waiting, and according to the officers' story, they shot and killed him when he reached for his gun. Two days later Jean Crompton was ordered to prison for a year and a day for violation of her parole.

"That's too bad," sympathized O'Leary when Dillinger broke the news.

The fires of wrath were in Dillinger's eyes. "We'll have to make a little trip out to Waterloo, Van, and take care of those guys."

Van Meter shook his head. "We won't have any time left for robbing banks, what with taking care of people."

The "black list" of those marked for death by the Dillinger gang was in fact mounting rapidly. First and foremost among those targeted by Dillinger was Harold Reinecke, the federal agent who he believed had mistreated Evelyn Frechette. Next in line were Captain Matt Leach and stool pigeon Art McGinnis. Of somewhat lower priority were Sergeant Reynolds of the Stege squad; Emil Wanatka, the proprietor of Little Bohemia; the three deputies who had fatally shot Hamilton near St. Paul; and now those responsible for the death of Tommy Carroll.

Dillinger paced about the house from one room to another. O'Leary gave him the package of money, and after taking it into the small bedroom, he came out and handed O'Leary twenty-five hundred dollars.

"Give this to Piquett for those St. Paul lawyers. Let's go and sit in the park for a while, Art. It's too hot in here."

The two walked over to Kosciusko Park, located only a few blocks from Probasco's, and seated themselves on a bench. O'Leary told Dillinger the details of his visit to Mooresville and mentioned that Art McGinnis was with Hubert. Just then a policeman walked up.

"Haven't you two birds any place to go?" he growled. "This park closes at nine o'clock." It was then about a quarter after nine.

"We didn't know that, officer," Dillinger replied.

"Well, you know it now."

"We're from out of town," Dillinger said amiably as the two got up to leave. "We wouldn't want to do anything against the law."[46]

The following afternoon Louis Piquett made one of his frequent trips to watch the Chicago Cubs play baseball. Dillinger, also an ardent Cub fan, had decided to take in a game the same afternoon. The paths of the two crossed in front of the park.

"H'yah, counsel," the outlaw called, waving his hand and heading in the attorney's direction. Piquett had already recognized another Cub fan as Captain Stege and was trying to avoid him, so the smiling Dillinger was anything but a welcome sight.

"Fuzz," hissed Piquett to Dillinger as he approached. "Big fuzz." This is an underworld expression denoting the presence of police, and the fugitive ducked into the nearest entrance.

Dillinger returned to the hideout in high spirits, after having witnessed his first ball game in nearly a year.

"Why don't you go to the ball games with me, Van?" he called out as he entered.

"You won't catch me running around the streets with my map all sliced to ribbons," snorted Van Meter.

"Well, you're going to Indianapolis with me tonight. We're going to start cutting down our list." And he told him about Art McGinnis.

The two outlaws were in Indianapolis the next morning, June 9. Perhaps McGinnis's suspicions had been aroused by O'Leary's visit, or Hubert Dillinger may have decided he wanted no part in a killing, for the police spy was no longer at the filling station when they arrived. They drove about the streets for some time, and finally spotted him in the business section of Indianapolis. McGinnis evidently saw them and mingled with the crowd of shoppers until he could make his way into a department store and disappear.

Their mission thus frustrated and McGinnis now on guard, Dillinger and Van Meter returned to Chicago that same afternoon.

Somewhere on the road in northern Indiana they had tire trouble, and Dillinger alighted to see what was wrong. Another car drove up and stopped, and two members of the Indiana State Police were about to get out when they found themselves staring into the muzzle of Van Meter's machine gun. Their journey was resumed instantly and at a high rate of speed, while the outlaws headed for a side road. No public mention of this incident is recorded—perhaps because the two officers had no desire to report either their failure to deal decisively with the desperadoes, or the fact that the desperadoes treated them like undersize fish to be tossed back in.

CHAPTER EIGHTEEN

THE PRIVATE LIFE OF A PUBLIC ENEMY

His month of residence with Jimmy Probasco was about the longest that John Dillinger had spent in any one place since embarking upon his adventurous career. Though hardly his first choice in accommodations or mode of living, the Probasco household required adjustments that afford insight into his character and that of his associates.

The house at 2509 North Crawford Avenue was a two-story frame cottage, once white, but now sadly in need of a revivifying coat of paint. Jimmy Probasco occupied the first floor. There was a small green hedge in front of the place, while a high board fence surrounded it on the side and extended back to the rear. The door of the house gives admittance to a small hall, from which the entrance to the Probasco apartment opens. This latter door leads directly into the living room, to the left of which is a small bedroom. A short hall connects the living room with the kitchen, and the bathroom lies to the right side of this hall. A larger rear bedroom is entered from the kitchen.

Dillinger and Van Meter occupied the small front bedroom, sleeping together on a folding couch. Probasco wished to purchase a more comfortable bed for their use, but the two fugitives, accustomed to sleeping on prison bunks, in the back of a truck, and even on the bare ground, declared that this arrangement was quite adequate to their needs. Peggy Doyle and Probasco shared a double bed in the rear bedroom. Peggy went away to work every morning and the two guests saw little of her, inasmuch as on her return she almost invariably went directly into her room and remained there.

In the large yard behind the house Probasco kept two vicious police dogs, King and Queen. It was an almost daily pastime of his to stand on the back porch and shout curses at the animals. Although he never struck them, it is remarkable that the two brutes, as savagely as they behaved toward others, cowered at the stentorian voice of little Jimmie Probasco. Dillinger and Van Meter approved of the dogs, inasmuch as they rendered an attack from the rear virtually impossible.

The back yard was also used as a parking place for automobiles. Dillinger had no car at this time, but Van Meter possessed a dark maroon sedan registered under the name of Henry Adams. Probasco kept two of his machines there, but the outlaws made no use of them.

Guns were kept in the clothes closet and the small bedroom. The arsenal consisted of four machine guns, four large-caliber rifles, and eight pistols, all of .45 caliber except for one .38-caliber pistol which Dillinger sometimes carried in his trousers pocket. The defensive armor included three bulletproof vests, as Van Meter always wore two when engaged in an expedition. In addition, there were many drums of machine-gun bullets, loaded clips of rifle bullets, and hundreds of rounds of ammunition in boxes.

Considerable mystery surrounds the sources of these weapons. There is no truth to reports that they made purchases from large and reputable sporting goods stores in Chicago. H. S. Lebman, a gun dealer in San Antonio, Texas, was arrested and convicted of supplying Nelson and others with machine guns.[47] Part of the equipment came from the police station robberies, but much of this was lost in various raids. No additional weapons were acquired while they were living with Probasco, although on one occasion O'Leary overheard Van Meter remark that he was going to St. Paul to obtain a couple of late-model rifles.

All of the food was prepared by Probasco himself, in spite of his eulogies of Peggy Doyle as a cook. Probasco was, in fact, a very competent chef, and the repasts enjoyed by Dillinger and Van Meter helped compensate for other inconveniences. The kitchen was completely equipped, and more than once a week Probasco would prepare twenty-pound roasts, cooked to perfection and served with tasty sauces and gravies. He was personally very fond of his native Italian dishes, and the two guests found that spaghetti formed a regular part of their diet.

The kitchen was stocked with cases of whiskey, gin, and beer, which served as both refreshments and a source of household income. Dillinger was a light drinker and restricted himself to one or two silver fizzes in an evening. Van Meter likewise drank sparingly. Men living lives as dangerous as theirs knew the importance of keeping their minds clear and alert at all times. Jimmy Probasco made up for the moderation of the others, and his normal condition may be described as half-drunk. But he exemplified the virtues of hospitality and was continually pressing food and drink on all who entered the house.

John Dillinger at this time was about five feet eight inches tall and weighed in the neighborhood of 165 pounds. He was finely constructed, with a large chest and sturdy legs, and possessed remarkable strength. A very neat and conservative dresser, he reluctantly confined himself to ready-made clothes, because of the risk involved in visiting tailors. Dillinger possessed a special vanity in always keeping his nails immaculately manicured.

There was not a killer instinct in the make-up of John Dillinger. On one occasion Probasco pressed him very urgently to "bump off" his partner in the tavern, with whom he had quarreled. The outlaw responded with laughter. In fact, probably no sum of money alone would have induced him to commit murder. But as to robbing banks—that was a different matter entirely. Dillinger once stated that he found bank robbery so easy that every time he passed a bank he felt an urge to hold it up. If he had to shoot a police officer in the course of a robbery, he saw this as the risk that went with their hazardous occupation, just as it went with his own. Much of Dillinger's success both as a bandit and as a gang leader was due to his ability to think clearly and quickly under pressure and to maintain self-control in emergencies. His gaze was unwavering and left no doubt as to who was in command of the situation. Otherwise, he was good-natured and amiable, and his friendly humor won him the devotion of his associates. He seldom used profanity, and preferred conversations about current events and baseball and other sports rather than about crime or his own exploits.

Homer Van Meter was of an almost directly opposite type, and yet the two men were close. He was taller than Dillinger, with wide shoulders and a narrow waist. The muscles and sinews of his arms stood out like bands of iron. He was a rough talker and lacked Dillinger's polish, but he possessed a measure of dry wit which he employed in jests uttered in a whining, complaining tone.

Van Meter gave much the impression of a caged animal. His fingers twitched, his eyes shifted nervously, his head turned continually from one side to the other. One entering the door of Probasco's home might see Dillinger reclining comfortably on a couch and reading a magazine, whereas Van Meter would never fail to be standing with machine gun in hand. Contrary to Dr. Loeser's testimony, Van Meter was not a drug addict. At the time of the operations Loeser himself provided tablets of morphine to ease the pain, but Van Meter did not routinely use narcotics.[48]

Although not a wanton killer, Van Meter had far fewer qualms than Dillinger about taking human life. Nevertheless he was anxious to live for his own part, and his great ambition was to amass a fortune of a quarter of a million dollars, so that he might flee to South America and live what he imagined to be the easy life of a gentleman planter. Perhaps it was this goal that rendered him close about money matters. As an example, the more open-handed Dillinger paid Probasco thirty-five dollars a day, whereas Van Meter haggled the price down to twenty-five.

For some days following the operations, Dillinger and Van Meter remained close to the house, but after that they began to go about more freely, much to the exasperation of Probasco, who feared that they might be recognized and followed. While they were indoors much time was passed playing cards, in which Probasco and Dr. Cassidy often took hands. Dillinger enjoyed reading, whereas Van Meter did not, and when his partner was thus occupied he would sit with ear glued to the radio that picked up police calls. Every few minutes he would deliver Dillinger a report on something he had just heard, until finally the latter would lower his paper or magazine and implore him to be quiet.

The radio and newspapers kept Dillinger and Van Meter well informed as to their own alleged escapades. On June 5 a deputy was slain in Louisville, Kentucky, and a posse set out in pursuit of the Dillinger gang. Another bulletin had Dillinger sighted at Baraboo, Wisconsin, on June 13. About ten days later John Dillinger and "Pretty Boy" Floyd were reported in a hideout in the Ozarks, but a raid by sixty federal agents and Missouri state police found nobody home. A short time before, Frederick A. Weber of Chicago was arrested because he looked like Dillinger. The gentleman became very much incensed and declared that he was considering plastic surgery. The irony was not lost on Dillinger.

Both Dillinger and Van Meter went about quite openly while living with Probasco, although Dillinger was far bolder in this respect.

"You're going to get it one of these days, running around so much," Van Meter would scold as Dillinger was preparing for another night on the town.

On several occasions the two remained away for a day or more at a time, and presumably were casing banks. Generally, however, their time was taken up with less serious business. Twice they went to the World's Fair, while Dillinger attended ball games at the Cubs' park on three or four occasions. Dillinger was passionately fond of gangster movies, and there were scarcely any he failed to see. Both of the outlaws liked to dance, and often went to cabarets, usually in the outlying neighborhoods. Once at the Grand Terrace Café, a black and tan resort,[49] Dillinger sat at a table close to the stage. He remarked that the chorus girls seemed to be eyeing him suspiciously, and noting that they whispered to each other as they left the stage, he lost no time in leaving the place. This was the only instance he felt he might have been recognized, for in addition to the facial surgery he disguised himself by dyeing his hair black, growing a mustache, and wearing glasses.

Dillinger occasionally patronized houses of ill fame, probably including one operated by a certain Rumanian immigrant at 3221 Warren Avenue, since it was less than two blocks from one of his favored meeting spots at Homan and Madison. Van Meter rarely went on these trips. Paradoxically, it was Dillinger who had little difficulty attracting women wherever he went, whereas Van Meter not only was rather homely but gave the feeling, as one party expressed it, of "something sneaking up on you." On their visits to cabarets, he would watch longingly as Dillinger departed with some young lady and the light of love in his eye.

One of the most remarkable aspects of the month-long residence of Dillinger and Van Meter at the Probasco hideout is the fact that O'Leary and Piquett were contacting them constantly during this time. O'Leary in particular visited the outlaws on an average of every other day, always losing any "tail" that was put on him by either federal agents or the Dillinger squad. Although all lines into Piquett's offices eventually were tapped, Dillinger called O'Leary regularly to make appointments. He would identify himself as "George" or "Fred" or by some other name which changed about every week, and nonchalantly invite him over for a game of cards.

It usually took O'Leary about two hours to complete the fifteen-minute journey from his abode on North Pine Grove to the hideout on North Crawford, less than five miles exactly due west.

After leaving his apartment, he would drive in one direction and then another until he came to a street on which no cars were parked. Here he would stop and wait for a minute or so to see if any car was following. After more of this aimless driving he would maneuver the machine into traffic, then suddenly pull into a parking place, toss his hat into the back seat, don a cap, and walk to the nearest elevated station. The next step would be to take a train to a point somewhere in the vicinity of Probasco's house. Here he would hail a cab, dismiss it about two blocks from the hideout, and cover the remaining distance on foot.

Piquett called at the cottage far less frequently, but he employed similar precautions. On one or two occasions, however, after having lingered too long at his cups, he drove directly to Probasco's in his large car and parked almost in front of the door. Had either the federal agents or the Chicago police used a skilled "tailer" to track O'Leary and Piquett, the hideout would inevitably have been discovered during the time both Dillinger and Van Meter were there.

In this same month of June, Piquett and O'Leary had a number of mysterious feminine callers which caused them to believe that there might be "G-women" as well as G-men. The first was a tall, dignified, well-dressed woman, with a beautiful figure, auburn hair combed straight back, and large blue eyes, who dropped by Piquett's offices about the time the facial operations were taking place. She was Pearl Hellman, or Pearl Elliott, and while living at Mishawaka, Indiana, she had come to know Dillinger and several of his old associates from Michigan City. A few days later she came back again.

"I'm suspicious of that dame," Piquett told O'Leary. "I think I'll take her out and get a few drinks in her, and see what this is all about."

A few hours later a much-excited Piquett telephoned O'Leary. "I'm over at Citro's on Halsted Street with the Hellman girl. Some of the boys over here just tipped me off that she's a G-woman."

"Get rid of her and come back here," O'Leary advised.

The saying, however, proved easier than the doing. When Piquett returned to the office, the auburn-haired beauty was still with him. O'Leary took her by the arm, and led her into his office.

"Mrs. Piquett is due here any minute," he informed her. "You'd better clear out, and clear out fast."

Pearl returned yet a third time, on this occasion with a man wearing a suit of obvious Michigan City prison manufacture.

"This is Joseph Byer," she declared by way of introduction. "He's an old sweetheart of mine, and I can vouch for him."

The sad-visaged Mr. Byer had a tale of woe to relate to O'Leary. He had spent many years in Michigan City, but had just been granted a three-day leave of absence to attend the funeral of his mother. The leave would soon expire, and being without friends on the outside, no other choice remained than to go back to the penitentiary—that is, unless word could be sent to Dillinger, whom he declared he knew, and Dillinger would consent to receive him into the gang.

"Write your story in a letter," O'Leary parried. "We have a contact man who sometimes sees Dillinger. He may come in today and he may not be in for a week, but when he does, I'll give him your letter."

That same afternoon O'Leary journeyed to the hideout, gave Dillinger the missive, and told him the story.

"Yes, I know that fellow Byer—he's a stool pigeon," Dillinger declared. "Have nothing to do with him. That puts Pearl Hellman off the list of right people, too, for bringing him around."

Later events would suggest that Dillinger probably misjudged the lady.

The second visitor to Piquett's offices was likewise a beautiful auburn-haired woman, gorgeously attired in white silks.

"You take this one and see if you can find out what she's after," Piquett instructed O'Leary.

"I'm Mrs. Alvin Karpis," the fair one began. "I haven't seen Alvin in several years, and I have to work to support our little girl. Right now we're very hard up, and I don't know what to do."

"I'm very sorry to hear of your troubles, but I don't know Alvin Karpis," O'Leary told her.

"I know you don't, but I understand your office handles John Dillinger's legal affairs. Dillinger knows Alvin, and I'm sure that if he knew my situation he would either loan me some money or put me in touch with my husband."

"We very rarely hear from Mr. Dillinger. But if we do I'll give him your message. I suggest that you come back in a week."

After her departure O'Leary made his way to the Probasco house.

"Sure, I know Karpis," Dillinger said. "But I never heard him mention a wife or daughter. I don't know what to say about that woman. I think you'd better stay clear of her."

When the woman returned several days later, O'Leary simply informed her that Dillinger had not contacted them.[50]

The third siren was a striking little platinum blonde. She gave O'Leary a name which he promptly forgot, and stated that she was a friend and former roommate of Evelyn Frechette. Now she was desirous of renewing old relationships, particularly with Johnnie Dillinger, and reinforced her request by exhibiting a shapely pair of chiffon-clad legs.

The much-harassed O'Leary made yet another trip to the cottage, and recounted this new story.

"That's the bunk!" Dillinger fairly shouted. "She's nothing but a G-woman. Throw her out!"

When the young lady returned, O'Leary listened to her dulcet ramblings for about half an hour.

"Listen, you!" O'Leary finally interrupted. "We're on to you and all your friends. Now beat it, and quit bothering us."

The little blonde picked up her hat and marched out, never to return.

About the middle of June, Dillinger and Van Meter lost patience with their pursuers. A story had appeared in the newspapers to the effect that Attorney General Cummings had issued a "shoot on sight" order, and this filled both outlaws with righteous fury. When O'Leary arrived in the evening, Dillinger handed him a slip of paper. It bore the names "Harold H. Reinecke, 5737 Kenmore, Rav. 6369," and "Melvin H. Purvis, 11 Scott, Sup. 3719."

"I want you to check up on these addresses and see that they're right," Dillinger told him.

O'Leary placed the paper in his pocket, ostensibly to comply with the request. The next morning he showed it to Piquett.

"Johnnie asked me to check up on a couple of addresses. We can't have that sort of thing going on."

Piquett's eyes opened wide. "I'll say we can't."

The two lost no time in getting to the hideout.

"Art tells me you gave him this paper to check up on some addresses," Piquett told Dillinger. "Just what are you planning to do, Johnnie?"

"They're out to kill me, aren't they? Why should I sit around and wait for it? We're going to be parked in front of their houses one of these nights and get them before they get us. That's all."

"That's all? Have you gone crazy?"

Dillinger tilted back in his chair and smiled as the attorney waved his arms and orated in his best courtroom manner.

"Don't you realize what a stunt like that would mean?" Piquett fairly shouted. "They'd call out the army and place the town under martial law, and hang me from the nearest lamppost. Besides, Purvis has to carry out the orders that are given him.''

''We'll leave Purvis out of it then, but there's nothing going to stop me from killing that son of a ----- Reinecke. He pushed Billie around for days without letting her eat or sleep, and smacked her, and then he lied about her in court. Since all that happened he's been living on borrowed time.''

''You're not going to kill anybody. Just forget about it. Art and I have gone far enough for you as it is. If you try to pull off a general massacre, I'm not with you any longer, Johnnie.''

''All right, counsel,'' said Dillinger glumly. ''We'll let it ride for the time being.''

CHAPTER NINETEEN

THE LAST RAID OF
THE DILLINGER GANG

Somewhat chastened by her sentence of a year and a day, and pursuant to advice from the judge who had placed her on probation, Marie Comforti returned to her home and for the time sinned no more. However, the government was confident that sooner or later she would be contacted by Homer Van Meter, and federal agents kept her home under surveillance. The sharp-eyed Marie was not long in detecting this. One day as she left her house, Al Muzzey, one of the most likable of the Chicago agents, drove by in his car as though a stranger hoping to make her acquaintance and offered her a ride.

An instant later Marie was seated beside him, and for some minutes they drove along in silence.

"It's nice of you to give me a ride," she told him finally. "I didn't know that the federal government was supposed to do that for me."

Van Meter had been at the Probasco cottage almost three weeks when one evening Dillinger, dressed in his finest, prepared to sally forth on one of his nocturnal expeditions.

"Where are you going?" asked Van Meter.

"A man has to go out and have a little fun once in a while," Dillinger said, expecting another lecture.

"That reminds me of Marie," Van Meter muttered instead.

The next day, about June 21, Van Meter drove to Marie's

home and told her to pack her things. They then proceeded to the home of William Finerty and his wife Ella at 492 Freeland Avenue, Calumet City, Illinois, where they rented a room under the name of Mr. and Mrs. Henry Adams. Finerty, whom Van Meter had met in a gambling house, was a railroad brakeman who represented himself to be a former gambling-establishment operator connected with the Capone syndicate. Van Meter himself always insisted that Finerty never had knowledge of his true identity, and this is supported by the fact that he and Marie obtained room and board for only fifteen dollars a week. For any member of the notorious Dillinger gang, the price would have been some ten times that amount.[51]

Van Meter continued to visit Dillinger at Probasco's house, and on occasion would remain there for a day or two. When thus enjoying the Probasco hospitality, he continued to pay twenty-five dollars a day.

During these months Harry Pierpont and Charles Makley remained in the Ohio state prison near Columbus, awaiting their journey to the death house. Pierpont's mother, enduring agony as the day of execution drew nearer, made several visits to Piquett's office. On one of these she brought a note addressed to Dillinger which her son had smuggled out and which she showed to O'Leary. In it Pierpont asked Dillinger to attempt a rescue if at all feasible, and enclosed a map of the section of the prison where he was confined. He implored him to hasten any such attempt, as new electric gates would soon be installed which would render any break exceedingly difficult. It mentioned that Dillinger was under no obligation to help him, as they were now even, alluding to the exchange of assistance at Michigan City and at Lima, and ended, "If you can't make it, Johnnie, I'll see you in hell. Harry."

O'Leary delivered the note to Dillinger and informed him that Mrs. Pierpont was staying at a tourist home on the South Side of Chicago, where the outlaw visited her during the latter part of June. He told the grief-stricken mother that his lack of resources made it impossible to break her son out of the penitentiary, but he gave her a sum of money to assist in any legal efforts she might be making. Mary Kinder likewise delivered messages to Piquett's office from Pierpont, and also made a trip to Mooresville, where old John Dillinger gave her three thousand dollars at his son's request to aid the condemned man.

About this time Louis Piquett found his dangerous client evolving into a Frankenstein monster threatening to wreak destruction too close to home. O'Leary came into the office one afternoon laughing heartily.

"I've just been out to see the boys," he chortled. "They were talking over a new project. You should hear about it."

"What is it?" Piquett asked.

"They're going to your home town of Platteville and take all the banks there."

"What's so funny about that?" the attorney demanded.

Nearly bursting with indignation, Piquett pulled a hat over his snowy locks and stormed out the door, accompanied by the chuckling O'Leary. The moment they entered the Probasco house, Piquett began taking his client to task.

"What's this O'Leary tells me about you fellows wanting to rob all the banks in Platteville?" he began. "Don't you know that's my home town?"

Dillinger arched an eyebrow. "Platteville, Wisconsin?"

"Sure. That's my home town."

"Well, what of it? You don't own the banks, do you?"

"What the hell! Of course I don't own the banks. But my mother and my father and my brothers live there. I was raised there, and I know everybody in the town."

Dillinger shook his head. "I'm sorry, Mr. Piquett, but we've got all the banks cased, and our gets all made. We've gone to a lot of time and expense already, and anyway, it's too easy. Just take a look at this get." He spread the hand-drawn map on the table. "You see, after we take the jugs, we drive out to Weygant's store on the edge of town, follow the old Dubuque road into Fairplay, cross the bridge at Savannah, recross the river at Clinton, Iowa, and then hit back into Chicago."

"But those people up in Platteville are my relatives and my friends," Piquett insisted. "I'd feel terrible if anyone got hurt."

"There isn't going to be any shooting," Dillinger told him. "It will all be over in ten minutes. The three banks are so close together that two lookouts can take care of the whole bunch at once. And how can there be any shooting? The police department doesn't amount to anything, and there isn't any vigilance committee. I'll bet there isn't a gun in the whole town. I'm telling you, it won't take us more than ten minutes."

"Quit your beefing," Van Meter cut in. "If your family loses any money in the banks, we'll kick it back to you."

Piquett was now fuming, his face as red as a chorus girl's lips. "I'm telling you, Johnnie, you can't do this!" he sputtered. "Everybody knows I'm your lawyer. If you go up to Platteville, it will look like I cased the banks and put my home town on the spot.''

"I suppose that's true," Dillinger acquiesced.

"I can't stand for anything like that, Johnnie. You're getting mighty close to home now. If you go shooting up Platteville, I'm through with you, Johnnie. I mean it. You and I will be through.''

"All right, counsel, don't get so burned up about it. To be honest with you, I don't like the idea of that Mississippi River cutting off our retreat. That's bad. So maybe we'll just postpone your town.''

As the two left the house, Van Meter whispered to the beaming O'Leary, "Why don't you keep your mouth shut, anyway?''

Through special legislation, the federal government announced from Washington on June 23 that a reward of $10,000 would be paid for the capture of John Dillinger, and $5,000 for information leading to his arrest. At the same time prices of $5,000 and $2,500 respectively were put on the head of "Baby Face" Nelson. In addition, the states of Ohio, Michigan, Indiana, Illinois, and Minnesota offered rewards of $1,000 each for Dillinger.[52]

Dillinger excitedly showed the paper containing this news to Van Meter.

"Looks like my price is going up," he jested. "Watch Jimmy burn when he finds the government put a cheaper price tag on him than on me. And you, Van, you don't rate at all.''

"Nuts to you," Van Meter grunted. "You just better watch out somebody doesn't cash in on that reward.''

The day before, another item concerning John Dillinger had appeared in the newspapers. An advertisement inserted in the classified columns of an Indianapolis daily by Mrs. Audrey Hancock read, "Birthday greetings to my darling brother, John Dillinger, on his 31st birthday. Wherever he may be, I hope he reads this message.''

The final appearance of the Dillinger gang on the stage of American crime took place on Saturday, June 30, 1934, with the robbery of the Merchants' National Bank in South Bend, Indiana. The raid, which confirmed Dillinger as the modern Jesse James, was perhaps his most dramatic and netted the bandits $29,890. According to eyewitnesses and the authorities, the holdup was carried out by at least four men, although neither Dillinger nor Van Meter mentioned that they had any other companion than "Baby Face" Nelson. The state of Indiana later indicted Jack Perkins as a participant, and in fact almost every person with even the slightest connection to the Dillinger gang became a suspect. The height of something or other was reached when the portly, white-haired, unmistakable Louis Piquett was required to appear in a private lineup as a possible South Bend bandit.[53]

It was shortly before noon when the robbers drew up to the bank, located in the heart of South Bend's business district. Dillinger, carrying a machine gun, entered first, accompanied by an unidentified fourth man with a machine gun and Nelson with a pistol in his hand. Van Meter remained in front to act as a lookout. Customers and employees were forced to lie on the floor, and as Dillinger kept guard, the agile Nelson clambered over the cages and began scooping up the money.

Outside hundreds of shoppers ran screaming for cover as police arrived at the scene and opened fire on the bandits. Machine-gun bullets whizzed along the sidewalks and into the bank. Talking about it later, Dillinger said, "The streets were full of police and slugs were flying everywhere. It was a regular battle. I don't know what the people in the town thought."

There were more persons hurt in this affray than in any other Dillinger raid. Delos M. Coen, cashier of the bank, was shot in the leg, and Perry G. Stahley, a vice-president, was wounded in the hip. A stray bullet struck Jacob Solomon, a bystander, in the abdomen. The wounding of all of these persons has been generally attributed to the bank robbers. However, shots were flying in both directions, and they were just as likely struck by police bullets.

Out in the street Homer Van Meter was having a truly exciting time. Kenneth F. Beers, a farmer from Cassopolis, Michigan, chose this particular day to drive into South Bend in his coupe with his wife and child. While waiting for a traffic light his car stalled, and the next instant he found himself in the middle of the field of battle. Howard Wagner, a traffic policeman, took cover behind the stalled automobile and began firing at Van Meter. The bandit, spraying the streets with his machine gun to keep other police at a distance, threw an occasional shot at the rear of the car to prevent Wagner from venturing out too far and taking careful aim. It is remarkable that the usually savage Van Meter, who could easily have slain the policeman, refrained from doing so because it would have likely meant hitting the woman and her child. Just at this time farmer Beers managed to start his motor and speed away. Wagner, finding himself alone in the middle of the street, turned to run, but it was too late. The infuriated Van

Meter let loose a blast and the unfortunate officer fell, his body riddled with bullets.

Dillinger, leading the retreat from the bank, ran to the car and slid behind the wheel. Nelson, carrying the money, approached the machine from the same side.

"Move over," he called to Dillinger. Nelson hopped in and took the vacated place at the wheel. The next instant a bullet tore into the back of the car and passed directly through Nelson's hat. Had Dillinger, who was a much taller man, remained in the driver's seat, the bullet would have struck him squarely in the back of the head.

Van Meter turned and ran to join his companions. As he was about to enter the car, the owner of a nearby jewelry store appeared and fired at him from only a few yards away. A bullet, evidently from a .22-caliber revolver, struck the bandit in the forehead about at the hair line, drilled under the scalp, and emerged about six inches from the point where it entered. Although not a serious wound, the force of the shot creasing his skull was enough to knock Van Meter off his feet. He fell to his knees, but Dillinger's powerful arms shot forth, seized him by the collar of his coat, and dragged him into the car. Detectives Harry Henderson and Harry McCormick poured their fire at the bandit machine as it sped through the streets of the city. During this exchange, Samuel Toth, a motorist, was hit in the eye.

No organized pursuit followed the marauders as they returned to Chicago by way of Calumet City and Torrence Avenue. A hasty examination of Van Meter's wound revealed that it was not as serious as it first appeared, and it was decided to take him to Probasco's.

Art O'Leary returned to his apartment late on the night of Sunday, July 1, and found a message requesting that he call Jimmy. Instead of telephoning, he and Piquett drove over to the cottage the following morning. They found Dillinger in the kitchen, Van Meter seated on a couch in the living room, still groggy from his wound, and Probasco ranting and raving at the top of his voice.

"Where's that damn Cassidy?" screamed Probasco. "I called him a dozen times yesterday to come over, and the son of a ----- never showed up. If we had to rely on him, Van Meter would be dead now. It's just lucky I happen to be a pretty good doctor myself. Here, show them your head, Van."

Van Meter leaned forward and displayed where the former

veterinary had placed cotton and adhesive tape over the holes, all the while denouncing the absent Cassidy.

"I saved your life, didn't I, Van?" Probasco exclaimed. "Why, I was up all night picking hairs out of that wound."

O'Leary went to join Dillinger in the kitchen, and a few minutes later Cassidy's knock was heard at the door. Probasco greeted him with a tirade of curses, which the young physician shrugged off. He felt that his work with the gang had ended with the facial operations, and had he known the nature of the present summons, he probably would have ignored it entirely.

Cassidy inserted a probe into the wound and removed several pieces of chipped bone, after which he treated the two holes and placed bandages over them. The physician informed Van Meter that the wound was not serious and that he would be all right in a few days, but cautioned him to rest because of a possible concussion and to watch for any signs of infection.

Dillinger and O'Leary now returned to the room, and the former related the excitement of the South Bend robbery. Van Meter told of his encounter with the policeman. "He was hiding in back of the car throwing one slug after another at me, and every now and then I would have to stop and toss a few back at him. Finally the farmer got tired of that stuff and got out of there with his wife and kid. The copper tried to run, but then it was too damned late."

Van Meter, somewhat recovered, began to vent his wrath against the author of the shot, who was mentioned by name in the newspapers.

"You know, Johnnie," he said to Dillinger, "we'll have to go back to South Bend in the next few days and take care of that little Jew."

Dillinger smiled. "Sure we will, Van."

"No, I mean it. I'm serious. I was looking right at him when he came running out of his store. I'd never forget his face in a million years."

"We'll go down there, Van." Dillinger was now laughing outright at his furious companion. "We can't afford to let a guy go on living that can shoot that straight."

A number of amusing incidents occurred during this stay at Probasco's house as the fertile brains of Mr. Piquett and Mr. O'Leary hatched ideas for exploiting the publicity value of their client. That concerning "Red" Hamilton's body met, as we have seen, with an indignant refusal, but there were others to which the gang lent a more receptive ear.

At the time when the search for Dillinger was at its hottest, a reporter for a Chicago newspaper was offered an exclusive personal interview with the famous outlaw. He placed the idea before the editors of his paper, and reported back that they were interested. O'Leary informed him that the price would be fifty thousand dollars and that he would be permitted to bring along a camera, which in addition to written signatures would serve to establish authenticity. He might converse with Dillinger for three or four hours, if he so desired, and was instructed to bring along a considerable sum for traveling expenses. The idea, of course, was to convey the impression that Dillinger was then in Mexico, California, or some other faraway place.

Great enthusiasm seems to have prevailed at the newspaper office over the idea, and details were carefully worked out.

"You're to stand at the corner of Lawrence and Kimball avenues at the time I designate," O'Leary informed the reporter. "A man who you know and who knows you will drive up in a car, and you're to accompany him. The journey will be made partly by airplane and partly by automobile. You're not to yell 'Copper' for two hours after the interview, in order to give Dillinger an opportunity to get away. After that you can get in touch with the authorities in order to prevent your paper and yourself from being charged with harboring."

Dillinger was sounded on the proposal and readily agreed to it. The plans were for him to go to some quiet spot about fifteen or twenty miles outside of Chicago, while Van Meter would remain concealed to guard him. O'Leary was to drive the reporter around for several hundred miles on the less-frequented roads of northern Illinois, then convey him to the rendezvous for the interview.

At the last minute the reporter dashed in to say that his paper had decided too much moral stigma might attach to publicizing so notorious a personage as John Dillinger. Perhaps it was that—or perhaps, on more sober consideration, the price was deemed too stiff.

A second publicity stunt was even more audacious. This was nothing more or less than a joint autobiography to be written by John Dillinger and Homer Van Meter. A recording device was to be brought to Probasco's home, and the two outlaws planned to dictate the stories of their lives. O'Leary was then to engage an experienced writer to prepare the material for publication.

In conjunction with the joint autobiography would be a talking motion picture. Dillinger intended to purchase cameras and sound-recording equipment, while O'Leary found a suitable secluded location, either in the woods of northern Wisconsin or south of Cleveland, Ohio.

The movie would be of the customary "Crime Does Not Pay" variety. Dillinger and Van Meter were to exhibit their machine guns, pistols, and bulletproof vests, then give a detailed account of one of their bank robberies, tentatively either that at Sioux Falls or the one in Mason City, in which no one had been killed. In a message to the youth of America, Dillinger would warn against following in their footsteps. He would tell how they were hunted like rats, and driven from one crime to another simply to raise the money needed to buy another day's protection.

Both Dillinger and Van Meter were highly enthusiastic regarding the idea, and spoke of it constantly over a period of several weeks.

"You know, I'm the one who can really tell this part of the story," Van Meter would remark to Dillinger. "I'll give out a message to the youth of America."

"No, that's not the idea, Van. We just want to tell them that crime does not pay."

"Well, you tell them that crime does not pay, and I'll give my talk to the youth of America."

The proceeds from this scheme were to be divided three ways, between Dillinger, Van Meter, and O'Leary. In the event of their sudden demise, Dillinger's share was to go to his father, and Van Meter's to his brother in Fort Wayne, Indiana. O'Leary realized that making a motion picture starring John Dillinger and Homer Van Meter could not be construed as a protected legal service and would guarantee his conviction on a harboring charge, but he felt that the financial returns would more than compensate him for this inconvenience.

By now the Probasco roof had sheltered the outlaws for over a month, and that alone was sufficient reason for the fugitives to move. There were other contributing factors as well. Van Meter, especially, felt that the hideout was becoming too conspicuous.

"There are too many people coming up here," he told Dillinger. "I don't like so many people around me."

Jimmy Probasco, with his noisy outbursts, frequent quarrels, and blatant manner of life, was also a cause of concern. On one occasion he had a bitter argument over the telephone with a fellow alcohol peddler.

"I don't care if you bring the cops," he told his conferee. "Go ahead, and see what happens to them when they get here." Dillinger and Van Meter overheard the conversation and were not amused.

The culminating incident occurred on the Fourth of July, 1934. Piquett had dropped over in the morning, and he and Probasco felt obliged to celebrate the patriotic occasion. Dillinger and Van Meter were out at the time, but came back later in the afternoon in Van Meter's car. As was their custom, they circled the house two or three times before parking the machine. As they were about to enter, Piquett and Probasco, returning from their tour of the taverns, drove up and parked Piquett's large car halfway on the sidewalk, and walked to the cottage arm in arm. The two outlaws returned to their machine and waited.

Inside the house, Piquett found several large bundles of money stacked on top of the piano, but no client, and he and Probasco therefore decided to continue their rounds for a while longer. When they had departed, Dillinger and Van Meter packed up all of their possessions and left without so much as a note of farewell.

Returning to find that his well-paying guests had checked out, Probasco raged and cursed at Piquett, blaming him and his drinking for scaring his tenants off. The friendship between them was over, he declared, and he never wished to lay eyes on the attorney again. This stormy scene, seemingly no more than a drunken brawl of words at the time, came close to having fatal consequences.

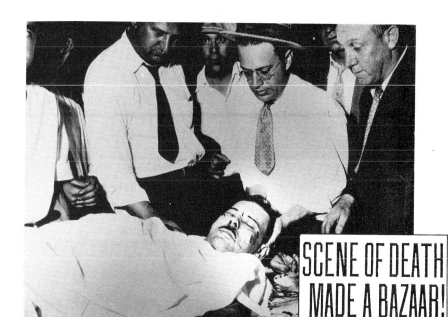

Posing with corpses was still in vogue for news pictures in the 1930s, and the Cook County coroner saw nothing out of line in holding Dillinger's body an extra day for the edification of the viewing public. *Dennis De Mark*

Spectators thronged to the Biograph Theatre after Dillinger was shot and solemnly posed around the puddles of blood in the alley where he fell. *Kathi Harrell*

SCENE OF DEATH MADE A BAZAAR!

"The spot" where John Dillinger was slain became a great bazaar yesterday, with gabby youngsters to tell you "eye-witness" stories for a coin and loud-mouthed men hawking handkerchiefs and bits of newspapers stained by the desperado's blood.

On the scene of Chicago's most famous "spot" in years gathered thousands of the curious, who proved eager bait for the scheming sidewalk spielers.

For a quarter you could buy a scrap of paper which they said had been dipped in Dillinger's blood. For 50 cents you could have a bit of a handkerchief likewise christened.

NECTIE SALE BOOMS.

And not far away in a haberdashery window hung a duplicate of the necktie Dillinger wore when federal men and East Chicago, Ind., police turned loose a fatal hail of bullets. The store advertised that there were plenty of ties like it for sale, and a curious public rewarded the notice.

No one really believed that all the bits of incarnadined paper and cloth for sale were genuine, but that didn't slacken the demand.

Showmen were quick to seize the opportunity provided by the arch-criminal's crimson death. They besieged police at the scene, demanding to be allowed to bid on Dillinger's personal effects.

BID ON CLOTHING.

One man offered the city $100 for four of the bloodstained bricks Dillinger fell on.

Another topped him by offering $1,000 for the shirt Dillinger was wearing, and still others wanted to buy the tie and hat.

Many hours after the shooting, the hawkers were still doing a big business. Dillinger's last stand had turned out to be a souvenir stand.

Chicago Herald

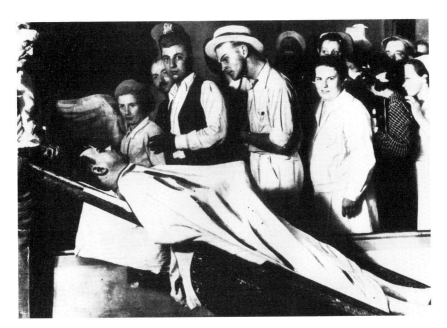

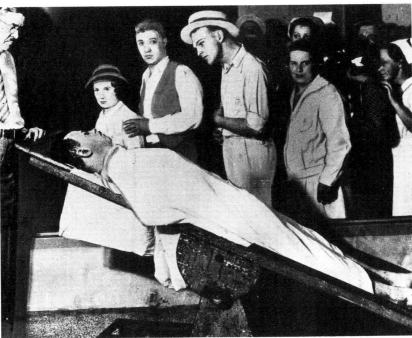

The *Chicago Daily News* rushed into print with a front-page picture of Dillinger's body that editors soon replaced with a view less suggestive of an erection. Though the effect was caused by his arm, other papers using the same picture had their photo retouchers flatten the sheet. *John Dillinger Society*

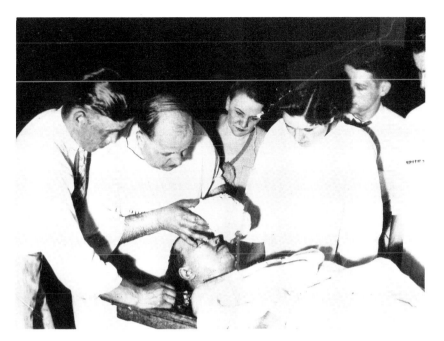

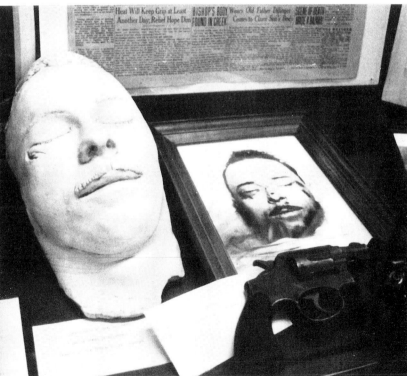

Some embalming college students had their unauthorized death mask of Dillinger confiscated by a Chicago cop, and it probably became the one now displayed at the Chicago police museum.
Marjorie Eker McDougall

```
                                        12-20 PM    CLE
                    CGO         7-22-34
DIV INVEST

JODIL
        DIRECTOR
LATE YESTERDAY AFTERNOON CAPTAIN ONEAL AND SERGEANT ZARKOVICH, OF THE
EAST CHICAGO INDIANA POLICE DEPARTMENT, CALLED MR. PURVIS AND MADE
AN APPOINTMENT TO MEET     MR. PURVIS AND MYSELF AT THE GREAT
NORTHERN HOTEL.  AT WHICH TIME SERGEANT ZARKOVICH ADVISED THAT HE HAD
A CONFIDENTIAL INFORMANT WHO HAD MET AND GONE TO THEATRES SEVERAL
TIMES WITH DILLINGER AND HIS GIRL FRIEND.  CAPTAIN ONEAL STATED THEY
WOULD LIKE TO GIVE THE INFORMATION TO THE DIVISION BUT REQUESTED TO
WORK WITH US WHICH ARRANGEMENT WAS ACCEPTED.  SERGEANT ZARKOVICH HAD
AN APPOINTMENT WITH THE INFORMANT LAST NIGHT AT 9 O CLOCK AND MR
PURVIS WENT WITH HIM.  THE INFORMANT PROVED TO BE A MRS. SAGE A
FORMER PROSTITUTE OF EAST CHICAGO AND WHO HAS BEEN ORDERED DEPORTED.
SHE IS ANXIOUS TO OBTAIN REWARDS AND NOT BE DEPORTED.  SHE WAS AD-
VISED THAT SHOULD HER ASSISTANCE BRING ABOUT THE APPREHENSION OF
DILLINGER WE WULD DO ALL WE COULD FOR HER.   SHE DOES NOT KNOW
WHERE DILLINGER LIVES AND HAS NO WAY TO GET IN TOUCH WITH HIM BUT HAS
TO WAIT FOR HIM TO CONTACT HER THROUGH HIS GIRL FRIEND, BETTY KEEL,
OF FARGO, NORTH DAKOTA.  SHE STATES DILLINGER HAS HAD HIS FACE
OPERATED ON.  REMOVING THE MOLE FROM BETWEN HIS EYES AND THE DIMPLE
FROM HIS CHIN AND THAT HE HAS ALSO HAD HIS FINGERS OPERATED ON.
INFORMANT     HAS ALSO ADVISED THAT HE HAS HAD HIS FACE AND HANDS
OPERATED ON.          STATED THAT HIS FACE HAD BEEN OPERATED ON.

        HOLD MIN
OPERATION ON HANDS  UNDOU BTEDLY FOR PURPOSE OF CHANGING FINGER PRINTS

              COWLEY

END
```

New York Daily News

In a last-minute teletype to Hoover the day of the Biograph ambush, Sam Cowley relayed Anna Sage's deportation concerns, and she assumed a deal was made. The Justice Department wiggled out on a technicality, but many Americans disapproved of what appeared to be a government doublecross.

The Dillinger case made Melvin Purvis more famous than J. Edgar Hoover, who inwardly seethed at this publicity setback, but felt obliged to send Purvis letters gushing with compliments. The director made Purvis's life so miserable that "America's Ace G-Man" resigned from the Bureau. He then prospered from endorsing products from Gillette razor blades to Dodge automobiles, and from heading up Post Toasties' "Junior G-Men," but Purvis's every effort to remain in law enforcement or security work was diligently obstructed by Hoover for the next 25 years. Purvis killed himself at home in 1960 with the ornate Colt .45 automatic he had received as a going-away present from fellow agents in 1935.

DILLINGER SLAIN BY PURVIS' MEN AT MOVIE HOUSE

Desperado Dies with Revolver in Hand in Lincoln Avenue Trap.

CB187 72 GOVT

IX CHICAGO ILL 10 1106A

J EDGAR HOOVER

1935 JUL 10 PM 12 19

DIR PERSONAL & CONFIDENTIAL FEDL BUR OF INV US DEPT OF JUSTICE
PENNSYLVANIA AVE AT 9 ST NW WASHN DC
I HEREBY TENDER MY RESIGNATION AS SPECIAL AGENT IN CHARGE OF THE
CHICAGO OFFICE OF THE FEDERAL BUREAU OF INVESTIGATION TO BECOME
EFFECTIVE AS OF THE CLOSE OF BUSINESS FRIDAY JULY TWELFTH STOP THE
BUREAU IN WHOSE SERVICE I HAVE ENJOYED THE ASSOCIATIONS OF SO MANY
FINE MEN WILL ALWAYS HAVE MY SINCERE BEST WISHES STOP IT WILL BE
APPRECIATED IF YOU WILL GRANT ME SUCH ANNUAL LEAVE AS HAS ACCRUED
RESPECTFULLY

MELVIN PURVIS.

FEDERAL BUREAU OF INVESTIGATION
U. S. DEPARTMENT OF JUSTICE
COMMUNICATIONS SECTION

FEB 29 1960

TELETYPE

5-24 PM EST   AJC

URGENT   2-29-60
TO DIRECTOR, FBI AND SAC CHICAGO
FROM SAC, SAVANNAH   1 P
MELVIN HORACE PURVIS, FORMER SPECIAL AGENT. INFORMATION RECEIVED THIS
DIVISION THAT MELVIN HORACE PURVIS COMMITTED SUICIDE TODAY. WIFE WAS
IN YARD AT TIME OF SUICIDE. FURTHER DETAILS WILL BE SUBMITTED.

END AND ACK PLS

REC-146

WA 5-23 PM OK FBI WA MS

MR. DELOACH

CC - Mr. De Loach
Mr. Callahan

OK FBI CG MS

MR. CALLAHAN

MELVIN PURVIS
JUNIOR
G-MAN
CORPS

Department of Justice

BUREAU OF INVESTIGATION

WASHINGTON, D. C.

February 24, 1927

To whom it may concern

This is to Certify that on January 25, 1927, the bearer, whose signature and photograph appear hereon, was regularly appointed a Special Agent of the Department and as such is charged with the duty of investigating violations of the laws of the United States and collecting evidence in cases in which the United States is or may be a party in interest

CANCELLED

Melvin H. Purvis Jr.

J. Edgar Hoover
Director, Bureau of Investigation.

Jno. G. Sargent
Attorney General

GOVERNMENT PRINTING OFFICE

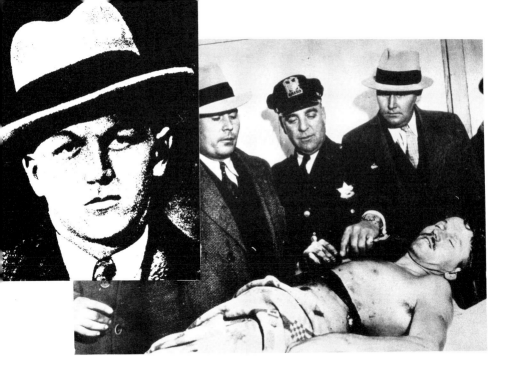

PURSUIT, DEATH BATTLE AND FLIGHT OF KILLERS

NELSON AND COMPANIONS TAKE FEDERAL CAR AND SPEED WEST ①

FEDERAL AGENTS IN CAR (No.1) CHASE NELSON'S CAR (No.2) ① ②

NORTHWEST HIGHWAY

FEDERAL CAR SKIDS TO STOP ①

ENTRANCE TO NORTH SIDE BARRINGTON PARK

FEDERAL MEN FIRE FROM BEHIND TELEGRAPH POLE AND FALL HERE.

NELSON'S CAR SUDDENLY TURNS OFF ROAD ②

BANDITS FIRE FROM BEHIND THEIR DAMAGED CAR

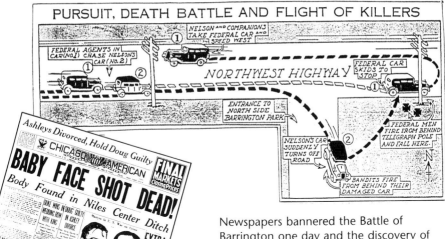

Ashleys Divorced, Hold Doug Guilty

CHICAGO AMERICAN FINAL MARKETS Closing Prices

BABY FACE SHOT DEAD!

Body Found in Niles Center Ditch

Herald Examiner 2 CENTS SPECIAL SPORTS

'KILL WIDOW OF BABY-FACE!' U. S. ORDERS GANG HUNTERS

Marina Becomes George's Bride in Glittering Pageant | Proclaimed Enemy of Nation; Identified by Call for Funeral

20 Pages of Comics in Color Sunday! Order Your Copy Now

Newspapers bannered the Battle of Barrington one day and the discovery of Baby Face Nelson's body the next, but the circumstances of his death went unreported, as did the exact location of the corpse. It was wrongly assumed that Nelson had died soon after the gunfight and his body had been dumped on the run, for part of the problem of finding it stemmed from wrong directions given by an anonymous phone caller. Police searched a wide area in two North Shore suburbs before discovering Nelson wrapped in a blanket next to St. Paul's Cemetery, at the southwest corner of what is now Conrad Street and Long Avenue in the township of Skokie. *Map courtesy of the John Dillinger Society*

Homer Van Meter's prison records display the old Bertillon method of identification by body measurements, used before fingerprinting became standardized and universal.

A crowd of onlookers ogle the body of Van Meter, who was shot by police in St. Paul on August 23, 1934.

John Dillinger. *John Dillinger Society*

CHAPTER TWENTY

PIQUETT FALLS
FROM GRACE

Whatever perils might have attended John Dillinger's stay at the house of Jimmy Probasco, he had found there the longest period of security in his criminal career. Once away, he quickly fell prey to the vultures always poised at the edges of the underworld. The end of the trail was in sight.

Art O'Leary learned of the outlaws' departure from the hideout during an excited visit from Piquett on the night of July 4. Cassidy heard from Van Meter the next day, and in accordance with instructions proceeded on a Western Avenue streetcar to the southern terminus of the line. Here he was met by Van Meter and conveyed by car to the residence of William Finerty in Calumet City. Cassidy remained there only long enough to redress the wounds, and returned to Chicago on an electric interurban railroad.

It was Saturday, July 7, when O'Leary received his next contact from Dillinger. The outlaw telephoned him at his office, and a meeting was arranged for that same day at Schiller Street and Sacramento Boulevard. Dillinger was hidden in the shadows on one side of the street, while Polly Hamilton, his latest light of love, stood in the parkway in the middle of the boulevard. O'Leary refused Dillinger's offer to introduce him to Polly, and after conversing for a few minutes regarding the Frechette appeal, the two men separated.

That same day Pat Reilly was arrested in Minneapolis for his part in the Little Bohemia episode, and held in bond of $50,000 on a charge of conspiracy to harbor Dillinger. He would be tried in September and sentenced to twenty-one months in prison and a $2,500 fine.

Two days later Cassidy called O'Leary and requested a ride to the Finerty home for another treatment of Van Meter, inasmuch as the place was hard to reach by public transportation. O'Leary, not wishing to visit outlaws in the presence of strangers, remained outside in the car while Cassidy was occupied within the house.

Louis Piquett had an appointment the same day, Monday, July 9, with Dr. Loeser at Wrightwood and Clark streets regarding the balance due the physician for his services. Unknown to the two, a third party was present at this conference in the person of C. G. Campbell, a federal agent. Campbell would trail Loeser to his new address of 1127 South Harvey Avenue, in Oak Park, whence he had moved and paid six months' advance rent to celebrate his new prosperity. This was the clue that ultimately enabled the federal government to learn of the Probasco hideout and plastic surgery.[54]

Two days later, on Wednesday, July 11, O'Leary had his next meeting with Dillinger. The two leaned up against a tree at the entrance of the park at Augusta and Sacramento boulevards, and talked for perhaps half an hour. Dillinger related that on the night before he and Polly Hamilton had gone to the World's Fair with Van Meter and Marie Comforti, and all had thoroughly enjoyed themselves. A policeman had begun to follow the party, and Van Meter, becoming apprehensive, departed with Marie. Dillinger and Polly, however, lost their pursuer in the crowds and remained for another hour.

The conversation switched to Evelyn Frechette and the possibilities of winning her freedom. The outlaw had evidently begun to despair of success through an appeal, and stated that he had recently made a trip to case the federal prison at Milan, Michigan, where she was confined. The local topography was such as to make any rescue extremely difficult, however, and the idea had therefore been temporarily discarded.

While they were thus absorbed in the exciting details of an exciting life, a police squad car was stealthily approaching. The driver slowed his machine to about five miles an hour, and all four occupants craned their necks to peer at Dillinger's face. After passing the tree, the two officers in the rear seat turned around and continued to stare out the back window. Dillinger nonchalantly returned their gaze until they passed from view.

"Get across the street and into your car," he ordered O'Leary. "I want you to get clear of this."

O'Leary hurried to the car, while Dillinger went on into the park and mixed with people watching a baseball game. O'Leary drove around the park to assure himself that the squad car was not lurking in the vicinity, then signaled by waving his hat. There was no difficulty picking Dillinger out of the crowd, for the outlaw was conspicuously attired in a new gray suit with a green pinstripe, white shoes, a bright green necktie, and a recently purchased straw hat.

"That was a close one," sighed the perspiring O'Leary as his companion seated himself in the car. "I don't think I'll play with you anymore. You're too hot. I'm going to get my damned head shot off."

Dillinger laughed.

"Do you think they recognized you?" O'Leary asked.

"Of course they recognized me. They couldn't help it."

"What would you have done if they had leveled a machine gun on you when they were right in front of us?"

"What else could I have done? I'd have gone up for them, just like they go up for me when I've got a chopper pointed at them. They had their chance then to take me, but they didn't have the guts to go through with it."

Dillinger and O'Leary were together again the very next evening. The outlaw had a meet arranged with Van Meter on the outskirts of Chicago, and requested O'Leary to drive him there. On the way Dillinger told of the Cubs baseball game he had witnessed that afternoon.

"There was a fellow sitting near me, and he was keeping a pretty close eye on me all through the game," he related. "I think he must have recognized me. I rounded several times, and each time there was this guy gunning me. I figured it would attract too much attention if I got up and left, so I just stayed to the finish and then mixed in the crowd. Anyway, it was too exciting a game to leave."

O'Leary drove out Torrence Avenue to the southern edge of Chicago. On one of the side roads Van Meter's car was drawn up in front of a barbecue stand. Van Meter himself was inside with a sandwich in one hand and a bottle of pop in the other, and ordered the same refreshments sent out to Dillinger and O'Leary in their car. Dillinger and Van Meter then proceeded to the latter's car, where they talked together for nearly half an hour. When they returned, Van Meter was speaking excitedly, and remained standing at the window of O'Leary's car after Dillinger had gotten in. "Baby Face" Nelson had been under discussion, and Van Meter was still on the subject.

"I had it out with Jimmy," he declared. "I told him I wasn't going to pay him any twenty-five hundred dollars. I never did care a hell of a lot about that guy, anyway."

"He was always complaining to me about you, too, Van," said Dillinger.

"Well, I don't see why I should stand half of that Milwaukee fall."

"If you don't feel you owe it, don't pay it," Dillinger told him.

"We had it pretty heavy there for a while. I thought we were going to draw guns on each other."

"Forget it, Van. We're through with Nelson, anyway. He's out of the gang."

"I suppose that's good. Don't forget about the 'soup.' I'll take care of everything else."

On the return trip Dillinger made no further mention of the Nelson incident, but he did elucidate regarding the "soup," or nitroglycerin.

"I'll let you in on something, Art. Van and I are going to pull off the biggest job of our lives. It will be one of the biggest jobs in the world. Just me and Van—we're not cutting anybody else in on this. I'll tell you what it is—we're going to take a mail train. We've got it spotted, we've been watching it for weeks, we know all its stops. We need the 'soup' to blow the door of the mail car. We also know how much money it will be carrying, and it's plenty. We'll have enough to last us the rest of our lives, and right after it's over we're lamming it out of the country."

This contemplated last great robbery was referred to again by Dillinger on several occasions, although he gave no further details, other than mentioning that it was planned for the week following that in which he met his death. In fact, it was the subject most on the minds of both outlaws at this time, and Dillinger in particular looked forward to it as the "one big haul" that would enable him to abandon his life of crime. Marie Comforti states that Van Meter disappeared for a day or two on several occasions while she was living with him at the Finertys' home, and it was on these trips that he and Dillinger "cased" the mail train.

Apart from these short journeys, neither of the outlaws left the Chicago area despite continual "sightings" of them in all parts of the country. On July 3 Dillinger was seen in Whitensville, Massachusetts, driving a car with a Michigan license. Reports from Boston four days later had him whizzing through that city in a car with three other men. The same day, July 7, he was "positively identified" in Iola, Kansas, as well as in Clinton, Iowa, although in the latter city police stated only that he might have been there. A tip reached Columbus, Ohio, on July 15 that Dillinger, under the name of Baker, had boarded a plane in Indianapolis bound for Washington, and eight policemen with machine guns were dispatched to the airport. The startled gentleman whom they greeted turned out to be G. Clay Baker of Topeka, commissioner of Workmen's Compensation for Kansas.[55] On this same date police in Fostoria, Ohio, were seeking him as the driver of a green sedan. The Chicago police on July 20 raided the Lawson Y.M.C.A. on Chicago Avenue following a report that Dillinger, Nelson, and the now-deceased Hamilton were dwelling there.

Cassidy requested O'Leary to accompany him on another trip to the Finerty home on July 13, inasmuch as Van Meter seemed in no hurry to pay for the work done on his head. Cassidy went into the house and in a few minutes brought Van Meter out to the car.

"Hello, Art," Van Meter called, extending his hand. "Come on in and have a beer."

"Thanks, Van, but I don't want these people you're living with to get to know me."

"Don't worry, they're not home. Anyway, they haven't the slightest idea who I am."

The three entered the house.

"What's this that Cassidy has been telling me about you not paying him for the work on your head?" O'Leary said.

"I think it ought to be included as a part of the other. I paid plenty to let them cut up my face, and the job was so rotten that I don't think I should be charged for this."

"I know, Van, but it was Loeser who did that other work. Cassidy isn't responsible for the way it turned out. This man has been risking his neck to come out and take care of you. I think five hundred dollars is a very good price for what he's done."

The ever-frugal Van Meter looked unhappy and said, "I'll take it up with Johnnie."

The matter evidently required little discussion, for the following afternoon Dillinger telephoned O'Leary and arranged a meeting at Kedzie and North avenues. Cassidy followed O'Leary, each in his own car, and upon their arrival they found that Dillinger had also brought Polly Hamilton. On this occasion she was introduced to them, but after exchanging a few words, Polly was sent to sit in Cassidy's car while the three men conferred in the other machine. Dillinger's first action was to produce his billfold and hand Cassidy five hundred dollars.

"Here you are, Doc," he told him. "I saw Van today and he asked me to give this to you."

The surprised Cassidy expressed his gratitude.

"There's another little matter of money, Johnnie," O'Leary said.

"I was over to see Jimmie Probasco the other day, and he mentioned that you still owe him some money for the time you were living there."

"I believe he's right. Give him this 'C' note. A hundred dollars ought to about cover it."

"By the way, Johnnie, your radio is still up at Probasco's. What do you want to do with it?"

"Do you want it, Art?"

"Sure. I'd like to have it as a remembrance of you."

"Tell Jimmy I said you could take it. I've got a rifle up there you can have. You don't have to be afraid. It's a clean gun. Nobody's been shot with it."

Cassidy, elated with his payment, went out that same night and purchased a new sport model roadster. The next day, Sunday, July 15, he and O'Leary went out to see Van Meter, and the young doctor exhibited his latest acquisition.

"That's a swell car you've got there," Van Meter said. "Let me try her out for you and see how she runs."

The outlaw jumped into the driver's seat and began racing the car at sixty-five or seventy miles an hour, while with every rise of the speedometer Cassidy's heart sank correspondingly.

"Runs swell," Van Meter informed the owner. "Maybe I'll borrow it from you the next time I heist a bank." He gave a wink to the grinning O'Leary.

It was the afternoon of Tuesday, July 17, before O'Leary found an opportunity to visit Jimmy Probasco. Cassidy went along with him, and they took possession of the radio and the rifle.

"Johnnie asked me to give you what he still owes," said O'Leary, handing the money to Probasco. "I'm sorry I didn't get a chance to bring it out before this."

"Is that all he sent—just a hundred dollars?"

"I guess that's all he figured he owed you."

"Well, it's really closer to two hundred and fifty dollars, but I'll take that up direct with Johnnie. That isn't so important. But here's something that is important."

Probasco then began a tirade against Piquett as a prelude to something more ominous.

"Piquett came up to see me the other day," he related, "and said he wanted to talk confidential. 'Jimmy,' he said, 'I haven't heard from Dillinger since the day he and Van Meter ran away from here. That was a dirty trick. But you know me—I just kept my trap shut and didn't say a word.' He goes on that way for a while, and then he tells me that he's tired of being mixed up with a guy as hot as Dillinger. Here comes the important part. He says why don't him and me clean ourselves and make a deal with the 'G' to put Johnnie on the spot, and have O'Leary knocked off with him? Me, I don't say yes and I don't say no. Then he goes away."

"But why me?" asked the startled O'Leary.

"Don't you get it? If he gets rid of you, that takes the heat off of his office. There wouldn't be anybody to hook him up with Johnnie. The government would be feeling sort of friendly, and instead of getting his nose burned in this mess, he figures he would be a big hero."

A multitude of thoughts raced through O'Leary's mind. His instincts told him that Piquett would never do such a thing. Had his nervous strain been less intense, he would have reasoned easily enough that Probasco's heart was now filled with animosity for Piquett, that the attorney had had numerous opportunities to betray Dillinger had he been so inclined, and that in any case, he would hardly want to expose himself to the vengeance of men like Van Meter and Nelson. But now he was thinking that Probasco had long been Piquett's friend, and he recalled that Piquett had mentioned an accidental meeting with Captain Stege at a movie. Piquett had also contacted Captain Dan Gilbert on several occasions, and when questioned regarding this had replied that he was only trying to see how much the authorities really knew. Piquett also mentioned that the police were looking for Dillinger in the vicinity of Fullerton and Lincoln avenues, and he wondered how they had obtained such accurate information.

Several hours later, at six o'clock, O'Leary met Dillinger in the park near Kedzie and North avenues. The outlaw was seated on a large white rock, at the side of the main driveway through the park, while a steady procession of automobiles whizzed by directly in front of him. Dillinger was possessed of one of his infrequent fits of anger, O'Leary soon discovered.

"Hello, Art," he said while getting into O'Leary's car. "Have you seen Probasco?"

"Yes. I was up there this afternoon."

"Did he tell you about Piquett?"

"Yes, but I don't believe any of that bunk."

"Well, I believe it."

"Oh, don't pay any attention to Probasco. You know he's drunk practically all of the time. He doesn't know what he's talking about."

"Well, there was that business about the Pierpont money, and Van Meter has also been warning me against him. He said he's been talking surrender too much."

Dillinger stared off in the distance for a minute or two.

"Art, I want you to get out of town," he began again. "Take your family, and go on up to the north woods or some place."

"What do you think you're going to do?"

"I'm going up to Piquett's office and leave him my card."

"You're crazy, Johnnie. You can't get away with anything like that. Anyway, Lou isn't going to double-cross you. He isn't that kind."

"All you have to do is just what I tell you. I'm telling you to get out of town for a week, and then I'll get in touch with you later. How soon can you go?"

"I can leave tonight, I suppose."

"That's fine. How are you fixed for money?"

"I've got enough."

Dillinger produced his billfold. "Here's five hundred dollars. That will take care of you for a while."

They parted, and that was the last time that Art O'Leary spoke with John Dillinger. It also marked the parting of the ways for Piquett and O'Leary. The latter never returned to the office, but left that same night for the wooded country of northern Wisconsin and Upper Michigan.*

Piquett left for Platteville, Wisconsin, on Friday of that same week. On the night of Saturday, July 21, a long-distance telephone call reached him, and much to his surprise he heard Dillinger on the other end of the line. The outlaw declared that he had reconsidered the matter of surrender, and made an appointment to discuss it further with Piquett on Monday, July 23. Perhaps he

---

*O'Leary told me that later, upon more mature reflection, he was convinced that the whole Piquett episode was an invention by Probasco. The latter had a noisy quarrel with Piquett, whom he blamed for Dillinger's departure. There were several occasions in the past when he had wished Dillinger to take care of his enemies. O'Leary declared that throughout this time he had never known Piquett to express any thought of turning in Dillinger.

was sincere and really desired to end his hunted-animal existence, or perhaps he planned to carry out his threat. His intentions will never be known, for even as he spoke long-distance to Piquett, teletype machines in Chicago and Washington had begun to clatter with discussion of an event that would swiftly culminate in the outlaw's violent death.

He had his weaknesses—women, for one thing,

and a flair for the spectacular.

—J. Edgar Hoover

PART V

According to legend and probably fact, Dillinger once told fellow robber William Shaw, "Never trust a woman or an automatic pistol." This mildly sexist allusion to unreliability reflected both the outlaw's sense of humor and his preoccupation with women, so the Dillinger legend, to be complete, required his betrayal by one. History had no right to expect so much, but that's exactly what happened. And that his betrayer should herself be immortalized as "the Woman in Red" might have been overdoing it in a fable, but not in real life.

So when author Girardin says in his preface that there can never be another Dillinger, he could also be referring to the odds against any criminal's life ever approximating his legend. The recurring claims that the famous outlaw was not killed at the Biograph were never credible enough to inspire frequent Dillinger sightings, but they affirm that the legend is too good to die.

Girardin revises the standard account as concerns John Hamilton, whom the authorities pursued long after his death, and the relationship between Dillinger and Anna Sage, who always maintained that she met and recognized the outlaw entirely by coincidence, through her friend Polly Hamilton. It appears now that Anna and Dillinger probably were acquainted, or at least had mutual friends in East Chicago who arranged for him to stay at her apartment while recovering from plastic surgery. While it's true she stood to benefit financially and otherwise from selling Dillinger out, the established story fails to note that the real plotters may have been northern Indiana gangsters who used her and a somewhat naive FBI to eliminate the man who might one day implicate them in various crimes as well as his own "wooden pistol" jailbreak.

FBI records suggest that the Bureau picked up rumors to this effect, but from hostile sources and at a time when it was not disposed to complicate its own tidy version. The same records largely confirm Girardin's contention that Dillinger died carrying not the paltry seven dollars that proved to newspaper readers how poorly crime paid, but a roll of several thousand evidently stolen off his body by Anna's friend, colleague, lover, and co-conspirator, Martin Zarkovich of the East Chicago police.

CHAPTER TWENTY ONE

THE WOMAN IN RED

Who played the role of the Judas Iscariot in the life of John Dillinger? Many of the details are locked in the bosoms of persons whose instincts for self-preservation have no doubt sealed their lips forever. But before he died, Dillinger revealed enough to identify most of those responsible.

In Lake County, in the northwestern corner of Indiana, a number of cities have sprung up and flourished on the sandy shores of Lake Michigan. Compared to the slow but steady growth of most communities, theirs has been almost an overnight arrival, due partly to their proximity to Chicago and their selection as a center of the steel industry. This sudden creation, coupled with the characteristics of most such mill towns located near a great metropolis, made them breeders of crime and the resorts of the underworld. A few have outgrown these early larval stages and blossomed into progressive American cities; in others the ties of the underworld are still wrapped closely about their throats.

Among these lake cities of Indiana is East Chicago, long bearing an ill repute for the close alliance between the worlds of politics and crime. From East Chicago were to come a number of the dramatis personae of the Dillinger saga.

Let us look first at Anna Sage, a typical product of a steel-mill town. Born Aňa Cumpanas in Rumania, she came from that country in 1909 with her first husband, Michael Chiolak, when only seventeen years of age, and a year later gave birth to a son, Steve. Possessed of a certain coarse beauty and an undemanding code of morals, Anna employed herself in the ancient profession of a prostitute. About 1919 she went to work in "Big Bill" Subotich's place on Guthrie Street, in East Chicago, and here she met and entered into a mésalliance with Martin Zarkovich of the East Chicago police force. Apparently husband Michael Chiolak lacked tolerance for the professional and charitable amours of his spouse, for about this time their bonds of matrimony were severed. Certainly Mrs. Zarkovich resented the connection, for she divorced her mate for being too friendly with Mrs. Sage.

Upon the death of her employer, "Big Bill," Anna took over the running of his establishment. In 1923 she expanded her operations by opening the Kostur Hotel in Gary, Indiana. This place soon attained considerable notoriety as a wide-open disorderly house, and no more bawdy and noisome a brothel ever plagued the local landscape. In the basement of this honky-tonk establishment was a saloon which earned the cognomen "Bucket of Blood" for the many stabbing affrays within its shady depths. Anna became known about northern Indiana as "Katie of the Kostur Hotel," and, swelling with pride in her growing enterprises, she referred to it as "the Kostur Hotel with forty-two rooms."

Although retaining her connections in East Chicago and Gary and with Officer Zarkovich, Anna removed herself to Chicago in 1927 and two years later entered into holy matrimony with Alexander Sage. They soon separated, but as Mrs. Sage she only extended her fortunes by opening new centers of prostitution in the larger city. Her houses were raided on numerous occasions over the years. In Indiana she was fined sixty dollars in 1930, and while criminal actions were taken against her also in February and November of 1931, court records indicate no disposition. In the following year she received two pardons from Governor Harry G. Leslie of Indiana. Meanwhile, the Chicago police raided her house at 2862 North Clark Street, and the federal government began proceedings to deport Madame Sage to her native Rumania as an alien of low moral character.

Martin Zarkovich, Anna's friend as well as paramour, was a good-looking dark-haired, dark-eyed Slav who had attained the rank of a sergeant on the East Chicago police force. His relationship with Mrs. Sage was commercial as well as amatory, for the connection between the madame of a dive and a police officer was mutually advantageous.

The third member of this triumvirate was Polly Hamilton, at this time twenty-six years old and a former inmate of the renowned Kostur Hotel. She had been married to Roy Keele, a Gary policeman, but later was divorced by him. Polly had also come to live in Chicago, at the Malden Plaza Hotel, 4615 Malden Avenue, and combined her activities as a "hustler" with working as a waitress at the S & S Sandwich Shop, 1209½ Wilson, in the brightly lighted Wilson Avenue district of the neigborhood known as Uptown.

According to the carefully rehearsed narratives broadcast to the world by Sage, Zarkovich, et al., the Rumanian brothelkeeper had never laid eyes on John Dillinger until a few days before his death. He was then brought to her house, as merely a visitor, by her young friend Polly Hamilton, who had met him entirely by chance in a cabaret. Anna Sage professed total ignorance of Dillinger's identity until she recognized his picture in a newspaper. Then she became horrified and frightened, and hurried to tell Sergeant Zarkovich, who dutifully informed the federal agents, and that was how it all happened.[56]

That the federal government would accept such an explanation defies both reasoning and common sense, but it evidently did. Out of the thousands of girls in Chicago, John Dillinger happens to meet one whose friend, Anna Sage, has operated "resorts" in Gary and East Chicago, Indiana, where Dillinger has his closest underworld affiliations, and who presently operates a house in Chicago two blocks from the corner where he has meets. Moreover, this Anna's long-time associate and paramour happens to be the East Chicago police officer Martin Zarkovich, who knows Dillinger's friends in that city, as well as Arthur O'Leary in Chicago.

As we have seen, from the inception of his career, John Dillinger, as well as Van Meter, Hamilton, and other members of the gang, had good contacts in Lake County, and particularly in East Chicago, where they maintained hiding places. That city's most prominent underworld figures included Hymie Cohen and Jimmie Regan, whom Indiana authorities identified as associates of Dillinger both before and after the Crown Point escape. They were also aware of the relationship between Cohen and Sergeant Zarkovich, and of the rumors that the First National Bank of East Chicago had been put "on the spot."

In any case, following the Crown Point escape, Captain Tim O'Neil of the East Chicago police announced that he would conduct his own investigation of the escape, while two weeks later

Zarkovich disclosed that he likewise had been investigating the alleged aid given Dillinger and his gang by certain East Chicago politicians and hoodlums, not including himself. The two officers must be lauded for their zeal in launching independent investigations, if we disregard reports that they were attempting to divert suspicion and ascertain how much was already known by other investigators. Assertions from Indianapolis that O'Neil and Zarkovich participated either directly or indirectly in the deaths of officers O'Brien and Mulvihill would be particularly uncomfortable when viewed in this light.

Dillinger needed underworld associations to operate in any city, but especially in a small one the size of East Chicago, where police and underworld figures are familiar with one another. Whether that acquaintance is in the line of duty or savored of connivance is not all-important in this particular instance; the characters and events of the one world simply cannot fail to be well known in the other. And although John Dillinger never mentioned which resorts he patronized in East Chicago and Gary, the house at 3221 Warren Avenue in Chicago, near his Garfield Park meeting place, was operated by the Rumanian immigrant Aña Cumpanas, later Anna Chiolak, now Anna Sage, from East Chicago and Gary.

Before his departure from Probasco's, Dillinger had begun casting about for a new hideout. Whether or not he knew Anna Sage personally, he almost certainly was sent to her by their mutual friends, and it would have been she who introduced Dillinger to Polly instead of the other way around. In any case, Dillinger found the pretty waitress to be an adequate substitute for his true love Evelyn, then inconvenienced by the authorities, and he saw her frequently thereafter. It was while Dillinger was recounting Polly's charms that Van Meter became so reminded of Marie that he virtually kidnapped her the next day.

In the beginning Dillinger had told Polly that he was Jimmy Lawrence, a stockbroker's clerk, and had explained that the scars on his face were the result of an automobile accident. But even before he departed the Probasco hideout, his true identity was no longer a secret.[57]

Piquett asserts that O'Leary, after one of his visits to Dillinger and Van Meter while they were living in the truck around East Chicago, reported that two men had also visited the outlaws, and that he had been introduced to them under the names of West and Roy Keele, who would have been Polly's former husband. The two names may only have been borrowed for the occasion, but if they are authentic, it indicates an even longer association between Anna and Polly and John Dillinger.

Tentative arrangements had been made for a new hideout while Dillinger was still living with Jimmy Probasco, and on July 4 he moved in bag and baggage with Anna Sage, bringing his arsenal of machine guns, pistols, bulletproof vests, and ammunition. That same day Polly called her place of employment and reported that she had had an "accident," and was rarely seen thereafter at her hotel or the sandwich shop. Dillinger, Anna Sage, her son Steve, and Polly Hamilton all resided together in the "call house" at 2420 North Halsted Street, in the Lincoln-Fullerton neighborhood.

Van Meter was greatly disturbed when he learned of the connections his friend had formed.

"I've got no use for that whole East Chicago bunch," he protested to Dillinger. "You're going to get yourself killed."

Zarkovich must have been aware that Dillinger was living with Mrs. Sage during this period, and both stood to benefit substantially from selling him out. The federal government was preparing to deport Anna for her activities in the realm of vice. The state of Indiana was investigating corruption in East Chicago and casting menacing looks in the direction of Sergeant Zarkovich and others. Washington was so anxious to get Dillinger that these relatively minor matters would perhaps be taken care of by U.S. authorities. But best of all, there was a reward of fifteen thousand dollars on the outlaw's head, and that was attractive indeed to those who gained their living off the baser instincts of mankind. Sergeant Zarkovich would cut in Captain Tim O'Neil, and he would take care of the details. Polly Hamilton would serve as the innocent bait to hold the victim until the trap could be prepared.

Sometime after the middle of July, Sergeant Martin Zarkovich journeyed to the offices of Melvin Purvis to recite the story worked up by him and Anna Sage. The information he conveyed naturally excited great interest. An appointment with the lady was arranged for the night of Thursday, July 19. Zarkovich drove the car, while Purvis and Mrs. Sage conversed in the rear seat.

"Kostur House Katie" told her story to the federal men, and all arrangements were made. Zarkovich and O'Neil would share in the reward and receive other considerations. Anna would also be paid, and Purvis promised to employ his influence toward quashing the deportation proceedings. The federal agents would be notified of the first opportunity for carrying out the deed.

On the afternoon of Sunday, July 22, 1934, Anna Sage telephoned Purvis and told him to get ready. Dillinger had invited Anna and Polly to a movie that evening, and it would then be a simple matter to put him on the spot. If they attended the Biograph Theatre in the near vicinity, Anna would be bareheaded; if they were going across town to the Marbro, as also discussed, she would wear a hat. In order that there be no mistake, as had happened too often in the past, Anna was to wear a white blouse and a bright orange skirt, a combination which would not fail to be detected.

There was a gangster movie playing at the Biograph, one of Chicago's oldest neighborhood movie houses, located at 2433 Lincoln Avenue on Chicago's Near North Side, just around the corner from Anna's apartment on Halsted. Dillinger liked gangster pictures, and so Anna Sage was hatless when they left the house. It had been an extremely hot day, and the outlaw wore only a white shirt, a pair of neatly pressed gray trousers (the same he had worn on a recent visit to the World's Fair and when meeting O'Leary in the park), white shoes, and a straw hat.[58] Polly Hamilton had been working in the morning and early afternoon, taking the place of a friend in the sandwich shop. She was also hatless that evening, and had on a tan skirt, white blouse, tan hose, and white open sandals.

The Dillinger party arrived at the theater about half past eight. A force of more than twenty federal agents, commanded by Purvis and Inspector Samuel P. Cowley, were summoned from the office and the Marbro stakeout and deployed in the doorways of nearby buildings. With them were Zarkovich, O'Neil, Glenn Stretch, Peter Sopsic, and Walter Conroy of the East Chicago police force. They settled down for a wait of two long, nerve-wracking hours.

Elaborate precautions were adopted to avert a repetition of the Little Bohemia affair. The principal members of the party remained about the front of the theater, while other groups were posted to the north and south and flanked by secondary parties, with the rear exits guarded as well. The theater manager and some nearby merchants, alarmed at the gathering of men and the repeated inquiries of Purvis as to the feature time, decided that a holdup was contemplated and called the police. A Chicago squad car responded, but accepted the agents' explanation of a federal stakeout, and obligingly left the area. It is interesting to speculate as to what Dillinger would have made of the convention of lawmen had he emerged from the show about this time.[59]

Purvis and two of his men made a tour of the interior of the theater, but were unable to locate their quarry in the darkness. Meanwhile, anxious thoughts must have coursed through the mind of Anna Sage as she watched a motion picture with the man who through her duplicity would lie dead before the night was finished. Did she experience any pangs of conscience, was she afraid lest a stray bullet might strike her down, or was she merely counting in her mind the dollars she would receive as reward for the betrayal?

It was 10:35 P.M. when Dillinger came out of the theater, with Anna and Polly walking on either side of him. Purvis nervously tried to light his cigar—the agreed-upon signal. The federal agents and police understood his movements and made a rush forward. What happened next is somewhat confused. Purvis, in his account given after the shooting, makes no mention of calling out to Dillinger. Later he seems to have remembered saying, "Stick 'em up, Johnnie." Some versions state that there was a call of "Hello, John," or simply "John." Others declare that nothing at all was said.

Somebody pushed Anna Sage aside, and pistols barked. A bullet entered the back of Dillinger's neck and came out his right cheek, just under the eye. Another slug entered his left side. Dillinger took two or three mechanical steps forward, then plunged face downward onto the bricks at the entrance of the alley.

The federal agents pushed back the crowd that gathered as if by magic. One said he took a pistol from the dying man's hand, while another turned him over with his foot. Zarkovich went through his pockets. Dillinger was then placed in the back of a police wagon that had arrived quickly on the scene, but died within five minutes, while on the way to the Alexian Brothers Hospital. Admittance there was refused because he was already dead, and so he was conveyed to the Cook County Morgue.

As was the case in most affrays involving Dillinger, bystanders were shot. Five bullets were fired. Two or three struck or grazed Dillinger, and two other persons were wounded. A young woman, Miss Theresa Paulus, screamed and lifted her skirts to discover a bullet hole in her thigh. Another passerby, Mrs. Etta Natalsky, was hit in the ankle.

Did Dillinger carry a pistol on the night he was killed? Probably he did. Anna Sage first stated that he had no gun, but later changed her story to declare that he carried a pistol stuck in his belt. This seems unlikely, as Dillinger was coatless, although Chicago police reports and others state that the gun was inside the front of his shirt. Some of the agents and the East Chicago men relate that a .38-caliber pistol was taken from a trouser pocket. Art O'Leary and others had seen a small-caliber pistol in Dillinger's arsenal, and when going out on the street he always carried it in his right-hand pants pocket. But O'Leary said he had never seen Dillinger with the model of gun pictured in the next day's newspapers as the one that the agents recovered.[60]

Who killed John Dillinger? No one seems to know, or to want to find out. The federal men say they fired the fatal shot, while the East Chicago police say that it was a member of their force.[61] It should be borne in mind, however, that if the G-men had no compunctions about seeing Dillinger killed, they would have considered it a greater feat to capture him alive. Some members of the East Chicago police department felt otherwise. A living Dillinger might talk, especially when he learned the identity of his betrayer, and what he would say, combined with what the state of Indiana already suspected, might have darkened the future for Sergeant Zarkovich in particular. A newspaper article under the name of East Chicago detective Glenn Stretch, who was present at the slaying, includes this statement: "In the first place, I want to say that Dillinger would never have been killed that night if it hadn't been for the East Chicago police."

Was any effort made to capture Dillinger? Inspector Cowley testified at the coroner's inquest that the outlaw drew a gun from his pants pocket. Sergeant Zarkovich says that he was shot before he could draw his pistol. Melvin Purvis, writing after his resignation from the government service, states: "He [Dillinger] whirled, tugged at his pants pocket. I know what happened. His gun was in that pocket and the hammer caught on the cloth as he tried to pull it out. He ran. We fired."*

Purvis, of all persons, should have been aware that the weapon recovered was a "hammerless" automatic, perfectly rounded with no projecting parts, and that anyone as familiar with the use of guns as John Dillinger would never carry one likely to snag in the lining of a pocket. Furthermore, Dillinger had developed the habit of always sliding his thumb over the top of any gun to avert this very problem.

Dillinger's killers naturally do not wish it thought that his

---

*In my later conversation with J. Edgar Hoover, he indicated displeasure with Purvis. He said that while Purvis could act with celerity and personal bravery, Little Bohemia had been badly mismanaged, and that at the Biograph he had wanted Dillinger taken alive. He suspected, as I did, that Zarkovich was there to make sure Dillinger was killed, and that Purvis should never have agreed to the presence of the East Chicago officers.

death was simply an execution. It must be remembered that the authorities firmly believed they were dealing with perhaps the most dangerous criminal of all time, so claims that he resisted arrest should be weighed against evidence from past performances. When trapped in the apartment of Mrs. Longnacre at Dayton, Ohio, Dillinger made no attempt to use his guns. When challenged by police in Tucson, Arizona, he was carrying a machine gun but surrendered without a struggle. When surprised by a Chicago police car while with O'Leary in the park, he would have submitted to arrest if confronted by guns. In other words, Dillinger showed no desire to die and surrendered peaceably on all occasions when he felt resistance to be futile. This makes it hard to believe that upon leaving the Biograph, finding himself outnumbered and surrounded on all sides, he would have attempted to use his pistol knowing it would mean certain death. However it came about, John Dillinger was shot down from behind, with no attempt worthy of the name made to capture him alive.

Arthur Brisbane, writing in his newspaper column, has a few words to say on the Dillinger killing:

"Chicago supplies a photograph of the dead bandit Dillinger lying on his back, bloodstains from various bullet wounds showing on his shirt.

"Sitting above him, looking down with satisfaction and triumph, you observe a detective and wonder how that detective's expression would change if Dillinger suddenly came to life."

J. Edgar Hoover, from behind his desk in Washington, declared of Dillinger, "He was just a yellow rat."

An inventory of the dead outlaw's personal belongings was made at the county morgue. Among other objects taken from his body was a gold pocket watch. At the time of his last conference with O'Leary, just a few days before his death, Dillinger had mentioned this watch.

"Art, I wish you would take my watch and give it to my dad," he told him.

"Take it to him yourself. You'll be going that way sometime." And so he did return to Mooresville, although he made the journey in a coffin.

"Well, I just got to thinking things over the other night. You never can tell what might happen."

At the same time he asked O'Leary to find him a bronze crucifix of the type distributed by Father Coughlin, the nationally known radio priest, to carry in his pocket. Dillinger seemed to feel the net about him was being drawn closer, and that he had little time left.

The case of Dillinger's watch contained the photograph of a girl. Chicago police declared it to be a likeness of Evelyn Frechette. Purvis identified it as Mary Longnacre. Anna Sage knew it was Polly Hamilton.

What happened to Dillinger's money? A total of $7.71 was officially inventoried and turned over to his father.[62] This led to false claims that Dillinger was short of funds at the time of his death. He had given O'Leary five one-hundred-dollar bills when sending him out of town, and this amount had been taken from a formidable bundle of others of the same denomination. Certainly this large sum had not been dissipated in the intervening five days. John Dillinger always carried thousands of dollars about his person and in a leather billfold in his left hip pocket. This was his "get" money, in case he was spotted and had to take flight. Anna Sage must have known of this money during the weeks he lived in her house, for he was constantly redistributing it in the pockets of his coats and trousers. Did she tell her friend Zarkovich? Detective Stretch, in his series of newspaper articles, makes this unadorned statement: "Zarkovich searched him and took some money from his pockets."[63]

There was much congratulation and backslapping after Dillinger had been killed. Melvin Purvis stated, "I believe that Mrs. Sage has performed an invaluable service ranking among the highest of those needed by our country at this time." Mr. Purvis was called to Washington to receive the personal commendations of J. Edgar Hoover, who also dispatched a letter of praise expressing "Highest esteem and best regards" to O'Neil and Zarkovich.

The Indiana authorities seem not to have shared Mr. Hoover's admiration for the East Chicagoans. Captain O'Neil became Sergeant O'Neil, and Sergeant Zarkovich became Detective Zarkovich. Captain Matt Leach intimates that Indiana would have gone even farther in these left-handed rewards had not Inspector Cowley and others warned the state to "lay off."

Others likewise failed to share in the general enthusiasm. The killing of Dillinger was widely heralded abroad, especially in London; and the *Voelkischer Beobachter* in Berlin asked, "Is a policeman calling a man by his first name before shooting him down sufficient trial? Does a country in which this happens deserve the name of a country of law and order? With a 'Hello, John,' and nineteen [sic] bullets America arrested, tried and killed her greatest criminal, Public Enemy Number One."

At home also were heard some discordant notes. Judge Robert Cowie, addressing a convention of the Wisconsin Bar Association, said that the Department of Justice was being built into a secret police comparable to those in Germany, Russia, and Italy, and described the G-men as being as lawless as the elements they seek to suppress. Referring to the killing of Dillinger, Judge Cowie stated, "The criminal in death stands out a bigger figure than he ever was in his bandit days, because of the glamour and gunplay indulged in to effect his ending."[64]

Louis Piquett was driving home from Platteville late Sunday night when the radio in his car carried a bulletin that Dillinger had been slain. The attorney only smiled. He had heard such reports a dozen times before. They were always killing Dillinger someplace or other. But now the details began coming in, and his face grew serious. Perhaps this time they really had him.

Upon reaching Chicago, Piquett drove straight to the Biograph Theatre. An excited crowd was still milling about. He saw a policeman whom he had known for years.

"What's this about Dillinger?" he asked.

"It's right. They got him."

"Where's his body?"

"At the morgue."

"Jump in the car. Let's drive over there."

Piquett and the officer forced their way through a mob of spectators, reporters, and police to the slab that held the body.

"That's Dillinger, all right," Piquett muttered to his companion.

New heights—or depths—of morbidity followed the slaying of John Dillinger. Supposedly civilized citizens soaked paper bags, newspapers, and handkerchiefs in the pools of his blood in the alley and cherished them as souvenirs or hawked them in the streets.

At the morgue hordes of the curious began arriving that night, and all day Monday the procession continued—thousands upon thousands of them—until the doors of this house of the dead were finally closed at midnight. The ghoulish parade included prosperous professional and business men, society matrons, politicians, police officials, housewives, meek-mannered clerks, painted and perfumed nightclub "cuties," idlers of the streets, giggling high-school girls—all seeking a vicarious thrill. There on the cold slab of the morgue lay the outlaw's body, partly covered with a sheet, his face torn with wounds. They passed before him—the men gaping with open mouths, the women shuddering and covering their eyes, or emitting short hysterical screams.

The inquest, held during the day, lasted only thirty-five minutes. Coroner Frank J. Walsh presided, assisted by Deputy Coroner Jacob Schewel. The police, whose strength and patience were taxed in maintaining order at the morgue, had to control the crowd here as well. Federal agent Earle Richmond was called and testified that he had identified the body as that of John Dillinger by means of the fingerprints, which had defied removal. Inspector Cowley followed him and gave a brief recital of the shooting. The coroner's jury brought in a verdict of justifiable homicide and added a few words of praise for the slayers. That was all.

It was late Sunday night when the news reached Mooresville. Virtually all inhabitants tumbled out of bed and congregated in the streets. Shortly after midnight the town's druggist opened his store, and it served as a meeting place until the break of dawn. Mooresville will long remember the death of its most famous citizen.

A grim procession made its way to the silent white farmhouse on the outskirts of the town. The terrific heat of the day and an attack of indigestion had caused old John Dillinger to retire early that night, and the callers needed to knock repeatedly on the rear door before he was aroused. The old man donned a shirt and a pair of overalls and appeared at the door barefoot. When told that his son was dead, he sagged wearily against the side of the door.

"I knew this was going to happen," he said softly. "I've been expecting it for a long time."

For a while old John Dillinger just stood there. The crowd stared curiously into his face, but his mind seemed miles away. Finally, he spoke.

"You're sure it's true this time? You know they've said that before."

Without waiting for an answer, he turned back into the simple living room and collapsed into the large chair, where he remained with his head buried in his hands.

Audrey Hancock heard the news and hurried over from Maywood. She had been fighting desperately to preserve her calm, but in her father's arms she broke into loud sobs, and her weeping aroused the two little girls, Doris and Frances. Clad in their nighties, they, too, learned what it was all about. Big brother Johnnie had just been killed.

A physician had been summoned for old John Dillinger, but by early morning he had recovered his strength and was ready to set out for Chicago. Accompanied by his son Hubert, he climbed into the seat of the old hearse belonging to E. F. Harvey, the local undertaker. Late Monday afternoon they arrived in Chicago, where he was shoved around by the curious throngs until finally induced to take some rest at midnight.

Early the following morning several men and women, claiming to be a professor and his students from a college of embalming, appeared at the county morgue and implied that they had the permission of Coroner Walsh and Melvin Purvis to make a death mask of the slain outlaw. The police, however, later decided that the mask was intended for commercial use and confiscated it.[65]

Old John Dillinger called at the coroner's office on Tuesday, and asked for young John's clothes and personal effects. A neatly wrapped brown package was handed him, and his fingers began to fumble nervously with the string.

"I'd wait until I got home to open that, if I were you," Coroner Walsh told him. The package included Dillinger's bullet-torn shirt, stiffened and dark with dried blood.

The reporters crowded around him. The old man had been through a terrific ordeal, and for an instant his pent-up emotions broke through.

"They didn't give my boy a chance. They just shot him down in cold blood. I wouldn't want to see a dog shot down like that. Why, he had fifteen or twenty men trying to kill him. That isn't fair."

The cold clay that had once been John Dillinger was taken from the county morgue to the McCready Funeral Home at 4506 Sheridan Road. Thrillseekers had been gathering since early morning, and soon there were thousands of persons besieging the mortuary. Only a few had the pleasure of seeing the wicker basket that held the corpse, but when old John and Hubert arrived, the onlookers felt at least partially rewarded.

Inside the undertaking establishment, father and son met for the first time since that memorable Sunday at Mooresville.

"My boy! My boy!" That was all old John said. There were no tears.

"I want to thank all of you good people who have been so kind to me," the old man said. "I intend to see that Johnnie has a good Christian burial, just like his mother would have wanted him to have if she were still alive."

That afternoon the Dillinger party left Chicago, bearing their dead with them. A crowd of over a thousand persons waited at the funeral parlor in Mooresville, but the body was taken first to the home of Mrs. Audrey Hancock, in Maywood. All through the night a steady parade of automobiles moved along the roads between Indianapolis and Mooresville and Maywood. Some waited in line for hours just to drive past the house and stare at it.

Early on the morning of Wednesday, July 25, they buried the body of John Dillinger, Public Enemy Number One, in the Crown Hill Cemetery at Indianapolis. Within its quiet grounds lie the remains of President Benjamin Harrison, Vice-Presidents Charles W. Fairbanks and Thomas Marshall, and the beloved Hoosier poet, James Whitcomb Riley. Cemetery officials and police feared that the expected crowd of fifteen thousand or more would wreak havoc on the burial plots, and so the final rites were conducted in secret with the general public barred. The lavender casket was lowered into the ground, and the Reverend Charles Fillmore, retired pastor of the Hillsdale Christian Church, spoke a few words at the side of the grave.

A large tombstone bearing the name of Dillinger marks the burial plot, and beneath it are two smaller headstones with the names of old John's two dead wives. Someday, when the Dillinger family can afford it, there will be a headstone for John Dillinger as well.

CHAPTER TWENTY TWO

KILL DILLINGER HERE!

When banner headlines declared that John Dillinger had been shot and lurid pictures of his stripped and blood-smeared body appeared in every newspaper, there was a general scurrying among his former associates. Homer Van Meter, certain that Dillinger had been sold out, feared that his own whereabouts might be known as well, and he left that same night for St. Paul with Marie Comforti. Nelson, suddenly finding himself acclaimed as the new "Public Enemy Number One," left immediately for California.

Anna Sage had been seized after the shooting by a Chicago detective, but was rescued and turned loose by a federal agent. Her troubles did not end with the success of the conspiracy, however. It would soon be discovered that two keys found on the body of the dead outlaw opened the doors to Anna's apartment and her clothes closet, where Dillinger had stored his arsenal. Before this was known, Mrs. Sage and her associates had removed the machine gun, the bulletproof vest, and ammunition under cover of darkness and dumped them in a nearby channel in Lincoln Park. Although they were found the next day by bathers, the ordnance no longer occupied a place that would have required much explanation concerning Dillinger's term of residence, and Anna breathed a bit more freely.[66]

Polly Hamilton fled the scene of the shooting and made her

way to the sandwich shop. There she found a friend, Maxine Dunne, also a waitress, and the two went out drinking. After the turmoil subsided, she lost herself in the city and presumably has followed her former profession.[67]

The first of the Dillinger harborers taken into custody was Dr. Wilhelm Loeser, who had been under surveillance by the federal agents for some time. Early on the morning of July 24, two days after the slaying, Louis Piquett called at his home in Oak Park and was admitted by Anna Patzke, the wife who did not know she was married.

"Hello, Anna," the attorney said. "Is the doc in?"

"No, Lou, he's taking a walk."

"Well, tell him that he better take a long walk."

"What do you mean?" she asked.

"You've been reading the papers, haven't you?"

"Yes, but nobody's bothered me. Do you think the government is after him?"

"I don't know, but if they are, it won't do him any good to hide behind a tree."

Dr. Loeser returned home soon after Piquett had left and was arrested by federal agents. Once in custody, the German physician required no great amount of persuasion to reveal the identity of the others. His part in the proceedings is outlined in a lengthy plea for clemency which he prepared for the United States Parole Board under the date of April 12, 1935. This statement was borrowed from him by Mr. O'Leary and is still in his possession. An excerpt from it follows:

> After I was in custody about one day I asked to see Mr. Purvis and told him that I would aid the government to the best of my ability, providing I would get a square deal in return. Mr. Melvin Purvis called the late Inspector Sam Cowley and said that Inspector Cowley was in complete charge of the Dillinger case, and anything Inspector Cowley did, and agreed to, he—Mr. Purvis—would back up 100 percent. So I told Inspector Cowley that I desired to aid the gov't., providing he would do what's square for me in return. I especially told him that I wished my parole violation squared up, and a chance given to me to live through this parole. Inspector Cowley assured me that he would recommend to his superiors in Washington that my parole violation be squared, and that this parole would run from the time I was taken into custody in the Dillinger-Piquett matter. Inspector Cowley also said that he would recommend to his superiors in Washington that I would not receive any sentence. My secretary, Anna Patzke, who visited me in the Bankers' Building, was present, and heard this conversation between

Inspector Cowley and myself. About one week later—when Inspector Cowley visited the apartment in the north part of Chicago, where we were kept in protective custody, he reiterated the same promise again in the presence of Anna Patzke. He was very enthusiastic and very much pleased with the aid I had given to the government, especially since my aid had saved three lives—one of them a supervising agent of the government—and *entirely built up* the government's case.

The physician told an elaborate tale suggesting that he, Dr. Loeser, was an innocent victim of circumstances, and that the real villains were O'Leary and Cassidy. It was Cassidy, Loeser said, who had performed the operations on Dillinger and Van Meter, while he merely stood by in the capacity of consultant, occasionally tossing in expert advice. All of this time the outlaws were tickling his nose with machine guns, while O'Leary was frightening him with threats of being shot, and Nelson was marching about the house brandishing a machine gun of his own. His "confession" being duly recorded and signed, Loeser was removed from the federal offices and kept in custody in various apartments in the far northern part of the city.

As soon as Loeser revealed the address of Jimmy Probasco, the little man was taken into custody along with Peggy Doyle. That was the night of July 25. The next morning he was dead. Inspector Cowley, in charge of questioning Probasco, stated that when left alone for an instant, he leaped from a window on the nineteenth floor of the Bankers' Building. He vehemently denied that the prisoner had been ill treated or intimidated by third-degree methods.[68]

Nevertheless, rumors quickly circulated regarding Probasco's death. One was that Probasco, almost seventy years old and frail, had been beaten to the point of death, and was dropped from the window so that the federal agents would not be found with a battered corpse on their hands. Another version is given by Mrs. Doris Lockerman, former secretary of Melvin Purvis, in a series of articles written for a Chicago newspaper.

It has been said that the G-men hung Probasco out a window to frighten him, that they lost their hold, and dropped him to his death.

Now, the room from which Probasco leaped is directly across an alley from the Rookery building. People working there could see into our offices, and we into theirs. Probasco leaped about 10 a.m.

Is it likely that the agents, even had they been in the habit of hanging prisoners out windows, which they were not, would have hung a kicking, yelling, 250 pound man out in broad daylight, in full sight of the office workers across the way?

The discrepancies in Mrs. Lockerman's story are that the windows of the adjoining building do not reach to the nineteenth floor of the Bankers' Building, and that James Probasco weighed not more than half of the 250 pounds ascribed to him.

Melvin Purvis, quoted in the same series of articles, gives this account:

> Little Jimmy Probasco, the odd old man who rented his house as a hide-out, came to a tragic and surprising end. One day while I was in Washington on an official mission he was questioned in my private office. It was not the first time Probasco had been there for questioning, and no one knew he had reached an emotional crisis. In the middle of a routine inquiry, he rose from his chair, and before anyone could bar his way, rushed to the window and thrust himself through. He fell nineteen stories.

Inasmuch as Mr. Purvis was in Washington at the time, he perhaps cannot be expected to know the details of what took place. But the windows of his private office front on Clark Street, whereas Probasco's body was found in the Rookery court, on the other side of the building.*

But stories alleging ill treatment are common in the criminal world, and one instinctively hesitates to credit accusations of this nature against the federal government. In further extenuation of the G-men, it may be mentioned that all subsequent prisoners in this Dillinger case were kept manacled to one arm of a chair, with the explanation that "one of you fellows jumped out the window, and we don't want it to happen again."

Arthur O'Leary was the next one caught in the federal net. Following his departure from Chicago the week before Dillinger was shot, he had proceeded to the Squaw Lake resort in northern Wisconsin near the Little Bohemia Lodge, and mostly to occupy his mind began looking for a site where the unlikely motion picture might be filmed. Hearing of the outlaw's death, he returned to Chicago immediately, but the newspapers informed him that the government had Loeser, and that meant the other members of the group would soon be taken into custody. He contacted Cas-

---

*O'Leary told me that when in custody he heard federal agents discussing the Probasco death. From their conversation, it sounded like Cowley had been battering the old man around but was dissatisfied with his answers. Supposedly he said something along the lines of "I know how to make you talk," and while holding Probasco over the edge of the window lost his grip on the struggling man.

sidy, who was then living at the Commonwealth Hotel under an assumed name, and the two fled to Wisconsin in their cars. After passing the next ten days at Lake Geneva, Milwaukee, and Fox Lake, the suspense became too much for O'Leary, and he returned to Chicago to telephone Piquett.

"How is everything?" he asked the attorney.

"Everything's fine. Come on up to the office. I want to talk to you."

"What do you mean, 'Everything's fine'? It can't be. Don't you read the papers?"

"I'm telling you, it's all right. Just come to the office."

Piquett, confident he could beat any charges that might be placed against him, wanted to confer with his investigator on a common strategy. O'Leary, however, recalling the whisperings of Probasco, now became certain that Piquett was leagued against him. The wires into the lawyer's offices had since been tapped, and the call was traced by the listeners. But the agents who were quickly dispatched went by mistake to a drugstore a few doors from the garage at Ashland Avenue and Irving Park Boulevard where O'Leary was making his call.

O'Leary told Cassidy of what had happened, and the two set out again, this time for Madison, Wisconsin. Cassidy took a room at the Y.M.C.A. and waited while O'Leary went on to Dubuque to pick up his wife and daughter. They separated finally at Madison, O'Leary and his family proceeding to St. Louis, while Cassidy drove to the Squaw Lake resort. The federal agents in Chicago had meanwhile seized O'Leary's trunks and discovered circulars and advertisements for Squaw Lake. There they found Cassidy instead of O'Leary, but refrained from picking him up until the others had also been located.

For two weeks O'Leary lived at the Congress Hotel in St. Louis, endeavoring to get Missouri license plates to replace his own from Illinois, whose numbers were being broadcast. Unsuccessful, on August 24 he drove to Fort Wayne and secured a set of Indiana plates from a garage. He returned to Chicago on the following day and located his former employer, Lewis Mack. He asked Mack to call Piquett in regard to giving himself up. Mack promised to do so, and made an appointment with him that evening in the lakefront city of Evanston, which adjoins Chicago on the north.

O'Leary had supper in an Evanston restaurant with his wife and daughter. As he stepped outside afterwards, he found himself looking into the barrels of a half-dozen machine guns. It must be remembered that for the last month the federal agents had been listening to Loeser's wild talk of O'Leary running about with a Tommygun, and they pictured the legal investigator as a very desperate character. The government agents were taking no chances, and there were probably a dozen men in the party.

The running and yelling of the G-men brought a large crowd to the scene.

"Make a move and we'll blow you to pieces!" they shouted. "Put your hands up! Higher! Higher!" By this time O'Leary had almost pulled his arms from their sockets.

Led by a squad of Evanston motorcycle police with sirens screaming, the motorcade sped from the North Shore suburb to the Chicago "Loop" and the federal offices in the Bankers' Building. Inspector Cowley and one of his agents conducted the questioning. O'Leary later denied from the witness stand that he had been subjected to any third-degree methods. Piquett, who saw him a few days after his arrest, said he looked "worked over" and was being treated for six broken ribs.*

The story O'Leary told the federal agents had met with complete disbelief, as it disputed much of what they had been told by Loeser. Finally, after several days of questioning, the two men were brought face to face. O'Leary was manacled to a chair in one corner of the room, and the German in the other.

"Dr. Loeser, you're a man old enough to be my father," O'Leary told him. "If you'll only raise your eyes from the floor and take a look at the condition I'm in, I am sure that it might induce you to begin telling the truth." One wonders why O'Leary should have made such a request if he showed no signs of wear and tear.

O'Leary was then led from the room, and several hours later it was announced that Dr. Loeser had changed his story of innocence and intimidation. Perhaps the physician required a trifle persuasion to tell this more incriminating version. Anna Patzke, who saw him shortly thereafter, told her friends that "they smashed his nose all over his face." However it occurred, a significant change took place in Loeser's appearance during the time he was in custody.

*O'Leary said that on the whole he was well treated while in federal custody, perhaps because they wished him to be a friendly witness in the Piquett trials. The one exception was Cowley, who slapped him frequently while he was being questioned. On one occasion, Cowley, exasperated at O'Leary's refusal to sign a statement that he had been the driver in the South Bend robbery, pulled him from the chair, threw him to the floor, and kicked him in his ribs.

The Chicago G-men had in fact been receiving some unwelcome publicity for their methods of questioning. "Boss" McLaughlin claimed that his teeth had been knocked out and that he had been dangled from the nineteenth-story window by his ankles. Jack Perkins also complained of mistreatment while in custody. Mrs. Lockerman, who was present in the offices and should know something of what went on, admits that the persuasion was sometimes more than oral.[69]

She writes: "It was about this time, however, that some of the agents did handle prisoners overroughly. They had read about the 'third degree' and tried to use it without knowing how. Their attempts were stupid and useless. They picked the wrong men to hit and got little information for their pains. These instances were isolated and few. The older and wiser heads in the organization quickly brought the men who tried it, victims of misdirected enthusiasm, back into line."

On the whole, the prisoners in the Dillinger case had little cause for complaint, other than in the instances already mentioned. They were permitted access to legal counsel and family members at all times, and enjoyed cigars and good meals and sleeping accommodations.

Dr. Cassidy was picked up in Wisconsin the day prior to O'Leary's arrest. Marie Comforti, William Finerty, and his wife Ella were taken into custody about the same time. Louis Piquett was the last to be arrested.

An attempt to detain Piquett had been made several days before. The attorney demanded to see a warrant, and none was forthcoming.

"You can murder me here on the street," he declared, "but I'll not go with you willingly without a warrant."

The agents obtained the warrant, and Piquett was seized the night of August 31 in front of his home. United States Attorney Dwight H. Green said, "We consider this arrest the most important in years."

The prisoners were arraigned before United States Commissioner Edwin W. Walker the following day. Before appearing in court, Piquett and O'Leary were allowed to confer.

"What are you planning to do, Art?" Piquett asked.

"I think I'll take a plea of guilty and have it over with."

"And how about Cassidy and Loeser?"

"They're going to do the same thing. You should, too, and see if you can't make a deal so we each get a year and a day."

"Not me. I'm fighting this. My relationship with Dillinger was strictly lawyer and client."

Loeser, Cassidy, and O'Leary went before the commissioner first and pleaded guilty to conspiring to harbor John Dillinger. Piquett's turn came next, after he had listened to his associates.

"Not guilty. I've been framed!" he shouted.

CHAPTER TWENTY THREE

THE BATTLE OF BARRINGTON

The ensuing months saw an intensive effort by federal, state, and local police to round up the remaining members of the Dillinger gang. For several weeks Homer Van Meter and Marie Comforti managed to stay out of sight in St. Paul. During this time Van Meter began consorting with a young waitress, Opal Meliga, and it was believed that Marie, in a fit of jealousy, had betrayed her sweetheart.

But it was his quarreling with "Baby Face" Nelson that resulted in Van Meter's undoing. A feud existed between the two men. Their dispute had been discussed at a meeting of Dillinger, Van Meter, and O'Leary in Chicago, and Dillinger had mentioned it again after leaving the conference.

"I hope Van and Nelson don't meet," Dillinger remarked to O'Leary. "If they ever come face to face again, they'll kill each other."

It had been Nelson's intention to seek Van Meter out in person, but upon more sober reflection he recalled that his enemy was very quick on the draw. While in St. Paul, he learned of a meeting planned between Van Meter and another underworld character, and decided that the ends of vengeance would be just as well served by simply informing the police.

Late on the afternoon of Sunday, August 23, Van Meter was hurrying to keep his appointment. A St. Paul police car, containing Chief of Police Frank Cullen, former chief Thomas Brown, and detectives Jeff Dittrich and Thomas McMahon, was waiting for him at the corner of University Avenue and Marion Street. When the officers commanded him to surrender, Van Meter drew his gun and began running toward an alley, but blasts from police machine guns knocked him headlong into the mud. His body was riddled with bullets, and fingers were shot off both hands. Van Meter's mangled remains were taken for burial to his home town of Fort Wayne, Indiana.[70]

Marie Comforti was quickly arrested and confined for several months in Chicago. In December of 1934 she was tried in Duluth, Minnesota, along with Thomas Kirwin, William A. Gray, and Mrs. Marie McCarthy, on charges of harboring Homer Van Meter. All of the defendants were found guilty. Marie and Mrs. McCarthy received sentences of a year and a day, Kirwin two years and a $10,000 fine, and Gray eighteen months and a $5,000 fine.

Within the thick walls of the state penitentiary at Columbus, Ohio, Harry Pierpont, Charles Makley, and Russell Clark had seen their last hopes of outside help dashed by the death of John Dillinger. Recalling, however, his successful sortie from the Crown Point jail, Pierpont and Makley contrived fake guns from soap and the pieces of a jigsaw puzzle. With these they managed to get out of their cells on September 22, and proceeded to release Russell Clark and six other convicts. But they were delayed by the new steel doors which had been recently installed, and the riot squad arrived in time to open fire on them with high-powered rifles. The first shots wounded Pierpont and Makley, and the others retreated to their cells. Makley died within an hour.

Harry Pierpont was badly wounded in the head and spine and almost totally paralyzed. Had events been permitted to take their natural course, he probably would soon have died. However, in the early morning of October 17 he was carried from his bed to the electric chair, and five minutes later the murder of Sheriff Sarber had been legally avenged.

"Baby Face" Nelson was the next to fall, but at a terrible price. Late in July he and his wife, Helen Gillis, were reported in northern Wisconsin. Several weeks later they were in St. Paul. From there they fled back to California, where Nelson joined up with John Paul Chase, a former bootlegging associate from San Francisco. But Nelson's new prominence as a Public Enemy made him less than welcome in his old criminal haunts, and the three returned to the Midwest.

The lake region of northeastern Illinois and southeastern Wisconsin has long been a favorite hideout of fugitives, who find it easy to move undetected among the crowds of visitors thronging the numerous resorts. It was here that Nelson, his wife, and Chase planned to take up residence, and arrangements were made to rent a cottage near Lake Geneva, Wisconsin, for the winter. But the season was now late and vacationers too few to render concealment easy, and in any case the G-men had learned of his intentions.[71] They were lying in wait at the house of his prospective host on November 27, 1934, which would prove to be a day of terror and tragedy for all concerned.

Nelson, Chase, and Helen Gillis headed straight to the trap, driving their car into the yard of the cottage, but a young agent walked out on the porch and revealed the ambush. The outlaws' car reversed itself and raced southeast in the direction of Chicago, about seventy-five miles away, while its license number was flashed to the federal offices in that city. On the road they encountered a northbound federal car bearing agents Thomas McDade and William Ryan, who turned around only to discover that Nelson had done the same. The two cars passed each other a second time, and now Nelson, seemingly more anxious to seek a fight than to avoid one, quickly turned around again and began pursuing his pursuers. Nelson was driving, with his tiny wife Helen beside him and Chase in the rear seat aiming a powerful automatic rifle.

As they overtook the federal car, Nelson, perhaps unsure of his target, yelled "Pull over!" while Chase leveled the rifle.

Instinctively, McDade pushed the gas pedal to the floor and regained a lead, while Ryan broke out the roadster's rear window with the butt of his Colt automatic pistol. For some miles the two machines raced toward Chicago at top speed, exchanging shot for shot.

Nelson soon found himself in new difficulties. Another federal car, containing Inspector Cowley and Special Agent Herman E. Hollis, had taken the same route as McDade and Ryan, the Northwest Highway, and now were surprised to observe the two warring machines flash past them with the wrong car in flight. They turned about and joined the chase, intending to assail the bandits from the rear. Meanwhile, however, a lucky shot from Ryan's gun had punched through the front of Nelson's car and broken the fuel pump, which quickly caused engine failure. This allowed McDade and Ryan to escape with their lives, and a few miles down the road they jumped out and concealed themselves in some tall grass, expecting the outlaw's machine to soon come limping by. When Nelson failed to appear, they decided against any rematch at that time and returned to Chicago, unaware that Cowley and Hollis had since joined the battle.

"Baby Face" Nelson made his last stand at the entrance to the city park at the northwest edge of the town of Barrington. Chase had been firing through the front windshield with his rifle, and as the car came to a stop, Helen Gillis leaped out and threw herself into a ditch. Her husband and Chase collected their weapons and took up positions. Cowley and Hollis, armed with a shotgun and a Thompson, stopped their machine as well and employed it as a protective cover against Nelson's fire. When Hollis tried to reach a nearby telephone pole, he fell with a bullet through his head, and died almost immediately. Inspector Cowley also was mortally wounded, but managed to fire several more shots at the outlaws before losing consciousness. He was rushed to a hospital, and an operation was performed in an attempt to save his life, but death came within a few hours.

The lives of agents Cowley and Hollis were not sacrificed in vain. Nelson had been hit more than a dozen times and was bleeding profusely from a .45 wound in his left side. Their own car too crippled for further use, the three still managed to escape in the federal car, with Chase driving, and headed toward the North Shore suburbs of Chicago.

The next day police found the nude remains of "Baby Face" Nelson, wrapped in a blanket. He had died during the night, and his body had been laid out carefully next to St. Paul's Cemetery in Niles Center [now Skokie], just outside of Chicago. The bullet-punctured federal car was abandoned at the side of the electric railway tracks near the neighboring town of Winnetka.[72]

Helen Gillis was arrested a short time later and sentenced to a year in the federal prison at Milan, Michigan, for harboring her fugitive husband. John Paul Chase fled to California and for some time avoided capture. Information reached the federal offices in Chicago that he was hiding at Mount Shasta, in the northern part of the state, and on December 24 a party of agents set out by airplane to bring him back. Before they could reach the fairly remote town, Chase had been picked up and jailed by the local police. He has since been tried for murder in the federal court in Chicago and sentenced to life imprisonment in the federal penitentiary on Alcatraz Island.[73]

Of the fugitives identified with John Dillinger, only two, John Burns and Joseph Fox, remained at large. Both had participated in the famous prison break at Michigan City, and the state of Indiana was still eager to effect their capture. Burns and Fox themselves had but little involvement with the Dillinger gang, but the manner in which they were taken affords an interesting illustration of police undercover methods.

Indiana dispatched Edward Barce, assistant attorney general, and Meyer Bogue, the paid informant who preferred the title of investigator, to Chicago in search of Burns. Bogue believed that the escaped convict's whereabouts were known to the "moll" Pearl Hellman, who knew Bogue only as an ex-convict from the Michigan City penitentiary. Contact was made through Harry Forrester, then serving a sentence for robbery. Bogue and Barce went to Pearl's home, where Barce was introduced under the name of Roth as a gangster from St. Louis whom Bogue supposedly was hiding in the Morrison Hotel in Chicago. Pearl stated that she believed she could locate both Burns and Fox through a man named Dick Day, and promised to advise them as to her success.

An elaborate trap was prepared in the Morrison Hotel, where Barce rented a suite of three rooms. Bogue was to meet Pearl in the middle room, where microphones were hidden, while Barce and his secretary, Jacqueline Roth, listened from the two adjoining rooms.

Bogue had concocted an elaborate story to impress his visitor. He stated that he had a friend in Peoria employed by a large distillery who would tip him off when a trailer truck loaded with whiskey was leaving for the wholesalers. The load was worth $75,000, and he would need help to take it. Bogue declared that he did not wish any of the Chicago mobs in on the deal, representing them to be unreliable and nothing but a lot of cowboys, but he knew Burns, Fox, and Day to be dependable, and if they could only be located, he and his friend "Roth" could work with them very nicely.

Completely duped by the story, Pearl promised to get in touch with Burns that afternoon, and Bogue drove her out to 69th Street. From the mirror in the car he watched her go into the building at 700 West 69th Street, and a few minutes later she came out with Burns and walked to the corner, where they separated. Pearl then returned to the car and informed Bogue that Burns would contact Fox and Day and enlist their help in hijacking the load of whiskey.

Several days later Pearl telephoned Bogue and stated that Burns wished to discuss plans with him on Sunday morning, December 17. Barce and Bogue immediately called Captain Stege of the Chicago police and postal inspector John McWhorter, who suspected Burns of complicity in the robbery of a money wagon in Brooklyn. It was Stege's desire to wait until the meeting was in progress in order that all three might be taken, but McWhorter argued that one was better than none in case the meet did not come off, and this latter view prevailed.

Burns, who resided in the second-floor apartment at the 69th Street address, had prepared an elaborate device to avoid capture. The front door was always kept locked, but a specially wired machine gun was fixed at the head of the stairs so that if the door was forced open the gun would automatically fire.

The raiding party was composed of Barce, Captain Stege, and officers Smith and Benson of the Chicago police, Chief of Detectives Sandor Singer of Hammond, Indiana, and postal inspectors John McWhorter and John McCarthy. They fortunately approached by the rear door instead of the front, and carried bulletproof shields that covered their bodies above the knees. Burns was in his pajamas at the time, and with his trap ineffective he offered no resistance.

"Come on in," he called as the raiders appeared at the door. "I guess the jig is up."

With him in the apartment was a woman whom he represented to be his sister, but who was really a farm girl from Benton Harbor, Michigan. The authorities seized an arsenal that included two machine guns, three rifles, two pistols, and three hundred rounds of ammunition. Burns was returned to Michigan City to complete the serving of a life sentence.

Pearl Hellman soon learned of the part she had unwittingly played in the capture. Barce and Bogue were hoping to retain her confidence and use her again in some future operation, but Attorney General Philip Lutz, elated at the success, spilled the details of the trick to the Indianapolis newspapers.

Considerable time would elapse before the roundup ended with the capture of Joseph Fox. Investigators learned that various fugitives frequented a house at 11434 Harvard Avenue, in the extreme southern part of Chicago, and the house was placed under surveillance by Bogue and the Chicago and federal officers. Finally a tip came that Fox would be there within a few days, and Bogue was dispatched to Indianapolis for Captain Matt Leach and

Chief of Detectives Harvey Hire, who wanted Indiana to share credit for the capture.

Before the arrival of those officials, however, Fox was taken into custody, about eleven o'clock on the morning of June 4, 1935. The arresting party consisted of postal inspectors McWhorter and McCarthy and sergeants Frank Fuerst, Tom Prindiville, and Harry O'Connell of the Chicago police.

Fox was returned to Michigan City for the remainder of his life term, but Indiana, resentful at being left out, blamed Bogue and dismissed him from its service.

In the backwash of the Dillinger case there reappeared Anna Sage, whose misdescribed orange skirt gained her worldwide notoriety as "the Woman in Red," to her considerable annoyance. After issuing corrections as to the actual color, she next complained that the federal government was taking advantage of her trusting nature and double-crossing her in regard to deportation.

Following the sensational events of July 22, 1934, Mrs. Sage and Polly Hamilton had been taken to Detroit by federal agents and maintained there for two weeks to ensure their silence as much as their safety. Anna then boarded a bus for California, where she was visited by Inspector Cowley, who paid her five thousand dollars in cash for spilling Dillinger's blood. She later returned to Chicago, and after the death of "Baby Face" Nelson again breathed easily.

But Anna did not feel the government was keeping its other part of the bargain. On September 29, 1935, she was back in the news complaining that Cowley and Purvis had promised to stop the deportation proceedings, and yet she was now finding herself closer than ever to an ocean voyage home. Inspector Cowley was dead, killed by "Baby Face" Nelson. Melvin Purvis had suddenly and rather mysteriously resigned from the service at what should have been the start of a long and rewarding career, and rumor had it that a factor in his decision was the government's failure to honor its pledge to Mrs. Sage.

"I did inform her that I would bring to the attention of the appropriate officials in Washington her action in aiding the government in this respect," Purvis admitted, "and that I would recommend that some step be taken to prevent her deportation, if possible. I have done that."

The source of Anna's troubles was her convictions for operating disorderly houses in Indiana. She therefore made a trip to

Indianapolis on October 1 to petition Governor McNutt for a pardon such as she had received from his predecessor when inconvenienced by similar convictions in the past. This governor, however, summoned Captain Matt Leach, who had interrogated Anna.

"Has Mrs. Sage revealed any information that might be of value to the state of Indiana in the Dillinger matter?" McNutt inquired.

"She has not," Leach replied. "Whenever I asked her any pertinent questions she merely squirmed around in her chair and refused to answer."

Anna Sage returned empty-handed to Chicago, where her arguments were heard before federal judge John P. Barnes on October 16.

Zarkovich and O'Neil, who, thanks to Anna, had divided a five thousand dollar reward between them, appeared to testify in her behalf. The government confined itself to replying that the Department of Labor alone possessed the authority to offer immunity in such a case and was in no way bound by any promises, actual or implied, made by eager gangbusters in the Justice Department. The United States Court of Appeals on January 22, 1936, agreed.

On April 25, 1936, the "Woman in Red" found herself on a deportation train carrying "undesirables" from Chicago to Ellis Island. Four days later, Anna Sage, neé Aňa Cumpanas, prostitute, madame, harborer and betrayer of criminals, and friend of the police, resentfully boarded the steamship *President Harding*, bound for her native land, declaring that she expected to be back soon.[74]

CHAPTER TWENTY FOUR

PIQUETT PAYS THE PRICE

The task of removing Dillinger completed, the next government intention was to convict any and all of his associates. Many of the prisoners had pleaded guilty; others did not possess the means to put up much of a fight. With Louis Piquett, however, the attorney general's office nearly met its match.

From the very beginning it was apparent that the battle would be a bitter one. Piquett's bond had been set at $50,000, double that for Loeser, Cassidy, and O'Leary. Finerty was placed under bond of $10,000, and his wife and Marie Comforti were held for half that amount. All of the prisoners were removed to the county jail.

Piquett had been incarcerated for several weeks before he was able to get his bond reduced to $20,000 and obtain his freedom. Early in November O'Leary, Cassidy, and Loeser were transferred to the county jail at Waukegan, Illinois. Under an obliging Sheriff Lester Tiffany, this establishment resembled the jail of comedians' jokes. Files and other tools lay about, and some bars in the place were partially sawed through. Prisoners were permitted to have their own radios and electric cookstoves, and meats, groceries, and pastries could be ordered by telephone. The more favored inmates were permitted to take evening strolls through the town. The good times came to an end, however, when it was discovered that Charles Foster, held on a charge of wholesaling narcotics, had absented himself from his cell in order to marry his sweetheart, Caroline Taft, before a local justice of the peace. The prisoners in the Dillinger case were again removed, this time to Wheaton, Illinois, where the regimen was more in accordance with jail traditions.

After numerous delays, Piquett's trial began in Chicago on January 8, 1935, in the federal court of Judge William H. Holly. The government was represented by United States Attorney Dwight H. Green, who had prosecuted Capone, and assistant district attorneys Horace Hagan and J. Albert Woll. Piquett led his own defense, of course, but associated himself with Edwin T. Peifer and Henry E. Pieruccini. Before the opening of the trial, Helen Gillis was brought from the Milan penitentiary to reveal whatever secrets of the gang she might possess.

Few trials in the history of the federal courts have excited as much interest as the prosecution of Louis Piquett on the John Dillinger charges. Not only was there to be the ever-interesting spectacle of a great criminal lawyer fighting his own defense, but the public expected to learn much of the secret operations of the famous outlaw. Piquett was openly branded the "brains of the Dillinger mob" and the "swivel-chair mastermind of the Dillinger gang." Attorney Pieruccini almost described his client as a lawyer who engaged in criminal practice, but realizing that this would lay him open to his opponents' jibes, he amended it to a lawyer who specialized in criminal law.

The government's case was outlined in considerable detail in the opening statement of Prosecutor Woll. As he concluded, Piquett snorted, "That's a lot of bull." Dr. Cassidy, pale-faced and nervously twitching his hands, was the first to take the stand, and related his part in the now-famous plastic operations. He seemed somewhat confused, however, as to whether Piquett or O'Leary had paid him the second half of his fee. Mrs. Lillian Holley testified that Dillinger had stolen her car, and Warden Lou Baker affirmed that the outlaw had escaped from his jail. Deputy Blunk, with spirits greatly restored by his own exoneration, talked freely of his experiences with the outlaw, while mechanic Saager told his story of intimidation.

The increasing animosity between Piquett and O'Leary culminated during the course of the trial, and a stormy scene occurred when the latter took the stand. As he finished relating his experience with Dillinger, Piquett whispered hoarsely to the reporters, "I'm going to cross-examine this guy myself, then watch the fireworks.'' Throughout the cross-examination there were many veiled allusions which attorney and witness understood, but which mystified the others in the courtroom. An attempt was made to hook up O'Leary and Cassidy in a previous connection with Dr. Eye and Dillinger. For two hours the battle on the witness stand surged back and forth, with many vital points mentioned, but never quite reaching the stage of complete disclosure. [See chapter 16, endnote 3.]

The government closed its case with the testimony of Dr. Loeser and his girlfriend, Anna Patzke. As they concluded, Piquett announced, ''Now I'll talk, and I'll talk plenty.''

Piquett's testimony in his own behalf proved to be the highlight of the trial. He spoke calmly and deliberately, at times waving his pince-nez to emphasize a point. The attorney began with a somewhat lengthy recital of the story of his life and career. The sobbing of his wife could be heard throughout the courtroom, and the jury sat in rapt attention. It was Jimmy Probasco, he declared, who had arranged the hideout for Dillinger and the plastic surgery. ''Probasco was a horse doctor or something,'' he said. ''He told Dillinger of some operation he had performed on a dog.'' He himself had counseled the outlaw to surrender, he insisted, but O'Leary would always undercut him on the idea. Piquett scored heavily when Judge Holly, in sustaining an objection, stated, ''It is not required of a lawyer to surrender his client or to inform law-enforcing agencies of his whereabouts.''[75]

The tension that had characterized every minute of the trial continued to the very end. Defense Attorney Peifer had begun his closing arguments when suddenly his face turned gray and he fell to the floor. Ada Martin, a trained nurse and a friend of the Piquett family, rushed to his assistance. At first many suspected the veteran attorney of performing a courtroom stunt, but an examination by physicians determined that Peifer had really suffered a heart attack and was unable to continue. Piquett then took up the torch and presented a closing argument with thunderous oratory. The scene was a fortuitous one for Piquett, whose deft handling of the crisis undoubtedly impressed the jury.

Nevertheless, Piquett awaited the outcome with foreboding, for he felt that the government was determined to ''put the finger'' on him. But the attorney's luck held; despite the testimony of the men who by their own admissions had conspired with him, the jury was out but four hours, and only five ballots were needed to bring in a verdict of acquittal. The coterie of relatives and friends attending Piquett staged a noisy celebration in the courthouse hall.

The government prosecutors, certain theirs was an airtight case, stood speechless. Piquett had become the only one of fifteen defendants to beat a Dillinger "rap." Prosecutor Green shook a finger in the defendant's face and declared, "Mr. Piquett, you are a very lucky man." It was announced that charges of conspiring to harbor Homer Van Meter would now be pressed with the utmost energy.

Attorney General Cummings commented on the case in a magazine article published shortly after the Piquett trial.

"It is useless for me to say that I am utterly disgusted with the outcome of that case. The Department of Justice has another charge against this attorney which it intends to prosecute diligently."

The second trial of Louis Piquett, this time for conspiring to harbor Van Meter, differed greatly from the first. Now federal authorities were determined to secure a conviction, and there would be no holds barred. If anything, Piquett had only firmed the government's resolve by crowing about his victory on the Dillinger charges and showering his tormentors with choice epithets. As though to avenge itself, Washington this time dispatched Brien McMahon, the ace prosecutor who had convicted John Paul Chase. Assisting him were Austin Hall and Harry N. Connaughton.

On the other side, the pugnaciousness and fighting spirit which had carried Piquett through to victory before seemed now to desert him. He placed his defense in the hands of John Elliott Byrne, who was assisted by Peifer. Byrne, although a former employee of the Department of Justice and a competent attorney, differed greatly from Piquett in matters of strategy, and there was scant accord between the two men. But the defendant's major handicap was having no copy of the transcript of his first trial. Notes taken by his stenographers had not been written up since his acquittal, and now they had been misplaced. Piquett knew that the government prosecutors would be scrutinizing his previous testimony, and Byrne's continued warnings to avoid perjuring himself rendered his defense weak and uncertain.

Selection of a jury began on June 18 in the courtroom of Federal Judge Philip L. Sullivan. As the trial opened, Piquett displayed his expected confidence. "There can be only one outcome—acquittal," he declared. "I am charged with harboring Van Meter, who harbored Dillinger, who harbored a stolen automobile. In other words, it is a continuing offense, and if a precedent is not set in this case, there are no limits to which it may not be carried. Was I to be expected to turn up the men? I'm not a stool pigeon.''

The same government witnesses took the stand, and their testimony closely followed that given previously.* Dr. Loeser told virtually the same story as before, amplifying it only in regard to the medical aspect of his work and the details of the Van Meter operation.

The physician was considerably embarrassed by the admittance of the first statement he had given the federal agents, in which he virtually exonerated Piquett and bestowed the culpability on Cassidy and O'Leary. As Loeser finished his testimony, Piquett declared, "If this isn't double jeopardy, then I don't know anything about law." Byrne moved for the withdrawal of a juror and for a mistrial on the ground that the same facts had been adjudicated already. Judge Sullivan denied the motion.

Anna Patzke, her testimony somewhat impeded by chewing gum, added one new element to the proceedings. She stated that when Piquett came by on July 25, he gave her five hundred dollars to aid in Loeser's flight, and that this money had been taken from her the same day by the G-men.

Piquett denied making any such payment and denounced the evidence as a deliberate plant. The money itself looked somewhat suspicious, as it consisted of fifty ten-dollar bills, all uncreased and bearing consecutive serial numbers. Furthermore, Loeser had been paid several thousand dollars only a short time before.

Arthur O'Leary appeared somewhat confused on the stand, in contrast to his sharpness in the previous trial. Piquett might have seized the opportunity to tear into his former investigator, but the fighting spirit was gone. The attorney wearily seated himself in a chair, and conducted the cross-examination in an almost disinterested fashion.

The rout was completed when Piquett took the stand in his own defense. Under withering cross-examination by Brien McMahon, the veteran attorney appeared tired and uncertain. Reflecting his fear of perjury charges, his testimony was a constant repetition of "I don't remember" and "My mind is hazy." The odds were heavily against him in the Dillinger trial, yet Piquett

---

*O'Leary, Cassidy, and Loeser had been released on their own recognizance on March 29. The former two were placed under a year's probation on September 21, while Loeser was sentenced to one day in the United States Marshal's Office on the Dillinger and Van Meter charges and then returned to Leavenworth because of his parole violation.

had scored a brilliant victory. The Van Meter trial was thus stacked in his favor on some legal points if not on others, but it was becoming apparent to all that he was losing.

In oratory, the closing arguments were far superior to those of the Dillinger trial. Austin Hall, who delivered the opening summation for the government, described Piquett as a "lawyer with the soul of a serpent" and "a seasoned lawyer operating in the hell hole of crime." O'Leary was described as "an upright young man who is telling you the truth," and Loeser and Cassidy as men who had been led into crime by Piquett.

"Louis Piquett is a master criminal," Hall declaimed. "He is guilty of the charges in the indictment. Gentlemen of the jury, find him so guilty."

As Hall walked back to the prosecution table, Piquett laughed and whispered, "I don't think he likes me."

Following Hall, Defense Attorney Byrne spoke in a calm, conversational tone and reminded the jurors that the government had found it necessary to apologize for its witnesses.

"Disinterested witnesses have been lacking in this case," Mr. Byrne said. "Everyone the government has called is a man who is paying back favors." Then he added, "It seems the government is making Piquett's memory the issue in this case. The cross-examination of Piquett was nothing more than a memory test. A man can have a faulty memory, and still not be sent to prison for it."

Piquett sat gloomy and discouraged as his attorney argued in his behalf. He might not have risen to speak except for Byrne's strenuous urging, but once he engaged the enemy a trace of the old fighting spirit returned.

The last courtroom battle of the colorful attorney was one that will long be remembered. He delivered a stirring appeal in a voice that would soften to a whisper or rise to a shout. Tears ran down his cheeks, and at times he sank on one knee before the jurors.

"I am called upon today to repeat what has been the most important act of my life," Piquett began. "On January 14, 1935, twelve of my peers heard the same evidence that has been spread before you in this case, and they brought in the verdict which told my old mother in Wisconsin that her boy was innocent.

"The government imported men from Washington to prosecute me in that case as they have in this. They have acted on the word of Homer Cummings, the attorney general, that the criminal lawyer must leave. Homer Cummings is trying to get me."

Brien McMahon rose to his feet and walked to the bench.

"In justice to the attorney general," he said, "I think his name should be left out of this."

"Don't interrupt me!" Piquett shouted. Order was restored and he went on, reciting his objections to the case and the prosecution's tactics.

"This is the greatest frameup since the crucifixion of Christ. They are trying to railroad me to the penitentiary—my government—your government—through the attorney general's office.

"I am nauseated that the government should take after me. Even the man who killed Lincoln had the right to have an attorney represent him, and so did the men who killed Garfield and McKinley and Cermak. I, too, had a right to represent a criminal.

"I never expected to be tried again. My memory was hazy on cross-examination. I didn't have the record. I was convinced that if you came back with a not-guilty verdict I would be indicted for perjury. I had to be awfully cautious.

"I'm not a lily-white reformer. I've represented a lot of criminals. That's my business. I think as much of my profession as Hall does. I will practice the best I can for the rest of my life if you will let me.

"This case doesn't mean much to Mr. McMahon or to Mr. Hall, but it means so much to me. I am past fifty years of age. I have never been arrested before. Hall told you and warned you that I would ask for your sympathy. I don't care. You have everything I possess in the world in the palms of your hands. I haven't murdered anybody, or robbed any widows or banks. All I have done was to represent a criminal.

"If you see it your duty to send me to the penitentiary, I won't receive it with tears. Give me what consideration you can. I alone have had to protect myself against the great and mighty government.

"If you have a scintilla of doubt, let it resolve to me. I could not pull witnesses from trees. My witnesses are dead. I am a defendant now, not a lawyer. May God speed you in your verdict!"

The concluding argument for the government was made by Brien McMahon, who spoke with anger and sarcasm.

"It is the criminals' mouthpiece," McMahon cried. "It is their front men like Piquett who allow desperadoes so often to escape justice.

"Louis Piquett was Dillinger's lawyer. Dillinger escaped from jail. And whom did he meet in Chicago? Louis Piquett. Here is a man who meets desperadoes just out of jail. And what did Public

Hero Number One have to say to him? He told you that he advised this man who had escaped from jail three hours before to surrender. And he wants you to believe that his illustrious client agreed.

"Piquett said to Mr. Hall that after this was over he did not think Hall would have anything against him. I have a different opinion. If he tried to shake hands with me he would not get very far. I haven't vengeance in my heart, but self-respect.

"I have a zealous respect for my duty as a member of the bar and for the traditions of this country not to fraternize with— that," McMahon said, pointing at the defendant. Piquett had incurred the wrath of the government prosecutors by cursing them roundly on several occasions, and the feeling on both sides was one of great hostility.

"This mouthpiece stands and asks for sympathy. That is a claim every man on trial makes. The only thing he can do is to beg for mercy.

"It is the government's attitude in this case that there are two separate and distinct cases—the conspiracy to harbor Dillinger, and the conspiracy to harbor Van Meter. Piquett has frequently referred to his acquittal on the charge that he aided Dillinger. Well, gentlemen, that is probably not the first time that a guilty man escaped justice.

"Let word go out to young men entering the legal profession that they must be decent and straight. Let those who are tempted to dealings with a mob know they cannot do it without incurring punishment. Think of the innocent victims of the criminals!

"I have a duty, and you have, to ascertain whether or not Piquett is guilty of the crime charged. Gentlemen, I have every confidence that you will see your duty and do it."

Piquett, resigned to defeat, sat gazing out the window, seemingly indifferent to what was going on about him. The jurors received their instructions from the bench and returned within two hours. "We, the jury, find the defendant, Louis Piquett, guilty as charged in the indictment."

Two days later, on June 27, Piquett's motion for a new trial was denied, and he was given the maximum sentence—two years in prison and a $10,000 fine.

"It is always very hard for me to deprive a man of his liberty," Judge Sullivan declared before passing sentence, "especially a man who belongs to the same profession as I do, and whom I have known for fifteen years. I have always found Mr. Piquett to be amiable, jovial, and a gentleman. But he is too easily led."

On October 1, 1935, the commissioners of the Illinois Supreme Court recommended Piquett's disbarment. His conviction, when it reached the United States Court of Appeals, was sustained. In desperation, Piquett approached the United States Supreme Court but was denied a hearing.

In spite of a lifetime of experience with hardship and hard knocks, Piquett's conviction struck him with devastating force. The thousands of dollars expended on his trials and appeals far exceeded any payments received in the Dillinger case, until at length he found his entire fortune dissipated and himself heavily in debt. The right to practice law which he had labored so hard to earn had been taken from him, leaving him deprived of any future means of livelihood. The constant worry and strain destroyed his health, and it was a broken, sallow-faced man who mechanically entered the United States Marshal's Office in Chicago on May 4, 1936, to surrender.

Just before this time the bitterness between Piquett and O'Leary burned itself out, and there occurred a reconciliation. It was O'Leary's lawyer, Hubbard C. Mullins, who represented Piquett before his nemesis, Brien McMahon, in a request for a stay of the mandate, which would give Piquett the time he still needed to place his affairs in order. But McMahon probably would not have given Piquett the time of day, and did not hesitate to deny the request.

CHAPTER TWENTY FIVE

CASUALTIES

The reign of terror ostensibly led by John Dillinger was at an end. America had battled the most daring criminal menace of this century, and now the monster lay dead at her feet. The struggle was a thrilling one from beginning to end, and victory was gained only at a terrific cost.[76]

The Dillinger gang had directed its efforts entirely to the robbing of banks. Naturally a great many holdups were erroneously ascribed to the band. The following is a confirmed list of their depredations, although there is often a considerable variance between the losses claimed by banks or reported in the papers and what Dillinger declares he actually obtained.

July 17, 1933—Commercial Bank, Daleville, Indiana, $3,500

August 4, 1933—Montpelier National Bank, Montpelier, Indiana, $6,700

August 14, 1933—Bluffton Bank, Bluffton, Ohio, $6,000

September 6, 1933—Massachusetts Avenue State Bank, Indianapolis, Indiana, $21,000

October 23, 1933—Central National Bank and Trust Company, Greencastle, Indiana, $76,000

November 20, 1933—American Bank and Trust Company, Racine, Wisconsin, $28,000

December 13, 1933—Unity Trust and Savings Bank, Chicago, Illinois, $8,700

January 15, 1934—First National Bank, East Chicago, Indiana, $20,000

March 6, 1934—Securities National Bank and Trust Company, Sioux Falls, South Dakota, $49,500

March 13, 1934—First National Bank, Mason City, Iowa, $52,000

June 30, 1934—Merchants National Bank, South Bend, Indiana, $29,890

Heavy though the financial losses may have been, they are of little moment compared to the toll of dead and injured. Of persons unconnected with the gang, that is, officers of the law and private citizens, one finds that fifteen were killed and seventeen wounded:

Killed

October 12, 1933—Sheriff Jesse Sarber, killed at Lima, Ohio, by Harry Pierpont

December 14, 1933—Sergeant William T. Shanley of the Chicago police, killed by John Hamilton

December 20, 1933—Eugene Teague, an Indiana state trooper, accidentally killed by an Indiana policeman at Paris, Illinois, in the capture of Edward Shouse

December 21, 1933—Louis Katzewitz, Charles Tattlebaum, and Sam Ginsburg, minor hoodlums, mistaken for members of the Dillinger gang and shot by Chicago police

January 15, 1934—Officer William P. O'Malley of the East Chicago police, attributed to John Dillinger

March 16, 1934—Undersheriff Charles Cavanaugh, shot by Herbert Youngblood at Port Huron, Michigan

April 22, 1934—Eugene Boisoneau, a CCC adviser, killed by federal agents at Little Bohemia Lodge, Rhinelander, Wisconsin

April 22, 1934—Federal Agent W. Carter Baum, killed by "Baby Face" Nelson near Little Bohemia Lodge

May 24, 1934—Detectives Martin O'Brien and Lloyd Mulvihill of the East Chicago police, attributed to Homer Van Meter

June 30, 1934—Policeman Howard Wagner of South Bend, shot by Homer Van Meter during a bank robbery

November 27, 1934—Inspector Samuel P. Cowley and Federal

Agent Herman E. Hollis, killed by "Baby Face" Nelson at Barrington, Illinois

Wounded

September 26, 1933—Finley Carson, a clerk in the Michigan City penitentiary, shot in the thigh and abdomen by John Burns in a prison break

September 30, 1933—Herbert McDonald of Beanblossom, Indiana, accidentally wounded in the arm by fellow citizens in the killing of convict Joseph Jenkins

November 20, 1933—H. J. Graham, cashier of the American Bank and Trust Company of Racine, Wisconsin, and Sergeant Wilbur Hansen of the Racine police, wounded in a bank robbery

March 6, 1934—Motorcycle policeman Hale Keith of Sioux Falls, South Dakota, wounded by bank robbers

March 13, 1934—R. H. James, secretary of the school board, shot in the Mason City, Iowa, bank robbery

March 16, 1934—Sheriff William Van Antwerp, Deputy Howard Lohr, and Fields, a Negro, wounded by Herbert Youngblood at Port Huron, Michigan

April 22, 1934—John Morris and John Hoffman, citizens of Mercer, Wisconsin, shot by federal agents at Little Bohemia Lodge

April 22, 1934—Federal Agent J. C. Newman and Constable Carl Christensen, shot by "Baby Face" Nelson near Little Bohemia Lodge

June 30, 1934—Perry G. Stahley and Delos M. Coen, bank officials, and Jacob Solomon and Samuel Toth, citizens of South Bend, Indiana, wounded in a bank robbery

July 22, 1934—Miss Theresa Paulus and Mrs. Etta Natalsky, wounded by stray bullets at the time Dillinger was killed

The casualties of the Dillinger gang and its associates were likewise very heavy. The list shows eleven persons killed and twenty-three sent to prison.

Killed

September 30, 1933—Joseph Jenkins, escaped convict from the Michigan City penitentiary, killed by citizens of Bean Blossom, Indiana

March 16, 1934—Herbert Youngblood, killed by police officers at Port Huron, Michigan

April 3, 1934—Eddie Green, shot by federal agents in St. Paul, Minnesota, died on April 11

April 23, 1934—John Hamilton, wounded by police at St. Paul Park, Minnesota, died about April 27

June 7, 1934—Tommy Carroll, killed by police at Waterloo, Iowa

July 22, 1934—John Dillinger, killed in Chicago by federal agents and East Chicago, Indiana, police

July 26, 1934—James J. Probasco, killed by a fall from a window of the federal offices in Chicago

August 23, 1934—Homer Van Meter, shot by police in St. Paul, Minnesota

September 22, 1934—Charles Makley, shot to death in an attempted prison break from the state penitentiary at Columbus, Ohio

October 17, 1934—Harry Pierpont, electrocuted at the state penitentiary at Columbus, Ohio

November 27, 1934—George "Baby Face" Nelson (Lester Gillis), died from wounds inflicted by federal agents at Barrington, Illinois

Imprisoned

September 29, 1933—James Clark, escaped convict, surrendered in Hammond, Indiana, and was returned to Indiana State Prison to complete a life sentence

November 19, 1933—Harry Copeland, arrested in Chicago and returned to Indiana State Prison

December 20, 1933—Edward Shouse, arrested in Paris, Illinois, and returned to Indiana State Prison

December 24, 1933—Hilton Crouch, captured in Chicago and sentenced to twenty years in Indiana State Prison for bank robbery

January 6, 1934—Walter Dietrich, escaped convict, captured in Bellwood, Illinois, by state's attorney's police from Chicago and returned to Indiana State Prison

March 24, 1934—Russell Clark, sentenced to life imprisonment for the murder of Sheriff Sarber, in the state penitentiary at Columbus, Ohio

May 5, 1934—Mrs. Beth Green, wife of Eddie Green, sentenced to fifteen months for harboring John Dillinger

May 23, 1934—Evelyn Frechette, sentenced to two years in the federal prison at Milan, Michigan; and Dr. Clayton E. May, sentenced to two years in the federal penitentiary at Leavenworth, Kansas, for conspiring to harbor John Dillinger

June 9, 1934—Jean Delaney Carroll, sentenced to a year and a day for violation of parole

July 7, 1934—Patricia Cherrington and Opal Long, sentenced to two years in the federal prison in Milan, Michigan, for harboring

December 7, 1934—John Burns, escaped convict, arrested in Chicago and returned to Indiana State Prison to complete a life sentence

December 22, 1934—Thomas Kirwin, sentenced to two years and a $10,000 fine; William A. Gray, to eighteen months and a $5,000 fine; Marie Comforti and Mrs. Marie McCarthy, to a year and a day each, for harboring Homer Van Meter

June 4, 1935—Joseph Fox, escaped convict, arrested in Chicago and returned to Indiana State Prison to complete a life sentence

June 7, 1935—Mrs. Anna Steve, sentenced to three months in jail for harboring her brother, John Hamilton

September 21, 1935—Arthur O'Leary and Dr. Harold Cassidy, after eight months in custody, placed on one year's probation for conspiring to harbor; Dr. Wilhelm Loeser, sentenced to one day in the U.S. Marshal's Office on the same charges, then returned to Leavenworth Penitentiary for his parole violation

May 9, 1936—Louis Piquett began serving a sentence of two years at Leavenworth Penitentiary

In other words, there were a total of twenty-six persons killed, nineteen wounded, and twenty-three sentenced—truly a terrible cost in bloodshed and misery. Added to this is the monetary cost of three hundred thousand dollars taken in bank robberies, and at least a million dollars expended by the federal and state and local governments, as well as by private organizations, for protecting against and running down the Dillinger gang.

What moral lesson, if any, can be derived from a life such as that lived by John Dillinger?

Dillinger was the only criminal designated Public Enemy Number One by a federal official, Attorney General Cummings. Well-meant as such designations undoubtedly are, they serve only to increase the glamour and publicity upon which the criminal ego feeds.

Let there be no mistaken belief that famous underworld characters are indifferent to the attention they excite. There was scarcely a day when John Dillinger and the members of his gang did not eagerly read the papers and listen to the radio news for a mention of their names. According to O'Leary, Dillinger derived a particular delight from jesting with Van Meter over their respective news value.

"Well, I see I made the headlines again today," Dillinger would remark to his companion. He would then turn to the fourth or fifth page of the newspaper. "Let's see if we can find a little something about you, Van." Dillinger would next turn to the classified columns and scan the advertisements. "No, they don't even mention your name."

Van Meter would express his profound indifference to the attention showered on his associate, but Dillinger knew that he inwardly burned with envy. Dillinger, in fact, cooperated with efforts to exploit his popularity and keep him in the public eye.

One thing is certain—there will never be another John Dillinger. Dillinger was an atavism, a throwback to the days of the buccaneers and the bandit chieftains who appear and flourish when society finds itself in an unsettled condition. Historical circumstances and certain personal qualities enabled him to rise to a paramount position in the annals of crime, and there is small likelihood of such a combination ever recurring again. Along with nerve and courage, Dillinger possessed an exceptional alertness of mind, and it was this quick thinking under pressure that enabled him for so long to escape from traps and keep a step ahead of his pursuers. The police, sensing this aptitude but not comprehending it, contented themselves with speaking of "Dillinger luck."

Luck played a part, but a great deal of the outlaw's success must also be ascribed to the uncoordinated and antiquated methods of his pursuers. When bound closely to the earth by reposing confidence in mass strength, reliance on informers, and the use of brutal third-degree methods, law enforcers cannot expect to cope with an extraordinary antagonist of the Dillinger type. The doctrine of brawn over brain and the medieval torture chamber have no place in modern life. It is only when strength of arm and the power of political connections give way to reason and the principles of scientific detection that the crime problem will begin to yield to the rule of law.

Did Dillinger find happiness or attain any of his goals? Time and again he answered these questions in remarks we can generalize:

"I'd give anything in this world to have my life to live over. I certainly would never do this again. I'm nothing but a hunted animal. There isn't a place in this world where I can lay my head at night with any confidence I will be alive the next morning. I'm a human being, and I want to live like other human beings. What pleasure do I get out of my money? Every cent I got I have to hand out just to be allowed to keep on living, and when the money runs low there's nothing left to do but go out and get some more. There's no going back now. I'm traveling a one-way road, and I'm not fooling myself as to what the end will be. If I surrender, I know it means the electric chair. There's no place left where I can hide. If I go on, it's just a question of how much time I have left. I guess I've just gone too far.''

Arthur O'Leary feels much the same. ''They're all gone—all of those men I knew during that mad, wild summer. Dillinger, Van Meter, Nelson, Hamilton, Carroll, Probasco—all dead. Piquett and Loeser may as well be, and there seems no place left for me to go except back to the orphanage.''

On the morning of May 9, 1936, the doors of Leavenworth penitentiary closed on the drooping, white-haired form of Louis Piquett, and with them closed the saga of John Dillinger.

Epilogue

Hoover's triumph over Dillinger and the Depression desperadoes firmly established the FBI as the country's premier crimebusting organization—as the story is told by the U.S. entertainment industry and the FBI itself. Popular accounts ignore the animosity that often existed between the Bureau and other police agencies because of professional jealousy, resentment of the FBI's self-promotion, and its attitude of superiority, often reflecting a well-justified distrust of the locals.

Also resented by other law-enforcement professionals was the way the FBI often received more than its share of credit for doing less than its share of the work. The new federal laws were tailored to "box office" crimes that were also the easiest to solve, especially once local authorities had been pressured into using the Bureau's national facilities and coordinating their efforts. Besides its centralized fingerprint files, the FBI's most highly touted facility was its crime lab, patterned after (some would say pirated from) the Scientific Crime Detection Laboratory pioneered in Chicago by Colonel Calvin Goddard. (In his papers, Goddard describes with some annoyance how the Bureau enrolled men in his courses, replicated his equipment and techniques in Washington, and then publicized its national crime lab as though the forensic sciences were an FBI invention.) Of course the task of dealing with ordinary and largely unsolvable crime was left to local authorities (as the

Constitution conveniently specified); and a careful reading of the new federal code could either find or not find a federal violation, depending on whether the crime would lend itself to a satisfactory solution that improved the Bureau's statistics and reputation. Although the Bureau did make some forays against racketeering when a federal law permitted, it wasn't until the 1960s that Hoover grudgingly conceded the existence of nationally organized crime.

The power that Hoover would wield in future years was not his to enjoy immediately, however. Throughout the thirties he and the Bureau still had enemies in high places, but the director demonstrated a genius for seducing some (like the American Civil Liberties Union), intimidating others, eluding their traps, or silencing them with publicity stunts.

Hoover prevailed in one test after another, and began building files on the private lives of public figures that would make him impossible to remove from office before his death in 1972. He early on purged the Bureau of the one agent who had briefly joined him in the spotlight of national publicity. Melvin Purvis had incurred Hoover's wrath after the Battle of Little Bohemia, and the director had sent his own man, Sam Cowley, to Chicago to take over the Dillinger hunt. Without demoting Purvis, his memos assign Cowley to every case of any importance. But when Dillinger's death occurred in the public and sensational manner in which it did, the press still made Purvis the celebrity-in-charge—and there was nothing either he or Hoover could do about it. Purvis, not Hoover, became "the man who got Dillinger," and head-line writers like names with few letters, whatever they may be. Moreover, Purvis looked more like an accountant than a gangbuster, which appealed to journalists' sense of irony. The fact that Purvis fired no shots at the Biograph was largely ignored. When Pretty Boy Floyd surfaced in Ohio unexpectedly and died in a hail of gunfire on October 22, newspapers gave the kill to Purvis although others had fired the shots. When Cowley and Hollis were killed by Baby Face Nelson on November 27, Purvis became their personal avenger who, it was said, had raced to the dying Cowley's bedside and taken an oath in blood. Whether figuratively or literally wasn't clear, but Hoover could tolerate no more. He yanked Purvis off the case and sent him on an endless round of inspection tours that kept America's new "Ace G-Man" off the streets and out of trouble. And out of the headlines. From internal memoranda, it looked as though Purvis would be exiled to some remote city as soon as his news value diminished. It does not appear that Purvis courted publicity or even particularly liked it, beyond the normal enjoyment of evidence of public approval. His personal modesty may even have worked against him, as journalists find that an attractive quality in any newsmaker.

Nevertheless, Hoover managed to make Purvis's life miserable with unreasonable demands and fanatical office inspections calculated to fault his abilities as agent-in-charge. One of Hoover's famous file memos records a rumor that Purvis became drunk at a party and waved a gun, which Purvis had to deny in correspondence that amounted to an informal disciplinary hearing. Finally, on July 10, 1935, the discouraged (and now disgruntled) agent wired the director that he was quitting the FBI, giving what amounted to two days' notice. This took Hoover by complete surprise, for only a few weeks earlier Inspector Clegg had reported that Purvis was intensely loyal to the Bureau and that "his high personal regard for the Director continues unabated in spite of what he probably feels to be some sort of punitive administrative action." The terse three-sentence resignation launched a flurry of frantic messages between Washington and Chicago, but left the embarrassed director with no clue as to any specific grievance and no explanations—except a lame one that Purvis was quitting for personal reasons, to pursue his own interests.

Newspapers speculated that Purvis had resigned to protest the Justice Department's reneging on its deal with Anna Sage, and though this had little to do with his decision, he denied it unconvincingly. When pressed, he offered the feeble explanation that his unwelcome notoriety had diminished his value as a crimefighter, as though his cover were blown. For the present, he wanted nothing more than to spend some time with his family and relax with a pipe. He seemed thoroughly upbeat in his newsreel farewell, which he ended with the crimefighting note that more wholesome activities for youngsters today would pay off in good citizens tomorrow.

Job offers poured in, but the furious Hoover managed to sabotage anything remotely connected with law enforcement or security or consulting work. Purvis was soon reduced to the embarrassing if lucrative business of endorsing consumer products ranging from razor blades to Dodge automobiles, and heading up the "Melvin Purvis Junior G-Men" club for Post Toasties breakfast cereal. When a young visitor to the FBI building thought his credentials as a junior G-man made him a privileged auxiliary agent, Hoover sent his researchers to the law books for the regulations on counterfeit credentials.

In 1936 Purvis published *American Agent,* a laudatory history of the FBI in which the director had no name (except as buried in a historical list of Justice Department officials). Hoover retaliated with *Persons in Hiding* (1938), which ignored Purvis altogether and gave credit for his cases to Sam Cowley, who was no longer alive to be interviewed. Purvis even vanished from the official FBI map of the Biograph Theatre ambush, a deletion noticed by some newspapers; and his voluntary resignation from the Bureau became a "termination with prejudice." In Don Whitehead's authorized history *The FBI Story,* which must have rivaled the Bible in sales, Purvis is present at the Biograph, but his name doesn't appear in the index.

Purvis tried to patch things up, and Hoover would respond with glowing letters of enduring friendship and personal invitations; but he dodged Purvis's visits to Washington and for the next twenty-five years continued to subvert his every opportunity. None of Purvis's ventures in lawyering, newspaper publishing, or radio-station ownership took off, and his health gradually failed. Shortly before noon on February 29, 1960, Purvis's wife Rosanne was working in the garden outside their home at Florence, South Carolina, when she heard a shot. She rushed into the house to find Purvis dead in an upstairs hallway, killed by a bullet from the nickel-plated Colt .45 automatic he had received as a going-away present from fellow agents twenty-five years before. Following the funeral his widow wired Hoover:

FEDERAL BUREAU OF INVESTIGATION
U. S. DEPARTMENT OF JUSTICE
COMMUNICATIONS SECTION

MAR 7 1960

WESTERN UNION

BIA002 (1052 AME MAR7 60) AA057 A

FEA047 PD FLORENCE SOCAR 7 956AME

J EDGAR HOOVER

DIRECTOR F B I WASHDC

WE ARE HONORED THAT YOU IGNORED MELVINS

DEATH. YOUR JEALOUSY HURT HIM VERY MUCH BUT UNTIL THE END I

THINK HE LOVED YOU

ROSANNE MELVIN JR ALSON AND CHRISTOPHER PURVIS.

Anna Sage also fared poorly in the years after Dillinger's death. Upon her arrival in Rumania in 1936, authorities refused to let her go on stage for a vaudeville company; and a restaurant-nightclub she opened in Timosuara attracted extortionists who had heard exaggerated accounts of her wealth. To shake off her tormentors, she changed her name and fled, moving from city to city in Europe. In Budapest she even underwent plastic surgery that deliberately disfigured her face with scars to suggest a tropical skin disease called chafar that would gain her admittance to a private sanitarium on the outskirts of Cairo, Egypt. In July of 1939, newspapers helpfully announced that reporters had tracked her there, where she was living in seclusion. The press apparently lost her trail during World War II, and her name made no further news until her death from a "liver ailment" on April 25, 1947, in Rumania.

Evelyn Frechette completed her harboring sentence in 1936 and toured for a time with Dillinger's father in a crime-does-not-pay carnival show. Her first remarriage failed, and a second was in trouble when she became ill with cancer and died on January 13, 1969, in Shawano, Wisconsin, at the age of sixty-one. Polly Hamilton went into hiding but eventually got her life back together. She returned to Chicago to work as a waitress under such names as Kay Sullivan and Kay Donahue, and married a Chicago salesman named William Black. They apparently lived a quiet life in pleasant circumstances at 1942 Mohawk, on Chicago's Near North Side, until her death as Edythe Black on February 19, 1969, barely a month after Evelyn's.

Opal Long served her harboring sentence and returned to obscurity. Her sister Pat Cherrington completed her own sentence on July 27, 1936, toured for a while, and then returned to working as a waitress, tavern hostess, and dice girl in gambling joints on North Clark Street. In 1938 she and two men were accused of fleecing a pool player of $9,000. But, in general, her adventures had ended with the Dillinger days, and after that she lived frugally in rooming houses. On May 3, 1949, an employee found her dead in her room at the Burton Hotel, 1439 North Clark Street. In her possession were several love letters from Harry Copeland, saying that he hoped to get out of prison in November, and $2.16.

Helen Gillis left the federal prison for women in Milan, Michigan, on December 13, 1936, and returned to the Chicago area. She apparently kept the name Helen Nelson in places where she worked, but carefully avoided publicity or even recognition for the next fifty years. She lived quietly with her son Ronald before her death in 1987, and was buried in the Gillis family plot in a western suburb of Chicago.

Louis Piquett fared poorly after his conviction for harboring Van Meter. He was fined $10,000 and disbarred, and entered Leavenworth on May 6, 1936. After his release on January 11, 1938, he worked in restaurants and saloons and in 1945 was tending bar at Coburn's Tavern, 112 South Clark Street. Otherwise, he lived quietly with his wife Nell at 661 West Sheridan, a block south of his old place at 659 Irving Park Boulevard, avoiding nearly everyone he had known. Despite Hoover's continuing opposition, Piquett received a presidential pardon from Harry S. Truman in January 1951, and applied for reinstatement to practice law. That was still pending when he suffered a heart attack on the street and died two days later, on December 12, at the age of seventy-one.

Arthur O'Leary received a suspended sentence in return for his testimony that helped send Piquett to prison. Then he dropped out of sight and eventually retired to Dubuque, Iowa, where he died, probably around 1970. What became of Dr. Loeser isn't known, but Dr. Cassidy killed himself on July 30, 1946, at the home of a sister in Chicago.

Sergeant Zarkovich proved to be a survivor. Despite a liquor-smuggling conviction in 1930 and a demotion for refusing to discuss Dillinger with Indiana's governor, he later made chief of detectives in East Chicago and served as chief of police there from 1947 to 1952. After retirement he remained employed by the city as a probation officer and died there on October 30, 1969, at the age of seventy-three.

J. Edgar Hoover not only survived but became an institution, after dodging a few close ones. On January 16, 1935, his agents located and surrounded the hideout of the Barker-Karpis gang near Oklawaha, Florida. Following a four-hour, one-sided gun battle, agents ordered a black gardener to enter the house and see if anyone had survived. Newspapers do not indicate how much the gardener enjoyed that assignment, but he did as told and came back with good news and bad news: The good news was that the fugitives were dead; the bad news was that the FBI had killed somebody's mother.

The Bureau had learned that Alvin Karpis and the Barkers usually traveled with a dowdy middle-aged woman with the unlikely name of Arizona Clark Barker, or Kate, identified as the Barker brothers' mother. But the public didn't know this, and the discovery that agents had just wasted Mrs. Barker required fast thinking. Within hours Justice Department press releases were describing "Ma" Barker as a hillbilly harridan who had raised her "spoor" to become the worst gang of bank-robbing kidnappers ever to terrorize America. For by this time the Barker-Karpis gang had been identified as the abductors of both William Hamm and Edward Bremer, and the perpetrators of several major and bloody robberies since 1931. So Hoover pulled out all the stops, turning "Ma" into a maternal menace and criminal mastermind whose evil "brood" illustrated the consequences of parental overindulgence. As he said of her, in the purple prose of ghostwriter Courtney Ryley Cooper, "The eyes of Arizona Clark Barker . . . always fascinated me. They were queerly direct, penetrating, hot with some strangely smouldering flame, yet withal as hypnotically cold as the muzzle of a gun."

The public had no problem with that. Women outlaws were part of the national tradition, and the surprise discovery of a "Ma" Barker only added a nice twist—a mother-and-sons outlaw team, for the other body was that of her boy Fred Barker. Herman was already dead, Lloyd in prison, and Arthur, aka "Doc," had just been picked up in Chicago when he left 432 Surf Street for a stroll without his gun on January 8, the same day federal agents killed Russell Gibson and captured Byron Bolton in a noisy shootout at 3920 North Pine Grove. That left Karpis, by popular consensus, the new Public Enemy Number One. Like Dillinger, Karpis was good at eluding FBI traps, so when a hostile U.S. senator made disparaging remarks about the Bureau's incompetence and Hoover's lack of actual police experience, the furious director ordered his agents to nail Karpis down so he could perform the capture personally.

The Public Enemy era, for all practical purposes, ended on May 1, 1936, when Hoover nabbed Karpis as he stepped out of an apartment building in New Orleans. The director had rushed to the scene when advised that Karpis was located, and the Bureau tried to make the *mano a mano* capture the crime news of the decade. It did generate enough news coverage that no one ever again impugned J. Edgar Hoover's courage or lawman skills—except Karpis himself, who later said he was disarmed and held at gunpoint by a crowd of agents who then turned him over to Hoover for the news photos. He also said that "Ma," however frightful she looked, had neither the experience nor the brains to lead anyone in crime, and was trucked around mainly as camouflage.

But Dillinger remained the outlaw the public best remembered, and he soon occupied an almost mystical place in the legend of the FBI. Not only did he become the ultimate trophy from the Bureau's glorious war on crime, but his enshrinement in the anteroom outside Hoover's office may also have helped the director vanquish the ghost of Melvin Purvis. Wrote Jack Alexander unflatteringly in 1938, "A tourist is dull-witted indeed if he fails to comprehend, as he gapes at the display cases, that he is looking upon the rude implements and superstitious talismans of a barbarous race that is slowly perishing under the relentless impact of a superior one." Dillinger's death mask seemed a particularly eerie artifact, and grouped about it were

> the straw hat he was wearing, a wrinkled snapshot of a girl which was fished from his trousers pocket, and the silver rimmed glasses he was wearing to heighten his disguise, one of the lens rims snapped by a bullet. There is a La Corona–Belvedere cigar he was carrying in his shirt pocket that summer night, still banded and wrapped in cellophane. . . . There is an almost unholy shriek of triumph in these stark, simple objects.

Dillinger and Hoover became a study in mutual mythmaking. If today's federal criminal laws owe something to Dillinger, the outlaw's memory owes as much to the director of the FBI, whom he in turn rewarded with glory and power that Hoover would forever wear before critics like a bulletproof vest. Not until Hoover was twenty years dead, and showed no signs of returning, would biographers dare to describe some of his personal peculiarities and apparent corruption or criticize the power he held over people from the president on down.

In the clash of those Titans of American mythology, Hoover's reputation as the world's greatest crimefighter has lately been losing ground to his nemesis John Dillinger, who broke the law honestly and had only himself to hide. As a truly loyal girlfriend put it,

> "Johnnie's just an ordinary fellow. Of course he goes out and holds up banks and things, but he's really just like any other fellow, aside from that."

A Dillinger Chronology

June 22, 1903 John Herbert Dillinger born at 2053 Cooper St. in Indianapolis, son of grocer John Wilson Dillinger and Mollie Lancaster Dillinger; mother dies when he is three and he is reared by sister Audrey

March 1920 Family moves to Mooresville, Ind.; father takes up farming

1920–1923 Quits school; works in machine shop and furniture factory; hangs out in Martinsville playing pool and baseball

July 24, 1923 Joins navy after being jilted by Mooresville high school girl

October 28, 1923 Goes AWOL for one day

November 7, 1923 Sentenced to 10 days' solitary confinement

December 4, 1923 Deserts navy and is later dishonorably discharged

April 12, 1924 Marries Beryl Hovious

May 1924 Steals 41 chickens from Homer Zook

Summer 1924 Excels as upholsterer in Mooresville furniture factory

September 6, 1924 Ed Singleton and Dillinger get drunk and fail in an attempt to hold up elderly Mooresville grocer Frank Morgan after closing time

September 16, 1924 Sent to Pendleton Reformatory as prisoner #14395 to begin a 10-to-20-year sentence; Singleton gets off with 2 to 14

October 20, 1924 Receives a 30–day extension of his sentence for escape attempt

February 25, 1926 Punished for gambling and disorderly conduct

October 1928 Punished for destroying property; meets fellow prisoners Harry Pierpont and John Hamilton

June 20, 1929 Divorced by Beryl Hovious, who marries a Morgan County farmer

July 15, 1929 Transferred from Pendleton to Indiana State Prison in Michigan City as prisoner #13225; robbery victim Frank Morgan and Brother Fillmore, Dillinger family minister, petition for his release

May 22, 1933 Released on parole; hitchhikes to Gary, Ind., where he meets with Hilton O. Crouch and Harry Copeland

June 10, 1933 Robs bank in New Carlisle, Ohio, of $10,600

June 24, 1933 With William Shaw, attempts to rob Marshall Field thread mill at Monticello, Ind.; Dillinger shoots assistant manager Fred Fisher in leg

June–July 1933 Dillinger visits ex-convict Frank Whitehouse in Lebanon, Ky.

July 3, 1933 Dillinger takes Frank Whitehouse and wife to Chicago World's Fair; visits other ex-cons along the way

July 15, 1933 With Harry Copeland, William Shaw, and Noble (Sam) Claycomb, robs Bide-a-Wee tavern in Muncie, Ind.

July 16, 1933 Mr. and Mrs. William Shaw, Noble Claycomb, and Paul ("Lefty") Parker captured in Muncie, Ind.; Dillinger and Copeland escape

July 17, 1933 Robs Daleville, Ind., bank of $3,500 with Harry Copeland

July 19, 1933 Suspected of robbing bank in Rockville, Ind.

July 20, 1933 En route to Chicago, Dillinger, with Mary Longnacre and Mary Ann Bucholtz, visits father at Mooresville farm

July 21, 1933 Dillinger and the two girls check into Crillon Hotel in Chicago, then spend three days at baseball games and World's Fair; photographs policeman

July 24, 1933 While returning to Dayton, Ohio, Dillinger stops at Michigan City prison so Mary Longnacre can visit her brother, James Jenkins

August 4, 1933 Robs First National Bank in Montpelier, Ind., of $10,000 with Copeland and Sam Goldstein; Dillinger associates Clarence "Whitey" Mohler, George Whitehouse, and Fred Berman arrested by Indiana State Police in East Chicago

August 8, 1933 Suspected of robbing bank at Gravel Switch, Ky.

August 14, 1933 Robs Citizens' National Bank at Bluffton, Ohio, of $2,100 with Copeland and Goldstein

August 18, 1933 Suspected of $30,000 bank robbery in Grand Haven, Mich., to which Eddie Bentz later confessed, implicating Homer Van Meter, Tommy Carroll, and Baby Face Nelson (aka Lester Gillis)

August 22, 1933 Sam Goldstein arrested by state police in Gary, Ind.

September 6, 1933 Robs State Bank of Massachusetts Avenue in Indianapolis of $25,000 with Copeland and Crouch

September 12, 1933 Dillinger throws guns over prison wall for his inmate friends; guns are found by other prisoners and turned in

September 22, 1933 Dillinger arrested at Mary Longnacre's house in Dayton, Ohio, jailed in Lima, charged with robbing banks in Indianapolis; Farrell, Pa.; and Bluffton, Ohio

September 26, 1933 Harry Pierpont, Charles Makley, John Hamilton, Walter Dietrich, Russell Clark, James Clark [no relation], Ed Shouse, James Jenkins, Joseph Fox, and Joseph Burns break out of Indiana State Prison with guns smuggled to them by Dillinger (box of thread was cover story); Machine Gun Kelly arrested same day in Memphis

September 28, 1933 James Clark recaptured in Hammond, Ind.

September 30, 1933 James Jenkins killed by vigilantes near Beanblossom, Ind.

October 3, 1933 Pierpont, Makley, Russell Clark, and Hamilton rob First National Bank at St. Mary's, Ohio, of $11,000

October 12, 1933 Pierpont, Russell Clark, Makley, Copeland, and Hamilton kill Sheriff Jesse Sarber while freeing Dillinger from Lima, Ohio, jail.

October 14, 1933 Dillinger, Pierpont, and Walter Dietrich raid Auburn, Ind., police station for guns and bulletproof vests

October 21, 1933 Same three raid Peru, Ind., police for more guns and vests

October 23, 1933 Dillinger, Pierpont, Makley, Clark, and Copeland rob Central National Bank in Greencastle, Ind., of $75,000; Baby Face Nelson, Tommy Carroll, and others rob First National Bank at Brainerd, Minn., of $32,000

October 24, 1933 Dillinger accused of $5,000 bank robbery in South Bend; actual robbers later apprehended

October 26, 1933 Indiana Governor McNutt calls up National Guard; Dillinger gang flees to Chicago

November 15, 1933 Trap is laid for Dillinger outside office of Dr. Charles H. Eye, dermatologist at 4175 W. Irving Park Blvd., but Dillinger and Evelyn Frechette escape after running gun battle east on Irving Park

November 17, 1933 Harry Copeland arrested in car at Harlem and North Avenue in Chicago, after pulling gun on girlfriend in argument; later sentenced to 25 years for Greencastle robbery

November 20, 1933 Dillinger, Makley, Hamilton, Clark, Pierpont, and Leslie "Big" Homer rob Racine, Wis., bank of $27,000, wounding a policeman and an assistant cashier and kidnapping another policeman, the bank president, and a woman employee

November 24, 1933 Dillinger gang member Leslie Homer arrested at LaSalle and Ohio streets in Chicago with ex-con Jack Liberty; Homer later sentenced to 28 years for Racine, Wis., bank robbery

December 1933 Chicago police include eight Dillinger associates, among them Mary Kinder and Pearl Elliott, on their Public Enemies list

December 11, 1933 Police Detective H. C. Perrow killed by Tommy Carroll in San Antonio

December 13, 1933 Dillinger, Hamilton, Clark, and Makley suspected of looting Chicago's Unity Trust and Savings Bank safe-deposit vaults, 2909 W. North Ave.

December 14, 1933 John Hamilton kills Chicago police sergeant William Shanley at garage on North Broadway

December 15, 1933 Visits sister Audrey in Maywood, Ind., and father in Mooresville

December 16, 1933 Chicago Police Capt. John Stege organizes 40–man "Dillinger Squad"; State's Attorney Thomas Courtney announces suspected connections between Dillinger, Touhy, Klutas, and Harvey Bailey–Verne Miller gangs

December 17, 1933 Chicago fence and Dillinger gang contact Arthur "Fish" Johnson (aka Johnston) arrested at 1742 Humbolt

December 20, 1933 Indiana state patrolman accidentally killed by fellow officer in capture of Ed Shouse at Paris, Ill.; Dillinger gang travels to Daytona Beach

December 22, 1933 Chicago cops raid apartment at 1428 Farwell and kill three minor gangsters they mistake for Dillinger gang

December 23, 1933 Hilton Crouch arrested at 420 Surf St., Chicago, later sentenced to 20 years for Indianapolis bank robbery

January 1, 1934 Dillinger gang celebrates New Year's by firing machine guns on beach at 901 S. Atlantic Ave. in Daytona Beach; wrongly suspected of robbing Beverly Gardens nightclub in Chicago and machine-gunning two cops

January 6, 1934 Walter Dietrich captured at Klutas gang hideout in Bellwood, Ill.; "Handsome Jack" Klutas killed; Joseph Aiuppa (aka Joey O'Brien), alleged supplier of machine guns to Dillinger gang, arrested nearby on same day

January 15, 1934 Dillinger, Hamilton, and unidentified men rob First National Bank of East Chicago of $20,000; Dillinger accused of killing police officer William P. O'Malley; Hamilton wounded and goes into hiding

January 25, 1934 Dillinger, Makley, Clark, and Pierpont captured by Tucson, Ariz., police, along with Mary Kinder, Evelyn "Billie" Frechette (aka Ann Martin), and Opal Long, when firemen fighting a blaze at their hotel recognize them from detective-magazine pictures. Dillinger extradited to Indiana to face charge of murdering Patrolman O'Malley

January 30, 1934 Transferred to Lake County Jail in Crown Point, Ind.; poses for pictures with Prosecutor Robert G. Estill

February 5, 1934 Trial date is set for March 12; Indiana judge William Murray refuses to transfer Dillinger to state prison

March 3, 1934 Displaying a whittled wooden gun, Dillinger breaks out of Lake County Jail, taking with him black prisoner Herbert Youngblood and two hostages, Ed Saager and Ernest Blunk, in the stolen car of Sheriff Lillian Holley

March 6, 1934 Dillinger, Hamilton, Baby Face Nelson, Homer Van Meter, Eddie Green, and Tommy Carroll ("Second Dillinger Gang") rob Security National Bank at Sioux Falls, S.D., of $49,500

March 8, 1934 Federal complaint filed in Chicago against Dillinger for interstate transportation of stolen auto (Dyer Act)

March 10, 1934 Suspected in gun battle with police in Shiller Park, Ill.

March 13, 1934 Dillinger gang robs First National Bank at Mason City, Iowa, of $52,000; Dillinger and Hamilton wounded

March 16, 1934 Herbert Youngblood killed by police in Port Huron, Mich.

March 22, 1934 Roy J. Frisch, witness in U.S. mail fraud case against Reno gamblers Bill Graham and Jim McKay, murdered near Reno by Baby Face Nelson, according to Nelson accomplice John Paul Chase; body never found

March 24, 1934 Harry Pierpont and Charles Makley sentenced to death at Lima, Ohio, for murder of Sheriff Jesse Sarber; Russell Clark sentenced to life

March 31, 1934 Dillinger, with girlfriend Evelyn Frechette, shoots his way out of FBI trap at an apartment in St. Paul, Minn.; Homer Van Meter also escapes

April 3, 1934 Eddie Green shot by G-men in St. Paul; deliriously spills wealth of information to FBI before dying on April 11

April 5–8, 1934 Dillinger visits father and family at Mooresville at height of "country's greatest manhunt"; April 6, rides with half-brother Hubert to Leipsic, Ohio, to contact relatives of Pierpont; on return trip, Hubert falls asleep and crashes car, goes for repairs while Dillinger hides in haystack with machine gun

April 9, 1934 Evelyn Frechette captured by Melvin Purvis when she and Dillinger go to State & Austin Tavern of Larry Strong, 416 N. State, Chicago; Dillinger gets away unseen

April 13, 1934 Dillinger and Van Meter raid Warsaw, Ind., police station for guns and vests

April 17, 1934 Local newspaper reports FBI trap for Dillinger in Louisville, so Dillinger, Hamilton, and Pat Cherrington head instead to Sault Ste. Marie, Mich., to visit Hamilton's sister

April 23, 1934 Dillinger gang shoot their way out of FBI trap at Little Bohemia Lodge near Rhinelander, Wis., with Baby Face Nelson killing one federal agent and wounding two other officers; FBI mistakenly shoots three innocent customers, killing one, but captures Helen Nelson, Jean Delaney, and Marie Comforti; after fleeing Little Bohemia, Dillinger, Hamilton, and Van Meter battle deputies near St. Paul; Hamilton mortally wounded

April 27, 1934 Hamilton dies at Aurora, Ill., apartment of Barker-Karpis gang member Volney Davis; buried by Dillinger, Van Meter, and members of Barker-Karpis gang at gravel pit near Oswego, Ill.

April 30, 1934 San Antonio gunsmith H. S. Lebman arrested for supplying guns to Dillinger gang

May 1, 1934 Dillinger and two others suspected of slugging and disarming three policemen in Bellwood, Ind.

May 3, 1934 FBI tipped that Dillinger is aboard SS *Duchess of York,* bound for Glasgow, Scotland; search of ship turns up former German spy Trebilsch Lincoln (aka Abbot Chao Kung)

May 4, 1934 Dillinger and Van Meter suspected of robbing bank in Fostoria, Ohio

May 5, 1934 Ten of 12 federal anti-crime bills proposed by Attorney General Homer Cummings approved by U.S. House

May 18, 1934 Dillinger and Nelson suspected of robbing bank in Flint, Mich.; Tommy Carroll (wanted for post office robbery) and Dillinger indicted by federal grand jury at Madison, Wis., for conspiracy to harbor one another; Nelson and Van Meter indicted for conspiracy to harbor Dillinger and Carroll

May 23, 1934 Evelyn Frechette and Dr. Clayton E. May, St. Paul doctor, are convicted of harboring Dillinger, fined $10,000, and sentenced to 2 years; Bonnie and Clyde killed near Gibsland, La.

May 24, 1934 Dillinger and Van Meter accused of killing two East Chicago cops; five state governors collectively post $5,000 reward for Dillinger's capture; *Liberty* magazine offers $1,000

May 27, 1934 Dillinger and Van Meter undergo plastic surgery by Drs. Wilhelm Loeser and Harold Cassidy at house of bar owner James Probasco, 2509 N. Crawford Ave. [now Pulaski], Chicago

June 2, 1934 Pat Cherrington and sister Opal Long (aka Bernice Clark) arrested at Chateau Hotel, 3838 N. Broadway, Chicago; Jean Helen Burke arrested same day

June 4, 1934 Indiana State Prison escapee Joseph Fox recaptured in Chicago

June 7, 1934 Tommy Carroll killed at Waterloo, Iowa

June 8, 1934 Dillinger indicted by federal grand jury at South Bend for interstate transportation of car stolen from Sheriff Lillian Holley

June 14, 1934 Ramsey County grand jury indicts Dillinger and Van Meter for assault in connection with their March 31 gun battle in St. Paul

June 15, 1934 About when Dillinger meets Polly Hamilton, friend of Anna Sage

June 22, 1934 Dillinger officially named Public Enemy No. 1; celebrates his 31st birthday at French Casino nightclub, 4812 North Clark St., with Polly

June 23, 1934 Attorney General Cummings posts $10,000 reward for Dillinger, but only $5,000 for Baby Face Nelson; Dillinger and Polly again visit French Casino, this time to celebrate Polly's birthday

June 24, 1934 Sixty state and federal officers raid ranch near Branson, Mo., on a tip that Dillinger and Pretty Boy Floyd are there recovering from wounds

June 27, 1934 Albert "Pat" Reilly, who was with gang at Little Bohemia, arrested by FBI in St. Paul and claims Dillinger is dead; later sentenced to two years for harboring Dillinger

June 30, 1934 Dillinger, Nelson, Van Meter, John Paul Chase, and unidentified man rob South Bend, Ind., bank of $30,000; one policeman killed and four citizens wounded

July 6, 1934 Pat Cherrington convicted in Madison, Wis., of harboring Dillinger and sentenced to two years

July 22, 1934 Dillinger killed as he leaves Biograph Theatre at 2433 N. Lincoln, Chicago, with Polly Hamilton and betrayer Anna Sage

Chicago Hideouts and Hangouts

4631 N. Paulina (Dillinger, at Opal Long's apartment)

2318 W. Sunnyside (Harry Copeland)

2649 N. Kedzie (Dillinger)

115 N. Parkside and 150–54 N. Parkside (Dillinger, Pierpont, and others)

1740 Humboldt (Harry Pierpont, Russell Clark)

1850 N. Humboldt (various)

4310 N. Clarendon (Dillinger, Pierpont, and girlfriends)

3154 N. Racine, Bel Ray Hotel (various)

1015 N. Clark, Olympia Hotel (Harry Copeland)

1343 W. Argyle (John Hamilton and Joseph Burns)

2530 N. Sacramento, Loganwood Apartment Hotel (John Hamilton)

2120 W. Washington, Vel Mar Hotel (Homer Van Meter)

2959 W. Washington (Homer Van Meter)

5510 N. Winthrop (Harry Pierpont)

901 Addison (Evelyn Frechette's apartment at the time she meets Dillinger, around 10/33)

840 W. Montrose (Harry Copeland arrested 11/17/33)

420 W. Surf (Hilton Crouch arrested 12/23/33)

3512 N. Halsted (apartment of Evelyn Frechette's sister Patsy, used by Dillinger after his escape from Crown Point, 3/4/34)

416 N. State, State & Austin Tavern (trap set for Dillinger results in Evelyn Frechette's arrest 4/9/34)

4849 W. Fullerton, Fullerton Hotel (used following South Bend robbery 6/30/34)

2300 W. Division, Clarence Lieder's Oakley Auto Construction Co. and hideout (Dillinger and Van Meter)

7190 W. North Ave., Jimmy Murray's Rainbo Barbecue restaurant and hideout (Dillinger, Baby Face Nelson, probably Van Meter)

700 W. 69th (Joseph Burns arrested 12/17/34)

11434 S. Harvard (Joseph Fox arrested 6/4/35)

Louie Cernocky's roadhouse, Fox River Grove (patronized by major midwestern gangs)

2246 W. Grand, Doc's Tavern

2350 W. Grand, Pioneer Restaurant

2242 S. Cicero, Hy-Ho Club

550 N. Clark, Nut House tavern and nightclub

4825 W. Cermak, Town Club

3925 N. Sheridan, Sheridan Billiard House

4541 N. Broadway, Barrel o'Fun Tavern (Dillinger introduced to Evelyn Frechette, fall 1933)

4812 N. Clark, French Casino nightclub (Dillinger celebrates 31st birthday with Polly Hamilton)

2509 N. Crawford [now Pulaski] Ave. (plastic surgery performed at cottage of James Probasco, 5/28/34)

3838 N. Broadway, Chateau Hotel (Pat Cherrington and Opal Long arrested 6/2/34)

3504 N. Sheffield, Sheffield Hotel (operated by Anna Sage, 1933)

3324 N. Clark (Anna Sage and her son Steve, 1933)

2862 N. Clark (Anna Sage "resort" raided by police)

2225 N. Seminary (apartment of Anna Sage)

3321 Warren Blvd. ("resort" operated by Anna Sage)

5542 N. Kenmore (residence of Anna and son Steve)

2838 N. Clark (apartment where Anna meets Dillinger before moving to her Fullerton apartment)

2420 N. Fullerton (Dillinger's residence with Anna Sage when he is killed)

4506 N. Sheridan Rd., McCready Funeral Home (receives body of Dillinger after its release from Cook County Morgue)

100 and 228 N. LaSalle (offices of Louis Piquett)

659 W. Irving Park (apartment of Louis Piquett and wife Nell)

661 W. Sheridan Rd. (apartment of Louis Piquett when he died in 1951)

2738 N. Pine Grove (residence of Arthur and Grayce O'Leary)

4175 W. Irving Park (office of Dr. Charles H. Eye, scene of Dillinger escape)

1956 W. Irving Park (office of Dr. Harold Cassidy)

1123 W. Argyle (offices of Dr. Cassidy and Dr. Eye)

1102 W. Leland (drugstore and office of Dr. Wilhelm Loeser)

1127 S. Harvey, Oak Park (Dr. Loeser and Anna Patzke arrested following plastic surgery on Dillinger)

942 N. California (Baby Face Nelson born Lester Gillis, 12/6/08)

944 N. California (childhood home of Nelson)

1627 Walnut, Wilmette (Jimmy Murray hideout where Baby Face Nelson dies after killing two federal agents at Barrington on 11/27/34)

1155 Mohawk Rd., Wilmette (residence of Father Coughlan, with his sister, at the time of Nelson's death)

51 LeMoyne Parkway, Oak Park (home of Jimmy Murray, 1934)

After the Facts

FURTHER INVESTIGATIONS BY WILLIAM J. HELMER

In the course of my research for this book, I came across important material not available to Girardin at the time he wrote his manuscript. Some of the following are notes proper, some enlarge upon Girardin's original information, and others are simply interesting little side trips through the life of one of this country's legendary outlaws.

1. The FBI evolved out of efforts of President Theodore Roosevelt to investigate land-fraud and anti-trust cases involving some U.S. senators and congressmen. With no investigative division of its own, the Department of Justice traditionally had "borrowed" agents from the Treasury Department, whose Secret Service had been organized following the Civil War to enforce tax laws, combat counterfeiting, and (somewhat belatedly) protect the president. Several national leaders thought the Justice Department logically needed its own investigators to "detect and prosecute crimes against the United States" (since that was the attorney general's job), but Congress effectively limited Executive Branch police powers by appropriating enforcement funds on a case-by-case basis. And when its own members were accused of corruption, Congress shamelessly amended an appropriations bill to forbid the borrowing of Treasury agents to do Justice Department work. Roosevelt, a former New York City police commissioner, responded simply by ordering his attorney general to set up his own investigative service, and the scandals it uncovered in 1908 caused enough favorable public commotion that when President Taft took office the following year he formalized the order, creating the Justice Department's first Bureau of Investigation. Before the outbreak of World War I, the B.I. had become as politicized and corrupt as other government agencies, but made up for its incompetence against German saboteurs by despotically deporting thousands of aliens during the notorious Red Raids of 1919–20.

During the backlash over those excesses, a young John Edgar Hoover was made B.I. director in 1924 with explicit orders to professionalize the agency; and though a zealous Red-Raider himself under Attorney General Mitchell Palmer, he proceeded to sanitize his office with a bureaucratic vengeance. By the time another Roosevelt became president in 1933, Hoover had ruthlessly created perhaps the first "clean" law-enforcement agency in U.S. government history—one so careful to avoid even the appearance of a national secret police (as feared by its opponents) that the Bureau still insists it only "investigates" suspected federal crimes, leaving prosecution entirely to the attorney general's office. (Of course, the same can be said of local and state police, who catch criminals and file charges but leave the rest to their respective prosecutors.) In July 1933, the Bureau was given additional enforcement duties and became a Justice Department "division," and once the new Division of Investigation had captured the public's imagination with its G-men and their War on Crime, Hoover lobbied for the formal title of Federal Bureau of Investigation. Attorney General Cummings authorized the change on July 1, 1935, to the annoyance of Hoover's rivals in other departments, especially Treasury, which resented the impression it created that the Justice Department's agents were the only federal investigators. Hoover did not improve peer group relations by ordering new letterheads featuring the name "Federal Bureau of Investigation" printed in a type size nearly twice as large as "U.S. Department of Justice."

2. Girardin's description of Dillinger's boyhood derives mainly from interviews with family members and so portrays young John less as a juvenile delinquent than as a victim of circumstances. His relationships with his stepmother and father were less harmonious than depicted here, but apparently no worse than in other families with unruly children. Most commentators viewed Dillinger's criminality according to their own position on nature versus nurture, which had become the central argument in the criminology of the day. H. L. Mencken regarded Dillinger as a plain bad apple who would have ended up in trouble one way or the other, while reformers such as Warden Lewis E. Lawes of Sing Sing blamed the justice system for transforming a rowdy kid into a hardened criminal. Fred Pasley, whose 1930 biography of Al Capone distinguished him as one of the few intelligent crimewriters of the day, interviewed Dillinger's boyhood acquaintances for a series of newspaper articles in the spring of 1934; and Joe Pinkston and John Toland looked closely at his upbringing for biographies of Dillinger published in 1962 and 1963 respectively. In their more balanced accounts, Dillinger emerges as a rebellious but likable youngster with a penchant for excitement that might have made him a poor spouse or shopkeeper, but who retained the American value system that has always combined strong moral principles with situational flexibility. Pasley guessed at the time that Dillinger's downfall would be his enthusiasm for women.

3. Other accounts have grocer Morgan giving the Masonic distress signal. Girardin could not recall the source of his information on this minor point but reminded me that during the twenties, the Klan in some states, including Indiana, became more a political than a racist organization. Later writers may have decided that a Masonic distress signal would avoid wrong impressions.

4. Girardin's description of the Michigan City breakout differs from others in one significant aspect. Virtually all published accounts have the guns smug-

gled into the prison in a box of thread, or some variation on this. In chapter 5, Girardin says escaped convict Walter Dietrich invented this story at the time of his arrest to conceal Dillinger's involvement as well as his own involvement with the Dillinger gang. FBI documents likewise credit the story to Dietrich, but Girardin notwithstanding, the amount of detail he provides still gives it some credibility. Before the box-of-thread story got into general circulation, another escapee talked about one package of guns being thrown over the wall and picked up by the wrong people, but does not say how the other guns arrived or mention the box of thread.

5. The Thompson submachine gun was a classic example of a gun gone wrong. The weapon was conceived as the world's first hand-held machine gun by General John T. Thompson, a retired U.S. Army ordnance officer who believed that Allied infantrymen needed more individual firepower than afforded by the bolt-action rifle. Called a "sub" machine gun to denote that it fired pistol instead of rifle ammunition, the strange-looking firearm was not completed in time to see battle, but still was optimistically marketed in 1921 as a state-of-the-art police "anti-bandit" gun that would shred armed robbers' getaway cars (a new development on the U.S. crime scene); and as a new concept in all-purpose, peacetime military ordnance that combined the best features of a pistol, rifle, and shotgun into "the most effective portable firearm in existence." Despite some imaginative marketing efforts (including portrayals of cowboys with Tommyguns shooting cattle rustlers), neither the police nor the military displayed much interest. It was a revolutionary weapon whose time had not yet come, and might well have ended up on the scrapheap of history but for a challenging new problem that arose out of Prohibition. Chicago's warring bootleggers had already invented the "one-way ride," and their subsequent need to perfect the "drive-by" shooting was nicely met by the Tommygun.

The Thompson Automatic Gun
Equipped With Cutts Compensator

Neal Trickel

Introduced by the Saltis-McErlane gang in the fall of 1925 and soon adopted by Al Capone, the "Chicago typewriter" debuted in New York three years later with the killing of Frankie Yale. During the early 1930s the Thompson became the mark of any serious gunman, and by the time state and federal laws began to restrict sales, the lethal appearance of its finned barrel and drum magazine and its bloody reputation (the St. Valentine's Day Massacre) had made it a symbol of that era—the gangster equivalent of the cowboy's six-shooter. Police eventually acquired Thompsons to maintain parity, but soon realized that machine guns could not be safely fired in many situations without doing in bystanders, and ended up using them mostly when posturing for pictures.

Shortly before his death in 1940, General Thompson wrote a melancholy note to a former employee in which he said, "I have given my valedictory to arms, as I want to pay more attention now to saving human life than destroying it. . . . It has worried me that the gun has been so stolen by evil men & used for purposes outside our motto, 'On the side of law & order.' " In the meantime, a Connecticut speculator had taken over the company, the Germans invaded Poland with their own version of the submachine gun, and the U.S. Army, after ignoring the Thompson for nearly twenty years, ended up buying more than two million of them.

6. The term "automatic" technically describes a machine gun, but in this manuscript and in common usage it describes firearms that are semi-automatic, or autoloading, with each shot requiring a separate pull of the trigger. Also, the terms "pistol" and "revolver" are sometimes used interchangeably, but properly, a pistol is any handgun whose cartridge chamber is part of the barrel, while a revolver has multiple cartridge chambers in a revolving cylinder that is separate from the barrel. In some instances here, the term ".38 automatic" is used in a general way that includes the lighter .380 automatic cartridge.

7. Leach always believed the book came from Dillinger, and the story is now part of the lore, but Joe Pinkston discovered that the joke actually was perpetrated by a pair of veteran Indianapolis newspaper reporters.

Matt Leach considered Pierpont the brains of the gang but thought that labeling Dillinger its leader would cause internal dissension and make their apprehension easier. The psychology failed, as Pierpont didn't care about publicity, and Dillinger only tried harder to live up to his image.

8. Dillinger and other gang members seemed always to meet their girlfriends entirely by accident at bars, taverns, and cabarets, which avoided the need to name the mutual friends and relatives whom the police and FBI would then add to their list of gang contacts and associates. Evelyn eventually admitted to her FBI interrogators that she had been introduced to Dillinger in early November 1933, by one of two sisters—Pat Cherrington, née Patricia Wilson and formerly Pat Young (possibly born in McClure, Arkansas, in 1903); and Opal Long, née Bernice or Frances M. Wilson, aka Bernice or Beatrice Clark (born probably in 1900, either in Louisville or on a ranch in Missouri)— who figure in the Dillinger story almost from start to finish. However, Evelyn and her friends fed the Bureau so many conflicting stories that sorting fact from fiction may never be possible.

Not long after arriving in Chicago around the age of eighteen, the admittedly "wild" Evelyn met and married an exciting young hoodlum named Welton Sparks, who had been robbing banks with a buddy named Arthur (or

Bob) Cherrington. In 1932 Sparks and Cherrington committed a mail robbery that landed them both in Leavenworth. Evelyn remained pals with Cherrington's wife Pat, whose older sister, Opal, had been living with a truck driver named Russell Clark (whom she claimed to have married) until he was convicted of bank robbery in 1927. When Clark and nine others broke out of the Michigan City Prison six years later, Opal was still waiting. Now preferring the name Beatrice or Bernice Clark, she introduced her sister, Pat Cherrington, to Russell and other members of the fledgling Dillinger gang who were assembling in Chicago; and Pat introduced her friend Evelyn to John Dillinger, who promptly fell in love.

Pat Cherrington managed to confuse the issue by claiming to be the girlfriend of Harry Copeland, who had been committing armed robberies with Dillinger before the Michigan City breakout that united Russell Clark with Opal Long. When Copeland was arrested in November, John Hamilton was still involved with a Stevens Hotel waitress who had even more names than the others—Elaine Dent Sullivan Burton DeKant was the name she gave to police—but the shooting of Detective Shanley concluded that relationship and left Hamilton available to Pat Cherrington, who remained devoted to him to the end.

A 1933 Essex Terraplane

9. The car was a 1933 Terraplane. Joe Pinkston affirms that while Dillinger liked the fast and maneuverable V-8 Fords that replaced the Model A in 1932, his car of choice was the Essex-Terraplane 8 that Hudson introduced the following year as its high-performance model. It had better acceleration (0–60 mph in 14.4 seconds compared to the Ford's 16.8) as well as a slightly higher top speed (about 83 mph compared to 81.8), and when the 1934 model was introduced at an auto show in St. Louis, Dillinger was waiting to buy the first one that appeared on the showroom floor. The Ford Motor Company has a letter allegedly from Dillinger complimenting them on their new V-8s that leave other cars "in the dust," but Pinkston has shown a copy of the letter to an Indiana State Police handwriting expert who doubts it is authentic.

10. The Unity vault robbery was sufficiently out of character for the Dillinger gang that its involvement has been questioned, partly because of the

tendency of holdup victims to prefer being robbed by Dillinger. Girardin's information came from Piquett's and O'Leary's discussions of the trouble they had later helping one of the gang's girls get money and "slum" jewelry from a safe-deposit box at another bank. Edward Shouse also attributed the Unity job to the Dillinger gang in his statement to the FBI.

THE RADIO POLICE CAR

11. In 1933 police radio was still a novelty. Many police departments had seen radio as a possible countermeasure to the new "motorized bandits" who appeared after World War I, but it was not until 1929 that the independent Chicago Crime Commission took the initiative of inspecting the country's first police radio system that was operating in Detroit. The *Chicago Tribune* covered the visit, and its publisher, Colonel Robert R. McCormick, reading his own paper, was so impressed that he virtually coerced Police Commissioner William F. Russell into giving it a try. McCormick would donate not only $10,000 worth of police car radio receivers, but also the services of his newspaper's radio station, WGN (for "World's Greatest Newspaper"). Soon the entire city of Chicago was enthralled by the police calls that frequently interrupted WGN's regular broadcast programming. McCormick next proposed an independent Technical Radio Advisory Committee that would advise the city on its radio needs, like it or not. Commander Eugene F. McDonald, Jr., president of the Zenith Radio Corporation, was named director of the committee, and on July 10 the Chicago City Council decided it might as well authorize Russell to buy the necessary equipment. A year later, on June 16, 1930, the new system was ceremoniously launched with five receiver-equipped squad cars, loaded with city cops and city aldermen, racing to crime scenes announced by the Chicago police dispatcher. The system was such a hit that by the end of 1931 the city had put receivers in a total of 179 cars—the Detective Bureau's five-man "cruisers" (traditionally Cadillacs) and the district stations' two-man "squads" (which now were enclosed Nash sedans instead of Model A Fords). This was the "calling all cars" era of police radio. Using an official police frequency of 1712 kilocycles (before "kilohertz") at the top end of the standard broadcast band, the dispatcher called two or more squads by car number and hoped that at least one heard the order. In the late 1930s transmitters were reduced from room-size to car-size, permitting two-way communications on multiple channels and on shortwave frequencies that were less convenient to monitor. But for several years the dials on the more expensive home radios continued to list both the call letters of the country's major broadcast stations and a frequency for "Police."

In an interesting coincidence, the Chicago Crime Commission began inspecting the Detroit police radio system on February 14, 1929, about the time Al Capone's machine-gunners were decimating the gang of Bugs Moran. The St. Valentine's Day Massacre inspired the founding of the country's first scientific crime-detection laboratory under Colonel Calvin Goddard, whose friends included Zenith's Commander McDonald. The two Thompson submachine guns used in the Massacre were located a few months later and ballistically confirmed by the Goddard laboratory, but led to no convictions. One of them later was loaned to the FBI, and the other gun disappeared. According to Eloise Keeler's biography of her late husband, Leonarde Keeler, the laboratory's polygraph pioneer, it went to Commander McDonald.

12. As mentioned in connection with the Unity vault robbery, the police, including the FBI, never ceased trying to link the various gangs of bootleggers, bank robbers, and kidnappers into one great criminal confederation. While the different groups did not work together the way the law-enforcers imagined, they did share many of the same doctors, lawyers, bail-bondsmen, fences, gun dealers, and car dealers, who became a kind of underworld support group, and they fraternized with one another regularly at the same hoodlum hangouts around Chicago and St. Paul, Minnesota. It can be fairly said that the St. Paul police then were as much a part of the underworld community as the celebrity criminals who helped finance local elections so they could harbor there in peace. In Chicago, the system was more complicated. Elected officials were beholden not to numerous independents who donated to certain fundraisers, but to the now-citywide "syndicate" forged by Al Capone. Thus it was the Chicago Syndicate that decided who should enjoy protection and who needed to be either disciplined or "put on the spot" for bringing on too much "heat." This is one reason some believe the Unity Savings robbery was not the work of Dillinger, unless he had the mob's permission. Dillinger enjoyed good relations with the Chicago underworld until his notoriety made him too dangerous. Likewise Baby Face Nelson, a Chicago native with a bootlegging background, enjoyed close personal ties with Rocco de Grazia, "Tough Tony" Capezio, and other upwardly mobile mobsters until killing a federal agent made him a liability. In pursuing both Dillinger and Nelson, the FBI found that the outlaws' principal Chicago contacts were also syndicate-connected in one way or another.

The Barker-Karpis gang was even closer to the mob, having members who virtually divided their time between the crime syndicate and the outlaw gang. The FBI had to keep in mind that the Bremer kidnapper whom Alvin Karpis called "Shotgun George" Ziegler was also the St. Valentine's Day gunman whom the Capone mob called Fred Goetz. After Byron Bolton's arrest in 1935, the *Chicago American* declared the 1929 massacre "solved" on the basis of information from Bolton implicating himself and Goetz, but which he had not bothered to share with his FBI captors. J. Edgar Hoover fired off blistering memos to Chicago and St. Paul demanding to know why he was being kept in the dark, and division offices sheepishly responded that Bolton's "confession" was also news to them. Hoover promptly issued statements flatly denying that there was any truth to the story, and the press dropped the matter in the belief that the Bureau would not lie. Meanwhile, however, agents let Bolton know how greatly he had embarrassed them, and Hoover soon received (but never released) a lengthy statement in which Bolton described the crime in detail. His account contradicted the one pieced together by the Chicago police and generally accepted by historians, but Bolton's version was later corroborated by the wife of one of the gunmen, by a maverick police detective who had personally stayed on the case, and eventually by Alvin Karpis himself, who added the name of "Tough Tony" Capezio, Baby Face Nelson's friend, to those involved in the mass murder. Supposedly Bolton had thought that the mob tipped the FBI to his whereabouts and decided to blow the whistle, but when Hoover dismissed his story of the Massacre, so did everyone else.

13. Arthur "Fish" Johnson, or Johnston, attained much notoriety as Chicago's leading fence and a primary contact for the Dillinger gang. Starting out in his mother's delicatessen at 2838 Armitage on the Near Northwest Side, he expanded his operations to include illegal gambling, trading in stolen bonds and securities, and providing such services as renting apartments for fugitives. At a later time when Baby Face Nelson was part of the gang and wanted to upgrade his private arsenal, he sent Johnson and Jack Perkins, another close associate, to New York with $750 to purchase a Monitor machine rifle, the commercial version of the Army's Browning Automatic Rifle (BAR), which he would use in his final battle with federal agents the following November. Johnson somehow survived the Dillinger era and prospered in the stock market before retiring in northern Indiana.

As for the disorderly conduct and lewdness charges that the police often filed, these were euphemistic violations of state and local sex laws against cohabitation, fornication, and so forth, which came in handy for harassing unmarried couples.

14. The "public enemies" campaign is a confusing one that grew out of efforts of the Chicago Crime Commission to turn public sentiment against Al Capone. In his 1989 monograph on the CCC, Professor Dennis Hoffman states that George A. Paddock, the commission's finance committee chairman, conceived the idea and suggested it to president Frank Loesch and operating director Henry Barrett Chamberlin, who released the first list of Chicago's twenty-eight top "public enemies" in April 1930. Capone was declared Public Enemy Number One, and newspapers responded with such enthusiasm that the Chicago police and the state of Illinois also developed lists, creating a virtual Public Enemy competition. In October 1933, Loesch generously invited the U.S. Justice Department to create a national Public Enemy list.

While that was not done officially, Attorney General Cummings joined the crowd on June 22, 1934, by calling Dillinger the country's leading public enemy and offering a federal reward of $10,000 for his capture. After Dillinger's death exactly a month later, Baby Face Nelson and Pretty Boy Floyd contended for top honors. When Floyd was killed on October 22, Nelson's promotion was undisputed; and with his death on November 27, the title went instantly to his wife, who, for at least a few days, became the country's first female Public Enemy Number One—until the newspapers learned to their annoyance that the FBI had kept her surrender secret. After that the title went variously to Alvin Karpis, Floyd Hamilton (of the Barrow gang), or whoever was making the most news, confirming J. Edgar Hoover's objection that a "Number One" position only provided egotistic criminals something to strive for. The enormous publicity generated by the first Public Enemy campaign had made Capone the "Babe Ruth of American gangsters" and Chicago the gangster capital of the world, to the everlasting annoyance of civic leaders. Dillinger's promotion to Public Enemy Number One was a major step toward immortality for both the outlaw and J. Edgar Hoover in spite of his

DILLINGER USED NUN'S DISGUISE, HOOVER RECALLS

Posed as Writer and Vault Salesman.

Washington, D. C., July 23.—[Special.]—J. Edgar Hoover, head of the division of investigation, today retold brief pages out of John Dillinger's history.

Dillinger at times disguised himself as a nun, Hoover said, so that he could scout around the scene of an intended holdup or raid.

At one time he posed as a writer of detective stories and persuaded an Indiana police detachment to show him its whole array of firearms. A couple of days later he returned and raided the entire arsenal, taking it to arm his mob, Hoover said.

During his first visit to ...

misgivings, and Hoover himself could not resist trafficking in Dillinger stories that embellished the outlaw's legend. Thus later writers have told, usually on the strength of a Hoover anecdote, how Dillinger hoaxed a banking association into inviting him to address its annual meeting, or how Dillinger sometimes masqueraded as a nun. Here it may be that Hoover simply lost track of which stories had been debunked. One FBI memo does in fact discuss a report that Dillinger had been spotted disguised as a nun on Chicago's Far North Side, conspicuously unaccompanied and wearing men's shoes. When it turned out that there was a Catholic convent in the same neighborhood, the division office decided that "possibly the informant did see a nun with masculine appearance unaccompanied in that vicinity."

In any event, the FBI could never shake the popular belief that it named and ranked public enemies, so it eventually relented, in a way. In 1950 it established an official list of the FBI's "Ten Most Wanted," which satisfied the public without singling out an individual criminal—although this system made it even easier to gain national recognition.

15. As related by Dietrich, the box-of-thread story does not involve Dillinger but rather a theater owner named Omar Brown who had ties to the

northern Indiana mob. According to FBI documents quoting Dietrich, Brown ordered a crate of thread from the American Thread Company in Chicago, planted three .38 automatics inside, changed the return address to the "East Coast Thread Co.," and shipped it on to the prison shirt factory. Most writers accept some version of the box-of-thread story but make it the work of Dillinger.

16. Road atlases of the thirties give the distance from Daytona to Chicago as 1,138 miles. To make the trip in the allotted time, Dillinger and Pierpont would have had to average between 40 and 50 miles per hour over two-lane blacktop highways interrupted by hundreds of crossroads, intersections, traffic signals, and towns.

17. Any gunman who tried to fit a Thompson into a violin case would have discovered that this was an artistic and literary convention. Submachine guns would fit in trombone and saxophone cases, but the preferred packaging was the nondescript factory "hard case," which somewhat resembled a black musical instrument case compartmentalized to hold the gun, buttstock, magazines, and accessories.

18. In some accounts, Dillinger deliberately fired low, and O'Malley either fell into the line of fire or was hit by a ricochet off the sidewalk.

19. Most of the underworld's physicians were recruited by way of this country's anti-abortion laws. Dr. Moran had distinguished himself as a pilot during the First World War, graduated with honors from Tufts Medical School in Boston, and then returned to his home state of Illinois to practice in the town of LaSalle. Like many sympathetic doctors and some simply dishonest ones, he performed the procedure at people's homes or under other less than ideal conditions. The death of a young woman patient in 1928 cost him his medical license and landed him in the Joliet state penitentiary at the age of thirty-three. He soon became the de facto head of the prison hospital, and did such a commendable job as both an administrator and a surgeon that Warden Henry C. Hill helped him obtain a parole in 1931 and also wrote letters to the American Medical Association. Illegal abortion was such a common infraction by even respectable physicians that the AMA reinstated Moran's license without much deliberation. He resumed the practice of medicine in the small town of Bureau, Illinois, only to be arrested, mainly on suspicion, for another abortion that he probably did not perform. That was enough to violate his parole, and he went back to Joliet consumed with bitterness. His second parole was fixed by a grateful and well-connected jewel thief named Oliver Berg, whom he'd treated during his previous incarceration, and Berg further rewarded him with introductions to some of Chicago's top gangsters and racketeers. If Moran's small-town practice had paid the bills, treating wounded hoodlums was a veritable gold mine, and with this new medical career came an exciting and boozy lifestyle that "Doc" Moran found irresistible. About 1933 he moved into the Irving Hotel at 4845 Irving Park Boulevard (seven blocks west of the office of Dr. Eye) and opened an office at 4861. The abortions he now performed regularly would have put him in the same circles as Louis Piquett, who represented other abortionists;

but his wealth came from treating gunshot victims who were wanted by the police. It was through Ollie Berg that Moran had met another jewel thief named Russell Gibson, whose wife knew Piquett already. While trying to raise bail for her husband following an arrest a few years earlier, she was advised by helpful officers that the bother of bond money, arraignment, indictment, trial, imprisonment, and other legal technicalities could all be avoided by paying five hundred dollars to their district's designated fixer, Lou Piquett, who had streamlined the criminal justice system to everyone's satisfaction. When not stealing jewels, Gibson worked with the Barker-Karpis gang, which made "Doc" Moran its primary health-care provider and introduced him to the Dillinger gang. However, following the Battle of Little Bohemia in April of 1934, he refused to treat the badly wounded Hamilton, because of some dispute with Dillinger, or possibly because the Chicago Syndicate was now denying sanctuary to federal fugitives. In any case, Hamilton died from his wounds at a Barker-Karpis hideout in Aurora, Illinois, and word of Moran's refusal to help tarnished his good name in the outlaw community. This may have contributed to his problems with the Barker-Karpis gang, who were also becoming alarmed at Moran's excessive drinking and bragging about his influence in the underworld. After Dillinger's death, the gang supposedly took Moran for a sobering boat ride in the fresh air on Lake Erie and didn't bring him back. Even J. Edgar Hoover relates this version by way of his ghost-writers. However, Herbert Corey, who had access to FBI files, and Alvin Karpis himself say that Moran was simply murdered and buried.

20. The same reporters who were inclined to describe Dillinger as bold, daring, audacious, fearless, or brazen seemed to delight in vilifying Baby Face Nelson, who received the worst press of any of the Depression outlaws. Only his mother had anything good to say, and that was in a short series of newspaper stories which began appearing barely a week after Nelson had killed two federal agents and was not a good candidate for sympathy. Nor did Mrs. Gillis's efforts to describe her son as a victim of injustice seem to be backed up with strong evidence.

The source of the nickname "Baby Face" is a matter of disagreement, but George Nelson, alias Jimmy Burnet, Jimmy Burnell, Jimmy Williams, and so on, was born Lester Joseph Gillis on December 6, 1908, at 942 North California Street on Chicago's Near West Side. His parents were young Belgian immigrants from respected families who married in the U.S., prospered enough to build a classic three-story townhouse, and raised four daughters and one other son who led apparently commonplace lives. His mother, Mary, had taught French two years before coming to America, where she tried to provide her children with the best of educations. Her husband, Joseph, was a skilled tanner who had worked his way up to assistant superintendent in a local leather company before his death in 1925, which the FBI describes as a suicide by natural gas while in a state of intoxication.

Lester was the youngest of the children and small for his age, but nice-looking and always well-groomed. He entered the first grade at Lafayette Public School and later transferred to St. Mark's Parochial School, but by the fourth or fifth grade was being shuttled back and forth between the two because of behavioral problems and a declining interest in scholarship. At one time he was enrolled in a respected Catholic boarding school attended by one of his sisters, but kept running away.

Mary Gillis blamed his descent into truancy and then delinquency on a restless spirit that could not tolerate confinement in a classroom. Whether or not she blinded herself to Lester's problems, that impression is created by the series of melancholy newspaper articles that carried her by-line. In them she labored to understand the man that her boy had become, but tended to excuse everything from car theft ("borrowing") to gunplay ("an accident with a revolver") as youthful peccadillos for which his late father had to share some blame. It was father Gillis's refusal to let Lester drive the family car, she believed, that had forced the lad to steal them, just as Lester's later practice of shooting people might be traced to his father's refusal to let him have toy pistols. No amount of spanking helped, she said, as Lester took his punishment stoically and would never shed a tear.

After finishing his first stretch at the St. Charles Reform School, where his behavior was always exemplary, Lester quickly fell "under the influence of a full-grown man" who "organized young boys into theft gangs"; and after that it was the police who "pushed him over the line into a definitely antisocial life." They taught him to bribe them whenever he was caught speeding, and soon their persecution "hounded" him into the bootlegging business, where, she supposed, "he met men who must have been crooks." She never claimed to know all of the devilment these bad influences put him up to, but "sometimes, if I asked him about some wrongdoing, he would simply nod and I knew he had done it. I'd ask him about something else and he'd say, 'Mother, I didn't do this.' " Mother Gillis "believed him every time, for I know that one thing he couldn't stand was a lie."

Thus Mrs. Gillis soon was able to know which banks Lester robbed and which he didn't, because he told her. She believed that Lester had not robbed banks in Hillside or Itasca, for instance, but juries believed otherwise; and it was then Les declared to his worried mother "that there was no use trying to live right."

But Lester had done one thing right, at least by some reckonings. He had met a tiny, dark-eyed, rather pretty sixteen-year-old salesclerk named Helen Wawrzyniak, which had so many spellings that her family shortened it to Warwick. Lester and Helen were married in Indiana in June of 1928, and ten months later their son Ronald was born. Ten months after that they had a daughter, Darlene. In a surprising departure from the criminal norm, the two seem to have been deeply devoted to one another; and even when Lester's increasingly serious offenses plunged them into a nightmare existence of running, hiding, and killing, Helen endured a lifetime's worth of terror and grief to stay by her husband's side.

Nor did his mother's love and loyalty diminish. While popular writers and J. Edgar Hoover competed to portray him as evil incarnate, she pointed up his little kindnesses and domesticity, though this was no small feat. "Even when he was the most hunted man in America," she wrote, "he met issues squarely, never ran from them. And he never shot a man in the back." Which was more than anyone could say for the feds who killed John Dillinger, seemed to be the implication.

Nelson had his own bank-robbing operation independent of Dillinger's prior to 1934, when the two pulled their first job together at Sioux Falls, South Dakota. But the Nelson gang included Dillinger's friend Homer Van Meter, and Nelson and Van Meter are said to have fronted the bribe money for Dillinger's Crown Point escape in the expectation that he would pay them back out of his share of the Sioux Falls loot. How Nelson and Van Meter met isn't known, but they no doubt had many underworld friends in common in both Chicago and St. Paul. The guns seized from the Dillinger gang in Tucson include some that were custom-made and may have come from Nelson, who does not seem to have been in Tucson at that time but may already have been supplying Dillinger with "gangsterized" rifles and pistols from a gunsmith in San Antonio, as described in endnote 46.

21. Every account differs. In some, the firemen become suspicious because of the weight of the luggage; in others, because a suitcase breaks open, or comes open just enough to reveal a protruding gun barrel. The probable tipoff, as Girardin says, was the generous payment, which also ranges from $12 to $50, depending on the report.

22. Girardin obviously liked Piquett and gave him the benefit of the doubt. Certainly the attorney was flamboyant, interesting, humorous, shrewd, and possibly loyal and good-hearted in his own peculiar fashion, but he seems also to have been a consummate con man whose ventures usually ranged from the merely dubious to the cheerfully fraudulent. One that demonstrated Piquett's creativity was his effort to form the "Order of St. Francis," the ostensible purpose of which was to promote the Catholic faith. Membership in the order required an initiation fee of ten dollars plus one dollar a month in dues, and of the 400 trusting souls in the first audience he addressed, 390 signed up. Unfortunately for Piquett, word of the new order reached Cardinal Mundelein, who exposed the scam in an official Catholic publication. Some of Piquett's other swindles were considerably less benign.

23. Around noon on June 9, 1930, Lingle was shot in the back of the head by a lone gunman in the busy pedestrian underpass at Randolph Street and Michigan Avenue. The killer escaped in the crowd, and every Chicago paper joined the *Tribune* in declaring Lingle a martyr to investigative journalism. Only after huge rewards were posted did newsmen discover that the $65-per-week reporter had been living like a king, was tight with Al Capone, and was up to his neck in the rackets. Brothers was later arrested and convicted on somewhat dubious evidence.

24. O'Leary was born in Parnell, Iowa, on April 3, 1894, and had a brother and two sisters. Both parents died when he was young, but he stayed in school working at various railroad and restaurant jobs until moving to Chicago about 1912. For a time he sold photographic enlargements house to house, then became a stock salesman for the Elgin Motor Car Company in

Argo, Illinois, in 1916. He was assigned to the company's territory around Dubuque, where he met Grayce Kabat, whom he married at Prairie du Chien, Wisconsin, the following year. They soon had a daugher, Anne, and a son, James. He remained a salesman for several companies in Iowa and Colorado before moving back to Chicago, where he began selling securities and working with Lewis Mack. He met Louis Piquett while selling questionable stock in a Pennsylvania lime company in the early 1930s, and went to work for him in January 1934 as a legal investigator.

25. Most of Girardin's information about the northern Indiana mob was added to this manuscript only in the weeks before his death. Here he also reveals how Dillinger came to hire Louis Piquett as his attorney, and that Arthur O'Leary not only came up with the Crown Point escape plan but had the wooden gun made by a Chicago woodworker who was not entirely clear on the concept. This may be the only discussion of Piquett's association with abortionist Ada Martin, who would prove to be a friend indeed to Nell Piquett when her husband's luck ran out.

26. This probably refers to Walgreen's. Some years ago the owner of that drug chain donated a crudely fashioned wooden pistol to the Chicago Historical Society, with Ernest Blunk's affidavit attesting that it was the fake gun used by Dillinger in his escape from the Crown Point jail. Shaped more like a revolver, with double-edged razor blades representing the cylinder, it is pictured in some articles and at least one documentary film, but it bore little resemblance to Dillinger's wooden pistol, which went to his family and was not displayed to the public until his father was hired months later by Emil Wanatka to operate a small museum at his Little Bohemia Lodge. The "real" phony gun can be seen fairly clearly in Dillinger's right hand in the family snapshots of him posing with his submachine gun in Mooresville. To further confuse the issue, most reproductions of that famous picture are a mirror image of the original, because the enlargements widely circulated by a major photo service were made from a copy negative that was printed "wrong side up."

In the aftermath of the Dillinger case, the newspapers and the public suffered what might be called a post-Dillinger letdown. The FBI received criticism and applause in nearly equal amounts as well as in combination, but its future as the national symbol of new-age crimefighting was no longer in doubt, and with Hollywood about to launch an era of G-man films, Hoover's legend was beginning about where Dillinger's left off. With Dillinger gone, newspapers began finding it unseemly that the father would try to "capitalize" on the death of his outlaw son by going on tour and then tending a museum that Emil Wanatka established at Little Bohemia. Most reporters put a negative spin on this news, and a tone of mild disgust could be detected in many editorials and letters to the editor. When the Dillinger family, Evelyn Frechette, Pat Cherrington, and other survivors of the Dillinger days began wearing thin as crime-does-not-pay carnival attractions, newspapers were quick to observe that the performances did not pay, either. A fickle press that first delighted in reporting that Dillinger's grave outdrew James Whitcomb

Riley's, later found news value in the fact that it didn't. The one person who survived this freak-show period with his own dignity intact was Dillinger's aging father. The tourists who flocked to Little Bohemia were generally respectful, particularly when they perceived a tired old farmer offering no excuses for his boy's criminality and making the best of what had to be torture. Old John Dillinger took visitors' quarters, patiently answered naive questions, and spoke appreciatively of Emil Wanatka as "a good man to work for." The experience was obviously humiliating, but he handled it with a diplomatic honesty that won him respect. "The reason I'm here," he would explain, "is because I buried two wives and there was that trouble with John, and my barn burned on me. I just had to do something."

Emil Wanatka treated the elder Dillinger with kindness even as he used him to increase the business that the historic battle generated. Nor was Emil above some more dubious forms of promotion. Stories circulate that he periodically salted the grounds with spent .45-caliber shell casings for visitors to find and treasure as souvenirs.

27. As usual, there are several versions of this minor transaction between Dillinger and his hostages when they were freed outside of Peotone, but the four-dollar one reported by Girardin also seems best supported by FBI interviews with Blunk and Saager. As for the location of Lilley's Corner, few present-day residents have heard of it or know their community's role in the Dillinger escape. An FBI document places the intersection at two miles east and one mile north of the community, near the house of a farmer named Bert Lilley, or Lilly. Some former residents put Lilley's farm three miles east and one mile north, near the intersection of Eagle Lake and Will Center roads; and a few think the corner was at Beecher Road and the old Dixie Highway and was named for Lillian Whitehead's restaurant, the White Lilley.

28. The Hargrave Secret Service was hired by Indiana to investigate the escape and discovered that Piquett had met Judge Murray at the World's Fair in Chicago. Piquett readily admitted seeing Murray there, but said it was entirely a coincidence and that the two merely exchanged greetings. Hargrave's put this together with informants' talk of bribes and concluded that Murray had been paid by Piquett to smuggle Dillinger a real gun. A somewhat wackier story had a real gun smuggled to Dillinger by Anna Sage, thought by some to be the mystery woman who had visited Dillinger with Piquett claiming to be his wife (it was actually Evelyn Frechette) and who supposedly managed to get it hidden in the bottom of a wastebasket. There is even a story that has Anna Sage working as a paid informant of Hargrave's.

29. Several sources support this account, particularly the involvement of Van Meter and Nelson in supplying the East Chicagoans with the funds used to fix the Crown Point escape. And of course Dillinger immediately joined up with Nelson and Van Meter to rob the Sioux Falls bank. Baby Face Nelson partisans make the point that the gang at this time could rightly be called Nelson's, Dillinger's having been broken up by the arrests in Tucson. However, Dillinger disliked working with the temperamental and trigger-happy

Nelson, and it galled Nelson that the public and the authorities automatically considered Dillinger the leader of any gang he was in.

30. Girardin's account of the jailbreak generally supports the charges of complicity on which Blunk and Cahoon were later acquitted. Indiana authorities evidently learned about the payoffs but could never confirm the rumors or separate the facts from the fictions of Meyer Bogue.

31. By this time, the Bureau already was on bad terms with Indiana authorities, particularly Matt Leach, and decided to excuse itself from the Crown Point mess on the ground that the jailbreaking itself was not a federal crime. If anything, the Bureau deliberately undermined Leach's efforts to investigate the northern Indiana gang by blandly concluding that Dillinger had escaped with a real gun somehow smuggled to him by Evelyn Frechette. Little support for this shows up in any FBI documents, but as in the case of debunking Byron Bolton's Massacre "confession," newspapers accepted Hoover's as the final word on the matter.

32. Watching from the sidelines, the FBI assumed that Esther Anderson was merely a girlfriend of Piquett's and that the lawyer's problems with the local authorities stemmed from his drinking and carousing, for which he had a considerable reputation. Although Girardin mentions elsewhere that he did not think Piquett's bad habits included philandering, the lawyer may have had a girlfriend named "Babe," who is mentioned in passing in several FBI reports. But since the FBI always thought the worst of Piquett, any woman he associated with might have been classified as his "paramour," to use one of the Bureau's favorite terms.

33. When Green proved to be unarmed, the FBI struggled to describe his actions in a way that justified the overkill. Inspector Hugh H. Clegg finally came up with the wording "assumed a threatening attitude and accompanied by menacing gestures," which still failed to convince reporters that the killing was not cold-blooded. Two high officials of the Treasury Department's Secret Service took it upon themselves to "investigate" Green's death with the obvious intent of giving the FBI a black eye, but Hoover's favorite crimewriter, Courtney Ryley Cooper, tipped him off that rival investigative agencies were virtually conspiring to embarrass the Bureau, and Attorney General Cummings came down so hard on Treasury Secretary Henry Morgenthau that the two principal plotters, Joseph E. Murphy and Grady Boatwright, were sent to Secret Service Siberia.

It was from the delirious ramblings of Green that the FBI learned much about the St. Paul underworld and the Barker-Karpis gang, with which he also had worked. It was Bessie Green who confirmed the involvement of Karpis and Doc Barker in the Bremer kidnapping, which she said had been planned by Harry Sawyer, a local mobster who operated notorious criminal hangouts and served as liaison between the police and visiting gangs; and with the Hamm kidnapping, which the Justice Department had tried to hang on Chicago's Roger Touhy. (Touhy was acquitted, but later framed by Al Capone for a bogus kidnapping that removed him as competition.) Bessie also mentioned in passing that Karpis and the Barker brothers usually traveled with a woman they called "Mother," who had not yet attracted much FBI attention.

34. Two federal agents were stationed at a neighbor's residence some distance away and were watching the Dillinger house through binoculars. The comings and goings of several cars and many family members aroused their curiosity and inspired much note-taking, but they could not believe that one of the visitors might be John Dillinger himself. After observing so much activity, they decided that one of the departing cars was particularly suspicious because of the way the passenger was trying to conceal his face, and the truth finally dawned. With as much stealth as possible, they began tailing the machine, only to discover that they had been tricked into following Dillinger's half-brother Hubert and nephew Norman Hancock. Humiliated, the Bureau descended on the Dillingers with a vengeance, grilling every relative and neighbor and generally terrorizing the town. It was further annoyed to learn that Dillinger's escape from Crown Point had violated no state law, which prohibited breaking out of prisons and reformatories but not local jails; and that Indiana law also exempted Dillinger's father (and possibly other close relatives) from prosecution for harboring a known criminal. In the end, agents advised Washington that many citizens of Mooresville were sympathetic to Dillinger and his family, and that any efforts to prosecute them on federal harboring charges could turn into a public-relations disaster. With great reluctance Hoover decided to let the matter pass. What happened to the agents conducting the surveillance is not recorded in the Dillinger files.

35. For his determination to lead a life unblemished by lawful activity, James E. Murray deserves more recognition than accorded him in FBI documents. Murray had briefly studied law and clerked in the Chicago court system before reaching the age of 30, but mostly he toiled as a precinct captain in the city's West Side wards until striking it rich at the dawn of Prohibition. With breweries selling out and closing down, he joined Joseph Stenson and other former beer barons in buying up plants around Chicago and southern Wisconsin and relicensing them to manufacture a nonalcoholic "brew" that had to start out as the real thing. The resultant "near beer" was a watery amber beverage containing less than one-half of one percent alcohol by law, and if not very popular with consumers, it at least provided an excuse to operate the brewery. This allowed some of the real beer to be diverted through creative recordkeeping, and some of the near beer to be salvaged later by "needling" the alcohol back into the keg with a large hollow needle, like a horse doctor's. The reconstituted product would have won no gold medals, but a keg that cost one dollar to manufacture could be sold for around $30; and eventually Jimmy Murray owned a nice home in Oak Park, summer houses in Michigan and Wisconsin, a cottage for fugitives in the little resort town of Wauconda, a fleet of expensive automobiles, and a boat or two on Lake Michigan.

A less ambitious criminal might have stopped to smell the roses, but Murray must have enjoyed the action. On the evening of June 12, 1924, he led a mixed bag of Chicago and St. Louis gangsters and cowboy bank robbers

James Murray.

from Texas and Oklahoma in what would become the country's last great train robbery. The bandits stopped the Chicago, Milwaukee, and St. Paul mail train at the Rondout crossing 32 miles north of Chicago, drove the clerks out of the express car with formaldehyde bombs, and made off in automobiles with loot worth two million dollars. The carefully planned caper took only 35 minutes and might have succeeded had one bandit not mistakenly shot another in the dark. Two nights later the sight of a wounded man outside a house at 53 North Washtenaw caused neighbors to call the police, who didn't buy the flimsy explanations and began arresting people—including one James Mahoney, who turned out to be James E. Murray. The former politician was convicted and sentenced to twenty-five years in Leavenworth, as was William J. Fahy, Chicago's "ace" postal inspector, who had been leading the investigation until a misstep exposed him as the inside man on the job.

The indomitable Murray served five years and then traded $385,000 in unrecovered bonds for a fresh start in life. He wanted to demonstrate, he said, that a man could learn from past mistakes and become an asset to the community, in his own case by opening a sandwich shop on the outskirts of Chicago. Probation officials were dubious, but the deal went through, and on the northeast corner of North and Harlem avenues soon arose one of the most palatial "hotdog stands" in America. The Rainbo Barbecue at 7190 West North Avenue was styled like an Alpine lodge and set Murray back what was then an extravagant $30,000, but its costly construction bought more than the eye could see. Two stairways, one hidden, led to a second floor that was specially outfitted to provide fugitives with sanctuary, comfort, and the peace of mind that came with a machine-gun tower (complete with machine gun) affording a 360-degree field of fire. This feature was added later for the benefit of Murray's celebrity guests, including John Dillinger, Homer Van Meter, and Baby Face Nelson, who used the place while shopping for other hideouts. Murray also handled stolen bonds and provided other criminal services, but FBI documents describe him as being so politically well connected that police simply refused to serve any arrest warrants that happened to come their way. Murray's virtual immunity from prosecution would make an interesting case study in Chicago and Cook County political corruption, and his role in the Dillinger story will remain an active one.

36. Hamilton's sister was a former PTA president, mother of six children, and respected local resident whose crime of harboring amounted to not calling the police on her brother and his well-armed friend. The Justice Department received a good deal of criticism not only for prosecuting Mrs. Campbell, but also for opposing a petition for executive clemency from the city council and 1,500 citizens.

37. Why the gang selected the Little Bohemia Lodge is open to specula-tion. It may have been suggested by Louis Cernocky, whose roadhouse near Fox River Grove was about the most popular hoodlum hangout in the Chicago area, and who probably knew Emil Wanatka as a former Chicagoan. Or Little Bohemia may have had its own place on the hoodlum circuit, as some neigh-bors claimed. In any case, Baby Face Nelson's group arrived at Little Bohemia carrying a letter of introduction from Cernocky asking Wanatka to take good care of his friends. This would have been an obvious tip-off to Wanatka that his guests were important hoodlums, whether or not he knew their identities. The fact that Wanatka ended up on Dillinger's personal revenge list would suggest that the outlaw felt betrayed by a friend rather than reported by an honest citizen, which he considered an occupational hazard. There are unconfirmed stories that when Emil Wanatka operated his Little Bohemia restaurant in Chi-cago in the 1920s, his lawyer was Louis Piquett.

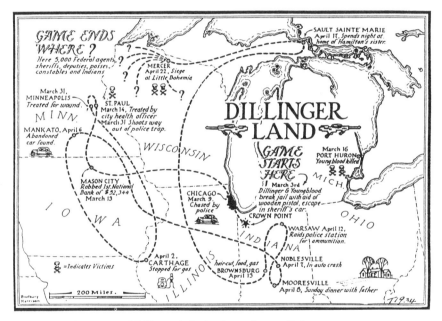

Time magazine map of Dillinger's flight from Crown Point.
Copyright 1934 Time Inc. Reprinted by permission.

38. Van Meter probably obtained the ransom money from Baby Face Nelson, who shared contacts with the Barker-Karpis gang in Reno, St. Paul, and Chicago, and who participated an underworld money-laundering net-work that involved crooked bankers in several cities. Some of the Bremer money was passed through Dr. Joseph Moran, and more was found after the arrest of Nelson accomplice John Paul Chase.

39. From voluminous FBI reports it seems clear that the Little Bohemia disaster occurred because news of the gang's imminent departure caused the agents to race there unprepared and set off a gun battle before getting

vote for

JOHN

YOU ALL KNOW ME
for

BANK EXAMINER

Fearless   Courageous   Cunning   Efficient

After the bungled Battle of Little Bohemia, some Wisconsin residents playfully circulated posters promoting Dillinger for bank examiner.

organized. Hoover blamed Purvis personally, however, and dictated a file memo containing unsubstantiated claims of a mutiny in which several agents went "all out of control" and locked Purvis, W. A. Rorer, and H. H. Clegg in a shed for the duration of the shooting. The ostensible purpose of the memo was to record that rumor (as heard by Assistant Attorney General Joseph B. Keenan) and order its full investigation, with the comment that it contradicted the accounts received from Purvis, Rorer, and Clegg. Students of Hoover have since discovered him to be a master of the carefully worded memo with which he could cover himself and either create instant history or disseminate derogatory information without vouching for its accuracy.

40. The death of John Hamilton has been one of the mysteries of the Dillinger saga, and some have always doubted that his was the body found at Oswego. It seems the Bureau was tipped off to the location not by Helen Gillis, as Girardin suspects, but by Edna Murray, girlfriend of Barker-Karpis gangster Volney Davis. Accounts differ on minor points, but Dillinger and Van Meter apparently took Hamilton to the Seafood Inn, a mob hangout in Elmhurst, Illinois, but were told to keep moving. Doctor Moran also refused to help, either because of some grievance he had with Dillinger or on orders of the Chicago Syndicate. The best the outlaws could do was transfer Hamilton to the car of Volney Davis, who carried him back to his apartment at 415 Post Street in Aurora, Illinois, and stayed with him until he died. According to the FBI, the burial party consisted of Dillinger and Van Meter, and Davis, Doc Barker, Harry Campbell, and William Weaver of the Barker-Karpis gang, who dug a shallow grave at a gravel pit near Violet Patch Park on East River Road northeast of Oswego, on property belonging to a Mrs. Augustus Shoger. Fatso Negri claims that he and Baby Face Nelson were also present, and Girardin indicates that Nelson, at least, knew the grave's location. The FBI's secretiveness left the deceased outlaw still robbing small-town banks that wanted the prestige of a Dillinger-gang holdup, but the Bureau had enough confidence in its dental identification that it exhibited Hamilton's teeth at the 1939 midwinter meeting of the Chicago Dental Society.

41. The Dillinger story has always included speculation that O'Brien and Mulvihill somehow died in an

JOHN HAMILTON

encounter with Dillinger and Van Meter, and that Zarkovich had some part in it. Most versions, including this one from O'Leary, make the killings the result of a more or less accidental encounter, but Matt Leach was convinced that Zarkovich set the two up deliberately, and might even have been the shooter. The subject arose while Dillinger was staying with Anna Sage and Polly Hamilton, and he gave it a slightly different interpretation. Without admitting his involvement or elaborating, he commented that the two had been after money.

42. In Chicago, Dillinger and Van Meter first holed up in the large yellow brick garage of the Oakley Auto Construction Company, 2300 West Division, at Division and Oakley Avenue. They would park the truck in the garage's elevator, and raise it halfway between floors. The garage was owned by Clarence (or Clary) Lieder, a 28-year-old naturalized Polish immigrant and long-time friend of Baby Face Nelson, who also fenced stolen auto parts and worked on Nelson's dirt-track racing car. Lieder's chief rival for the gangster trade was Joe Bergl, whose Bergl Motor Sales happened to be identically located just off Oakley but 34 blocks to the south, at 2346 West Cermak Road [22nd Street]. Bergl's garage was conveniently situated halfway between two former headquarters for the Capone mob, the Lexington Hotel at Michigan Avenue and 22nd Street, just south of the Loop, and the Hawthorne Hotel at 4833 West Cermak in Cicero. His customers included such visiting underworld notables as Machine Gun Kelly, and he is credited with inventing the auto smokescreen generator used by Capone gunmen as well as the Barker-Karpis gang to elude pursuers. The device squirted motor oil into the hot exhaust manifold to produce white smoke that came billowing out of the tailpipe, and Lieder is said to have built a competing model.

Lieder's inconvenient elevator arrangement (and perhaps his anxiety) sent Dillinger and Van Meter to Jimmy Murray's place, where Dillinger soon wore out his welcome. Instead of secluding himself upstairs, the outlaw fraternized with the regular customers, some of whom remarked upon his resemblance to John Dillinger. Worse, he began flirting with the waitresses. Murray complained to Piquett, and this may have convinced the lawyer to take James Probasco up on his offer of a hideout. When Dillinger was killed, Murray hurried to sell the Rainbo to a man named R. G. Williams, who renamed it the Pickininny. This was not a step toward personal reform, however, as Murray would remain in the service of Baby Face Nelson.

43. John J. McLaughlin was a Chicago political boss, fixer, bagman, and all-around crook in the tradition of "Bathhouse John" Coughlin and "Hinky Dink" Kenna, who reigned well into the Prohibition era and set the venality standards by which Chicago politicians would forever be judged. McLaughlin was already under indictment for involvement in a 1932 mail robbery committed by the Barker-Karpis gang, but had enough integrity to save his son from prison by confessing his own efforts to move some of the Bremer ransom money that he had gotten from Dr. Moran.

44. Loeser was born in Barby, Prussia, on November 8, 1876, and emigrated to the U.S. with his mother, sister, and four brothers in 1888. The

family lived in Minden, Iowa, for ten years and then moved to Kansas, where Loeser began the medical studies that he completed in Chicago in 1905. Besides practicing medicine, Loeser opened a pharmacy and office at 1102 Leland in the Uptown district, and it was probably there, about 1925, that he met Louis Piquett in connection with political activities. Six years later he was convicted of selling drugs, and Piquett helped him make parole after serving eighteen months. Loeser fled to Mexico when he learned, probably from Piquett, that it would cost him $10,000 in bribes to stay out of prison. He returned to Chicago broke in January 1934, and Anna Patzke told him of the favors done by their attorney. It now seems likely that Piquett scared Loeser into leaving town to forestall his learning about some of them.

While Loeser was in prison, the conscientious Piquett had taken Anna to dinner on several occasions, and after one of them she came home to discover smoke escaping from the windows. When firemen extinguished the blaze, she further discovered that the fire had been started by a safe-blower, who had gotten away with more than $3,000. Now even more sympathetic, Piquett encouraged Anna to recoup this loss by mortgaging her house, and then invested her money in some manner that made it disappear. To get her mind off these setbacks, Anna took a vacation in California, only to learn that in her absence no payments had been made and the mortgage had been foreclosed. The hapless Dr. Loeser decided he should talk with Piquett about his and Anna's money problems, and the lawyer wanted to help. But he had to warn Loeser that he was in danger of arrest as a parole violator. Loeser countered by showing Piquett how successfully he had obliterated his fingerprints with a special caustic soda treatment. Impressed, Piquett happily informed Dr. Loeser that his new investigator, Arthur O'Leary, just happened to have a cousin, Dr. Harold Bernard Cassidy, who was interested in that kind of work; and that it was Dr. Loeser's further good fortune to know an attorney with a special client who wanted his fingerprints removed. This was in the spring of 1934, and Piquett's special client was the then-notorious confidence man William Elmer Meade, who had been on the run for years, and who would stay on the run by jumping bail as soon as his prints were altered. Loeser agreed to "supervise" Dr. Cassidy's work on Meade and probably was still waiting to be paid when an even greater opportunity presented itself. On the evening of May 28, 1934, at the house of James Probasco, Loeser was introduced to a man he recognized as Piquett's most special client of all, John Dillinger.

45. Cassidy was born in Port Washington, Wisconsin, on February 19, 1902, and obtained his medical degree from the University of Illinois in 1927. He opened an office at 1123 Argyle in Chicago's Uptown district and there knew Dr. Charles Eye, who had an office in the same building. Both doctors were suspected of performing illegal abortions. Cassidy moved to 1956 Irving Park Boulevard in 1930, and Eye to 4175 Irving Park, where Dillinger barely escaped the police trap on November 15, 1933. By most accounts, Dillinger went to Dr. Eye on the recommendation of Art McGinnis, but the fact that Eye and Cassidy were friends and that Cassidy was O'Leary's cousin would suggest a more complicated set of relationships. In any case, Harold seems to

have been the black sheep of an otherwise respectable family that included two sisters and a lawyer brother, John Cassidy, who shared an apartment with their mother at 1830 Lawrence Avenue. Cassidy's divorced wife Freida lived in Elmwood Park with their young son, Harold Jr., and pursued him relentlessly with writs of attachment for overdue child support. Cassidy usually claimed to have met O'Leary through his uncle four or five years previously and to be the O'Leary family doctor, but the uncle lived in the same building as O'Leary and the two apparently were related. FBI records also list an office for Cassidy at 4802 Broadway, which may have been an outpost of Dr. Joseph Moran as well. Those offices are above the Green Mill, a historic Chicago nightclub that featured such entertainment celebrities as Joe E. Lewis and "Texas" Guinan during its Prohibition heyday, when it represented one of the Capone mob's principal North Side holdings.

Cassidy's perjury problems of December 1933 stemmed from alibi testimony he gave in behalf of a client of Louis Piquett, who then represented Harold Cassidy.

46. After his death, a debate arose over Dillinger's practice of hiding in plain sight, and three Chicago high school students wrote to Melvin Purvis suggesting that the outlaw's going about in public was not only "heroic" but a smart way to avoid being caught. Their poor choice of words brought a humorless response from Director Hoover, the Bureau's only spokesman, who paraphrased their question to express his disapproval of pro-Dillinger sentiment: "I cannot agree that there was anything heroic or intelligent either in the life which John Dillinger led or the manner in which he met his death." Still, the public feasted on tales of Dillinger's fearlessness around police, as when taking pictures of them at the world's fair, or enlisting one's aid in capturing a runaway puppy that he had bought in St. Louis for Evelyn.

47. On several occasions Dillinger either used or left behind what newspapers called "baby machine guns," which were never described but aroused the curiosity of gun collectors who saw one displayed in the old FBI building's "Dillinger" exhibit. These were Colt .38 "Super Automatic" pistols (essentially the Army M1911 .45 automatic chambered for .38) fitted with clips holding twenty-two cartridges, plus a Cutts-type compensator (to reduce barrel climb), a vertical foregrip from a Thompson gun, and mechanically modified for fully automatic fire. The gun left behind at Little Bohemia was traced from Colt's in Hartford, Connecticut, to a Fort Worth, Texas,

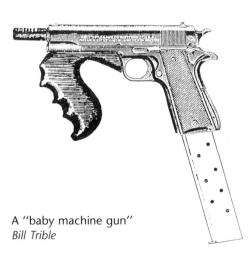

A "baby machine gun"
Bill Trible

distributor called Wolf & Klar (the source, as it happens, of Machine Gun Kelly's Thompson), which had sold it unmodified to a San Antonio gun dealer named Hyman S. Lebman at 111 South Flores Street. H. S. Lebman supplied these and other weapons to the Dillinger gang by way of Baby Face Nelson, who apparently had met him through veteran bank robber Eddie Bentz in the summer of 1933. Nelson purchased both the custom-made machine pistols and some Thompson submachine guns, which Lebman obligingly rustled up from different sources and shipped to Nelson and Tommy Carroll, usually in St. Paul. In November of 1933, Nelson, his wife Helen, Homer Van Meter, and Marie Comforti enjoyed Thanksgiving dinner with the Lebmans, at which time Van Meter placed a personal order for one of the custom-made pistols in caliber .45. On December 11, Carroll fatally wounded a San Antonio detective who tried to question him as a "suspicious character," but made good his escape after ducking into Lebman's shop to borrow a pair of trousers.

When arrested the following April, Lebman could not be held on any federal charge except suspected possession of stolen government property—a U.S. Army .45 automatic. Nothing would come of that, but the Lebman raid was publicized as evidence of the need for a federal machine-gun law, as there was a Thompson on the premises, and Lebman further admitted that he was converting Van Meter's pistol to fire "full-auto." As it happened, Texas had passed a state machine-gun law the previous October, and for violating that Lebman received a five-year sentence in 1935. The conviction was reversed on appeal, however, and during a retrial in 1936 the jury deadlocked at eleven to one for conviction. The U.S. attorney suspected that the holdout juror had been bought, and for the next five years tried to persuade Texas authorities to try the case again. However, the state attorney's office kept citing witness problems and a crowded court calendar, and finally dismissed the indictment in 1941.

The machine pistol recovered in St. Paul was traced to a distributor in California, but apparently reached Dillinger also through Lebman. That investigation disclosed that a Los Angeles police officer had developed and patented the " 'Steady Fire' Riot and Anti-Bandit Gun with 'Multi-Shot' Magazine," which was merely a Colt .45 or .38 Super Automatic with a large-capacity magazine and an attachable shoulder stock, such as further modified by Lebman. The Bureau found that Dillinger's guns contained special parts that had been patented by the policeman and produced by the Monarch Arms Company in Los Angeles, which probably became the Western Arms Company. These dealers and Lebman, in some combination, may have been the source of exotic guns also for the Barker-Karpis gang, Pretty Boy Floyd, and even the Touhy bootlegging gang. Another reputed arms source for the Dillinger and Barker-Karpis gangs was a Chicagoan known as Joey O'Brien, who operated popular hoodlum taverns on his way to becoming Joey Aiuppa, head of the Chicago Syndicate in the 1960s. Although patently false, a persistent rumor had the Auto-Ordnance Corporation giving complimentary Thompson submachine guns to famous gangsters for promotional purposes.

48. While Loeser's testimony may have propagated the story that Van

Meter was a drug addict, the FBI considered him a drug user prior to that, and its reports occasionally name individuals believed to be his suppliers.

49. Black and tan resorts were jazz-age nightclubs patronized by both white and "colored" couples, which made them especially disreputable as places of entertainment.

50. In his many years as a fugitive, Karpis had loved and left any number of women, some of whom did not know his identity and were understandably dismayed when charged with harboring him. The one woman for whom Karpis professed genuine affection was Dolores Delaney, who bore him a son while serving her sentence for harboring. After his capture, Karpis claimed that he had made financial arrangements for the support of her and the little boy, but did not mention any wife who might have given him a daughter.

51. The Finertys later admitted knowing Van Meter's identity but managed to avoid conviction by claiming ignorance of the fact that he was a federal fugitive, so the economical rates that Van Meter enjoyed were due either to the Finnertys' good will or to Van Meter's haggling power.

52. As discussed elsewhere, the Justice Department never created an official Public Enemies list, but Attorney General Cummings evidently used the term in such a way that it sounded like an official declaration, and this is the occasion usually cited as the time of Dillinger's promotion to national Public Enemy Number One.

53. With many of its hangouts now under surveillance, the Dillinger gang had taken to meeting at night on the grounds of a white frame schoolhouse on the northwestern outskirts of Chicago. It was located on the west side of the road two or three miles north of the intersection of state highways 62 and 53 and was so situated as to provide a good view of all approaches, which also allowed for headlight signaling by arriving gang members. Here the South Bend job was planned, and most accounts place the number of robbers at five or six. Some witnesses identified one of the bandits as Pretty Boy Floyd—but some also identified one as John Hamilton, who had been dead two months. Yet several documents and statements contain clues that Floyd, though never known to have met Dillinger, may indeed have joined him on this one occasion. A South Bend suspect interrogated later said that he had turned down the job for other reasons, but had been told by its promoters that the gang was specially assembled and included a bank robber who was "famous" in the west. After his arrest as a friend of Nelson, Fatso Negri told the FBI he inferred that Floyd was in the group because he overheard references to Adam Richetti, who was Floyd's regular partner in crime. Negri added that while planning the South Bend job, Nelson took an intense dislike to the unidentified robber whose friend was Richetti, and later griped when Floyd was killed by the FBI instead of by him. While testifying in court, Negri was asked if he knew Floyd, and he said yes, without elaborating. Though less than reliable in some of his claims, Negri later confirmed the planning of the Murray-sponsored mail-train robbery and said Floyd was expected to participate. Since Richetti had served time in the Indiana State Prison, he might have been Floyd's contact with either Dillinger or Van Meter during this period.

The train robbery was supposed to help Dillinger finance his escape to Mexico; and while the FBI never learned any details, it did turn up evidence that Dillinger had intentions along those lines. In April of 1934, a Los Angeles federal agent interviewed the airplane pilot who had flown Dillinger as a prisoner from Tucson to Douglas, Arizona, en route to Indiana. The flyer reported that after Dillinger's escape from Crown Point, he was approached by a Chicago policeman wanting to know if he could pick up Dillinger somewhere outside Chicago and fly him to Mexico. Purvis was not sure what to make of the story, and nothing seems to have come of it, but from their subject's description of the policeman, agents guessed that he might be First District detective Frank Bauler, who was Evelyn Frechette's uncle.

54. The FBI's informant was Meyer Bogue, who had overheard Piquett arguing money matters over the telephone and setting up the meeting. The area was quickly staked out by agents who followed Loeser home without yet knowing who he was or what they had. They learned from a postman that the resident's name was Robeind, but did not connect him with a mystery doctor called Robeint who was said to be altering fingerprints. Dr. Loeser remained under surveillance until July 24, two days after Dillinger's death, and was arrested only after agents saw Louis Piquett drop something off at the house. The terrified Loeser quickly fingered Probasco, who was picked up the next evening and plunged to his death a few hours later.

55. Among the many wrong people nabbed by the police or the FBI in their nationwide gangster search was Mrs. Chico Marx. Agents looking for Evelyn Frechette had seized her at the Newark airport the previous April, and then had put her and a frightened fellow airline passenger through the wringer before realizing their mistake. To make amends, the embarrassed agents spent the evening chauffeuring Mrs. Marx around town in search of Chico and then took her to her hotel, by which time she was treating the experience as a lark. Probably less amused was an unidentified couple pounced on at Chicago's Union bus station by shotgun-wielding G-men who handcuffed the woman and clubbed the man to the sidewalk in the belief they had caught Mrs. Baby Face Nelson and the ghost of the long-deceased John Hamilton.

56. Police in Chicago and northern Indiana suspected that Dillinger had been patronizing Anna Sage's "resorts" as far back as 1923, and that the gonorrhea described in his prison medical records was a souvenir of his early philandering (supposedly he confided to a fellow prisoner later that an absence of regular sex gave him headaches). The FBI had little interest in Dillinger's old affairs or affiliations, and so to protect Anna Sage, as well as to frustrate a local press that seemed to have too many inside sources, the Bureau became a fount of disinformation. Thus an eager *Chicago American* reporter was fed hints that produced a curious banner headline in at least one issue the following day: DILLINGER PUT ON SPOT BY MAIL BANDIT AND WIFE. "A mail robber, with a record and a new rap on stolen bond charges, and his wife traded John Dillinger to Uncle Sam for hope of his own freedom and a reward for her," the paper declared, adding that it would respect the

Justice Department's wishes to protect the couple's identity. In fact, the Bureau had just arrested James Murray for helping Dillinger gang member Harry Copeland obtain a car with stolen bonds, and the prospect of another long stretch in prison had led Murray to offer Dillinger up. Dillinger had meanwhile moved to Probasco's for surgery during the month of June, and thence to the Fullerton apartment of Anna Sage, who had plans of her own. The reporter may have put together a garbled version of betrayal schemes leaked by different G-men, and assumed the plotters were man and wife. On the other hand, it's likely that Murray and Sage did know each other and were racing to deliver the goods. This evidence that Murray had already turned informer could explain how he avoided prosecution over the bonds and some other matters later. The newspapers quickly enough identified Anna as the duplicitous "woman in red," so the public assumed that the mysterious "mail bandit," like the "Croatian gambler" and the "vengeful boyfriend" (who supposedly had lost his girl to Dillinger), were merely more federal fabrications to protect Anna Sage.

57. In her formal statements to the FBI, Anna Sage makes Dillinger sound (no doubt unintentionally) like a young woman's dream come true. He comes off as a well-groomed, good-humored, generous, and somewhat bashful suitor whom Polly met at a tavern and who had to be lured to her place with the promise of homemade pies. He's also described as a romantic fellow who took Polly for walks along the beach, sat up with her when she was ill, sang her lullabies and love songs, and (Polly later adds) called her his "Countess" while whispering sweet nothings. But then, as Anna tells it, she became suspicious of Polly's fellow, browbeat him with accusations, and confused him into revealing his true identity:

"I told Polly that I was going to make that man, meaning Jimmy Lawrence, admit that he was Dillinger or he could leave. . . . I told him to wait a minute and I went out in the other room and got several pictures which appeared in the newspapers and showed them to him and told him that if he was John Dillinger he would have a gun on him, and if he had no gun he was not Dillinger. He did have a gun in his pocket." She tried to reason with Polly, who wouldn't listen, and then called her friend Zarkovich for advice. Polly later admitted knowing Dillinger's identity all along, and, according to Anna, he even had warned her that this "might cause her lots of trouble and sorrow, but she told him that she did not care, as it was worth it."

58. Hot would be an understatement. Chicago was in the midst of a record-breaking heat wave that produced afternoon temperatures as high as 109 degrees at the municipal airport and was causing dozens of heat-related deaths. Considering that Dillinger was a serious gangster movie buff and that his choice was between Shirley Temple in *Little Miss Marker,* playing halfway across town at the Marbro, and Clark

Gable in *Manhattan Melodrama,* playing a block away at the Biograph, the FBI might have bet on the latter—especially since the Biograph displayed a huge banner proclaiming COOLED BY REFRIGERATION, which involved large fans blowing over slabs of ice in the basement.

59. It had become FBI policy to avoid including Chicago police or even informing them of its activities, partly in the belief that Dillinger had informants in the police department. This so irked Chicago authorities that no police from the Biograph's district attended the most dramatic inquest since the St. Valentine's Day Massacre, to the expressed annoyance of the coroner. The practice of excluding the police nearly had serious consequences the following January when agents laid siege to the Barker-Karpis hideout at 3920 North Pine Grove, killing Russell Gibson and capturing Byron Bolton. Chicago squads raced to the scene of a reported gun battle and nearly opened fire on the agents, who were afterwards scolded by every civic official who could locate a reporter.

Why the FBI did not confront Dillinger in or outside Anna Sage's apartment instead of at a busy theater caused the Bureau considerable criticism, but FBI records make it clear that Anna wanted no G-men storming her place, and Purvis evidently was so eager to get Dillinger that he did not argue the point—or even ask where her place was. This gave Anna the following day to clean house before Chicago police tracked down her address through a telephone number found at Polly Hamilton's. That the FBI could not imagine Dillinger residing at Anna's may be surprising, but a report written two weeks later advised that the Chicago office still was "exhausting every possible lead with reference to the location of the place where Dillinger was living prior to his death on July 22, 1934." The only Chicago address associated with Dillinger as Jimmy Lawrence was a phony one of 3967 North Pine Grove, a street which ends at Irving Park Boulevard with number 3959. Curiously, if number 3967 existed, it would be practically next door to Louis Piquett's apartment at 659 Irving Park—and diagonally across the street from the Barker-Karpis hideout at 3920 Irving Park.

Colt Automatic Pistols
.32 and 380 Caliber
Pocket Model—Hammerless

60. This was probably a failure of O'Leary and Girardin to communicate. The gun pictured in the newspapers was a .380-caliber Colt Pocket Model, probably the single most popular and common "civilian" automatic pistol of the day, if not the era. Hundreds of thousands were produced in outwardly identical .32 and .380 (9mm short) versions from 1903 until the 1940s, and these turned up in nearly every Dillinger arsenal seized. The

gun long displayed at FBI headquarters as the one carried by Dillinger that fateful night turned out to be a ringer, however. Chicago writer Jay Robert Nash, after antagonizing the FBI with his conspiracy theories in *Dillinger: Dead or Alive?*, caused it some actual embarrassment by confirming that the one in the case had not been manufactured by Colt's until after Dillinger's death. In Joe Pinkston's efforts to track the original gun, he learned that Hoover may have given it as a personal gift to a Hollywood personality, who never responded to inquiries. FBI records reveal that Hoover occasionally did give "famous" guns to people who were friends of the Bureau, especially if they were in the entertainment industry.

61. Different accounts place the number of shots fired at anywhere from three to nineteen (or even more), and the *Chicago American* disloyally gave the kill to the East Chicago officers. The Bureau itself had trouble pinning down the exact number and seems to have settled on five—two of which struck Dillinger in the neck and side, one that may have grazed his face, and two that missed—all fired by federal agents. It refused to identify the shooters, saying that Dillinger was brought down by efficient teamwork rather than any individual, and soon rumors had Zarkovich himself killing Dillinger to make sure he never talked.

FBI records are somewhat contradictory but seem to conclude that

```
DIV INVEST     CHICAGO      JULY 27, 1934     9-45 PM      EPH

DIRECTR

MATT LEACH OF INDIANA STATE POLICE CALLED AT THIS OFFICE TODAY AND

ADVISED THAT A CONFIDENTIAL INFORMANT HAD GIVENHIM INFORMATION

INDICATING THAT ANNA SAGE, POLLY HAMILTON AND SERGEANT MARTIN

ZARKOVICH PUT DILLINGER ON THE SPOT IN ORDER THAT THEY MIGHT GAIN

POSSESSION OF DILLINGERS WEALTH AND THAT ZARKOVICH HAD KNOWN WHERE

DILLINGER WAS FOR THE LAST SIXTY DAYS AND THAT THE ABOVE THREE

INDIVIDUALS WERE RESPONSIBLE FOR THE MURDER SOME TIME AGO OF TWO

EAST CHICAGO INDIANA POLICE OFFICERS WHO WERE KILLED BY DILLINGER

GANGSTERS.  MATT LEACH REQUESTED THAT THE DIVISION

COOPERATE WTH HIM IN INVESTIGATING THESE CHARGES.  I TOLD

MR. LEACH THAT THERE WAS NO CHARGE OF ANY FEDERAL VIOLATION AND THAT

CONSEQUENTLY THE DIVISION WAS WITHOUT AUTHORITY TOUNDERTAKE SUCH

AN INVESTIGATION.

END

OK EJC                    COWLEY           JUL 3 0 1934
```

Special Agent Charles Winstead fired first, then he and agent Clarence Hurt fired simultaneously, followed by fourth and fifth shots from Winstead and Hollis that missed, unless one nicked Dillinger's cheek as he fell. Because the second shots by Winstead and Hurt sounded like one, many witnesses, including other agents, reported hearing only three or four. The Bureau announced immediately that Purvis (who was starting to receive credit for the actual killing) had not fired any shots, but declined to be more specific. By the time Purvis was pressured into resigning from the Bureau, virtually all responsibility for getting Dillinger was being given, posthumously, to Sam Cowley, but many accounts still refer to Purvis as the G-man who shot Dillinger.

At first, the East Chicago officers went along with the FBI's idea of a team, as they could claim to be duly deputized members of it. By 1936, however, Captain Tim O'Neil could see that this modesty was getting him and Zarkovich nowhere in their efforts to collect the Indiana reward, and he announced, to the FBI's annoyance, that in fact it was he who had fired the fatal bullet. He and Zarkovich had already split the federal reward of $5,000 (less $250 each to officers Sopsic, Conroy, and Stretch), but Indiana had been holding out because of the East Chicagoans' failure to cooperate in the state's investigation of their own department.

62. As usual, different reports list different amounts of cash found on Dillinger's body, including $7.81, $7.80, $7.71, and $7.70, suggesting that coins were becoming personal souvenirs even as his possessions were inventoried. Unsuccessful efforts have been made to track down Dillinger's ruby ring, gold pocket watch with Polly's picture, and other personal items, but anything of value or interest quickly disappeared.

63. In her statements to the FBI, Anna Sage said that Dillinger had left her apartment carrying several thousand dollars, and the disappearance of his bankroll between the Biograph and the morgue led to an official if perfunctory inquiry. None of the agents then reported seeing anyone remove anything from the body, although agent D. P. Sullivan did say that he had felt "what appeared to be a roll of money or paper in the right-hand pants pocket"; and many years later he wrote in the FBI newsletter *Grapevine* that he actually had seen city officers in the police wagon going through Dillinger's possessions. At the time, however, Hoover discounted Anna Sage's story on the basis of Sam Cowley's somewhat ingenuous assurance that Dillinger was coatless that night and therefore could not have been carrying any large rolls of bills. So the Bureau had to ignore Glenn Stretch's published remark that he had seen Zarkovich take Dillinger's money. Joe Pinkston was told by "Tubby" Toms, a reporter close to Matt Leach and the Dillinger case, that the East Chicago police probably removed a money belt containing $6,000 or $7,000.

64. Although most papers suppressed their disappointment at the loss of such a newsmaker and praised the FBI, many questioned the wisdom of an ambush that put bystanders at such risk; and a few considered it just plain un-American to shoot a man in the back. The Clarendon, Virginia, *Chronicle* was particularly hard on the G-men, calling them "mostly cowards" and remark-

ing that "Dillinger died with millions of admirers because he was a brave man, and a figure of romance, appealing to the imagination, and a hunted man, and the underdog in the fight." Melvin Purvis came off poorly in the verse it quoted in an editorial ("Oh that men once more were manly, woman's pride and not her scorn / That again the pale young mother dared to boast a man is born") while Dillinger did much better ("He left a name at which the world grows pale, / To point a moral or adorn a tale"). The foreign press in some countries had only slightly loftier objections, likening the killing to an American gangland execution.

If many people had mixed feelings about Dillinger, those who expressed them to newspapers mostly did so anonymously. In the Chicago *Daily Times,* for instance, "D. J." declared, "I am a young girl, but I expect to be a woman some day, and it makes me sick to think that one of my sex would lead a man to his death . . . I certainly feel sorry for his father, and if I were a man and a member of Dillinger's gang I'd certainly avenge his death." Another "Reader" insisted that Dillinger "was accused of many things that he didn't do," and condemned the "stool pigeon who put a finger on him." And while literary fame may have eluded one New Orleans poetry journal editor, Darwin Kellogg Pavey found at least some measure of posterity in FBI files with his ditty titled "Dillinger—A Song of Hate":

> Outlaw judges on the bench,
> Outlaw cops with club and gun,
> Doing crimes whose awful stench
> Fills, with loathing, ev'ryone.
>
> Fifteen rats in ambush lay,
> Their sadist lust for blood to sate;
> A social rebel there to slay.
> Lured by a judas, to his fate;
>
> Fifteen rats, with slinking stealth,
> Who sought no captive in the dark;
> With cautious care of their own health,
> Laid, in cold blood, one rebel stark.
>
> Long forgot, our Law Supreme,
> With its sacred Bill of Rights;
> Now is but a troubled dream
> In this dark and fearsome night.

65. The carnival of the macabre that followed the slaying included efforts by several parties to beg, bribe, or otherwise get past police to make death masks of Dillinger's battered face. News of one such project appeared in Chicago papers on July 24, and when a mask showed up later and unbidden on Hoover's desk in Washington, along with a chatty letter about the method used to make it, the director ordered an investigation. Interviews yielded evidence that several masks had been made, one had been confiscated, a deputy coroner had been fired "for accepting or demanding gratuities," and

everyone was lying through their teeth. But Hoover learned enough to conclude that his gift was not obtained in a manner so blatantly criminal that it might become an embarrassment.

It appears that four different "masks" were made during the day and a half of chaos that began with Dillinger's arrival. A large crowd already had gathered by the time the body reached a slab in the basement's "cool room," and morgue personnel were practically trampled by policemen, hospital workers, city officials, local politicians, and miscellaneous fast-talkers before some order was restored. The only officials not present initially were Coroner Frank Walsh and Medical Examiner Jerry Kearns, leaving police in a postmortem quandary. Anxious to get the body into other authorized hands, they collared the first doctor they could find. This was Jim Pilot, the young resident on night duty at Cook County Hospital; and when told to perform an autopsy on the most notorious corpse in the country, Pilot frantically called an intern friend named David Fisher, requesting backup. Fisher had to make his way into the building through an underground passageway, and only after much shouting and shoving by the Chicago cops did the corpse get moved upstairs to a posting room. The two worked nervously but carefully and put their findings in a four-page report called a Coroner's Protocol, which Kearns signed. Later, Kearns would purport that he had performed the autopsy personally, and Walsh would have to say that he was present at the time.

The body was returned to the basement sometime in the night, and the first death mask was made. An unusual character named Kenneth "Doc" Coffman—whose résumé would eventually describe him as a photographer, sculptor, newspaper illustrator, theater publicist, sign painter, and amateur criminologist—got past police by waving a letter from Colonel Calvin Goddard, locally prominent for establishing the city's crime lab. Whatever the letter may have said, Goddard's name carried enough weight to make the mission official, and police beat back the crowd so that Coffman and a friend could work. This death mask—or, more accurately, the mold—was made by merely greasing the face with petroleum jelly and pouring on liquid plaster. The plaster quickly dried to produce a negative or female impression, which "Doc" Coffman spirited out before too many questions were asked. (It was Coffman's unschooled belief that criminality could be discerned in a person's facial structure—a variation on phrenology that survived into the late 1930s.) After preparing this mold to receive another pouring of plaster, Coffman ended up with a somewhat crude but recognizable masklike replica of Dillinger's face, in which he detected definite indications of criminality.

By eleven o'clock the next morning the crowd was nearly out of hand when Harold May, president of the Reliance Dental Supply Company, arrived to make a death mask. With him were an Irish police sergeant and a colleague, probably Jerome F. Nachtman, a recently licensed dentist who had worked his way through school playing piano in mob-owned nightclubs. May flashed a deputy sheriff's badge, and his friend the police sergeant took care of the rest. In less than half an hour he had used a new kind of dental-impression material called Reprolastic, marketed by his company, to make a mold of Dillinger's face—ostensibly to demonstrate that this new product had law-enforcement applications. In fact it did, but the ulterior motive, revealed much later, was to produce death masks of Dillinger to peddle at Chicago's Century of Progress fair. It was May who proudly sent a casting to J. Edgar Hoover with a letter promoting Reprolastic. Hoover liked what he saw, investigated, and soon was sending copies of the casting to any police departments that wanted one and to other privileged individuals, until the requests piled up so high that the Bureau got tired of fulfilling them.

By the time Professor A. E. Ashworth arrived to make a death mask, about seven P.M. Monday, crowds were still jamming the rooms and corridors to gawk at Dillinger's body, making access all but impossible. He implied that his mask was for a crime museum at Northwestern University, which sounded plausible since the Goddard crime lab was affiliated with that school, and police told him to come back at ten. Professor Ashworth taught at the nearby Worsham College of Embalming, and when he returned later with several students, the police moved the corpse once again. Worsham's technique was to cover the face with a plaster-and-cotton mud that dried to form the mold.

By this time, the police were beginning to wonder about the growing number of death masks, and one cop, Sergeant Alfred Mulvaney, decided that Professor Ashworth and his students lacked proper authority. In what student Marge McDougall (née Marjorie Eker) recalled was a "terribly officious and overbearing" manner, Sergeant Mulvaney announced that he was confiscating the mask in the name of the law. Unable to sway him from his duty (Mulvaney may have been the "Irish cop" who accompanied Harold May), Ashworth insisted that Mulvaney at least transport the mask to some safe place and make out an official receipt. Mulvaney grumpily agreed, and Marge McDougall made sure he complied. She trailed him upstairs to a large vault, asking questions, engaging him in conversation, and otherwise prolonging the trip. Before Mulvaney and the attractive embalming-college coed could complete their round trip to the basement, Professor Ashworth had poured another death mask, which a student smuggled out in a wadded-up sheet. When Dillinger's body reached the McCready Funeral Home the following afternoon, Ray McCready commented disapprovingly on the condition of Dillinger's face, which had lost skin and facial hair to the repeated moldmaking.

The body also had undergone another morgue experience that would cause a certain commotion. The McCready Funeral Home reported and the Mooresville undertaker confirmed that Dillinger's brain was missing, a discovery that inspired the New York *Daily News* to proclaim, SICK GHOUL STOLE BRAIN OF DILLINGER. Dillinger's father and half-brother Hubert angrily threatened to sue Cook County for desecration damages. Since nobody knew what monetary value to place on a famous outlaw's brain, the senior Dillinger decided on $20,000, the amount that would pay off his mortgage. An exhumation request convinced Cook County that the Dillingers meant business, and officials began to scramble. First, Coroner Walsh denied the brain had been tampered with at all, but its absence could hardly be disputed, and soon medical examiner Kearns acknowledged the removal of an ounce or two of gray matter for routine testing. Apparently unaware of Kearns's statement, coroner's toxicologist Dr. Clarence Muehlberger declared that he had half the brain in a jar of preservative, and thought the other half might have been placed in the corpse's stomach cavity in a moment of anatomical confusion. Before that statement reached Dr. Kearns, he remembered having sent Dr. Muehlberger two-thirds of the brain and keeping one-third for himself. On August 3, the Chicago *Daily Times* totaled the fractions that kept coming in and waggishly complimented the coroner's office on finally accounting for "seven-sixths" of the brain—one-sixth more than John Dillinger could have claimed.

After deciding that the brain had not been removed maliciously or for commercial purposes (a $10,000 carnival offer for the dead outlaw's body had been angrily rejected), the Dillinger family cooled off and let the matter drop, at which time the coroner's office quickly announced that the brain, or the several parts of it, had all been destroyed in the testing—without discovering any abnormalities that would account for Dillinger's criminality.

That left only the mystery of Dillinger's penis. The outlaw's dynamic love life not only had fascinated his public but had moved some pop psychologists to speculate that Dillinger's bank robbing was an effort to impress females (or variations on that theme). Some time after his death, the legend arose that Dillinger was endowed with a sexual organ of such impressive size that it had been placed on display at the Smithsonian Institution in Washington, D.C., or maybe at the National Medical Museum, which for many years had its building on the Smithsonian's grounds and indeed offered tourists a large room full of eye-catching and stomach-turning exhibits. The museum's curator said that one long-time employee recalled that tour bus operators in the city used to drum up business by implying that the organ was on display. Ronald L. Baker's *Hoosier Folk Legends* (1982) includes a tale that Dillinger's penis was twenty-three inches long and a genuine handicap to lovemaking, because the amount of blood it took to maintain an erection often caused him to pass out. Dillinger (as well as other famous criminals and popular cartoon characters) was even featured in one of the little "eight-pager" pornographic booklets that became popular in the thirties.

The Dillinger legend's origin has never been established, but folklorists know that folk heroes often are credited with great sexual prowess, and in Dillinger's case a small measure of truth may have combined with a widely published photograph to produce a museum-quality sex organ. The photo was one that dominated the front page of the *Chicago Daily News* on July 23 and showed a crowd of people staring at the corpse covered with a sheet, which appeared to be draped over a conspicuous erection. Other *Daily News* editions the same day carried a different picture; and in other papers that used the suggestive one, the tent-pole effect was eliminated by retouching. The rise in the sheet probably was caused by the corpse's arm, and after seeing what the original picture looked like in print, other editors evidently decided it could give the wrong impression.

Smithsonian Institution   Washington, DC 20560

Public Inquiry Mail Service

Visitor Information and Associates' Reception Center

In response to your recent inquiry, we can assure you that anatomical specimens of John Dillinger are not, and have never been, in the collections of the Smithsonian Institution.

Enclosed is a brochure describing our museums.

Your interest in the Smithsonian Institution is appreciated.

However the rumor got started, both the Smithsonian Institution and the National Medical Museum are still queried so often that they now respond with form letters politely denying that they have, or ever have had, any part of John Dillinger's "anatomy." If the legend tends to amuse Dillingerologists and perhaps even the museums, the FBI has failed to see the humor. In 1968, for instance, two California college students thought they could trick the Bureau into writing them a denial that they could use to "repudiate" the Dillinger penis rumor. In an interoffice memo, two Bureau officials discuss in all seriousness the alleged "biological phenomenon consisting of an appendage eighteen inches in length," and decide (with a handwritten "I concur" from Hoover himself) that "the inquiry from these students is impertinent, ridiculous and does not deserve a reply. They are not identifiable in Bufiles."

They are now.

Quite a few death-mask castings survive, copied from one of the Dental Reliance Company originals, from one belonging to the Chicago police (which may have come from the mold confiscated by Sergeant Mulvaney), or from one that belonged to a former employee of the Goddard crime lab, Joe Wilimovski, who kept microscopes and other equipment when the laboratory later went to the Chicago Police Department. When Wilimovski died, his collection passed to his brother Allan, who before his own death sold it as part of what he called the Goddard Collection to his collector friend Neal Trickle in Monroe, Wisconsin. This mask resembles the Chicago Police Department's in some significant respects, but might be the second Ashworth mask that the professor's students smuggled out. Trickle's understanding is that the mask came from Wilimovski's first wife, Adelyne (or Adeline), whom Wilimovski married about that time and who may have been connected with either the embalming college or the morgue. In any case, with this mask came the only surviving early mold, which was auctioned (along with two early castings) to a British collector in 1992 for $10,000.

The mold made by "Doc" Coffman was discarded by his widow, who later sold its only known casting at auction to a collector in Glenview, Illinois, for $850. The mold made by Harold May, his unnamed colleague (probably Dr. Nachtman), and his Irish policeman friend was used for pistol practice after they learned that their scheme to sell copies would require the Dillinger family's permission. Besides the casting that Harold May sent to J. Edgar Hoover, another from that mold somehow ended up with a dental-supply salesman in Brooklyn, who bequeathed it to family members now living in Saugerties, New York.

Despite its announced destruction, John Dillinger's brain may have survived both the testing and the confusion only to vanish a second time, if another dubious story can be believed. In this account, the threatened lawsuit led someone to hide the brain in the Northwestern University histology laboratory, where it lay forgotten until the lab was renovated in the late 1940s. It then became some professor's conversation piece, and he supposedly gave it to a doctor friend in Kansas, who supposedly sold it to a Chicago-area optometrist with the appropriate name of Brayne—none of which has ever been confirmed.

If that brain story is highly suspect, so are the rumors of the gang's buried treasures. One "Dillinger hoard" is supposedly contained in several suitcases buried at the far end of a pasture on the old Pierpont family farm near Leipsic, Ohio. A second hoard, amounting to $150,000 in jewelry taken from the Unity Trust and Savings Bank, is purportedly buried on a remote part of the old Dillinger farm near Mooresville. A third treasure, consisting of $200,000 in cash, is supposed to be buried 500 yards due north of the Little Bohemia Lodge. As Girardin indicates, Dillinger did make reference to loot that had been hidden one place or another, but the gang's living expenses were so great that cash was often in short supply, and if any robbery stash remains to be found by treasure hunters, it would probably turn out to be nonnegotiable securities.

Various Dillinger legends are deliberately propagated by the John Dillinger Died for You Society (a spoof on Elvis Presley– type fan clubs), along with rumors that it was not Dillinger but a *doppelgänger* who died outside the Biograph. After the shooting, one person or another would say that the body didn't look like the Dillinger they had known, and this was usually good for a short news item. There were also hoaxes. In 1937 newspapers reported that Indiana's assistant attorney general had been through Mooresville and found many residents believing that a letter to Dillinger's sister, supposedly from the outlaw himself, was authentic. "They are certain that Dillinger is alive, and nothing you can say will convince them otherwise," he told a reporter. This notion was argued with all seriousness in *Dillinger: Dead or Alive?,* published in 1970 by a Chicago author who had based a complex conspiracy theory on the errors and discrepancies found in official documents. The Dillinger Society accepts any of these things as proof that "Dillinger Lives," at least in the hearts and minds of men.

66. Agents liberated Anna Sage from the Chicago police, but seemed to take little interest in her place of residence, where Dillinger had been living since the Fourth of July, or in her personal associations, which became embarrassing when Chicago newspapers turned up snapshots of her with Zarkovich. Even after some boys found Dillinger's Thompson and other ord-

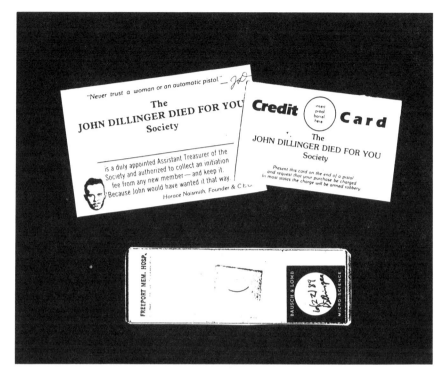

Among the Dillinger Society's possessions is some eyebrow hair
(*bottom*) found embedded in one of the Dillinger death masks.

nance which Anna had thrown into Lake Michigan, the Chicago office merely
accepted possession and shipped the items to Washington. Matt Leach kept
pestering the Bureau to investigate Zarkovich as having known Dillinger's

whereabouts for many weeks. He finally stirred
up the *Chicago Tribune*'s Colonel McCormick
into making speeches charging conspiracy and
cover-up, which only confirmed the frustrated
Leach as a loose cannon and helped get him
fired.

67. Soon after Dillinger's death, Chicago
newspapers rustled up several girlfriends of Dillinger gang members and paid them to tell their
stories. To the less sensitive journalists of the
time, these girls were merely "floozies" who
became "gun molls." In the *Chicago Herald &
Examiner,* Bernice Clark (Opal Long) and Mary
Kinder each published somewhat skimpy
memoirs under their own bylines, with a little
help from staff writers; but from the accounts of

Evelyn Frechette ("What I Knew about John Dillinger—By His Sweetheart," 8/27/34 to 9/1/34) and of Polly Hamilton ("Dillinger's Last Hours with Me—By His Sweetheart," 10/25/34 to 10/27/34), it was apparent that each wished to be remembered as Dillinger's one true love. The following excerpts provide a few clues to Dillinger's personality and the style that tended to win him friends, as well as the hearts of restless young women.

In her account, Evelyn writes:

> Only one big thing happened to me in my life. Nothing much happened before that, and I don't expect much more from now on—except maybe a lot more grief. The one thing that happened to me was that I fell in love with John Dillinger.
>
> John was good to me. He looked after me and bought me all kinds of jewelry and cars and pets, and we went places and saw things, and he gave me everything a girl wants. He was in love with me.
>
> Falling in love with John was something that took care of itself. I like John's kind. I don't mean because he was a criminal and carried guns around, and wasn't afraid of police or any one. There was something else. I always figured that what he did was one thing and what he was another. I was in love with what he was. I liked going out where people were laughing and having a good time and cutting up.
>
> It was a cabaret on the North Side where I met John Dillinger. It happened the way things do in the movies. I was 25 years old and I wasn't any different from all the other girls that were 25 years old. Then I met John and everything was changed. I started a new kind of life.
>
> It was in November, just about a year ago now, I remember. I was sitting at the table with some other girls and some fellows. We were having a good time.
>
> I looked up and I saw a man at a table across the room looking at me. He didn't look away when I looked up. He just stared at me and smiled just a little bit with the corner of his mouth. His eyes seemed to go all the way through me.
>
> A thing like that happens to a girl often and it doesn't mean anything. This was different. I looked at him and maybe I smiled.
>
> Anyway, he knew one of the girls I was with and pretty soon he came over to our table and spoke to the girl and she said, "Billy, this is Jack Harris."
>
> I didn't know then he was the John Dillinger everybody under the sun was looking for. To me that night he was just Jack Harris—a good looking fellow that stood there looking down at me and smiling in a way that I could tell he liked me already more than a little bit. He said:
>
> "Where have you been all my life?"
>
> For a long time after our meeting in the cabaret John Dillinger was just Jack Harris to me. Once in a while I thought he acted kind of strange. There were places he said he wouldn't go or didn't want to and he wouldn't say why or maybe he'd just say he didn't like the place or it wasn't safe.
>
> I didn't ask any questions. Why should I. He was good to me. From the very first night I met him there was nobody else in my life, and I didn't want anybody else. He treated me like a lady.

The following spring federal agents, acting on a tip, arrested and jailed Evelyn but missed Dillinger. Although he arranged for her defense, he observed the tradition that if you can't be with the one you love, you love the one you're with—namely Polly Hamilton, who was likewise swept off her feet by the Dillinger charm:

John Dillinger, the outlaw? I didn't know him. The man I knew, and loved, was Jimmy Lawrence, a Board of Trade clerk. A smiling Jimmy Lawrence, whose mouth twitched at the corners when he told a funny story. The Jimmy Lawrence who gave me my amethyst ring.

Jimmy Lawrence wasn't grim, wasn't a killer, any more than he was a Board of Trade clerk.

I wouldn't let him call for me, because they thought he was a sissy, with his gold-rimmed glasses and trick mustache that the authorities say now he used for a disguise.

He'd stand outside the place I worked and make faces at me through the window to see me laugh.

I met him one night early last June at the Barrel of Fun night club. He came up and asked:

"What would happen if I called you up some night?"

He didn't lose any time when I told him to try and see. The very next day he called, and that night he was waiting for me outside the restaurant where I worked at 1209 Wilson av. He grinned and said:

"The name's Jimmy Lawrence, if you've forgotten."

One of the shyest fellows I ever saw, but I liked that in him. Off we drove in a taxicab to the Stables to dine and dance. After that it was almost every evening.

We rode in more taxis than I'd ever known there were in Chicago, and it didn't matter where we had dined, we always had to have a red hot [hotdog] before he'd go home. Only twice in all the time I knew him did he drive a car.

Lots of things happened that should have told me he was John Dillinger. The scars from having his face altered and removing that mole might have warned me. I asked him about them, though, and he said, "Listen, Countess, I was in an auto accident."

He called me Countess at first, and sometimes Cleopatra. Honey was the name I liked best, just the same.

It may not have been love at first sight. He wasn't much for flattery. But you knew he meant it when you heard him say to somebody:

"She's all right. I like her just like she is."

But as for who he was, I had another clue. One of the girls I knew said one time, "He looks just like John Dillinger."

But I didn't think so. You judge people you know by the way they act as well as by the way they look, and he was better to me than any other man I ever knew.

He wasn't exactly a fashion plate. He wore the same gray suit all the time I knew him, which shows he wasn't trying very hard to disguise himself. He told me he wore his clothes until he grew tired of them, and then threw them away.

He was simply crazy about cards, and he always seemed so much more talkative when he was in a game. He was an awful tease, too.

It wasn't any fun for him to play without some money up, but he knew the rest of us didn't have much to lose; so he always made the stakes low enough that we could all play.

It was at Mrs. Sage's that we found out what a great big Indiana farm boy he was. All he asked was a home-cooked dinner.

Baking powder biscuits and chicken gravy, just like they have on the farm, were what he liked best. Tomatoes, green onions, and radishes he had to have, too. When it was hot weather, he always brought ice cream, for he liked it so. Sometimes he'd bring half a dozen boxes of strawberries.

He liked steak for meat, but when he was feeling particularly happy, nothing but frogs legs from Ireland's [restaurant] would do. He used to bring them out and stand over them while we cooked them.

And would you believe it, he'd wash the dishes.

There wasn't much pretense about him. He said he was just an Indiana farm boy, and he insisted I was a farm girl, too. When he really wanted to tease me, he'd say:

"There's Polly now. She just proves that you can take the girl away from the country, but you can't take the country away from the girl."

If he thought I didn't like it, though, he'd mighty quickly explain that he was only kidding.

John Dillinger, or Jimmy as he was known to me, never liked to hurt anyone's feelings. He was what you'd call on the up-and-up with me and all his friends every minute.

I don't know whether he was in love with me or not, but I was goofy about him. The two-day party we had celebrating his birthday on the 22nd of June and mine on the 23rd was just about the most important thing that ever happened to me. He sent me two dozen roses and bought me the amethyst ring, and we spent the evenings at the French Casino.

He must have been in love with me. Lots of times he talked about a home and kids of his own. He used to say he was going to retire from his Board of Trade job and buy a chicken farm, but I never took him very seriously on that.

You probably don't think of a machine gunner as singing. He sang, all right, in a low, rollicking voice. His favorite songs were "All I Do Is Dream of You," which he always sang to me, and "For All We Know."

When he was being funny, or winning at cards, he'd sing, "Hey, Hey, How Am I Doin'?"

He was more affectionate than you would think, although he did not like to show it. He didn't like others to show affection either. When we played cards, he collected a fine of a nickel each for a kiss and he made everyone pay up.

There was the night at a near North Side night club. Jimmy was always interested in the entertainers, for he loved a good floor show, and he and I were chatting with one of them when a police squad car, one of those big ones, drew up in front, full to detectives.

You may think that Jimmy got out a machine gun, or slipped through the back door. Well, when he heard about the squad he hurried right up to the front to see it, just as interested as could be. Afraid? Why, not at all. The police could have caught him right there if they'd known.

That must have been why it took so long to catch him; he was always right under their noses, where they weren't looking for him.

He said, when the detectives had left: "I wonder what they wanted?"

He was usually like that about the police. Whenever he saw any officers, we waited around to see what they were going to do. Just curious, I guess.

He always was interested in the squads that passed when we were riding in a taxicab, but he never seemed the least bit afraid, or tried to hide.

Now that I think of it, and know what a hunted thing he was, it takes my breath away to think what happened one night at the Grand Terrace. We were dancing there when a fellow at another table got a little impertinent.

Jimmy—he's always Jimmy to me—just burned. His eyes stopped twinkling and seemed to look through that fellow. It was one of two occasions when I ever saw him really angry.

When we got out on the floor the other man purposely bumped into us. Jimmy stopped dancing and demanded:

"What do you want—the whole floor?"

The other man snapped:

"Yeah, what are you going to do about it?"

Jimmy was all for hitting him and getting into trouble—Jimmy, mind you, who was really John Dillinger. Why, if he had ever been arrested it would have been all up with him.

I got him off the floor and persuaded him to sit down. But he said: "I'm burning up. I'd like to take a sock at that guy. . . ." At the French Casino, the Chez Paree, at all the swanky places on the North Side he and I danced, right along with the best people. He knew the managers of some of the places and talked to them about their floor shows, but they didn't know him.

Next to card playing, he liked dancing, and he was a good dancer, too, although he didn't know many fancy steps. The carioca was his favorite dance tune. He'd beg the orchestra leaders to play it again and again.

Talk about hiding! We were always the first to begin dancing when the music started, because he liked us to be the only couple on the floor so everyone could see us step.

He liked night life, but the odd thing about it was that he never drank much. On very special occasions he'd have two gin fizzes in an evening. One was usually his limit, though, and often he drank only a glass of beer. He never smoked very much, either, and I don't believe I ever heard him swear.

We went to Riverview Park often. He couldn't get enough of the rides. We never went on one and then stepped off. Three times on each one he liked was the quota, and some times we rode more than that. You would have thought he had never grown up. He'd yell like an Indian all the way down, and then he'd lean over and kiss me when we went around the curves.

Boy, did we have fun!

Our car on one of the rides stuck away up at the top in one of the amusement parks one day. That didn't bother him; I guess he wasn't afraid of anything.

Now that I know he was John Dillinger, I can understand why he always liked the shooting galleries so. Customers would line up to watch him knock over the targets.

On the Sunday afternoon before he was killed, Dillinger watched Anna Sage's son Steve play sandlot baseball while the girls went for bike rides. Polly later admitted that she had long been aware of Dillinger's identity.

We got back in time to see Jimmy being introduced to the crowd. It pleased him so much he bought beer for both teams and distributed the bottles in person right there in Jackson Park, while more policemen than there are bullets in a machine gun drum were looking for him. He had been awfully kind the night after

I read that the Dillinger gang had robbed the South Bend bank of $28,000. That night he bought me gardenias.

When he found out I wasn't feeling very well, he hunted up an electric fan for me and an extra pillow. It was about 5:30 in the evening. I remember there was some argument about how to cook the chicken for dinner, but we got it cooked. He must have had a premonition of death that Sunday we stepped out of the Biograph Theatre. He was so much more considerate, sweeter, I mean, than he had ever been to me before. Then, too, he carried a gun that day.

Jimmy insisted on going to the Biograph because he wanted to see "Manhattan Melodrama," the story of a New York gangster, that was playing there. We had a couple of games of pinochle and then started.

The theater was crowded. Jimmy and I got seats together in the third row from the front, but Anna had to sit by herself at the back. If he did have a premonition, Jimmy was a pretty good bluffer. He laughed and joked all through the show, and asked me for a kiss in a loud whisper, just to embarrass me. When the show was over, Anna joined us and we started away.

Jimmy had been insisting for a week or more that I take his arm when we walked together. Before he could ask this time, I slipped my arm through his.

As we stepped out, Jimmy seemed to step away from me.

Suddenly a gun roared, right beside me.

I jumped in fright, and Jimmy was lying there shot. . . .

With the possible exception of Polly, none of the Dillinger gang "molls" seem to have made the transition to a life of respectability.

68. As mentioned in connection with the Little Bohemia problems, J. Edgar Hoover made a practice of writing file memos that were much like entries in a diary. In response to Probasco's alleged suicide, he instantly wrote a memorandum that covered himself on several points:

Mr. Cowley telephoned from Chicago at approximately 10:30 A.M. [stating] that Probasco had just jumped out of a window at the Chicago Office, which is on the 19th floor. They had him in a room, where Mr. Chaffetz was taking his finger-prints. Mr. Chaffetz walked out for a minute, and the next thing they knew he had jumped out the window. I remarked that this was extreme carelessness. . . .

Mr. Cowley called immediately after the occurrence, and had not learned definitely that Probasco was dead, though there would be no question but that he was.

I told him he would have to make a statement to the press. I remarked that [this] shows extreme carelessness on the part of the Chicago Office. Mr. Cowley stated that when they took Probasco into custody they found a letter which indicated that he was on the verge of committing suicide. . . .

If agents found a letter contemplating suicide, it remains buried in Bureau files, but most newspapers obediently reported that an agent had carelessly turned his back and a despairing Probasco had jumped—except for one or two papers that earned the Bureau's eternal enmity by suggesting that Probasco had been dangled out the window to make him talk.

Newspapers never learned that Probasco's girlfriend Peggy Doyle tried to jump to her death while she and Dr. Loeser were in federal custody. The two were being held in an apartment building at 1648 Lunt when the woman locked herself in the bathroom on August 17th, less than a month after Dillinger died, and leapt from a third-floor window. She survived the fall with serious injuries and remained hospitalized until October 27th.

69. Perkins, whose day job was managing the Capone Syndicate's slot machines in Cicero, apparently also had interests in a pool hall called the Sheridan-Irving Recreation Parlor at 3925 North Sheridan, and in the betting parlor of Otis Murphy at 3939½ North Sheridan. He already had been "questioned vigorously and thoroughly" by the Chicago police and had resisted their "every means of persuasion," the Bureau euphemistically reported, and after that had continued providing the gang with logistical support in the way of guns, ammunition, and bulletproof vests. So the Bureau was understandably put out when a newspaper reported that he too had been interrogated by defenestration. When agents confronted him on this, Perkins insisted that he had been maliciously misquoted by irresponsible journalists and gave the Bureau a statement affirming his treatment as an honored guest. Once his lawyer reached the scene, however, he declined to sign it.

70. Baby Face Nelson and Van Meter apparently did have a falling out, as Girardin says, but it was more Nelson's hot-headed style to resent police interference in his plans for revenge. So the tip probably came not from Nelson, or from Marie Comforti (whom Homer was cheating on), or even from the parents of the young girl Van Meter was accused of seeing, but instead was simply a sellout. After her arrest, Marie Comforti told agents that Van Meter had been in St. Paul trying to collect $2,000 from a man she knew as Frank McCarthy, who was living at the farm of mobster Harry Sawyer and had been holding (as well as holding out on) Van Meter's money. She said Homer had been carrying that same amount or more in a money belt and at least $6,000 in a zippered portfolio at the time he was killed, and she had no doubt it was McCarthy who arranged the killing to save his skin. Meanwhile, Van Meter's father had begun his own investigation. After viewing Homer's tattered remains, Harry Van Meter concluded that his son was not shot while fleeing, as claimed by the police, but had been used virtually for target practice. In March 1935 he convinced an oddly sympathetic FBI that he was an honest and sincere old railroad man appalled by his son's crimes but needing to know the truth. The St. Paul police had been neither civil nor informative, he said, so he had talked to reporters and some detective magazines, which in the thirties were well-regarded publications. The consensus was that Homer had been "put on the spot" by crime boss Harry Sawyer, bagman for the police and associate of Jack Peifer, owner of the Hollyhocks and other hoodlum hangouts. Three years later the Bureau would decide that both the elder Van Meter and Marie Comforti were about as close to the truth as they were. In 1939, Thomas Kirwin, who had harbored Van Meter, told agents that Homer was betrayed by another harborer, Tom Gannon, in collusion with Peifer, who then divided ten or twelve thousand dollars of Van Meter's money with the St. Paul police, while Gannon kept his guns. Volney Davis and his girfriend Edna Murray previously had told the FBI that the Barker-Karpis gang

had cut ex–police chief Brown out of his share of the Bremer ransom for his killing of Van Meter.

71. On October 6, the Sausalito police arrested Sally Bachman at her apartment and turned her over to federal agents, who offered her a deal. If she would help them track Baby Face Nelson to his lair, they might take him by surprise and thus spare the life of her boyfriend John Paul Chase. Sally had traveled widely with Chase and the Nelsons and had a good memory for details. After checking out dozens of hotels and taverns in many small towns that looked much alike, she eventually led the agents to the Lake Como Hotel, a comfortable resort on the more secluded Lake Como, just west of Lake Geneva, Wisconsin (and still in business as the French Country Inn). Sally confirmed that this was the place where Baby Face intended to hibernate for the winter, and the reason for his choice soon became apparent. The hotel had been a deluxe speakeasy during Prohibition, and its owner, Hobart Hermanson, was a friend of Chicago's Bugs Moran (unless his marriage to Moran's ex-wife had strained that relationship). The Como still attracted more than its share of underworld characters, and Hermanson (yet another friend of Jimmy Murray's) was the perfect host who never asked for identification or looked askance at women who did not resemble wives. This was a bit risky in Wisconsin, which to this day retains (and occasionally enforces) archaic sex laws that prohibit fornication, cohabitation, oral sex, anal sex, extramarital sex, same-sex sex, and finally lewdness, to make sure it had left no loopholes. So the federal agents sent Sally Bachman home with their thanks, then assured "Hobe" Hermanson that they would not have to frighten off all his paying customers if he would lend them the use of his two-story house, situated maybe fifty yards from the hotel proper.

That was arranged on October 28, 1934, and after four weeks of scrutinizing every car and every face without spotting their desperadoes, some boredom had set in. Thus agent J. J. Metcalfe was not totally on his toes when a familiar-looking V-8 Ford drove up, and by the time he realized the occupants were not the unhappy Hermansons but the Baby Face Nelsons, it was too late to alert his colleagues, who were upstairs relaxing with rifles. Nelson, realizing he had blundered into an unset trap, exchanged a few casual words and sped off, worried by the close call but still highly amused at having caught the "G" with their pants down.

Not only had the agents blown their trap, but they had no way of giving chase, for fellow agent C. E. McRae had chosen that inopportune time to drive the FBI car into town for groceries. Metcalfe suffered embarrassment at the time and reproach from his superiors (Hoover scribbled "Very sloppy work" on the field report), but he could still consider himself lucky. Nelson had been ready to shoot the agent with a .38 automatic he was holding under a newspaper.

72. For all its drama, spectacle, and banner headline violence, the Barrington gun battle departed sufficiently from the script that newspapers were not sure how to play it and readers were not sure what to make of it. The

problem was that the good guys died, and the bad guy who killed them had acquitted himself (the unidentified accomplice did not yet count) in a fashion that came off as quite heroic—marching fearlessly into a blizzard of bullets that tore through his body without silencing his angry machine gun, was how the picture played. That was hardly the Baby Face Nelson that everyone loved to hate. So the discovery of his body one day later was anticlimactic—he must have died soon afterwards, and the whereabouts of the others was now anybody's guess.

The only clue left behind was Nelson's shout to his accomplice, "Drop everything and get me to the priest," and an unconfirmed report that a car carrying a badly wounded man had been turned away by monks at a Catholic monastery near the village of Techny on Waukegan Road, which led to Chicago's North Shore suburbs. Beyond that, all that the newspapers could learn was that an anonymous telephone call the following morning had led police and federal agents on a wide search around Niles Center [now Skokie] that for a while looked like a wild goose chase. Then the bloody clothing was found, and a few hours later the body, laid out next to St. Paul's Cemetery at the southwest corner of Niles [now Conrad] and Long avenues.

So on that score there seemed to be nothing else to report, and the newspapers concentrated on condemning the murder of two more federal agents, though some could not help hinting that Hollis and Cowley had been paid back for their ambush of Dillinger. With Nelson gone, the *Chicago Herald-Examiner* translated the Justice Department's overheated capture orders into "KILL WIDOW OF BABY-FACE!" who, at age 21 and 94 pounds, may have become the country's first female public enemy by mutual newspaper consent, but was also its most pathetic one. After her night of horror and a day of walking the streets, Helen Nelson had managed to reach her brother-in-law, Robert C. Fitzsimmons, who arranged her surrender the following evening on a downtown street corner where they felt she would not be shot on sight (such was the impression created by the press). The FBI kept her surrender a secret for nearly a week, but once the newspapers got wind that Helen was in their custody, the Bureau insisted that she had been "captured," which it eventually modified to "picked up." The male accomplice would be named and tracked down soon enough.

While Nelson remained "the trigger-nervous runt of the depleted Dillinger gang" (adding insult to his mortal injuries, for the "second" Dillinger gang could rightly have been called Nelson's), the emerging details of Helen Nelson's ordeal did evoke a degree of public sympathy. A few days after the Battle of Barrington, with Helen in FBI seclusion, the *Chicago American* published a chillingly understated account of the outlaw's death as the girl had related it to her family on the night she made it home:

"Les took the wheel and they called to me. They picked me up. Les tried to drive but couldn't make it. I knew it was no use trying to get a doctor. I knew as we rode that he wouldn't be my pal much longer."

Then she described how they made their way to a house "outside Chicago." Someone there helped Chase carry her husband inside, first to a reclining chair and then to a bed, where she removed his clothes and tied the only rag she could find around his waist to try to stop the bleeding.

"All three of us knew Les was dying. But there was nothing we could do. . . . After a while, Les said to me, 'It's getting dark, Helen—say goodbye to mother.' He mentioned all the family—his brothers and sisters and their children. When he came to our own children, he cried. A few minutes later, Les said: 'It's getting dark, Helen. I can't see you anymore.' "

Nelson died that evening at 7:35, she said, and "I didn't know what to do, so I sat there hour after hour with him. [The next morning] we carried Les' body to the car to find some place to put it. I had no idea where to go. We drove out toward Niles Center. We passed a cemetery and I decided that was the best place to leave Les' body. During the ride I sat in the back seat with Les, holding him up so he looked alive. We didn't dump him in the ditch like they said. When we stopped, I put my arms under Les' shoulders and the other man took his feet. It was too much for me, though, and I fell down, hurting my knee on the pavement. We lifted him out and put him down on the grass." Then she took an old blanket from the car and tucked it around the body, she said, because "Les always hated the cold."

That stark account of the outlaw's death had a sadness about it that threw J. Edgar Hoover into fits, and he was further infuriated when Helen had the temerity to tell a judge that she had left her children with relatives so she could dutifully remain with her husband, who did not have much time left. Upon reading this, Hoover—who had a way with words—expanded his repertoire of epithets from "yellow rats" and "vermin in human form" (lawbreakers) to "mawkish, maudlin, misplaced sentimentality (etcetera)" drooled by "sobsisters" of the press. The director wanted the heads of the people who had given the dying Nelson sanctuary and helped his criminal accomplices escape. Why he did not get them is one of the mysteries of the Baby Face Nelson case.

Under intensive questioning, Helen had little choice but to fill in some details, one of which was their desperate escape from Barrington and efforts to reach Father Phillip W. Coughlan, a Catholic priest with whom the Bureau was already acquainted. That she and Father Coughlan managed to keep their stories straight enough to confound the FBI remains one of the mysteries.

Father Coughlan's hoodlum connections had become known to the FBI the previous April when his card turned up in a Buick coupe driven by Tommy Carroll and abandoned at Little Bohemia. Questioning then had revealed that Coughlan's boyhood on Chicago's West Side had naturally made him acquainted with a few of the city's future bootleggers and gunmen. Instead of following in their footsteps, however, he would train for the priesthood at St. John's Seminary in Little Rock, Arkansas, and serve in parishes at St. Joseph and Medina, Missouri, before returning to Chicago in the early thirties. He first signed on as chaplain at the Oak Park Hospital and became acquainted with Tommy Touhy, who was there recuperating from either illness or some misadventure, of both of which he had many. Tommy (who once threatened to turn himself into a human bomb with vials of nitroglycerine) made his famous bootlegger brother, Roger "the Terrible" Touhy, look sane and saintly by comparison, but Tommy also had his good days, and on one of them he introduced Father Coughlan to a young friend called Jimmie Williams.

From Oak Park Father Coughlan had gone to Michigan City, Indiana, where from January through November of 1933 he did some kind of church work that included operating a chapel in the resort community of Long Beach. It was during the summer of that year, he said, that he quite by accident ran into young Jimmy Williams at the Willard Cafe in Michigan City, and they renewed their acquaintance. Being familiar with the area, it was no inconvenience to help Jimmy find and rent a summer cottage near Long Beach for the Williamses and some of their friends. When Jimmy, Helen, and their friends departed following a robbery of the Grand Haven, Michigan, bank, he did notice that the newspaper picture of one robber, who was captured by a fluke, looked a lot like one of Jimmie Williams's friends. Later he made a pleasure trip with Jimmie to St. Paul, and both enjoyed the hospitality of Louie Cernocky's roadhouse at Fox River Grove, without his knowing it to be a favorite watering hole of the Dillinger and Barker-Karpis gangs.

Most of this the FBI learned later. Although his card was in Tommy Carroll's car, they assumed that all they had turned up was an unusually naive whiskey priest a little less clean-cut than the Pat O'Brien kind, and they gave him the benefit of the doubt. For he convincingly professed dismay at learning that his young friend Jimmie Williams was otherwise known as Lester Gillis, and better yet as the notorious Baby Face Nelson, who had just killed a federal agent and wounded other officers in the Battle of Little Bohemia; and Father Coughlan readily acknowledged his secular duty to help fight crime. The somewhat gullible G-men told him to go and sin no more, and to let them know if he should hear again from Baby Face. Over the next few months the Bureau began to discover that quite a number of its fugitives and suspects were members of Father Coughlan's congregation, and that he had stored the car used in the Grand Haven bank robbery. Sensing an increase in the FBI's suspicions, Father Coughlan may have found it in his secular interest to also become an informant, officially or otherwise. In any event, the November 27th phone call from a panicky Father Coughlan came as no great surprise, though the story he gave still seems to have been taken at face value.

By Helen's account and that of other witnesses, the three fugitives had quickly left the Northwest Highway in the bloody and bullet-riddled government Hudson and raced back east on State Highway 22, a narrow blacktop road that still snakes through a heavily forested area in the direction of Chicago's North Shore suburbs. They turned south on Waukegan Road, which goes past the Techny monastery (where they may have briefly stopped), and then wound their way on side streets to 1115 Mohawk, an expensive home on the outskirts of Winnetka, where they made Father Coughlan's day.

Father Coughlan was now considered (at best) a spiritual adviser to hoodlums, and the last hoodlum that he wanted on the doorstep of his sister's residence was a gutshot Baby Face Nelson, bleeding from seventeen wounds and desperately needing help. Weighing unhappy alternatives, he said he could not take them in, but would lead the way to a safe place where Jimmy could get medical attention. He had no particular place in mind, he told the excited federal agents, and had thanked the Lord when the shot-up Hudson solved his problem by heading in another direction. The much-relieved priest then hurried to a telephone and advised the FBI of his terrible experience, complete with a few discrepancies that the agents wrote off to his hysterical state of mind. This all occurred between about 4:30 and 6:30, according to the different accounts.

Although new to the battle against day-to-day crime, the government's fledgling gangbusters had quickly come to appreciate the importance of the elaborate interstate network of underworld friends and supporters in helping fugitives stay a step ahead of the law. City police already knew this, of course, but jurisdictional limitations only abetted the problem; and in some cities— especially St. Paul, Chicago, Hot Springs, Toledo, and St. Louis—the police *were* the problem. So the Justice Department had broken new law-enforcement ground by declaring all-out war also on the harboring of fugitives—an interesting crime that often required proof of innocence rather than of guilt. Agents already had arrested scores of people in a dozen states who had in some fashion (and in some cases unwittingly) helped Dillinger and Baby Face Nelson; and so they continued to pressure Helen Nelson to reveal the hideout where her husband had gone to die.

Helen did not cooperate eagerly, claiming that Nelson had been conscious all the while and giving Chase directions. Besides, it was nearly dark, and she didn't know the roads or the area. But the agents persisted until she led them block by block and turn by turn to Walnut Street in the North Shore suburb of Wilmette, not far from Father Coughlan's and only a mile or so from St. Paul's Cemetery, where Nelson's body was found. On Walnut only one residence met her description of a gray stucco cottage with a garage in back and a front porch running the full width of the house. This was a bungalow at number 1627.

From the helpful postman and neighbors, the agents learned that the residents at 1627 were an unemployed truck driver named Ray Henderson and his wife Marie, whose domestic squabbles had annoyed nearby homeowners as well as the police. What clinched the location was the discovery that 1627 Walnut was a mailing address for a politician, brewery owner, train robber, stolen-bond trader, and retired barbecue czar named Jimmy Murray. Plus another known hoodlum or two.

Surveillance was established, visitors were identified, cars were described, and license plates were recorded, and finally the Hendersons and hoodlums were taken in for questioning. And that was it. No arrests were made and no charges filed, as far as records indicate. And for some equally unexplained reason, the crime reporters who had descended like locusts on James Probasco's house, climbing through the windows and picking it clean, remained content to repeat only that Baby Face had expired at a Chicago-area "hideout."

FBI reports on 1627 are conspicuously sparse and uninformative, but may offer a few clues to what didn't happen.

Four months after the Barrington battle, a "confidential" informant (a special class of informant whose names are blacked out in FBI documents) advised the Bureau that the person who helped Helen Nelson transport her husband's body was not Chase, as originally believed, but Jimmy Murray himself; and that Murray since then had been trying to dispose of Nelson's guns. Supposedly this ordnance, which included the Monitor machine rifle, was considered so hot that it already had been turned down by one of the informant's friends—indeed, a friend who had defrauded Dr. Wilhelm Loeser, of plastic surgery fame, out of $250,000 some ten years earlier. That scam had involved selling Loeser expensive equipment for illegal distilling, then tipping off the police so Loeser would lose it and have to buy more. A good suspect in such a swindle would be Louis Piquett, except that such a plum would never have gone unpicked. Not enough is known of Dr. Loeser's other friends to provide any clues to the swindler.

It was two years later, in March of 1937, before the Chicago field office received an unexpected visit from Sergeant W. R. Sumner, a policeman in the North Shore suburb of Kenilworth, with more information on the subject. It seems the Sumner family and the Hendersons were neighbors, and Marie Henderson occasionally dropped by to chat. On a recent visit she had remarked, in making conversation, that Sumner and his wife would be greatly surprised if they knew where Baby Face Nelson had died—and who was with him at the end. Sumner feigned only mild interest in hopes of learning more without alarming Mrs. Henderson, and this he was sharing with the FBI. Marie had not said explicitly that Nelson died at her house, but she did add more pieces to the puzzle. She mentioned that Jimmy Murray was an old and close friend who was presently trying to recruit her brothers to work as sluggers for the Yellow Cab Company. She added that she herself was a sometime girlfriend of one Guy McDonald, a known hoodlum who also used her address, and who was a partner of Murray's in some new brewery ventures in southern Wisconsin. She also mentioned the name of one Leo Heinz, a member of the Niles Center Board of Trustees, who, Sumner said, controlled the area's slot machines. Heinz had some connection with her house, Sumner believed, and perhaps with Nelson's going there. Moreover, she laughed at how another of her friends, a Catholic priest named Father Coughlan, had fed the Bureau a line—the implication being that he himself had led Nelson to the Henderson residence. She also remarked in passing that Father Coughlan had known the Newton brothers from his early priesthood days in Oklahoma, and through them had met Jimmy Murray, who had used them in the Rondout train robbery in 1924.

The most interesting revelation of Mrs. Henderson was that Nelson had taken refuge in what he thought would be the last place the FBI would ever think to look—because it belonged to one of the Bureau's own agents or informers (she wasn't clear which) who had been supplying Nelson with intelligence on the FBI's activities. Finally she mentioned that Baby Face Nelson's guns were still for sale, stashed somewhere in the town of Niles Center [Skokie], the last she heard.

No further reports have been found. Perhaps the FBI already had figured out that Father Coughlan led Nelson to 1627 Walnut (or wherever he died), but still was loath to prosecute a priest. Or, it may have had a problem with charging one of its own informants—conceivably Jimmy Murray, who had magically avoided prosecution for any number of crimes that by now were known to the FBI. Just as the threat of prosecution turns offenders into informers, so does the promise of immunity.

A piece that may or may not fit the puzzle is that the Buick coupe which yielded Father Coughlan's card in April 1934 had been sold the year before by a Heinz Motor Company of Niles Center for delivery to one Helen Ferguson, named in FBI records as a girlfriend to both the Barker-Karpis gang and Dillinger's; and that it may have been used by Charles Urschel kidnapper Albert Bates in an American Express robbery before it was seized at Little Bohemia.

73. Chase received a life sentence on March 28, 1935, and was promptly sent to the Rock. Fifteen years later he became eligible for parole, only to learn that Hoover was still on the case. The director knew that a certain Chaplain Clark had been agitating on behalf of the aging Machine Gun Kelly and now wanted to help John Paul Chase. Hoover not only scotched the possibility of parole in 1950, but remained ready to indict Chase on the second Barrington murder charge for which he had never been tried. On the bottom of a memorandum he wrote, "Watch closely & endeavor to thwart efforts of this priest who should be attending to his own business instead of trying to turn loose on society such mad dogs."

When Chase finally received a hearing in 1955, Hoover's letter of opposition already lay on the parole board's desk, and agents began scouring the country for the testimony it would need to convict Chase again. A federal judge refused to allow prosecution on a murder charge that had been kept on a shelf for twenty years, but not before Hoover had tracked down a score of elderly witnesses, including Father Coughlan, now in a Jasper, Indiana, rest home and too feeble to participate. It was the bad luck of former agent Thomas McDade, who had exchanged gunfire with Chase and Nelson in 1934, to have mellowed over the years. In a letter to Father Clark in 1952 he had expressed no objections to a parole for Chase, and for this Hoover declared him, in retirement, a traitor to the Bureau. Despite Hoover's continued and adamant opposition, Chase was finally paroled on October 31, 1966, and worked at minor jobs until his death from cancer on October 5, 1973.

Nor did Helen Nelson's ordeals soften Hoover in the least. When she completed her harboring sentence, a federal prosecutor advised the attorney general that the 22-year-old widow was clearly no threat to society and looked so pathetic that prosecuting her on still more charges, as Hoover wished, might inspire "blubbering brothers" to denounce the department as heartless. Undeceived by the effort to sound tough-minded, Hoover protested that sympathy would be less wasted on the widows of the two slain

G-men, and on the Bureau's copy of his letter he scribbled that the U.S. attorney appeared to be a "blubbering brother himself."

74. However Purvis had phrased it to Anna Sage originally, she clearly believed that she had a "deal" and later made the Bureau sound like welchers. Courts supported Immigration's position that it was not bound by any Justice Department promises, expressed or implied; but judging from correspondence between Hoover and his Chicago office, the director had fully expected to resolve matters informally and probably would have done so if Anna had stayed out of sight. The Bureau did not publicly acknowledge her as its informant and had tried its best to keep her away from Chicago, sending her first to Michigan and later to California, where on October 11, 1934, she was paid her $5,000 secretly and in cash. When she returned against the Bureau's wishes, Hoover washed his hands of the matter and righteously denied that any promises had been made. It probably did not help that Anna had gotten herself evicted from 2403 Orchard Street, where she had opened an alleged beauty shop, and that newspaper photographers found her hairstyling equipment piled outside on the sidewalk less than two blocks from the Biograph Theatre.

Extra!---Lawyer Jailed

FINALLY the law caught up with THE RIGHT MAN in the Dillinger case.

Louis Piquett, Chicago attorney accused of harboring Dillinger and the sinister Homer Van Meter, was denied an appeal for review of his conviction and sentences to two years in prison and a fine of $10,000!

For once the mouthpiece behind the smart crook IS ADJUDGED A CROOK HIMSELF!

When more crooked lawyers go to jail there'll be less crime. AND NOT UNTIL THEN.

Detroit Times, 5/5/36.

75. Everyone agreed that this explicit jury instruction won Piquett's acquittal. However, Piquett had already attracted attention by buying drinks for the house in a suburban bar and bragging that his trial was fixed. How fixed wasn't clear; he merely claimed that he had "more on Judge Holly" than the judge had on him. The acquittal astounded the FBI, whose interoffice correspondence describes the judge as being practically a member of the defense team; so the despair that crippled Piquett during his second trial may have stemmed from facing not only the biggest guns from the Justice Department, but also an impartial judge. Hoover gloried in Piquett's conviction on the Van Meter charges, vilifying him in speeches and in print as the kind of "mouthpiece" and corrupter of the judicial system who kept criminals in business. Long after Piquett had served his term and was venturing to hope that his license might be reinstated, Hoover made sure that anyone who might be sympathetic received a full accounting of Piquett's moral and professional shortcomings.

76. Another high cost could not be measured at the time. Ironically, it was the country's preoccuption with Dillinger and the other outlaws after 1932 that allowed locally organized crime to quietly metastasize into a nationwide condition. The imprisonment of Al Capone and the repeal of Prohibiton seemed to ring down the curtain on the familiar forms of crime associated with bootlegging. But if alcohol diminished as a source of criminal

R E L E A S E   and   R E C E I P T

WHEREAS, THE UNITED STATES DEPARTMENT OF JUSTICE did employ me to secure information leading to the apprehension of JOHN DILLINGER, alias Frank Sullivan, and,

WHEREAS, I, ANNA SAGE, did secure and deliver personally to an official of the DIVISION OF INVESTIGATION, UNITED STATES DEPARTMENT OF JUSTICE information as to the whereabouts of the said JOHN DILLINGER at a particular time, now, therefore,

KNOW YE, ALL WHOM THESE PRESENTS MAY CONCERN, That I, ANNA SAGE, for and in consideration of the sum of five thousand dollars ($5,000.00) lawful money of the United States of America, to me in hand paid by _S. P Cowley_, known to me as an official of the UNITED STATES DEPARTMENT OF JUSTICE, the receipt thereof in full is hereby acknowledged, have remised, released and forever discharged, and by these presents do, for my heirs, executors and administrators, remise, release and forever discharge the United States of America, the said UNITED STATES DEPARTMENT OF JUSTICE, or division thereof, and/or any of its officials, employees or the ATTORNEY GENERAL thereof, it, his or their heirs, executors, successors, and administrators, of and from all and all manner of action and actions, cause and causes of actions, suits, debts, dues, sums of money, reckonings, covenants, contracts, controversies, agreements, promises, variances, trespasses, damages, judgments, extents, claims and demands whatsoever, in law or in equity, which against I ever had, now have or which my heirs, executors, or administrators hereafter can, shall or may have by reason of the said employment, or by reason of any other matter resulting therefrom or connected therewith in any manner whatsoever from the beginning of the world to the date of these presents.

IN WITNESS WHEREOF, I have hereunto set my hand, seal and fingerprints, this _11th_ day of _October_ at _Los Angeles, Calif._ in the year one thousand nine hundred thirty-four.

Signed, sealed, fingerprinted and delivered in the presence of

Joseph E. P. Nunn   _Anna Sage_ (Seal)
O. H. Sackett

Before receiving her $5,000 reward money, Anna Sage had to sign a receipt and statement in quaint legal jargon that released the government from any further obligations it might have incurred since "the beginning of the world."

revenue, the traffickers in booze had already built an efficient underground highway system that racketeers also could travel. Capone's example had taught his successors the folly of high-profile crime, and when the federal government focused its efforts on chasing interstate fugitives, the mobs heaved a sigh of relief. They already had been sobered by public outrage over the St. Valentine's Day Massacre and the prospect of Repeal, so those with a business mentality prevailed over those with a gunman mentality and began to plan ahead.

The first national underworld conference took place in Atlantic City from May 13 to May 16, 1929, and included the senior statesmen in crime from most other parts of the country. Chicago's John Torrio, mentor of Al Capone, came out of ostensible retirement in New York to serve as gangster emeritus in meetings with the crime kings of the future: Frank Costello, Meyer Lansky, Lucky Luciano, Louis Buchalter, and others from New York; Max Hoff and his cohorts from Philadelphia; Torrio's old cronies from Chicago, including Capone and the ascending Frank Nitti; plus the mob chiefs from Cleveland, Kansas City, Detroit, Boston, and other major cities. Capone was under a cloud for having kept Chicago in an uproar, but he too seemed sick of the violence and willing to retire now that the bellicose North Siders had been brought into line.

The convention ended on May 16 with different cities allocated to their most capable crime bosses, who formed a national "commission" that could enforce unwritten treaties and agreements with more than moral suasion. Capone may have suffered some injury to his feelings, but he showed his support for the new order by going directly to jail. On the last day of the so-called convention, he submitted to arrest in Philadelphia on a gun-carrying charge and took what amounted to a year's sabbatical. Besides, Bugs Moran was still out there somewhere and likely harboring a grudge.

The understandings reached at Atlantic City provided the foundation for modern organized crime. A few holdouts had to be removed to make the dream come true, and Lucky Luciano is generally credited with purging the new federation of some recalcitrant "Mustache Petes." Two New York crime families in particular had been feuding for supremacy in the so-called Castellamarese War, but the attrition rate was low and would not have reformed the system in any case. So Luciano allegedly ordered a bloodbath known as the "Night of the Sicilian Vespers" in 1931, when the new guard is supposed to have wiped out the old in a sudden and well-coordinated orgy of murder, as thrillingly depicted in the *Godfather* trilogy. Unfortunately for that colorful bit of American gangster lore, some skeptical historians have scoured newspaper and police reports in an effort to document this milestone event. All have found it to be one of the myths that popular writers like to propagate as part of the Mafia legend, and one which accounts for the cast of unfamiliar characters who seem to come out of nowhere twenty years later. By the time they appeared before Senator Kefauver and other investigators in the 1950s and '60s, Meyer Lansky, Frank Costello, Albert Anastasia, Ben Siegel, Vito Genovese, Joey Gallo, Tony Accardo, Joey Aiuppa, Sam Giancana, and the others were all middle-aged men who had long since made their fortunes in every-thing from gambling to labor racketeering with little federal interference, and now were comfortably presiding over an "underground empire" in some ways as powerful as the government itself. They had prospered without machine-gun fire or banner headlines while Hoover waged his thirty-year war against interstate bank robbers, Nazi saboteurs, and the Communist threat.

As for the bank robbers, the Justice Department owed a considerable debt to the Dillingers and Pretty Boys and Baby Faces for its new role and image as the nation's first honest policeman, and it may have deliberately selected a crime war it could win for the greater purpose (at least initially) of raising the country's morale. Or, it may not have known any better. In 1933 nationally organized crime was still a concept not easily grasped, and it can be argued that the enormous admiration the FBI eventually inspired, by what-ever means, did more than any economic programs, political policies, or charismatic president to restore faith in the U.S. government. A war on the new "organized" crime would have been as frustrating then as it is now. Senator Kefauver, the Appalachin meeting, years of state and local investiga-tions, and Robert Kennedy's Justice Department finally forced J. Edgar Hoover to concede the existence of a "Mafia," or a "Cosa Nostra," or other short-hand for nationally organized crime, but only in recent years have the G-men had either the laws or the inclination to battle the Godfathers with the energy they devoted to the Depression desperadoes.

In 1993, British author Anthony Summers offered a startlingly different explanation for Hoover's apparent blind spot on organized crime. In *Official and Confidential: The Private Life of J. Edgar Hoover,* he claims that the coun-try's top mobsters possessed hard evidence that Hoover was homosexual, and successfully blackmailed him into laying off the rackets. That's a possibility, but even without such a sword above his head, Hoover had a unique set of priorities in which law enforcement was more a means than an end. He understood that a war on something as hard to define as racketeering would reward him with failure and embarrassment instead of personal gratification, public heroization, and the availability of more police power than enjoyed by a world-class Communist dictator.

Acknowledgments

A book of this kind owes more to the community of crime buffs, amateur researchers, and memorabilia collectors than to professional writers and historians. The Girardin manuscript was discovered in the course of exchanging information with several of these people, most of whom had become acquainted through Joe Pinkston's John Dillinger Historical Museum in Nashville, Indiana. Pinkston's introductions usually led to correspondence and often to personal friendships among members of an ever-growing network of history enthusiasts dedicated to learning as much as possible about Dillinger, mainly, but also the Barker-Karpis gang, Pretty Boy Floyd, and the others who represent the last of the all-American outlaws. The Dillingerologists who have become close friends are Rick Mattix of Bussey, Iowa, Jeff Maycroft of Muskegon Heights, Michigan, Neal Trickel of Monroe, Wisconsin, Kathi Harrell of Champaign, Illinois, and Sandy Jones of Ft. Collins, Colorado. Author John Toland, and Ken Craven and director Harold Billings at the University of Texas main library were generous with their time and efforts. Some particularly helpful crime buffs (who cover Prohibition gangsters as well) and moral supporters include, in no particular order, Chuck Schauer, Bill Trible, Mark Levell, John Binder, Sharon DiRago, Albert Vasquez, Alanna Nash, Tom Smusyn, Michael Webb, Richard Lindberg, Victoria Cirinich, Reg Potterton, Ellen Poulsen, Rick Cartledge, Jacque Ramey, Tom Hollatz, Elaine and Bill Sundin, Burt Nielson, Dr. Richard C. Mahron, Dr. Jonathan Lewis, Ed Baumann, Kenan Heise, Nate Kaplan, Richard Crowe, Ron Kovar, Mike Johnson, Tamara Shaffer, Sherry Zimbleman, Margaret Schmidt, Bernadette Doran, Dr. David Fisher, John O'Brien, William Balsamo, Karen Abbott and Paula DeSalvo at *Playboy*, eminent book dealers Patterson Smith of New Jersey and Tom Joyce of Chicago, Mrs. Maria Stiglich of East Chicago (who once worked for the police department and knew most of the people mentioned by Girardin), Marge McDougall (who helped make a Dillinger death mask in 1934), Loretta Walsh (who encountered Dillinger at Jimmy Murray's barbecue stand, and began putting together a scrapbook), and especially ace photographer Henry Scheafer (who was there the night Dillinger died). All contributed information, recollections, photographs, or enthusiasm to this volume, as did Russell Lewis of the Chicago Historical Society, who put me in touch with editor Bob Sloan at Indiana University Press, and ultimately with their world-class manuscript editor, Jane Lyle, and master designer Matt Williamson.

Special thanks go to Rick in Iowa and Jeff in Michigan, who can bring to famous crimes and criminals the enthusiasm and expertise which boring people try to bring to sports. Rick greatly expanded the Dillinger chronology and address collection and filled in many Dillinger connections with the Barker-Karpis gang.

Crime buff and collector Dennis DeMark not only made the greatest contribution to this project in terms of research, but serves award-winning barbecue—the kind John Dillinger would have liked—at his "Oh Dennis!" Saloon & Charcoal House in Racine, Wisconsin (where local police proudly display the machine gun that Dillinger once used to rob their bank).

Sources

Dozens of books, hundreds of articles, and thousands of newspaper stories chronicle Dillinger's career, but those providing either detailed or accurate information are rare enough (and this project different enough) that a lengthy bibliography would serve little purpose. Contemporary newspaper accounts are more exciting than factual, and in the absence of some unimpeachable source their frequent contradictions can be resolved with any degree of certainty only by independent corroboration, logical probability, and informed judgment. Many small discrepancies remain, but a surprisingly reliable source was the early detective magazines. Some were well written and edited and enjoyed large circulations; and without the pressure of several daily deadlines and intense rivalry among several newspapers in a city like Chicago, *True Detective* and a few others took at least some pains to screen out the false reports, wild exaggerations, reckless speculations, and utter nonsense common to earlier crime reporting. Some of these reporters also wrote articles and books with no greater concern for accuracy, and as these became the sources for still later authors, much erroneous material has been handed down from one writing generation to the next. This frequent disregard for facts would be appalling, except that it makes the work more interesting than simply discovering that everyone was right.

The only contemporary books that tell the Dillinger story in useful detail are long out of print and becoming fairly rare, but include *Ten Thousand Public Enemies* by Courtney Ryley Cooper (1935), *Farewell, Mr. Gangster!* by Herbert Corey (1936), *American Agent* by Melvin Purvis (1936), and *Persons in Hiding* by J. Edgar Hoover (1938). These are based on the gospel according to the FBI, which commonly opened its files to friendly writers, but more interestingly reflect the battle between Hoover and Purvis. Cooper was one of Hoover's kept writers whose magazine articles ignored, discounted, or even disparaged Purvis when Purvis's fame threatened to eclipse the director. When mistreated into resigning, Purvis retaliated with a highly complimentary history of the Bureau that referred to "the Director" only rarely and not by name. Hoover quickly put Cooper to work ghostwriting a self-authorized Bureau history that not only ignored Purvis entirely but replaced him with

Sam Cowley, whose death in battle with Baby Face Nelson had conveniently eliminated him as a source of competition.

Of the later books that covered the outlaw era with any accuracy, the most original and interpretive is *Dillinger Days* (1963) by John Toland, the respected historian whose travels, research, and interviews included all the major gangs of the period. The book that represents the most detailed and accurate study of the outlaw himself is *Dillinger: A Short and Violent Life* (1962) by Joe Pinkston and Robert Cromie, which preceded Toland's book without attracting as much attention, but which has since been republished in paperback by the Chicago Historical Bookworks of Evanston, Illinois. Pinkston has resumed his research on the subject and is amassing information that one day should be worthy of a definitive multi-volume Dillinger biography.

Many books now scrutinize J. Edgar Hoover and the FBI and find fault with their wars on crime, Communism, and critics. The first of these was Max Lowenthal's *The Federal Bureau of Investigation* (1950), an unfriendly treatment that flabbergasted a Hoover grown accustomed to unqualified hero worship. The Bureau fired back with *The FBI Story* (1956), which must have enjoyed sales of biblical proportions, to judge from the numbers still available in used book stores. It was a well-written, authorized, detailed history by Don Whitehead, enjoyed Hoover's imprimatur, and described the Bureau in the approving terms of a smart public-relations agency rather than the delightfully purple prose of Courtney Ryley Cooper. Especially since Hoover's death in 1972, FBI faultfinding has increased to the level of Bureau bashing that no one could have imagined in the Eisenhower or early Nixon years. With that still in vogue, probably the most scholarly and balanced (if still often critical) histories are to be found in Curt Gentry's *J. Edgar Hoover: The Man and the Secrets* (1991) and Richard Gid Powers's *Secrecy and Power: The Life of J. Edgar Hoover* (1987). Of greatest value to me was Powers's earlier book, *G-Men: The FBI in American Popular Culture* (1983), which describes the carefully orchestrated efforts of Hoover and his publicists to create a combination of image and organization unprecedented in law-enforcement history—and, it might be added, one which sold the American public on a lofty ideal of police professionalism that has never been realistic but did set the standards by which the country's cops soon found themselves judged, like it or not. (For years I had wondered why no one else was making the connection between the New Deal politics of 1933–34 and the convenient appearance of celebrity outlaws who invited the enactment of federal anti-crime laws. Author Powers not only picked up on the connection but devoted much of his distressingly rare *G-Men* book to analyzing it in glorious and entertaining detail.)

Because this work is based on a manuscript written almost sixty years ago, and since I've been reading on the subject for years, my efforts here have consisted mainly of sifting through FBI documents that confirm, support, or contradict the Girardin account, or elaborate on it. This material includes letters, reports, and memoranda of all kinds, as well as vast numbers of newspaper clippings harvested by local Bureau offices and forwarded to Washington. Because of their redundancy and problems with legibility, I soon abandoned efforts to identify individual items that often were duplicated or incomplete or whose serial numbers have been lost in the copying process. So the new information provided in the notes can be found, unless otherwise indicated, somewhere in the 36,000 pages of FBI material that is filed more or less chronologically as JODIL 62-29777, in the J. Edgar Hoover Building's basement reading room, whose staff is pleasant but whose furniture is less than user-friendly. Good luck.

Note: Neither the police nor the press took great pains to determine the spelling of names, nor did it seem to matter much to the individuals bearing them. Marie Comforti is usually misspelled Conforti, even though the FBI devoted a memo to the correct family spelling. Frechette is sometimes spelled Frechetti, Dietrich as Detrick, Zarkovich as Zarkovitch, and James W. Regan as Ragen or Reagan, and so forth. When possible, this book uses the spelling on licenses or tombstones, though even that can be misleading, as Louis Piquett is buried under the original family spelling of Piquette. Dillinger signed his letters "Johnnie," but reporters often spelled it Johnny, or gave his middle name as Herman instead of Herbert. To this day his headstone (replaced more than once because of vandalism) reads "John H. Dillinger, Jr.," even though his father's middle name was Wilson.

Index

Touhy, Roger (gangster), 44, 49, 294–95n33
Train robbery, proposed, 208
Treasures, buried, rumors of, 314n65
Tucson, Ariz., capture of Dillinger gang, 56–58, 125

Union National Bank (Streator, Ill.), robbery, 51
Unity Trust and Savings Bank (Chicago, Ill.), robbery, 43–44, 283–84n10, 285–86n12
Urschel, Charles, kidnapping of, 5–6, 65

Van Antwerp, William (Mich. sheriff), 120
Van Buskirk, John, 59, 61
Van Meter, Homer (gang member), 19, 39, 52, 56, 105, 134, 142, 293–94n29; activities following plastic surgery, 182–85; bank holdups, 114–15, 117, 198–200; events leading to his death, 231, 239–40, 259; killing of East Chicago policemen, 162–63, 298–99n41; Little Bohemia Lodge shootout and aftermath, 146, 148, 150, 152–56, 158; plastic surgery, 174–78

Wagner, Howard (South Bend police), 199–200, 257
Walsh, Thomas (U.S. atty. gen.), 3
Wanatka, Emil, 145–47, 148, 292–93n26

Weapons, 36, 48, 282n6, 286n13; available at Probasco residence, 187, 301–302n47; holdups to obtain, 35–36, 141–42; on Dillinger at time of death, 223–24, 306–307n60; used in Michigan City prison break, 27–28, 53, 287–88n15. *See also* Gun, wooden; Submachine gun
Wellnitz, Fred, 29
Weyland, Grover, 42–43
Wilgus, Hobart (East Chicago police), 53–54, 62
Williams, Joseph (judge), 17–18, 21
Wisconsin: proposed Platteville robberies, 197–99; Racine bank robbery, 42, 60; state efforts to extradite Dillinger gang members, 59–61. *See also* Little Bohemia Lodge
Woll, J. Albert (asst. dist. atty.), 248
Woman in Red, The. *See* Sage, Anna
Wooden Gun, Ind., 101
World's Fair, Chicago, Dillinger's visits to, 190, 206

Youngblood, Herbert (hoodlum): death of, 119–20, 258; role in Crown Point jail escape, 84–87, 90–91, 105n, 108

Zarkovich, Martin (East Chicago police), 66, 162–63, 218–20, 298–99n41; epilogue, 267–68; role in Dillinger's death, 216, 221, 223, 224, 226, 246

GEORGE RUSSELL GIRARDIN was a young Chicagoan trying to start up an advertising agency in 1934, the year of Dillinger's death, when a chance encounter with Dillinger's lawyer, Louis Piquett, gave him the idea to tell the true story of the criminal's life and career in crime. The articles Girardin wrote for the Hearst newspapers from information supplied by Piquett and his private investigator, Arthur O'Leary, became the basis for a book that was never published. Girardin later became the head of the advertising agency that bore his name and was known as an orientalist for his writing on Chinese and Japanese history and art. He retired in the 1970s and was living quietly among his books and collections when a chance encounter with Bill Helmer led to a new collaboration and the publication of the long-forgotten manuscript on Dillinger.

WILLIAM J. HELMER worked for several years on magazines in New York before returning to the University of Texas at Austin for a master's degree in history. His thesis topic was the Thompson submachine gun—"a case study in history and technology," later published by Macmillan as *The Gun That Made the Twenties Roar.* Helmer's credentials in writing, editing, history, and crime earned him a job on the National Violence Commission in Washington, D.C., and after that at *Playboy* magazine in Chicago, where he produced *Playboy's Illustrated History of Organized Crime,* headed up the Playboy Defense Team for the magazine's foundation, and otherwise specialized in social and legal issues as a senior editor in charge of the Playboy Forum department. He is still a contributing editor and a freelance writer, mainly on crime history and social change.

Book and Jacket Designer: Matt Williamson
Copy Editor: Jane Lyle
Production Coordinator: Harriet Curry
Typeface: Stone Sans and Bodoni Book
Typesetter: Weimer Graphics, Inc.
Printer and Binder: Maple-Vail Book Mfg.